LIVE JESUS IN OUR HEARTS

REVELATION

AND OLD
THE

TESTAMENT

High School Framework Course 1

CHRIS WARDWELL

saint mary's press

Thanks and Dedication

Thanks to May Lane and Brian Singer-Towns whose guidance made writing this a wonderful experience; to my former coworkers at St. Thomas High School who have shared their work and ideas with me over the years; to my friends and family for their encouragement, especially my wife, Christine, and son Jacob.

A very special thank you to our student contributors: Viva from Cotter High School in Winona, MN; Casey and Ifeoluwa, both from Mater Dei High School in Santa Ana, CA; Carolina from Providence Catholic High School in New Lenox; and Bella from Father Lopez Catholic High School in Daytona Beach, FL.

This book is dedicated to the Basilian Fathers, to whom I am eternally grateful for the love and support they have given me.

The Subcommittee on the Catechism, United States Conference of Catholic Bishops, has found that this catechetical high school text, copyright 2019, is in conformity with the *Catechism of the Catholic Church* and that it fulfills the requirements of Core Course 1 of the *Doctrinal Elements of a Curriculum Framework for the Development of Catechetical Materials for Young People of High School Age*.

Nihil Obstat: Dr. John Martens, PhD
               Censor Librorum
               November 15, 2018

Imprimatur: † Most Rev. Bernard A. Hebda
               Archbishop of Saint Paul and Minneapolis
               November 20, 2018

The nihil obstat and imprimatur are official declarations that a book or pamphlet is free of doctrinal or moral error. No implication is contained therein that those who have granted the nihil obstat or imprimatur agree with the contents, opinions, or statements expressed, nor do they assume any legal responsibility associated with publication.

The content in this resource was acquired, developed, and reviewed by the content engagement team at Saint Mary's Press. Content design and manufacturing were coordinated by the passionate team of creatives at Saint Mary's Press.

Cover image © Markus Pfaff / Shutterstock.com

Printed in the United States of America

1165 (PO6613)

ISBN 978-1-59982-946-3

CONTENTS

UNIT 1: God's Original Revelation 8

CHAPTER 1: God's Original Plan 10

Article 1: The Divine Architect and His Plans 11

Article 2: The Bible or Science—Which One Is Right? 18

Article 3: Right People, Wrong Turn 23

Article 4: Sin's Ripple Effect 30

CHAPTER 2: God's Revelation 36

Article 5: Natural Revelation: Finding the Artist in the Art 37

Article 6: Logic: It Just Makes Sense 41

Article 7: Divine Revelation: The Word from On High 46

Article 8: Inspiration: From God's Mouth to Our Hearts 51

CHAPTER 3: Overview of the Bible 58

Article 9: From Word to Text 59

Article 10: When Did It Happen? When Was It Written? 64

Article 11: Not One Book, but Many 67

Article 12: Bible Translations 72

Article 13: The Old Prepares Us for the New 75

Article 14: The New Fulfills the Old 77

CHAPTER 4: Interpreting the Bible 84

Article 15: Reliable Guides: The Magisterium and the Holy Spirit 85

Article 16: Exegesis: What Does It Mean? 88

Article 17: Making Sense of the Bible 91

Article 18: The Literature of the Bible 94

Article 19: Biblical Archaeology: Digging for Answers 98

UNIT 2: God Revealed to His Chosen People............ 110

CHAPTER 5: The Patriarchs: God Reveals Himself to a Chosen Family 112

    Article 20: Abraham and Sarah... 113

    Article 21: Isaac and Jacob 120

    Article 22: Joseph 126

CHAPTER 6: The Pentateuch: God Reveals Himself to His Chosen People........... 132

    Article 23: Exodus: Free at Last! 133

    Article 24: Covenant: The Ties That Bind 140

    Article 25: Leviticus and Numbers: Being Holy 145

    Article 26: Numbers and Deuteronomy: The Promised Land 152

CHAPTER 7: Joshua and Judges 160

    Article 27: What Goes Around Comes Around . . . Or Does It? 161

    Article 28: Joshua: The New Moses... 168

    Article 29: The Judges: New Authority Figures 172

    Article 30: Samuel: Reluctant Kingmaker 178

    Article 31: Ruth: An Unexpected Hero 184

CHAPTER 8: The Rise of the Monarchy... 190

    Article 32: King Saul: A Disappointing Start................................. 191

    Article 33: David: A New King Emerges 196

    Article 34: King David's Downfall... 201

    Article 35: King Solomon: The Last of the Good Old Days................... 205

    Article 36: The End of One Nation.. 210

UNIT 3: God Revealed through Kings and Prophets.......................222

CHAPTER 9: The Kings and Prophets of the Northern Kingdom 224

Article 37: Divided We Fall: The Kingdom Splits 225

Article 38: Prophets: God's Messengers 230

Article 39: Elijah and Elisha: Hard-Core Prophets.........................238

Article 40: Sex and Money: Hosea and Amos..........................245

Article 41: Jonah: Laughter Is the Best Medicine 251

CHAPTER 10: The Kings and Prophets of the Southern Kingdom 258

Article 42: Good Kings: Shining Stars on a Dark Horizon....................259

Article 43: Isaiah Part 1: Hope for the Hopeless 264

Article 44: Jeremiah: Outrageous Heart 268

Article 45: Ezekiel: Actions Speak Louder Than Words.......................274

Article 46: The Babylonian Exile: Far Away from Home 279

Article 47: Isaiah Parts 2 and 3: A Light in the Darkness 283

CHAPTER 11: The Messianic Prophecies 288

Article 48: Old Testament, New Testament: Woven Together.................289

Article 49: Messianic Prophecies: Pointing toward the Light 292

Article 50: Psalms: Guided by Poetry 298

Article 51: Previews: Moses, Joshua, David...........................303

UNIT 4: God Revealed through Holy People and Worship 316

CHAPTER 12: Rebuilding Jerusalem and the Temple 318

Article 52: Leaving Babylon, Going Home 319

Article 53: The Temple: Worship Central 323

Article 54: Rebuilding Jerusalem 327

Article 55: Psalms: Songs for Every Occasion 332

CHAPTER 13: Ordinary People Give Extraordinary Witness 340

Article 56: Tobit, Judith, Esther: A Happy Ending 341

Article 57: Maccabees Part 1: Fighting a Just War 349

Article 58: Maccabees Part 2: Witness Testimony 353

Article 59: Maccabees Part 3: Life after Death 357

CHAPTER 14: The Wisdom Books 364

Article 60: Wisdom from Above 365

Article 61: Job: Why Do Good People Suffer? 369

Article 62: Ecclesiastes: What's the Point? 376

Article 63: Song of Songs: Love Poems 379

Article 64: Ben Sira: Wisdom Far from Home 382

UNIT 5: God Revealed through Jesus and the Church 394

CHAPTER 15: The Gospels 396

Article 65: Sharing the Story 397

Article 66: The Synoptic Gospels: Similar but Different 401

Article 67: Major Events in the Synoptic Gospels 406

Article 68: Jesus: Storyteller and Miracle Worker 412

Article 69: From a Beloved Friend: The Gospel of John 418

Article 70: Jesus: God in the Flesh 425

CHAPTER 16: The Acts of the Apostles and the Letters 430

Article 71: Acts of the Apostles: Passing the Baton 431

Article 72: Paul's Letters: Time Machine and Guidebook 437

Article 73: Letters to Everyone: The Non-Pauline Letters 442

Article 74: The Book of Revelation: A Message of Hope...................... 445

Article 75: Passing It On 450

CHAPTER 17: Scripture in the Life of the Church 456

Article 76: Sacred Scripture: Food for the Soul 457

Article 77: The Prayer of the Church: Getting into the Rhythm 460

Article 78: The Lord's Prayer: An Essential Conversation 465

Article 79: The Right Thing to Do: Morality in the Bible..................... 468

Article 80: *Lectio Divina*: Listening to the Word 472

Article 81: Common Catholic Devotions 476

APPENDIX: Challenge Questions.................................... 488

GLOSSARY.................................... 491

INDEX 502

ACKNOWLEDGMENTS 511

UNIT 1
God's Original Revelation

HOW DOES
THE BIBLE
HELP ME
KNOW
GOD?

LOOKING AHEAD

CHAPTER 1 Page 10
God's Original Plan

CHAPTER 2 Page 36
God's Revelation

CHAPTER 3 Page 58
Overview of the Bible

CHAPTER 4 Page 84
Interpreting the Bible

The Bible helps me realize that God loves ME. The love revealed in the Bible completely applies to me individually as it does to everyone else. The Parable of the Lost Sheep, a personal favorite, reminds me that God is always there for me and will be waiting for me no matter how far I've strayed.

VIVA
Cotter High School

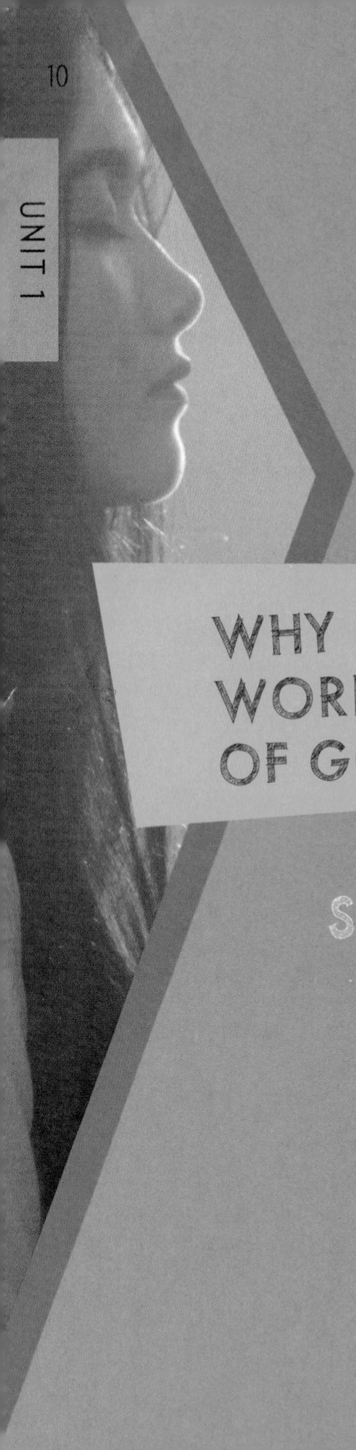

CHAPTER 1
God's Original Plan

WHY IS THERE EVIL IN THE WORLD? WAS THAT PART OF GOD'S PLAN?

SNAPSHOT

Article 1   Page 11
The Divine Architect and His Plans
• Pre-read: Genesis 1:1–2:3
• Pre-read: Genesis 2:4–25

Article 2   Page 18
The Bible or Science—Which One Is Right?

Article 3   Page 23
Right People, Wrong Turn
• Pre-read: Genesis 3:1–24
• Pre-read: Genesis 4:1–16
• Pre-read: Genesis 6:5–9:29
• Pre-read: Genesis 11:1–9

Article 4   Page 30
Sin's Ripple Effect

Article 1

The Divine Architect and His Plans

Is there a God? How do we know? Did something create God, or has God always existed? Did God create everything, or did the universe just sort of happen? Why did God create us? If God is good, why are suffering and evil part of creation? Each mystery leads to another greater mystery. Then your head just starts spinning with the immensity of it all!

The Bible, and in particular, the Book of Genesis, lays the foundation for our belief in the one true God, Creator of **Heaven** and Earth. It recounts the family histories of our ancestors in faith and the messy fall from grace because of their choices. This biblical text pulls no punches when it comes to facing the darker side of human behavior with its shocking portrayals of murder, rape, infidelity, tribal wars, and more. Even though human failings and **sin** get lots of attention, the important thing that Genesis teaches is that this is not how it started. It was not even the plan. On the contrary, God's plan was very good.

© Vadim Sadovski / Shutterstock.com

"In the beginning, . . . God created the heavens and the earth" (Genesis 1:1).

Heaven ➤ A state of eternal life and union with God, in which one experiences full happiness and the satisfaction of the deepest human longings.

sin ➤ Any deliberate offense, in thought, word, or deed, against the will of God. Sin wounds human nature and injures human solidarity.

In the Beginning

The Book of Genesis appropriately opens the Bible with the words "In the beginning." In Greek, the word *Genesis* means "beginning." The first few chapters address how God created everything, how the human race took a turn down the path of sinful disobedience, and how that path brought about a separation from God and one another. As you read these chapters, you may notice that the Bible has two complementary Creation accounts. The first account tells how God created everything in six days and rested on the seventh. The second account continues with a unique narrative focused on Adam and Eve, which many scholars believe was written centuries before the first one.

Why are there two Creation accounts in the Book of Genesis, and which one of them is true? The short answer is that both of them are true. Both express the religious or spiritual truths that God wanted to convey for the sake of our salvation. Each Creation account has its own complementary set of truths to teach us about God, humanity, and all of creation. And though these accounts use symbolic language and are not intended to be strict historical accounts, they do convey some historical truths. One such truth is that all humanity descended from a first set of parents, who are symbolically named Adam and Eve. (We will further explore Catholic principles for interpreting the Bible in chapter 4).

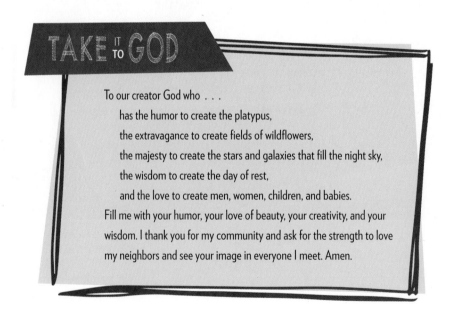

TAKE IT TO GOD

To our creator God who . . .

> has the humor to create the platypus,
>
> the extravagance to create fields of wildflowers,
>
> the majesty to create the stars and galaxies that fill the night sky,
>
> the wisdom to create the day of rest,
>
> and the love to create men, women, children, and babies.

Fill me with your humor, your love of beauty, your creativity, and your wisdom. I thank you for my community and ask for the strength to love my neighbors and see your image in everyone I meet. Amen.

It Was Good

Have you ever had a teacher who repeated something over and over in order to drive home a point to make sure you would remember it? When this happens, we know it must be something important. The author of the first Creation account does something similar. This account describes how God created the universe within a six-day period. Notice how the author declares, "God saw that it was good," as God finishes each act of Creation.

Then God said: Let there be light, and there was light. God *saw that the light was good*. . . .

Then God said: Let the water under the sky be gathered into a single basin, so that the dry land may appear. And so it happened. . . . God called the dry land "earth," and the basin of water he called "sea." *God saw that it was good*. Then God said: Let the earth bring forth vegetation: every kind of plant that bears seed and every kind of fruit tree on earth that bears fruit with its seed in it. And so it happened. . . . *God saw that it was good*. . . .

Then God said: Let there be lights in the dome of the sky, to separate day from night. . . . God set them in the dome of the sky, to illuminate the earth, to govern the day and the night, and to separate the light from the darkness. *God saw that it was good*. . . .

Then God said: Let the water teem with an abundance of living creatures, and on the earth let birds fly beneath the dome of the sky. God created the great sea monsters and all kinds of crawling living creatures with which the water teems, and all kinds of winged birds. *God saw that it was good*. . . .

Then God said: Let the earth bring forth every kind of living creature: tame animals, crawling things, and every kind of wild animal. And so it happened: God made every kind of wild animal, every kind of tame animal, and every kind of thing that crawls on the ground. *God saw that it was good*.

(Genesis 1:3–4,9–25, italics added)

UNIT 1

6 DAYS OF CREATION

In the first Creation account, God creates the world in six symbolic days. This graphic shows the key things God created on each day.

Finally, the author tells us that on the sixth day "God looked at everything he had made, and found it very good" (1:31).

This belief that all of creation is good is an essential part of our faith. It guides our interaction with other human beings and all of creation. We also learn something about the Creator: because everything he creates is good, we can conclude that God is also good.

The first Creation account also notes one thing that sets human beings apart from the rest of the created world: God made human beings in his own image (see Genesis 1:27). We share this wonderful gift with the angels, whom God also made in his image, having intellect and free will just as we do. All human beings—male and female, no matter the color of their skin, the country where they live, the religion they profess, or the sins they have committed— are made in God's image. This means that every person, without exception, is worthy of our care and respect.

These Creation accounts also teach us about the nature of God. Many creation stories from other cultures written during this time period depict creation resulting from violent struggles among many gods. This is not true of the Creation accounts in Genesis; there is only one God who created everything out

of love, not violence. His all-powerful nature is demonstrated in how he brings light, earth, sky, plants, animals, and human beings into existence by merely speaking. The God revealed in Scripture loves his creation and desires to be in close relationship with it, especially the human beings he created in his image.

Adam and Eve

In the second Creation account, we are introduced to the parents of all human beings, Adam and Eve. God first creates Adam, providing him with everything he needs for physical survival in the Garden of Eden, but God notes that it is not good for Adam to be alone. God then makes a companion for Adam (see Genesis 2:18–25). Here we learn God's desire for us to be part of a community. The most basic cell of a community is the family. By bringing Adam and Eve together, God establishes a community of people who are bound to him and to one another. The union of Adam and Eve with God **prefigures** the People of God called together by Jesus Christ to be his **Church.**

© agsandrew / Shutterstock.com

God created human beings in his image and likeness.

prefigure ➤ Similar to foreshadowing, it is an indication of a type of thing, person, or event that points to its future fulfillment. The meaning of what is contained in the Old Testament is unveiled in the New Testament.

Church ➤ The term *Church* has three inseparable meanings: (1) the entire People of God throughout the world; (2) the diocese, which is also known as the local Church; (3) the assembly of believers gathered for the celebration of the liturgy, especially the Eucharist.

The union of Adam and Eve is so close that the author of Genesis writes, "The two of them become one body" (2:24). The curious phrase "become one body" could refer to the sexual union that brings about children, but it also refers to the deep bonds created by people who love one another. Perhaps you know a friend who has lost a parent or someone else very close. You might not have even known the person who died, but somehow you are able to feel the loss and sadness your friend is experiencing. This is called compassion, which literally means "to suffer with." It occurs when one has a deep love for another. This bond is God's intention for us all—to be united in one body. Saint Paul calls the Church "the Body of Christ" and writes, "If [one] part suffers, all the parts suffer with it; if one part is honored, all the parts share its joy" (1 Corinthians 12:26).

Longing for . . . Something

A new phone, a new car, winning the game, getting an A on your test, finding your true love, fame and fortune. . . . The list goes on and on. Everybody wants something. It seems to be an unending cycle of craving, grasping, fulfilling, and repeating. Too often we remain unaware that there is a hole in our heart that only God can fill. We all have this empty place that longs for God's love and connection. In showing the close and intimate relationship between God and Adam, Genesis helps us to see that God's plan from the beginning has been for human beings to be in intimate relationship with him.

Though this emptiness can feel quite uncomfortable at times, the desire to fill that hole is nonetheless good because it is what draws us closer to God. It is like an empty stomach that hungers for food. Without the hunger, we do not know to seek nourishment. This healthy yearning for God is actually from God, because he desires to be in a relationship with us. It is God's way of drawing us nearer to him. The good news is that God fills that hole!

A Square Peg in a Round Hole

If we were to believe every commercial message we see on television, we might think our joy in life could be found in choosing the right toothpaste. How often has that worked? The media constantly bombard us with messages that happiness can be found by dressing in a particular way or participating in certain activities. Why would any of these be more likely to make us happier than the toothpaste? None of these things provide us with any lasting satisfaction, yet that is where we often go to fill the void. Trying to find a lasting happiness in possessions, experiences, and other worldly things is like trying to fit a square peg in a round hole. It just does not fit. The more you try to force it, the more pain and frustration it brings.

These things to which we gravitate in our search for happiness are what Saint Thomas Aquinas (1225–1274) called particular goods. A **particular good** is something that shares in the goodness of God but ultimately leaves us unsatisfied. Food, sporting events, scientific endeavors, relationships, sex, power, and so on—these are all things that can help us to experience the goodness of God, but any one of these by itself will not bring us deep and lasting happiness.

Aquinas says that the **ultimate good** is the source of our complete fulfillment. This fulfillment can be found only in our union with God. It is God alone who can bring us lasting peace and joy both in this life and in the next. Attempting to fulfill this fundamental desire elsewhere leads only to frustration and sometimes failure. Saint Augustine of Hippo (354–430) offered a similar sentiment when he said, "Our hearts are restless until they rest in you, O Lord." The Creation accounts in Genesis help us understand why we have this longing. ✳

OVERVIEW of the Book of Genesis

- **Themes:** The goodness of creation, sin and its consequences, covenant, and bringing good out of evil.
- **Important people:** Adam and Eve, Cain and Abel, Noah, Abraham, Sarah, Isaac, Jacob, and Joseph.

HMMMMM. . .
If some of our desires do not lead us to happiness, what might help us determine the desires that do?

particular good ➤ Something that shares in the goodness of God but ultimately leaves you unsatisfied.

ultimate good ➤ The source of our complete fulfillment, which can be found only in our union with God.

UNIT 1

Article 2

The Bible or Science—Which One Is Right?

The Book of Genesis says that God created the entire world and all of its inhabitants in only six days (see Genesis, chapter 1). Your science teacher may say that the universe started with the big bang over thirteen billion years ago. The Book of Genesis says that God created man "out of the dust of the ground" (2:7). Your science teacher may say that human beings evolved from apes. This seems to set up a conflict between the Bible and science. Which one is true? Actually, they are both true, just in different ways.

That may seem like a poor excuse for an answer, but consider this analogy. A baby boy is born into the world. One could say that the love his parents had for one another and their desire for a family is what brought this beautiful boy into existence. One could also say that the infant was the result of the fertilization of an egg by a sperm, which then began a nine-month-long gestation, followed by the baby's birth. Which one is true? Are they both true, just in different ways?

We "do not have to choose between religion and science because both are true." —Pope Leo XIII

UNIT 1

Did you know that a Catholic priest is responsible for the big bang theory, a scientific theory explaining how the universe began? It's true! The theory was first suggested by Fr. Georges Lemaître, a priest from Belgium. In the 1920s, he proposed that the universe originated from the explosion of a single primeval atom. Subsequent studies by Edwin Hubble and others have confirmed that the universe was indeed expanding. Though there are other hypotheses, Father Lemaître's big bang theory remains one of the world's best scientific explanations for the beginning of our universe.

Truth We Can Figure Out

What does it mean when a science book says that something is true? It is important to note that science deals strictly with *objectively measurable phenomena*. A *phenomenon* (sing.) is a fact, event, or situation that can be observed. *Measurable* means that one can calculate its observable qualities in a certain way. *Objective* means that one is describing something based on facts as they truly are, rather than being influenced by one's personal biases. For example, height, length, weight, and speed are all phenomenon that can be measured. They are also objective facts. They are objective because, if calculated correctly, they will be the same no matter who is measuring them. When numerous scientists find the same results in their measurements, they will declare something to be true. Even then, it does not mean it is true forever. With new information, scientists reevaluate and sometimes later come to different conclusions.

Often people equate the words *true* or *truth* with the scientific meaning of the terms. Yet some things that we know are true even though we cannot measure them objectively. For example, you might say that you are happy. Happiness is not a phenomenon that we can measure objectively. Even though you know it to be true, it cannot be scientifically proven.

A great deal of confusion could be avoided if people understood that religion and science address different kinds of truth and use different methods to discover what is true. For example, there are spiritual truths that are logical and can be known through human reasoning rather than through scientific proof. And there are some truths beyond the abilities of humans to know, except when they are revealed by God.

The Truth That Is Revealed

God gave human beings the wonderful gift of reason, which is the power of gaining knowledge through the use of logic. Human reason is limited though. First, we are not completely logical beings. We are often swayed by emotions, and our viewpoints can be tainted by selfishness or misunderstandings. Second, our knowledge is limited by our experiences. We do not have the benefit of being everywhere, all the time. But there is one who does have that benefit!

God is not constrained by his own creation. Our ability to grasp him is limited, but his ability to reveal himself to us is unlimited. Throughout history, God has done exactly this. The Bible is the record of how God has revealed himself and his plan to us. The most important truths revealed in the Bible are not scientific truths but religious truths. For example, in the first Creation account, we learn that God is good. This truth is not something that can be measured objectively. God's goodness has no height, weight, speed, and so on. The truth of God's goodness is outside the realm of science, but it is neverthe-less true. We look to the Church to help us relate the truths of faith to those of science. (We will explore God's Revelation more completely in chapter 2.)

The Truth Is Always True

Pope Leo XIII wrote, "Truth cannot contradict truth" ("Encyclical on the Study of Holy Scripture", number 23). You do not have to choose between religion and science because both are true, even though we come to know their truths through different methods. And if both are true, then one cannot inval-idate the other. "There can never be any real discrepancy between faith and reason"[1] (*Catechism of the Catholic Church* [CCC], 159). Ultimately, if the truths of religion and science appear to contradict each other, we have not fully understood one or both.

Faith and reason actually comple-ment each other. The sciences have greatly helped deepen our understanding of the Bible itself. Sacred Scripture has a divine source, but each of its many human authors lived in a particular location and historical situation, spoke a specific lan-guage, and had an understanding of the world that was unique to their place and time. Science helps us understand these

Pope Leo XIII was head of the Catholic Church from February 20, 1878, to July 20, 1903.

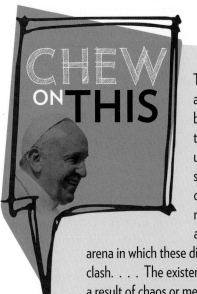

CHEW ON **THIS**

The issues you have been addressing . . . are of particular interest to the Church, because they have to do with questions that concern us . . . the beginning of the universe and its evolution, and the profound structure of space and time. . . . It is clear that these questions have a particular relevance for science, philosophy, theology and for the spiritual life. They represent an arena in which these different disciplines meet and sometimes clash. . . . The existence and intelligibility of the universe are not a result of chaos or mere chance, but of God's Wisdom, present "at the beginning of his work . . ." (Prov 8:22). . . . We ought never to fear truth, but welcome new scientific discoveries with an attitude of humility. (Pope Francis, "Greeting of His Holiness Pope Francis to Participants at the Conference Organized by the Vatican Observatory," May 12, 2017)

people, places, languages, and situations. The disciplines of archaeology and anthropology have been indispensable to bringing us a far better understanding of the written words of Sacred Scripture.

Looking at the Big Picture

Some Christians read the Bible literally. That is, they believe that every part of the Bible teaches not just religious truth but scientific truth as well. Because of this, they do not support the scientific theories of evolution or the big bang theory. This **fundamentalist approach** embraces an interpretation of the Bible that ignores the literary forms used by the Bible's human authors and the historical settings in which the writings were developed.

---

fundamentalist approach ➤ The interpretation of the Bible and Christian doctrine based on the literalist meaning of the Bible's words. The interpretation is made without regard to the historical setting in which the writings or teachings were first developed.

UNIT 1

Catholics do not read the Bible with a fundamentalist approach but rather with a **contextualist approach**. Our interpretation of the Bible takes into account various contexts in order to understand the truth God is revealing through the Bible's words. These contexts include the literary forms used, the historical situation at the time, the human authors' cultural beliefs and practices, and a number of other things. These contexts provide us with clues to help us better understand the intention of the human authors in expressing God's Word. (We will look more closely at this in chapter 4.)

Biblical Truth

Much of what is written in the Bible is scientifically and historically correct, but not all of it. The Bible was never intended to be a science or history book in the way we understand those fields of study today. Offering scientific explanations and recalling historical events are not its main goals; the purpose of the Bible is to reveal religious truth. In this sense, "the books of Scripture firmly, faithfully, and without error teach that truth which God, for the sake of our salvation, wished to see confided to the Sacred Scriptures"[2] (*CCC*, 107). When the Bible teaches what God wants us to know for our salvation, it is fully accurate and true. This is something we can count on! ✳

 **HMMMMM. . .** What might be the biggest challenge to understanding the intentions of the Bible's human authors?

---

contextualist approach ➤ The interpretation of the Bible that takes into account the various contexts for understanding. These contexts include the senses of Scripture, literary forms, historical situations, cultural backgrounds, the unity of the whole of Sacred Scripture, Sacred Tradition, and the analogy of faith.

Article 3
Right People, Wrong Turn

Kenoba's eyes were filled with tears as she texted her friend. "Why does it have to be like this?" she asked. "Why did Missy have to die in that accident? Why do my mother and brother have to fight all the time? Why can't everyone just get along and love each other?"

The Bible's answer in the Book of Genesis is that the world isn't supposed to be as Kenoba described. Instead, Genesis depicts Adam and Eve living with God in the Garden of Eden in a state of **original holiness** and **original justice**. Holiness refers to their loving union with God and being free from sin. Justice is a condition in which rights and duties within relationships are respected and everyone gets what is due to them. In other words, God created a world with no suffering or hatred or even death for our first parents to live in.

This original state of holiness and justice allowed Adam and Eve to share in the divine life of God, which certainly brought them complete happiness. They experienced this happiness because they lived their lives the way God intended—in full communion with God, with each other, and with the world God created.

We do not know how long this blessed state lasted for Adam and Eve. We do know that temptation came in the symbolic form of a snake and a forbidden fruit (see Genesis 3:1–13). Adam and Eve's sin of disobedience is where humanity takes a wrong turn and sin and evil enter history. This is sometimes simply called **the Fall**. Instead of following God's way, Adam and Eve decided to take on the role of God themselves—to "be like gods, who know good and evil" (Genesis 3:5). This **Original Sin** is how humanity lost its original holiness and justice and became subject to death.

---

original holiness ➤ The original state of human beings in their relationship with God, sharing in the divine life in full communion with him.

original justice ➤ The original state of Adam and Eve before the Fall, a state of complete harmony with themselves, with each other, and with all of creation.

Fall, the ➤ Also called the Fall from Grace, the biblical revelation about the origins of sin and evil in the world, expressed figuratively in the account of Adam and Eve in Genesis.

Original Sin ➤ From the Latin *origo*, meaning "beginning" or "birth." The term has two meanings: (1) the sin of the first human beings, who disobeyed God's command by choosing to follow their own will and thus lost their original holiness and became subject to death, and (2) the fallen state of human nature that affects every person born into the world, except Jesus and Mary.

Adam and Eve's sin of disobedience is where humanity takes a wrong turn and when sin and evil enter history.

The Tree of the Knowledge of Good and Evil

Numerous questions often arise from reading this story. If Adam and Eve had never eaten the fruit, would we all be happy now and never die? Why did God allow the serpent to be there in the first place? Why would God not want Adam and Eve to know the difference between good and evil? If they were supposed to stay away from the tree, why did God put it right in the middle of the garden?

These are all good questions, but they assume that these events occurred exactly as they are stated in the text. It is important to remember that this narrative is not intended to be a historical report. The author instead used fig-urative language to represent what happened to humanity's first parents, their disobedience to God, and the consequences for those actions. The account symbolically expresses several important truths regarding our relationship with God: sin is a free choice, sin destroys the harmony and union humans have with one another and God, and sin brings about pain and suffering.

Why was it wrong for Adam and Eve to eat from the Tree of the Knowledge of Good and Evil? It is important to recall the symbolic nature of this account and look at the tree within the context of the entire narrative. What happens immediately after they eat from the tree? Adam and Eve notice they are naked, and they cover up what makes them different—the things that separate them from each other. He is a man. She is a woman. Before this they were one body—"bone of my bones and flesh of my flesh" (Genesis 2:23)—who felt no shame in each other's presence.

Consider what it would be like to stand naked in front of a classroom of your peers. Most of us would run out of the classroom immediately or do what Adam and Eve did—try to cover our private parts! We would react this way in part because we fear others judging an intimately personal part of who we are and categorizing us as beautiful or ugly. In fact, we do this to ourselves all the time: What do people think of me? Am I loved? Am I worthy of being loved? We also look upon others with the eyes of judgment. We label one another— this person is good and that person is evil.

Adam and Eve hid from God after their disobedience because of their shame and fear of judgment. They pulled away from the one who loved them, and tried to hide the beauty that he had created. Like a parent saddened at the irreversible mess his children made, God asked Adam and Eve: "Who told you that you were naked? Have you eaten from the tree of which I had forbidden you to eat?" (Genesis 3:11). God knows that we cannot bear the burden of judgment on one another, "For by the standard by which you judge another you condemn yourself, since you, the judge, do the very same things" (Romans 2:1). If we were to see through God's eyes, we would know that his unconditional love is greater than any judgment or label we place upon one another.

MAKE IT SO

"Am I my brother's keeper?" (Genesis 4:9). Cain's response was just a dodge. The truth he did not want to face is that all of us are our brothers' and sisters' keepers. You are responsible for taking care of the clueless classmate who just transferred to your school; the lonely kid searching for a welcoming lunch table; the young, first-year teacher who has not gotten control of classroom discipline yet; or your mother or father, who had a bad day at work. They are all your brothers and sisters (yes, even your parents). Though you certainly cannot be everything to everyone, you can be something special to someone.

Am I My Brother's Keeper?

Let's consider the other accounts in the first eleven chapters of Genesis: Cain and Abel, the Flood, and the Tower of Babel. These stories are also considered prehistorical narratives, which is not to say that they did not happen; rather, these events simply occurred before the time in which human beings wrote down their history. Ancient people passed these stories on orally, and over time they were written down to become the Book of Genesis, reliably preserving the truths God intended to reveal. They offer us many important religious truths about the inherent goodness of humanity, the consequences of sin, and God's mercy.

After Adam and Eve are expelled from the Garden of Eden, Genesis moves on to the events surrounding their two sons, Cain and Abel (see 4:1–16). If you have brothers or sisters, you might find Cain and Abel's story of sibling rivalry and jealousy kind of familiar. Cain's jealousy reflects something that every human being feels to some greater or lesser degree: the desire to be noticed and appreciated. But when that desire becomes twisted and turns into jealousy, it reflects one of the consequences of sin: a self-centered temperament.

When asked about Abel's whereabouts, Cain avoids answering God's question with a dismissive and rude response, "Am I my brother's keeper?" (Genesis 4:9). Cain's comeback to God reflects an attitude that lies at the heart of sin: my life is about me, not about you or anyone else. When we take on

Cain's fierce jealousy of Abel drives him to commit murder.

UNIT 1

© Elena Elisseeva / Shutterstock.com

All of us are our brothers' and sisters' keepers.

this mindset, we tend to look at other human beings as objects who can either contribute to, or get in the way of, our own happiness. We delude ourselves and think that we are "like gods, who know good and evil" (3:5). Thinking we know it all, we look with eyes of judgment and decide who is worthy and who is not. This attitude can lead to something as commonplace as deciding who sits with us at the lunch table, and it can also lead to something as atrocious as genocide. Cain and Abel remind us that this self-centered temperament clouds our emotions and thoughts, and when we act on these emotions and thoughts, peace and harmony begin to disintegrate.

The Great Flood

The account of Noah and the Flood is probably one that is very familiar to you. Perhaps as a child you had a toy ark with a tiny set of Noah and his family, along with pairs of various animals from around the world. Noah's adventure has also been used as the plot for popular comedic movies as well. Images of rainbows and cheerful animals getting along together on a seafaring vessel might leave the impression of a happy-go-lucky story. On the contrary, the biblical account is a much darker experience for Noah and his family.

The account begins with God observing the wickedness of human beings. When he saw "how every desire that their heart conceived was always nothing but evil, the LORD regretted making human beings on the earth" (Genesis 6:5–6). God regretted creating human beings? That is pretty bad! It was so bad that it seems that God found it best to just start over with the one good man left on Earth: Noah. The plan was to use a great flood to wipe out every human being and animal on the planet, except for Noah, his family, and the pairs of animals they loaded on to the ark.

The Flood comes and the ark stays afloat on the waters for forty days (see Genesis 7:17). Forty is a number that you see often in the Bible. The biblical authors sometimes convey a deeper truth using symbolic numbers like forty. Moses was on Mount Sinai for forty days (see Exodus 24:18). The Israelites wandered in the desert for forty years (see Joshua 5:6). Jesus was tempted by the devil in the desert for forty days (see Matthew 4:1–2). So forty is a number indicating a period of testing, trials, or purification. Knowing this, we are able to connect God's purification of the world's sin by the Flood with other times of testing and purification in the Bible.

It is in this account that we see the first mention of the word *covenant* in the Bible. A **covenant** is a solemn agreement between human beings or between God and humans in which mutual commitments are recognized. Covenants play a significant role throughout the Bible. They are often accompanied by some sort of physical, outward sign that reminds those involved of the covenant. With Noah, God promises never to destroy all the creatures of the Earth with another flood and offers the rainbow as a sign of their covenant. "When the bow appears in the clouds, I will see it and remember the everlasting covenant between God and every living creature—every mortal being that is on earth" (Genesis 9:16). Covenants are a way that God expresses his desire to be in communion with his people, and a way that we express our love for and fidelity to God.

© Mike Mareen / Shutterstock.com

The rainbow is the sign of the covenant between God and Noah.

covenant ➤ A solemn agreement between human beings or between God and a human being in which mutual commitments are made.

UNIT 1

Stop Your Babeling!

The Tower of Babel is the last of the prehistorical events covered in Genesis. It is an interesting account of how sin separates us from God and one another. On the surface, the builders of the tower seem a little arrogant but rather harmless in the grand scheme of things. What is so wrong about building a tower? We can get a clue from understanding a bit of the Hebrew language that was used to write most of the Old Testament. "Babel" is the Hebrew form of the name "Babylon." For the ancient Israelites, the story of the Tower of Babel would call to mind the Babylonian Empire and all its evils.

The chief sin of the builders of the Tower of Babel was their pride. The tower they planned to build would bridge the gap between Earth and sky (Genesis 11:4). For them, the sky represented the dwelling place of god. They arrogantly believed they could bridge the gap between God and fallen humanity. This is the sin of many of the empires encountered by the Israelites: the Egyptians, the Assyrians, and the Babylonians. God thwarts their ambition by confusing the people's language (see Genesis 9:5–8), reminding them—and us—that God alone is the source of our salvation.

The Root of Evil

If you spend 30 minutes watching the world news, you will come across enough stories of war, poverty, human trafficking, and other types of violence that you might question the goodness of God. But the accounts from Genesis that we just reviewed make it clear that the source of evil in the world has nothing to do with God's action and everything to do with the actions of human beings. God created everything good, but humans have free will and can choose to do good or evil.

Imagine that your parents give you a car so that you can get to school, attend church youth group events, or participate in service projects. These are all good things, but what comes attached to those car keys is both freedom and responsibility. You can use the car to travel to school and church, or you can use the car to participate in selfish, illegal activities. If you are caught doing something wrong in the car, you cannot blame your parents for the choices you freely made. In a similar sense, God has given us many gifts for us to use for the good of all. If we use them selfishly, we cannot point the finger of blame at God. ✳

 How does the author of The Tower of Babel use language and location to represent the consequences of sin?

Article 4
Sin's Ripple Effect

If you toss a stone into the water, it sends circular ripples outward from the center point where the stone landed. If you were only able to see these waves going out in circles, you could still pinpoint the spot in which the stone landed. Similarly, the prevalence of sin in the world today can be traced backed to the disobedience of Adam and Eve.

© eyepark / Shutterstock.com

The negative effects of sin can ripple outward, affecting many other people.

The Consequences of Sin

The consequences of sin are quite natural: a loss of unity, harmony, and justice. For example, if your best friend was angry with you and posted something hurtful about you on social media, your friendship would certainly face some rough waters. Perhaps you both might hold a grudge and not talk to one another for a long time. Maybe this would even cause a split in your group of friends—some supporting you and others backing your friend. Sin brings about pain, suffering, a loss of unity, and a ripple effect that can be devastating.

The consequence of our first parents' sinful choice was a loss of their original holiness and justice. Their intimate union with God was disrupted. Humanity still suffers from the effects of their Original Sin; we lack the freedom and holiness that God intended for us. Our self-centered outlook distorts our sense of right and wrong. Because of Original Sin, our human nature is weakened. Our power to relate to God and choose what is good has been undermined, therefore we are inclined to sin. All human beings have inherited this tendency toward sin, which is called **concupiscence**. We experience concupiscence when we feel tempted to cheat on a test, to lie to our friends, or to post something mean about a classmate on social media. How this tendency is passed on is a mystery. One thing is certain: sin entered the world and its effects have been lasting.

Sin and Salvation History

We can see the effects of Original Sin throughout all of **salvation history**. Salvation history is the pattern of specific events in human history through which God clearly reveals his presence and saving actions. The Bible communicates salvation history, particularly how God never gives up on his people despite the times they turn away from him. The People of God repeatedly swing between faithfulness and unfaithfulness. They often seek the quick and easy route of self-satisfaction, rather than following God's will.

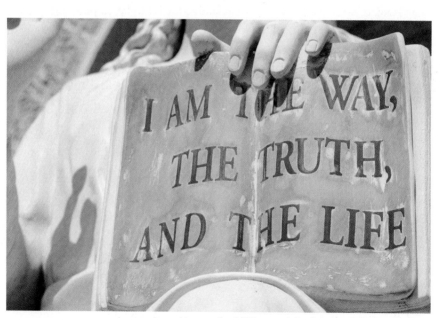

Jesus indicated he was the fulfillment of God's saving plan when he said, "I am the way, the truth, and the life . . ." (John 14:6).

---

concupiscence ➤ The tendency of all human beings toward sin, as a result of Original Sin.

salvation history ➤ The pattern of specific events in human history in which God clearly reveals his presence and saving actions. Salvation was accomplished once and for all through Jesus Christ, a truth foreshadowed and revealed throughout the Old Testament.

Ultimately, the good news is that sin does not have the final say. "For God so loved the world that he gave his only Son, so that everyone who believes in him might not perish but might have eternal life. For God did not send his Son into the world to condemn the world, but that the world might be saved through him" (John 3:16). The Bible repeatedly teaches that God still cares for us: God made clothes for Adam and Eve (see Genesis 3:21), and God protected Cain from being killed (see 4:14–15).

As we continue through this course, we will study how God has revealed himself, his love for us, and his plan for our salvation. Our guide will be the Bible, God's Holy Word. We will explore how the Bible came to be and how to understand, or interpret, its stories and teachings. We will take a close look at the accounts in the books of the Old Testament and what they mean for us today. And we will conclude with a brief look at the New Testament, in which the fullness of God's plan is revealed by the coming of his Son, Jesus Christ. ✳

A Little Fun!

The Book of Genesis has been a great source for Bible-based puns over the years. Have you heard any of these?

Q. Where is the first baseball game in the Bible?
A. In Genesis because it says "In the big inning, Eve stole first, Adam stole second, and Cain struck out Abel."

Q. How did Noah's family find their way around the ark at night?
A. They used floodlights.

Q. Why didn't they play cards on the ark?
A. Because Noah was sitting on the deck.

CATHOLICS **MAKING** A DIFFERENCE

Imagine an island far off the coast of California, whose inhabitants are all infected with a contagious, disfiguring disease. Now, imagine going there, by choice. This is what Saint Damien of Molokai (1840–1889) did. Leprosy is a deadly, contagious disease that damages the skin, limbs, nerves, and eyes. At the time of Saint Damien, it was incurable, so to stop its progress the authorities banished lepers to an isolated Hawaiian peninsula called Kalaupapa. Saint Damien was a Catholic priest from Belgium who was sent as a missionary to the Hawaiian Islands. He saw the inherent value of these people and the terrible way they were treated. He volunteered to move to Kalaupapa in 1873. He lived closely with the people he served and tended to their needs. Damien eventually contracted leprosy and died in 1889. He was canonized a saint in 2009.

HMMMMM. . .

Describe a time when you have you witnessed one sin leading to other sins.

---

canonize ➤ The act by which the Church officially recognizes a deceased Catholic as a saint.

1. What does it mean to say that both Creation accounts in the Book of Genesis are true?

2. "God looked at everything he had made, and found it very good" (Genesis 1:31). What important beliefs does this verse lead us to?

3. How can science and religion both be true?

4. Explain the differences between the fundamentalist and contextualist approaches to interpreting the Bible. Which approach do Catholics take?

5. Why do we consider longing for God to be something good?

6. Define *Original Sin* and explain the consequences that followed from it.

7. Use one of the prehistorical narratives to explain the ripple effects of sin.

ART STUDY

"AND GOD SAID IT WAS GOOD"

The two accounts of Creation in the Book of Genesis reveal that all creation is good.

1. What mood does this painting convey?

2. How does the artist show the perfection of God's creation?

3. What in the painting, gives you a hint of what will happen in Genesis, chapter 3?

CHAPTER 2
God's Revelation

HOW DO I KNOW GOD EXISTS?

SNAPSHOT

Article 5   Page 37
Natural Revelation: Finding the Artist in the Art

Article 6   Page 41
Logic: It Just Makes Sense

Article 7   Page 46
Divine Revelation: The Word from On High

Article 8   Page 51
Inspiration: From God's Mouth to Our Hearts

Article 5

Natural Revelation: Finding the Artist in the Art

Ever since Bianca was a little girl, she's loved making animals and people with clay. When Bianca was six years old, her parents took her to the Baltimore Museum of Art so she could see real sculptures created by famous artists. They were all so beautiful, but there was one she liked best of all: *The Thinker*, by Auguste Rodin. Bianca was fascinated by this big sculpture. To her, *The Thinker* looked uneasy, anxious, and seemed to be concentrating very hard. It made her wonder what the artist was thinking about when he created it: Was he trying to solve a problem? Was something troubling him? Was he missing something in his life?

August Rodin's famous sculpture *The Thinker*, on the grounds of the Musée Rodin, Paris, France.

© davidf / iStock.com

TAKE IT TO GOD

God,

Thank you for the gift of words.

In the beginning, you created everything with your words.

Your Word became flesh in Jesus Christ.

Your words in the Bible offer me guidance and hope.

Give me the courage to use my words honestly.

Inspire me to use my words to enlighten and encourage others.

Help me to hear you, even when your voice is beyond words.

I promise that I will listen.

I give you my word!

Amen.

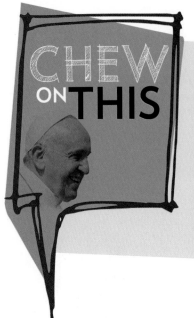

CHEW ON THIS

Creation is not some possession that we can lord over for our own pleasure; nor, even less, is it the property of only some people, the few: creation is a gift, it is the marvelous gift that God has given us, so that we will take care of it and harness it for the benefit of all, always with great respect and gratitude. (Pope Francis, "General Audience," Saint Peter's Square, May 21, 2014)

Now, as a high school teen, when Bianca visits the museum and sees the sculpture, she can relate to these questions herself. She often feels like she's never fully satisfied or happy even though she has much to be grateful for. Why is that? What's missing in her life?

Knowing God through Creation

Because we were created to be in communion with God, we will constantly be restless until we have fulfilled our desire to know God fully. There are numerous ways we can come to know God. When we look at any artwork, we can learn something about the artist. This does not mean that a painting physically resembles the painter, but rather it reveals something about her, such as her desires, beliefs, hopes, and so on. The American painter Edward Hopper said, "Great art is the outward expression of an inner life in the artist" (Smithsonian Archives of American Art). Similarly, the Bible itself states that we can come to know the "author" of creation through his work. "For from the greatness and the beauty of created things / their original author, by analogy, is seen" (Wisdom 13:5).

If we assume that God created the universe, then by observing the universe we can learn something about God. Saint Paul writes, "Ever since the creation of the world, his invisible attributes of eternal power and divinity have been able to be understood and perceived in what he has made" (Romans 1:20). So what do we learn about God from creation? For one thing, we learn that God is mighty and all-powerful, for the universe we observe is vast and complex beyond our imagination. From the stunning variety and beauty of solar systems, planets, animals, plants, and other life forms, we learn that God is infinitely creative. Seeing how all creatures thrive and are cared for (unless human beings mess things up) tells us that God is good and cares for his creation.

Similarly, because we are made in God's image (see Genesis 1:27), we can gain some understanding of God through our lives and our relationships with one another. Being made in God's image does not mean that we physically look like God. God does not have a height, weight, skin color, or hairstyle, nor does God have a gender. Instead, our **soul** is what reflects the image of God. Every human is endowed with an eternal soul, which finds its origin in God. Because our soul enjoys a freedom that desires truth and beauty and is drawn to goodness and joy, it is reasonable to assume that God is the source of freedom, truth, beauty, goodness, and joy.

Saint Augustine of Hippo (354–430) taught that the beauty of creation itself is a testament to the existence of God. We can see for ourselves the beauty of a tropical beach, a snowcapped mountain range, or a deep and expansive canyon cut by time and water. Though these things are temporary, there must be, argued Saint Augustine, an ultimate beauty from which they were formed. Augustine said that this ultimate beauty is God. By knowing the beauty of creation, we come to know something about its Creator.

Because we are made in God's image, we can gain some understanding of God through our lives and our relationships with one another.

soul ▶ Our spiritual principle, it is immortal, and it is what makes us most like God. Our soul is created by God at the moment of our conception. It is the seat of human consciousness and freedom.

All of these ways of coming to know God through what we can observe and experience is called **natural revelation**. Natural revelation is the process by which God makes himself known to human reason through the created world. We call it "natural" because it is a way God is revealed to us that does not have to be taught or learned. We acquire this information by using logic and observing the world. ✳

HMMMMMM. . . How might the animal or vegetable world reflect some aspect of our Creator?

---

natural revelation ➤ The process by which God makes himself known to human reason through the created world.

Article 6

Logic: It Just Makes Sense

Perhaps you have had the experience of doing something thoughtlessly and someone responded: "God gave you a brain. Use it!" Though that may be kind of a rude response, we must admit that there is truth in it. God did give us intelligence and an ability to discover and learn. Not only will this intelligence help us with our daily activities, it can also lead us toward knowing God.

In the Middle Ages, a number of theologians initiated a new approach in how they addressed and understood God's Revelation. These theologians were called scholastics, and they used philosophy to better understand revealed truth. Grounded in Sacred Scripture and the Church Fathers, **scholastic theology** employed the use of logic to back arguments supporting the existence of God and to come to a deeper understanding of the human experience.

Five Logical Proofs

The most prominent of these scholastic theologians was Saint Thomas Aquinas (1225–1274), a thirteenth-century Dominican priest who was greatly influenced by Greek philosophy. He is known for his systematic way of addressing theological questions, using reason and argumentation. The most well-known example of his work is the *Summa Theologica*, an extensive theological study offering a reasoned approach to the teachings of our faith. Within the *Summa*

Albertus Magnus, Dominican, medieval German scholar, theologian, and teacher of Saint Thomas Aquinas.

---

scholastic theology ➤ The use of philosophical methods to better understand revealed truth. The goal of scholastic theology is to present the understanding of revealed truth in a logical and systematic form.

Theologica, Aquinas provides his "five ways" or proofs of the existence of God. These "proofs" should not to be understood as scientific evidence but rather as "converging and convincing arguments" (*CCC*, number 31) that lead us toward the truth of the existence of God. The following are Aquinas's five proofs:

1. **The First Mover.** This argument rests on the idea that everything in the universe is constantly in motion. If you see a ball rolling on the ground, you can safely assume that something or someone put that ball into motion. Because there is movement in the universe, we can reasonably conclude that at some point there must have been an unmoved mover, which brought everything into motion. This unmoved mover is what we call God.

2. **Causality.** This proof is based on the idea of cause and effect. If there is an effect (such as the existence of something), we can safely say that there must have been a cause. Things do not create themselves but come into being because of a cause, so it stands to reason that there must have been a "first cause" that initiated all things into existence. This first cause is God.

3. **Contingency.** This argument follows the logic that the existence of something is dependent upon the existence of something else. Your existence is contingent on the existence of your parents. If everything depends on the existence of something else, then there must be a prior necessary being who is not dependent on anything else. This necessary being, which is the source of the existence of all creation, is God.

4. **Perfection.** This proof is based on our ability to observe the world and distinguish varying degrees of qualities. We can know the difference between bad, good, and better. For example, we can determine that one person is less healthy than someone else, or that murder is bad and healing a sick person is good. Aquinas said that we are able to make these distinctions because there is a standard of perfection, or ideal, by which we can measure what is perfectly good, true, and beautiful. This ideal or perfect being is God.

5. **Intelligent Being.** This argument is rooted in the orderly way that things behave. The universe is not a chaotic and haphazard existence. Light travels the same speed in the Milky Way as it does in distant galaxies. Human lungs absorb oxygen and exhale carbon dioxide. These behaviors were established by an intelligence outside ourselves. There must have been an intelligent being that gave order and purpose to everything in the universe. This intelligent being is God.

Some of these proofs can be easily confused with one another. Below is a chart that can help us distinguish between them.

UNIT 1

Proof	Addresses the question:	A Brief Reminder	Visual representation
First Mover	Where? (movement)	Things move. Something must have started movement.	
Causality	How?	Cause and effect. Something must have happened first.	
Contingency	What?	Everything depends on something else. Something must have existed first.	
Perfection	How much?	There's bad, good, better. There must be a perfect ideal by which the lesser qualities are measured.	
Intelligent Being	Who?	Things behave regularly and in an orderly fashion. An intelligent being must have given order to the universe.	

Reason Still Needs God's Help

Being made in God's image gives us the capacity to recognize his existence using our experience and reason. We are able to use reason to know God's existence with certainty. However, we are still only human and, because of Original Sin, we often do not use our reason honestly or effectively. For example, selfishness might be an obstacle to honesty. You would be less likely to tell the truth if it meant that you would lose something that is valuable to you. Sin obscures our ability to see things as they are. This includes our ability to know God as he is.

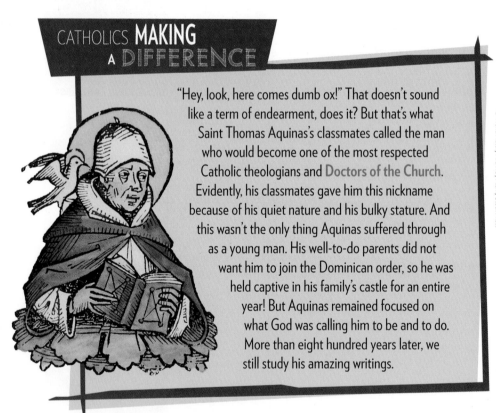

CATHOLICS MAKING A DIFFERENCE

"Hey, look, here comes dumb ox!" That doesn't sound like a term of endearment, does it? But that's what Saint Thomas Aquinas's classmates called the man who would become one of the most respected Catholic theologians and Doctors of the Church. Evidently, his classmates gave him this nickname because of his quiet nature and his bulky stature. And this wasn't the only thing Aquinas suffered through as a young man. His well-to-do parents did not want him to join the Dominican order, so he was held captive in his family's castle for an entire year! But Aquinas remained focused on what God was calling him to be and to do. More than eight hundred years later, we still study his amazing writings.

© World History Archive / Alamy Stock Photo

Doctor of the Church ➤ A title officially bestowed by the Church on saints who are highly esteemed for their theological writings as well as their personal holiness.

It is also important to note that God cannot be contained inside the realm of reason. God's power and understanding have no limits. Because reason is a human activity, it is limited. Humans need help from God so that we can know "those religious and moral truths which of themselves are not beyond the grasp of human reason so that even in the present condition of the human race, they can be known by all men with ease, with firm certainty"[1] (*CCC*, number 38).

Sometimes You Just Know

Human beings also have an inner sense that can help us come to know God. Perhaps you've had the experience of looking up at the night sky, far from city lights, and were amazed at the multitude and brightness of the stars, some of which are so far away that it took thousands of years just for their light to arrive here. Considering how vast creation is, you reaffirm your belief in an intelligent Creator. Some people, after overcoming great adversity, wake up one morning grateful to be alive, and somehow they just know that the gift of life must have a giver. Each of us has a soul that is tuned in to eternity. It basks in the beauty of creation, values truth, guides us toward moral goodness, and through our **conscience** recognizes our God who continues to reveal himself to humanity. ✻

HMMMMM. . .

Choose one of the first four of Aquinas's Five Proofs and apply it to something tangible (that has not already been addressed in the textbook). How does your conclusion compare with Aquinas's conclusion?

---

conscience ➤ The "inner voice," guided by human reason and Divine Law, that enables us to judge the moral quality of a specific action that has been made, is being made, or will be made. This judgment enables us to distinguish good from evil, in order to accomplish good and avoid evil.

Article 7

Divine Revelation: The Word from On High

Knowing *about* someone and *knowing* someone are two different things. You may know that George Washington was born in Virginia and that his wife's name was Martha. You may know that he was a general in the American Revolution and that he became the first president of the United States. Still,

Spending time, talking, listening, and being open are ways we can get to know someone.

you would never say that you *knew* George Washington. Knowing someone requires a relationship of some sort—an openness to each other, time spent together, ongoing communication, and so on.

Something similar could be said of God. We can know about God. We can say that he is the Creator of all things. We can explain that he existed before time and space. We can come to know these things by observing the world and by using reason, what we call natural revelation. This is knowing *about* God.

Knowing God requires something more. **Divine Revelation** is God's self-communication through which he makes known the mystery of his divine plan. Through Divine Revelation, God has revealed himself and has communicated his desire to be in intimate relationship with humanity. Divine Revelation is most fully realized in the life, Passion, death, Resurrection, and Ascension of Jesus Christ. Jesus himself testifies to this: "Whoever has seen me has seen the Father" (John 14:9). Jesus is claiming that he is our best avenue for truly knowing God. And one of the best ways to get to know Jesus is to meet him in Sacred Scripture.

Divine Revelation ➤ God's self-communication through which he makes known the mystery of his divine plan. Divine Revelation is a gift accomplished by the Father, Son, and Holy Spirit through the words and deeds of salvation history. It is most fully realized in the Passion, death, Resurrection, and Ascension of Jesus Christ.

The Divine Roller Coaster

The **Bible**, also called Scripture, is the collection of Christian sacred writings accepted by the Church as inspired by God. It is a testimony to the ways God revealed himself to us through his deeds and words throughout history. In the Bible, we learn how God made himself directly known to the first human beings, guiding them both before and after their sinful disobedience. His condemnation of evil with the Flood was followed by his everlasting covenant with Noah. God then made himself known to Abraham who "obeyed when he was called to go out to a place that he was to receive as an inheritance; he went out, not knowing where he was to go" (Hebrews 11:8). God established a great nation through Abraham's descendants, first through Isaac, then through Jacob, the father of the Twelve Tribes of Israel. Sarah, Rebekah, and Rachel equally trusted God, who gave them the gift of children even when it seemed impossible.

Years after the patriarchs died, their descendants became enslaved in Egypt. God revealed himself to Moses, who led the Israelites out of slavery to the Promised Land. This was the land of Canaan, which God had promised to

© Tommy Alven / Shutterstock.com

In the Bible, the relationship between God and his people was full of ups and downs like a roller-coaster ride.

Bible ➤ The collection of Christian sacred writings, or Scripture, accepted by the Church as inspired by God and composed of the Old and New Testaments.

the children of Abraham, God's **Chosen People**. God established a covenant with his Chosen People at Mount Sinai and gave them his Law to guide them. God's Law is summarized in the Ten Commandments. Even with faithful leadership and laws to follow, the Israelites strayed from their relationship with God. The prophets were chosen by God to speak his message of salvation, which was quite often a call for repentance. Idolatry and terrible treatment of poor and oppressed people topped the complaint lists of **prophets** like Isaiah, Jeremiah, and Amos. They repeatedly called the people to be faithful to their covenant with God. Some prophets even described their hope for a Messiah.

God also reveals himself through the wisdom literature of the Bible. These books offer practical guidance on how to live in accordance with God's Law. They also address the more complicated questions of life, such as the mystery of why bad things happen to good people.

Give It to Me Straight

Have you ever wished that God would just quit being so mysterious and come down here to answer our questions? We want God to give it to us straight. This is exactly what happens next as the New Testament begins. Carrying on in the tradition of the prophets before him, John the Baptist prepares the way for Jesus Christ. As part of that preparation, John calls people to a Baptism of repentance. This Baptism was a first step in the process of healing our wounded nature, a process that would find its completion in the saving work of Jesus Christ.

St. John the Baptist, by Anton Raphael Mengs, 1774. How did John the Baptist prepare the way for Jesus?

Chosen People ➤ Also called the Israelites or the Jews, these are the descendants of Abraham, Isaac, and Jacob, whom God entered into a special covenant with at Mount Sinai. God chose them to prepare for the coming of his Son, Jesus Christ, the Messiah and Savior of the world.

prophet ➤ A person God chooses to speak his message of salvation. In the Bible, primarily a communicator of a divine message of repentance to the Chosen People, not necessarily a person who predicted the future.

I DIDN'T KNOW THAT!

Don't eat shellfish (see Leviticus 11:10–12). Don't wear clothing with mixed materials (see 19:19). And don't curse your parents, or you could be put to death (see 20:9)! These laws from the Old Testament seem strange to us today, but they served two important purposes. They set the Israelites apart from other peoples, helping preserve their ethnic and religious identity. And they provided a high ethical standard for God's Chosen People to live up to, as an example for other peoples. The Books of Exodus, Leviticus, Numbers, and Deuteronomy say that Moses received 613 laws in total. Through these laws, God influenced every part of their daily lives.

In the writings of the New Testament, we learn that the separation between God and humanity is restored through the life, death, Resurrection, and Ascension of Jesus Christ, the only begotten Son of God. In Christ, the human and divine are brought together in one Divine Person.

> In the beginning was the Word,
>   and the Word was with God,
>   and the Word was God.
> He was in the beginning with God.
> All things came to be through him,
>   and without him nothing came to be.
>
> . . . .
>
> And the Word became flesh
>   and made his dwelling among us,
>   and we saw his glory,
>   the glory as of the Father's only Son
>   full of grace and truth.
>
>   (John 1:1–4,14)

UNIT 1

In Jesus Christ, God is most fully revealed. Christ gave the Apostles the responsibility to carry on his mission through the work of the Church, continuing the public Revelation of God's saving work. Because of this, God's public Revelation ended with the death of the last Apostle. Under the guidance of the Holy Spirit, the Church has overcome many challenges and obstacles. As members of the Church, we draw guidance and inspiration from following the struggles of the early Church as told in the Acts of the Apostles and the letters of the New Testament.

This is a very brief summary of **salvation history**, the pattern of events recorded in the Bible through which God clearly reveals his presence and saving actions. As you can tell from just reading Genesis, it is quite a bumpy ride. The history of our faith goes through so many highs and lows that you might think it was a roller coaster. When God's people keep the covenant, things tend to go well. When they fall away toward sin, things head downhill quickly. The good news is that through the ups and downs, God is always in the seat right next to us. ✳

In the Bible, the relationship between the people and God was full of ups and downs like a roller-coaster ride. How might this roller-coaster ride of the Bible be similar to an individual person's relationship with God?

---

salvation history ➤ The pattern of specific events in human history in which God clearly reveals his presence and saving actions. Salvation was accomplished once and for all through Jesus Christ, a truth foreshadowed and revealed throughout the Old Testament.

Article 8

Inspiration: From God's Mouth to Our Hearts

You may have heard of scientists or authors having an "aha! moment" when a new idea or a solution comes to them. When describing these special moments, these people will sometimes say that the idea just popped into their head. Sometimes we call these inspired thoughts. The word *inspire* means to "blow or breathe into," indicating that the thought seems to have come into us from something outside ourselves.

Inspiration takes on new and infinitely more important meaning when it comes to the Bible. Rather than ideas just coming to the writers from out of nowhere, the ideas were inspired by the Holy Spirit, the Third Person of the Trinity. **Divine Inspiration** is the divine assistance the Holy Spirit gave the human authors of the books of the Bible so these authors could communicate through human words the divine message of salvation God wishes to reveal. With this assistance, the human authors of the Bible were able to teach "solidly, faithfully and without error that truth which God wanted put into sacred writings for the sake of salvation" (*Dogmatic Constitution on Divine Revelation* [*Dei Verbum*, 1965], number 11).

The word *inspire* means to "blow or breathe into."

Divine Inspiration ➤ The divine assistance the Holy Spirit gave the authors of the books of the Bible so the authors could write in human words the message of salvation God wanted to communicate.

God Is the Author

There is a term in the publishing world called *ghost writer*. A ghost writer is someone who has a gift for writing and helps other people tell their stories. For example, ghost writers are often used to write celebrity autobiographies. Through interviews or recordings, the celebrity tells his or her life story, but it is the ghost writer who does the actual writing. The life story and its meaning belong to the celebrity. The celebrity is the true author. The ghost writer just had the gifts needed to put the story into written words.

The writing of the Bible is not exactly ghost writing, but it has some similar dynamics. The human authors of Sacred Scripture were inspired by the Holy Spirit to communicate the truths God wanted us to know for our salvation. Remember that the word *inspire* means "breathe into," implying that the Spirit was alive within the human authors, assisting them as they wrote. This does not mean that the Holy Spirit dictated the Bible word for word. Instead, God's truth was expressed using the human authors' skills and creativity. It is a collaboration of God's message combined with human expression. Because it is God's Word being conveyed, God is the true author of Sacred Scripture.

The human authors of the books of the Bible were divinely inspired, allowing them to communicate God's message of salvation through human words.

Just as the human authors of the bible opened themselves up to allow the Holy Spirit to speak through them, we too are called to open ourselves to God's voice in our lives. Set aside a little time each day for God to speak to you.

As the Creator of everything, God is our ultimate source of wisdom and knowledge. Simply put, God is never wrong. Because God is the true author of Sacred Scripture, we can count on the saving truths expressed within in as being inerrant (without error). The books of the Bible teach the truths of faith accurately and without mistake. This is called **biblical inerrancy**.

Because God is the primary author, the Bible is the sacred text for Christians. It is divided into two parts: the Old Testament and the New Testament. The New Testament recounts much of the life of Jesus Christ, the Son of God. It also tells us how his first followers, the early Church, overcame many obstacles to continue Jesus' saving mission. The **Old Testament** contains writings that remain sacred to the Jewish people also. Being Jewish, Jesus often quoted from these writings and found inspiration and comfort from them as well. For Christians, the Old Testament prepares us for God's full Revelation in the life, death, and Resurrection of Jesus Christ. We will look more closely at the meaning of the Old and New Testaments in chapter 3.

---

biblical inerrancy ➤ The doctrine that the books of Sacred Scripture are free from error regarding the truth God wishes to reveal through Scripture for the sake of our salvation.

Old Testament ➤ The Christian name for those biblical writings that record God's Revelation to the Chosen People. Christians believe the Old Testament anticipates and prepares for the New Testament.

His Message, Our Words

Like Jesus, the Bible has both a human and a divine aspect to it. The saving truths expressed in Sacred Scripture are truly divine, but the means of expression are truly human. Because God loves us, he communicates with us in ways that we can understand. If you were walking with a friend and saw that she was in danger of getting hit by a car, would you tell her to move using a language she did not understand? Of course not! Through the Bible, God speaks incomprehensible truths in ways we can comprehend.

However, we sometimes have to work to comprehend the words of the Bible's human authors. Because the human authors were writing two thousand or more years ago, we have to take into account the situations those authors were in. They had an understanding of the world that was unique to their time and place. To properly grasp what the human authors were trying to communicate, we "must take into account the conditions of their time and culture, the literary genres in use at that time, and the modes of feeling, speaking and narrating then current" (*CCC*, number 110). Accurately understanding what the human authors were trying to say allows us to better recognize God's message to us.

MAKE IT SO

We often mistake prayer as simply talking to God, sometimes forgetting the more important part of that conversation: listening to God. Consider what the human authors of the Bible did. They opened themselves up to allow the Holy Spirit to speak through them. In a similar way, we are called to open ourselves to God's voice in our lives. Saint Teresa of Calcutta said, "I always begin my prayer in silence, for it is in the silence of the heart that God speaks" (Carol Kelly-Gangi, *Mother Teresa: Her Essential Wisdom*, page 54). Take 5 minutes every day to sit prayerfully and silently. Set aside this time for God to speak to you. You might not hear a physical voice, but when you listen silently, God will speak to you in ways you never considered.

UNIT 1

But grasping the author's intentions is not enough. God may have communicated truths that were not apparent to the author. Therefore, we must also look for God's truth expressed in the Bible, and we can do so by remaining open to the guidance of the Holy Spirit. The same Spirit that guided the human authors of the Bible also guides us in understanding their words: "Sacred Scripture must be read and interpreted in the light of the same Spirit by whom it was written"[2] (*CCC*, number 111). This is the work of biblical interpretation, which we will look at more closely in chapter 4. ✳

 How does accurately understanding what the human authors of the Bible were communicating allow us to better recognize God's message for us?

1. What does it mean to be made in God's image?

2. Describe scholastic theology and offer an example of it.

3. What is the difference between natural revelation and Divine Revelation?

4. What is salvation history, and how is it like a roller-coaster ride?

5. In what way is God's Divine Revelation most fully realized? Explain.

6. How are Divine Inspiration and biblical inerrancy related to each other?

7. What does it mean to say that the Bible is both human and divine?

How God Reveals Himself to Us

God reveals himself to us through both natural revelation and Divine Revelation.

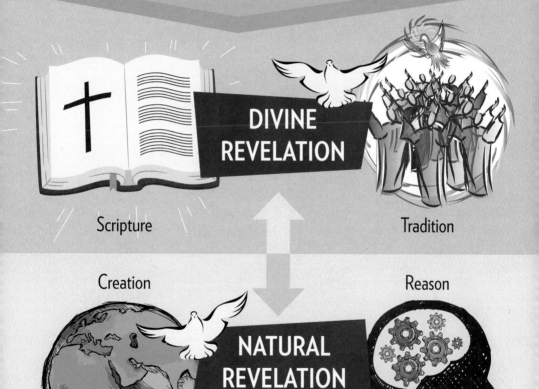

Scripture

Tradition

Creation

Reason

1. Why do you think the arrow points in both directions?

2. Can you give other examples of how God reveals himself to us?

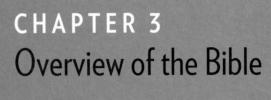

UNIT 1

CHAPTER 3
Overview of the Bible

WHY IS THE BIBLE SO COMPLICATED?

SNAPSHOT

Article 9   Page 59
From Word to Text

Article 10   Page 64
When Did It Happen? When Was It Written?

Article 11   Page 67
Not One Book, but Many

Article 12   Page 72
Bible Translations

Article 13   Page 75
The Old Prepares Us for the New

Article 14   Page 77
The New Fulfills the Old

Article 9

From Word to Text

What was the last article you read online from a reputable news organization? Whatever it was, it probably went through these five stages before it ended up on the computer screen in front of you:

1. Something happened: a memorable event occurred, someone said something significant, many people were affected by a horrible and terrifying tragedy, a joyous celebration took place.

2. The word got out: someone told someone else about it, several people shared the experience with others, someone called a news organization or the police.

3. Reporters investigated and wrote the story.

4. The story went through editing where it was changed, shortened, or maybe combined with a similar story from a different writer.

5. Finally, the story was deemed worthy enough to be included on the news website.

After an important event has occurred, reporters investigate and interview eyewitnesses before writing the story.

Many of the books of the Bible went through a similar process, just with more people and over a longer period of time.

A Significant Experience

The process started with something significant happening. Our ancestors in faith experienced something that affected their lives profoundly: Abraham heard God's voice call him to move to a new land, the Lord appeared to Moses in the form of a burning bush, the psalmist saw how tenderly shepherds cared for their sheep, Jesus multiplied the loaves and fishes for the crowd of disciples. Whether these were personal, internal experiences or events visible to crowds of people, God revealed himself for the sake of our salvation.

By Word of Mouth

When something momentous happens to you, your family, or your friends, what is the first thing you do? Most likely, you talk to or text someone to tell them about it. This is the second stage of the process. The events in the Bible were no different, except there were no phones for talking or texting. Nor did most people know how to read or write. Passing on the stories by word of mouth was the only way to communicate them to others. The handing on of the message of God's saving plan through words is called **oral tradition**. From generation to generation, people passed on the narratives, prayers, and prophecies of their ancestors. Some of the events in the Old Testament were told orally for many years before they were written down. Likewise, in the **New Testament**, the disciples traveled across land and sea to preach the Good News after Jesus told them, "Go, therefore, and make disciples of all nations, baptizing them in the name of the Father, and of the Son, and of the holy Spirit, teaching them to observe all that I have commanded you" (Matthew 28:19–20).

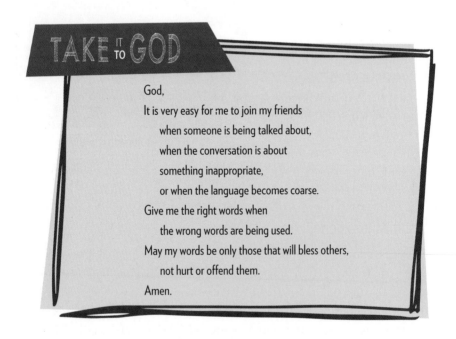

TAKE IT TO GOD

God,
It is very easy for me to join my friends
    when someone is being talked about,
    when the conversation is about
    something inappropriate,
    or when the language becomes coarse.
Give me the right words when
    the wrong words are being used.
May my words be only those that will bless others,
    not hurt or offend them.
Amen.

---

oral tradition ➤ The handing on of the message of God's saving plan through words and deeds.

New Testament ➤ The twenty-seven books of the Bible, which have the life, teachings, Passion, death, Resurrection, and Ascension of Jesus Christ and the beginnings of the Church as their central theme.

But how reliable is oral tradition? If you have ever played the game "Telephone" you know how challenging it can be to keep a simple story straight after passing through only six or seven people in just a couple minutes. How, then, can a complex story stay accurate after passing through a dozen generations over several hundred years? Several factors allow for this.

For example, unlike the game "Telephone," oral tradition is often passed on using song and poetry to help people remember details accurately. Think about how you learned your ABCs when you were a child—through song! Singing the alphabet helped you to remember it.

Also unlike the game "Telephone," oral tradition is held not by one person but by a group of people and passed on from one generation to the next. The events, experiences, memories, and knowledge held in common bind them together as a family, a tribe, a community, or a culture. Consider the alphabet song again. You are not the only person who knows it. This simple little song is shared in common by your family, your friends, and generations of Americans. No doubt you can still sing it to this day, despite having learned it so long ago, and most likely, you'll teach it to your own children and grandchildren in the future.

Finally, consider your own family's stories. How often have you heard the same stories about family trips and memorable events accurately told over and over again at family gatherings? Many families continue to pass down their stories through oral tradition. Some share stories that reach back to the settlers of the first thirteen colonies of the United States. Others have stories of ancestors who were slaves and escaped by way of the Underground Railroad. Historical records often verify the accuracy of these

© McIninch / iStock.com

Many families continue to pass down their stories through oral tradition.

stories. In terms of Scripture, not one, but thousands of Israelite families held their oral tradition sacred, and in doing so, passed it on from one generation to the next, protecting its accuracy as they did so.

The Word in Ink

As time went on, certain events in the lives of the Israelites prompted the need to preserve God's saving words and deeds in writing. This third stage is called the **written tradition**. Quite often these events were crisis moments. For example, one such crisis occurred in the sixth century BC when many Jewish people were captured and taken from the Promised Land to slavery in Babylon. This period is called the **Babylonian Exile**.

MAKE IT SO

Sharing accounts of God's love and saving power was important for our ancestors in faith. How can you participate in sharing the Good News? One way is to be a sharer of good news when you post on social media. Spreading gossip and rumors on social media does not require any skill and can lead to people being hurt.

Before you post something online, ask yourself: "Is it truthful? Is it helpful? Is it kind?" If you cannot answer "yes" to all three questions, do not post it.

written tradition ➤ Under the inspiration of the Holy Spirit, the synthesis in written form of the message of salvation that has been passed down in the oral tradition.

Babylonian Exile ➤ The period in Israelite history during which the Israelites of the ancient kingdom of Judah were held in captivity as slaves in Babylon. The period began with the Babylonians' destruction of the Temple and the city of Jerusalem in 587 BC and lasted until 539 BC.

During the fifty years of the Babylonian Exile, the Jewish leaders reflected on their situation and the possible effects this exile might have on the people. They were concerned that exposure to a foreign culture and a foreign religion would cause the people to lose their faith in the one true God. Scholars today believe that many of the books of the Old Testament were written during this time. A written record of their history and religious laws would help the Jews in Babylon maintain their faith in Yahweh. Inspired by the Holy Spirit, these human authors captured in writing what had been passed on in oral traditions and perhaps other written records. Other books in the Old Testament and New Testament were written during other times of crisis. ✳

HMMMMM. . . How does accurately understanding what the human authors of the Bible were communicating allow us to better recognize God's message for us?

Article 10

When Did It Happen? When Was It Written?

A young woman named Sara described her life before and after her decision to join a circus school when she was nine years old. "When I joined the school, I was a mess," she said. "I had no confidence in myself, and I was so shy I hardly talked to anyone. I felt like I couldn't do anything right. But my parents encouraged me, and over time, the circus school became my second family. They helped me see the goodness in myself and encouraged me to take risks." Now Sara is sixteen, a high-wire performer, and teaches classes on high-wire performance to other children and youth. "Looking back, I now see how God was active in my life when I joined the school, even though I couldn't see it at the time."

Sometimes only in hindsight do we discover how certain people and events have made crucial differences in our lives. When people go through difficult or painful times, they often are only aware of the discomfort or sadness they feel at that moment. But years later, they might look back and see that time as an important period in their life, a time when they learned about themselves and grew in their relationship with God, family, and other loved ones.

Looking back, can you think of a time when God could have been acting in your life to help you fulfill your potential and dreams?

Hindsight Is 20/20

The people we meet in the Bible are no different. For example, after God helps the Israelites escape slavery in Egypt, they complain about the difficulties of traveling in the desert! "The people grumbled against Moses, saying, 'Why then did you bring us up out of Egypt? To have us die of thirst with our children and our livestock?'" (Exodus 17:3). In the moment, the Israelites cannot see God's loving hand guiding their journey. Only with time and reflection are they able to gain some perspective and deeper understanding of their experience; it allows them to fully appreciate the liberating hand of God that saves them from the pharaoh.

UNIT 1

Sometimes there was a long period between the actual events in the Bible and when the final writing occurred. During this time, the accounts of God's actions were passed on orally from one generation to the next. At some point, guided by the Holy Spirit, human authors expressed how God acted in the lives of their ancestors who lived years, decades, or sometimes even centuries beforehand.

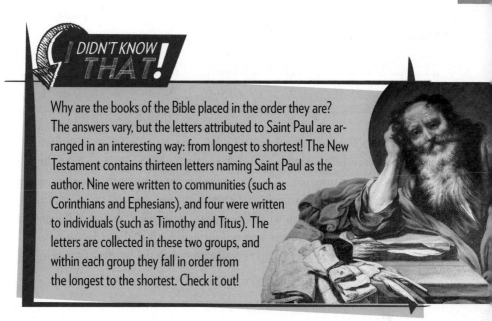

DIDN'T KNOW THAT!

Why are the books of the Bible placed in the order they are? The answers vary, but the letters attributed to Saint Paul are arranged in an interesting way: from longest to shortest! The New Testament contains thirteen letters naming Saint Paul as the author. Nine were written to communities (such as Corinthians and Ephesians), and four were written to individuals (such as Timothy and Titus). The letters are collected in these two groups, and within each group they fall in order from the longest to the shortest. Check it out!

Bouncing around in Time

The Bible starts at the beginning of time—literally "In the beginning . . ." (Genesis 1:1)—and ends looking forward to the second coming of Christ (see Revelation 22:20–21). This might give you the impression that the books of the Bible go in consecutive order from the beginning to the end. Though there are some chronological elements to it, this is not the case overall. The Bible tends to bounce around in time, going backward and forward, and sometimes events found in one book are repeated in another book.

The books are also not ordered by the dates they were written. For example, most scholars believe the Gospels were written between AD 62 and 100. Because these book record the life and ministry of Jesus, it made sense to place them first in the New Testament. However, most, if not all, of Saint Paul's letters were written before any of the Gospels.

UNIT 1

Books	Period Covered	Date Written
Genesis	Creation–1500 BC	900–500 BC
Exodus	1500–1250 BC	900–500 BC
Prophetic Books	922–300 BC	865–300 BC
Gospels	5 BC–AD 30	AD 62–100
Paul's Letters	AD 51–65	AD 51–65

All of this information might feel a bit mind-boggling, but do not let it overwhelm you! Just remember that as you read each book, it is always helpful to learn about the time period in which the events most likely occurred, as well as the date the book was probably written. Knowing this information can help you imagine the situation in which the events took place, and what the author meant in communicating these events. Ultimately, all of these details help us to better understand what God is revealing through the words of the human authors of the Bible. ✳

Give two reasons why it might be helpful that time passed between the events in the Bible occurring and their being written down in final form.

Article 11
Not One Book, but Many

By now you might be asking, "How did the Bible become the Bible?" This is a very important question. Let's take a closer look.

It's Like a Library

The word *bible* comes from the Latin term *biblia*, which means "books." This should give you a hint as to what the Bible is. The organization and structure of the Bible is like a library of books with the different kinds of writing grouped together. Like a two-level bookshelf, the Bible is divided into two main sections: Old Testament and New Testament. The Old Testament in a Catholic Bible contains forty-six books, divided into four sections: the **Pentateuch**, the Historical Books, the Wisdom Books, and the Prophetic Books.

The Pentateuch (a Greek word meaning "five books") is at the heart of the Old Testament. These first five books tell the origin stories of the Jewish People and their special relationship with God. The Pentateuch is also called the **Torah**, a word meaning "law" or "teaching." The Old Testament is the record of salvation history prior to the coming of the Savior, Jesus Christ.

Pentateuch ➤ A Greek word meaning "five books," referring to the first five books of the Old Testament.

Torah ➤ A Hebrew word meaning "law," referring to the first five books of the Old Testament.

The New Testament contains a total of twenty-seven books that focus on the life and teachings of Jesus Christ and the life of the early Church. It can be divided into four or five sections: the Gospels, the Acts of the Apostles, the Epistles or Letters, and the Book of Revelation. The four Gospels are at the heart of the New Testament, as they reveal the life of Christ, his divinity, and his saving mission.

Taken together, the seventy-three books of the Bible make up the **canon of Sacred Scripture**. The word *canon* comes from the Greek term *kanna*, meaning "cane" (as in sugar cane). The ancients sometimes used cane as a measuring stick. The word later came to mean a standard used to determine measurements or laws. Thus, the canon of Scripture is the collection of books that have met the standard to be approved as the inspired Word of God.

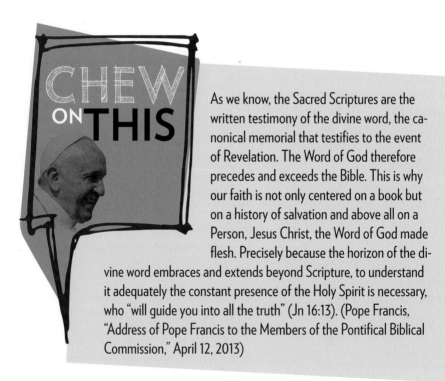

As we know, the Sacred Scriptures are the written testimony of the divine word, the canonical memorial that testifies to the event of Revelation. The Word of God therefore precedes and exceeds the Bible. This is why our faith is not only centered on a book but on a history of salvation and above all on a Person, Jesus Christ, the Word of God made flesh. Precisely because the horizon of the divine word embraces and extends beyond Scripture, to understand it adequately the constant presence of the Holy Spirit is necessary, who "will guide you into all the truth" (Jn 16:13). (Pope Francis, "Address of Pope Francis to the Members of the Pontifical Biblical Commission," April 12, 2013)

---

canon (of Sacred Scripture) ➤ The books of the Bible officially recognized by the Church as the inspired Word of God.

Protestant Bible? Catholic Bible?

You might be aware that there are Catholic Bibles and Protestant Bibles. What's the difference? It basically comes down to seven books in the Old Testament—Tobit, Judith, First and Second Maccabees, Wisdom, Sirach, Baruch—and parts of Esther and Daniel. Catholics call these writings **deuterocanonical**, meaning "second canon." Catholic and Orthodox Christians consider these books part of the official canon of Sacred Scripture, while Protestant Christians do not. Here's a brief summary of why:

1. The Jewish Scripture used by the early Christians was called the **Septuagint**. The Septuagint was written in Greek for Greek-speaking Jews. The earliest canon for the Old Testament of the Christian Bible was based on the Septuagint and contained forty-six books. This is the canon Catholics continue to use in their Bibles up through today.

2. Around AD 100, a council of Jewish leaders determined a new canon for the Jewish Scripture. They left out many of the books in the Septuagint, including the seven deuterocanonical books listed above. This new canon became the Jewish Bible that is still used today.

3. Many centuries later, during the Protestant Reformation (AD 1500s), Martin Luther and other Protestant reformers believed that the Christian Old Testament should include only the books contained in the Jewish Bible. So they removed the seven deuterocanonical books from their Old Testament. (Some Protestant Bibles include the seven books in a separate section called the **apocrypha**.)

Although this is a simple summary of a more complex history, the end result is that Catholic Bibles have forty-six books in the Old Testament, and Protestant Bibles have thirty-nine.

---

deuterocanonical ➤ Books of the Old Testament that do not appear in the Hebrew Scriptures but are accepted by the Church as part of the canon of Scripture.

Septuagint ➤ A Greek translation of the Old Testament begun about 250 BC. The Septuagint included the forty-six books of the Old Testament. It is often referred to by the roman numeral LXX, which means seventy, in honor of the legendary seventy rabbis who translated the Hebrew text into Greek in supposedly seventy days.

apocrypha ➤ Writings about Jesus or the Christian message not accepted as part of the canon of Scripture.

Who Decided?

The official canon of Scripture evolved over time. Guided by Apostolic Tradition, by the end of the second century AD, most churches were using a collection of books very similar to the Bible we have today. Then in the late fourth century, the early bishops of the Church gathered in two councils and discussed which writings met the standard. The bishops at the Council of Hippo, in the year 393, and at the Council of Carthage in 397, came to the same conclusion regarding the list of books to be contained in the Bible—the seventy-three books we have today.

However, it was not until much later, at the **Ecumenical Council** of Trent (1543–1563), that this list was officially approved by the Church.

© Saint Mary's Press

Why do you think various locations were selected for these ecumenical councils?

Ecumenical Council ➤ A gathering of the Church's bishops from around the world to address pressing issues in the Church and society. Ecumenical Councils are usually convened by the Pope or are at least approved by him.

How Did They Decide?

The decisions to include or exclude specific texts was not merely a random choice based on personal preferences. To be considered inspired by the Holy Spirit and included in the canon, each book had to meet these four criteria:

1. **Apostolic origin.** To pass this standard, the writing must have been based on the preaching and teaching of the Apostles and their closest companions. This criterion applied to New Testament books only.
2. **Universal acceptance.** If the book was accepted by all Christian communities at that time, it passed this standard.
3. **Liturgical use.** Were the texts being used in liturgical celebrations, especially in the Mass? If so, this standard was met.
4. **Consistency.** The Church leaders looked at the book's content to gauge if its message was consistent with other universally accepted Christian and Jewish writings.

What about the books that did not make the cut? Why were they excluded? The answer varies from text to text, but a good example is the gospels written by **Gnostic** Christians. *Gnostic* refers to the belief that salvation comes from secret knowledge available to only a select few. The Church rejects Gnosticism because God reveals his saving plan to all people, not just a select few. The Gnostics also believed that the material world was evil, so their Gospels placed little importance on Jesus' suffering and death, which is an essential element in God's plan of salvation. The Church decided these Gospels were contrary to the teaching of the Apostles and inconsistent with the other accepted biblical books. ✳

HMMMMM. . . Why did the Church take so many years to decide which books to include in the canon?

Gnostic ➤ Referring to the belief that salvation comes from secret knowledge available to only a select few.

UNIT 1

Article 12
Bible Translations

Some people are surprised when they realize that the Bible was not written in English. Unless you read ancient Greek and Hebrew, the Bible you are using is a translation. If you have learned or are learning a new language, you know how tricky and challenging, and sometimes funny, it can be to translate words from one language to another. The Bible is no different.

The phrase "lost in translation" refers to the experience of words losing their subtle meaning when they are translated from one language to another. Many concepts and words are unique to their original language and just do not translate easily into other languages.

However, our knowledge of ancient languages and history is continually growing, helping to ease many of the obstacles Bible translators face.

Can you think of any other examples of poor translations that could cause confusion or misunderstanding?

© Mr Doomits / Shutterstock.com

It's All Greek to Me . . . Except for the Hebrew and Aramaic

The Bible was originally written in three different languages: Hebrew, Greek, and Aramaic. The Old Testament was mostly written in Hebrew, but a few parts of it were written in Greek and Aramaic too. The New Testament was written in Koine Greek, which was the language most commonly used throughout biblical lands in the first century. There are also a few Aramaic words scattered in the New Testament. Aramaic was a common language used by many people living in Israel at that time and probably the language Jesus used most often in his public addresses.

It's the Same Thing, Just Different

The Bible has been translated into many languages since its books were first written. Saint Jerome, a Scripture scholar in the early Church, completed one of the earliest translations of the Bible. He completed his translation of the Bible into Latin in AD 405. Called the **Latin Vulgate**, the Church used this translation of the Bible for over a thousand years.

Latin Vulgate ▶ The Vulgate is a Latin version of the Holy Bible and largely the result of the labors of Saint Jerome (c. 345–420), who was commissioned by Pope Damasus I in AD 382 to make a revision of the old Latin translations.

UNIT 1

CATHOLICS **MAKING** A DIFFERENCE

Saint Francis Xavier (1506–1552) was one of the founding members of the Society of Jesus (the Jesuits). He also was one of the first Catholic missionaries to travel to Japan to spread the Gospel. He arrived in 1549, many other Jesuits following him. They translated parts of the Bible and other religious texts into Japanese. By the end of the century, the ruler of Japan began persecuting Catholics. A Jesuit priest, Saint Paul Miki, and twenty-five others were crucified in Nagasaki in 1597. Soon afterward, Catholicism was banned, but some priests stayed illegally and encouraged people to practice their faith in secret. Many of them gave up their lives in order to spread the Gospel to the Japanese people.

If you were to look online today to purchase a Bible, you would find a number of translations available. Not only are there a variety from languages all over the world, but there is also a large assortment of English translations. Translations are often done with a specific purpose in mind. Some are written so that younger children can understand the content, some use more contemporary language, and others seek to be more faithful to the literal meaning of the words.

There are four Catholic English translations that are used most often today: The *New American Bible, Revised Edition (NABRE)*; the *New Revised Standard Version, Catholic Edition (NRSV)*; the *New Jerusalem Bible (NJB)*; and the *Good News Translation in Today's English Version, Second Edition (GNT)*. The English translation we use for the Scripture readings at Mass in the United States is the *NABRE*. The Church in Canada uses the *NRSV* for its Mass readings. The *NJB* is a wonderful translation to use in prayer because of its poetic use of language. The *GNT* uses more basic, easy-to-understand vocabulary and was probably the translation you read when you were younger. Though the different translations vary in the specific words they use, each one is faithful in expressing God's Word to us. Compare the different translations of Matthew 5:13–16 on the next page. ✳

UNIT 1

Different Translations of Matthew 5:13–16

New American Bible, Revised Edition
The Similes of Salt and Light

You are the salt of the earth. But if salt loses its taste, with what can it be seasoned? It is no longer good for anything but to be thrown out and trampled underfoot. You are the light of the world. A city set on a mountain cannot be hidden. Nor do they light a lamp and then put it under a bushel basket; it is set on a lampstand, where it gives light to all in the house. Just so, your light must shine before others, that they may see your good deeds and glorify your heavenly Father.

New Revised Standard Version
Salt and Light

You are the salt of the earth; but if salt has lost its taste, how can its saltiness be restored? It is no longer good for anything, but is thrown out and trampled underfoot.

You are the light of the world. A city built on a hill cannot be hid. No one after lighting a lamp puts it under the bushel basket, but on the lampstand, and it gives light to all in the house. In the same way, let your light shine before others, so that they may see your good works and give glory to your Father in heaven.

New Jerusalem Bible
Salt for the Earth
and Light for the World

You are salt for the earth. But if salt loses its taste, what can make it salty again? It is good for nothing, and can only be thrown out to be trampled under people's feet.

You are light for the world. A city built on a hill-top cannot be hidden. No one lights a lamp to put it under a tub; they put it on the lamp-stand where it shines for everyone in the house.

In the same way your light must shine in people's sight, so that, seeing your good works, they may give praise to your Father in heaven.

Good News Translation
Salt and Light

You are like salt for the whole human race. But if salt loses its saltiness, there is no way to make it salty again. It has become worthless, so it is thrown out and people trample on it.

You are like light for the whole world. A city built on a hill cannot be hid. No one lights a lamp and puts it under a bowl; instead it is put on the lampstand, where it gives light for everyone in the house. In the same way your light must shine before people, so that they will see the good things you do and praise your Father in heaven.

Look again at the four translations of Matthew 5:13–16. How can comparing four translations of the same Scripture passage help you to better understand that passage?

Article 13
The Old Prepares Us for the New

"We were so late getting to the theater that we missed the entire first half of the movie! I couldn't keep track of who was who and what was what. It was just way too hard to follow. That's probably why the ending didn't make any sense!"

Missing the first half—or even the first 10 minutes—of a movie can leave you somewhat confused at the end. The end only makes sense because of what happens in the beginning. The same goes for the Bible. The second half, the New Testament, only makes sense because of what happens in the first half, the Old Testament. Knowing and understanding the Old Testament is key to fully understanding the New Testament. Without the Old Testament, we would only get half of the story.

The Two Testaments

Open up your Bible. Find the division between the Old Testament and the New Testament. Hold the pages of the Old Testament in your left hand, and hold the pages of the New Testament in your right hand. One thing you will notice is that almost two-thirds of Sacred Scripture is the Old Testament. These books are just as inspired by the Holy Spirit as those in the New Testament. It is through the events of the Old Testament that God prepares us for the coming of Christ.

We cannot fully understand the New Testament without understanding the inspired and revealed Word of the Old Testament.

God called a Chosen People, and over centuries he readied them to be open to and understand the Christ event. He prepared them through covenants, sacred promises to which God was faithful, even when his people were not. He sent them spirit-filled leaders who prefigured Christ. And even though it failed, the earthly kingdom he allowed them to build prepared them for the Kingdom of God established by Christ.

So why do we call it "Old" if it's so important? That's a good question. If you look up the word *old* in a thesaurus, you will find words and phrases like "outdated," "over-the-hill," "inactive," "broken-down," and "obsolete." This is *not* what we mean when we call the Old Testament "Old." We call it "Old" because it reveals God's covenants and saving actions prior to the coming of Jesus Christ. The Old Testament expresses an eternal wisdom that is as vibrant and relevant as it was thousands of years ago. Some say that it might also be called the "Original Testament."

Sadly, some Christians have wrongly thought that because we now have a New Testament, the Old Testament has become obsolete. This couldn't be further from the truth. It is very important to remember that Jesus was a Jewish person who practiced his faith. The writings of the Old Testament were sacred to him. In fact, he would often quote from the Old Testament. For example, when asked about the Greatest Commandment, Jesus quotes Deuteronomy and Leviticus (see Matthew 22:34–40). When questioned about marriage and divorce, he cites Genesis (see Mark 10:1–12). While on the cross, he prays Psalm 22 (Matthew 15:34). Most of the books of the Old Testament still serve as the Scripture for Jewish people today.

So rather than reject the Old Testament, we, like Jesus, venerate it as the true Word of God, "an indispensable part of Sacred Scripture"[1] (*CCC*, number 121), whose promises are fulfilled by our Savior, Jesus Christ. ✻

HMMMMMM. . . Describe some ways God was preparing his people in the Old Testament for the coming of Jesus.

Article 14

The New Fulfills the Old

Star Wars. The Lord of the Rings. The Fast and the Furious. These popular movie franchises work because even though each movie stands on its own, there are always a few loose ends left for a sequel to answer. If you are a fan, you wait impatiently for the next movie to be released so you can discover where the story goes next.

There is a similar connection between the Old and New Testaments in the Bible. Like the first movie in a two-movie series, the Old Testament leaves us with some loose ends. For one thing, the Israelites are left hoping for a messiah, a savior, promised by the prophets of the Old Testament. As the sequel to the Old Testament, the New Testament fulfills this hope with the Good News that Jesus Christ is the long-awaited Messiah. The New Testament reveals how God the Father sent his only Son, Jesus Christ, to initiate a New Covenant with his people. It is "New" because God had never before revealed himself like this. Certainly God had acted in amazing ways in the Old Testament. But, by becoming flesh in the

In the Transfiguration of Jesus, two key Old Testament figures, Moses and Elijah, appear with Jesus. What might be the symbolic meaning of these Old Testament heroes appearing with Jesus?

person of Jesus Christ, God established a **New Covenant** that fulfilled and perfected the **Old Covenant**. Here are a few examples of how New Testament events tied up the "loose ends" left in the Old Testament.

- The Old Testament leaves the sin of Adam separating us from God. In the New Testament, Jesus is the "New Adam" who reunites God and humanity.
- In the Old Testament, God establishes his Law through Moses, but the **Old Law** is not enough to save humanity from sin and death. In the New Testament, Jesus establishes his **New Law** of Love, fulfilling the meaning of the Old Law and bringing us the fullness of salvation.
- In the Old Testament, God provides priests, prophets, and kings to guide the people in keeping their covenant with him, but these earthly leaders are not enough to help the people stay faithful to the covenant. In the New Testament, Jesus completely and perfectly fulfills the roles of priest, prophet, and king, bringing the Old Covenant to fulfillment in his New Covenant.

Old Testament Prophecies Fulfilled

Jesus' disciples were with him on a daily basis. They lived with him, traveled with him, touched him, heard him teach, and saw his miracles and signs. They witnessed his Passion, death, Resurrection, and Ascension. They were well versed in Old Testament writings and began making the connections between Old Testament prophecies and things they had witnessed. They came to believe that Jesus was indeed the fulfillment of the Old Covenant, the awaited Messiah, the Son of God, the one to bring salvation to all the nations, "the one who is to come" (Matthew 11:3). This chart shows some prominent Old Testament prophecies and how the New Testament authors recognized their fulfillment by Jesus Christ.

New Covenant ➤ The covenant or law established by God in Jesus Christ to fulfill and perfect the Old Covenant or Mosaic Law. It is a perfection here on Earth of the Divine Law. The law of the New Covenant is called a law of love, grace, and freedom. The New Covenant will never end or diminish, and nothing new will be revealed until Christ comes again in glory.

Old Covenant ➤ The original covenant God established with Abraham and renewed with the Chosen People at Mount Sinai, in which he promised to be their God and they promised to be his people, obeying his Law and worshipping him alone.

Old Law ➤ Divine Law revealed in the Old Testament, summarized in the Ten Commandments. Also call the Law of Moses.

New Law ➤ Divine Law revealed in the New Testament through the life and teaching of Jesus Christ and through the witness and teaching of the Apostles. The New Law perfects the Old Law and brings it to fulfillment. Also called the Law of Love.

Event	Old Testament Prophecy	New Testament Fulfillment
The Savior will be born of a virgin.	**Isaiah 7:14**: "Therefore the Lord himself will give you this sign: the young woman, pregnant and about to bear a son, shall name him Emmanuel."	**Matthew 1:22–23**: "All this took place to fulfill what the Lord had said through the prophet: 'Behold, the virgin shall be with child and bear a son, and they shall name him Emmanuel,' which means 'God is with us.'"
The Savior will be born in Bethlehem.	**Micah 5:1–4**: "But you, Bethlehem-Ephrathah / least among the clans of Judah, / From you shall come forth for me / one who is to be ruler in Israel."	**Luke 2:4–7**: "And Joseph too went up from Galilee from the town of Nazareth to Judea, to the city of David that is called Bethlehem. . . . While they were there, the time came for her to have her child, and she gave birth to her firstborn son."
The Savior will be full of zeal for God's house, the Temple.	**Psalm 69:10**: "Because zeal for your house has consumed me, / I am scorned by those who scorn you."	**John 2:17**: "His disciples recalled the words of scripture, 'Zeal for your house will consume me.'"
The Savior will be filled with the Spirit of God.	**Isaiah 61:1**: "The spirit of the Lord GOD is upon me. . . ."	**Luke 4:16–21**: "[Jesus] unrolled the scroll and found the passage where it was written: 'The Spirit of the Lord is upon me.' . . . He said to them, 'Today this scripture passage is fulfilled in your hearing.'"
The Savior will come into his glory, arriving on an ass (donkey).	**Zechariah 9:9**: "Behold: your king is coming to you; / a just savior is he, / Humble, and riding on a donkey, / on a colt, the foal of a donkey."	**Matthew 21:4–5**: "This happened so that what had been spoken through the prophet might be fulfilled: . . . 'Behold, your king comes to you, / meek and riding on an ass, / and on a colt, the foal of a beast of burden.'"

Event	Old Testament Prophecy	New Testament Fulfillment
The Savior will be betrayed for thirty pieces of silver.	Zechariah 11:12: "And they counted out my wages, thirty pieces of silver."	Matthew 27:3: "Then Judas, his betrayer, seeing that Jesus had been condemned, deeply regretted what he had done. He returned the thirty pieces of silver."
The Savior will suffer and die.	Psalm 22: "My God, my God why have you abandoned me? . . . All who see me mock me. . . . As dry as a potsherd is my throat. . . . They divide my garments among them; / for my clothing they cast lots." (Read the whole psalm for many more connections to Jesus' Crucifixion.) See also Isaiah 52:13–53:12.	Mark 15:34: "Jesus cried out in a loud voice, 'Eloi, Eloi, lema sabachthani?' which is translated, 'My God, my God, why have you forsaken me?'" Mark 15:29: "Those passing by reviled him." John 19:28: "Jesus said, 'I thirst.'" John 19:24: "So they said to one another, 'Let's not tear it, but cast lots for it.'" (Read the complete accounts of Jesus' Crucifixion to see other connections.)
The Savior will be the Son of God and will overcome death.	Psalm 2:7: "I will proclaim the decree of the LORD, / he said to me, 'You are my son; / today I have begotten you.'" Psalm 16:10: "For you will not abandon me to Sheol, / nor let your devout one see the pit."	Acts 13:33–35: "It is written in the second psalm, 'You are my son; this day I have begotten you.' . . . That is why he also says in another psalm, 'You will not suffer your holy one to see corruption.'"

Jesus: Center Stage in Both Testaments

Let's take a step back to look at the big picture we have been painting so far. We have proposed that every human being has a longing for the love and connection that only God can fill. We have proposed that God reveals himself through natural revelation and Divine Revelation. And we've looked at how a unique and privileged mode for Divine Revelation is through God's Word in Sacred Scripture, for in Sacred Scripture the fullness of God's Revelation appears in the Word Made Flesh, Jesus Christ.

Now we are making the case that to fully understand Jesus Christ, we not only need to read the New Testament but we must also be familiar with the Old Testament. This is why many future chapters will be devoted to helping you become familiar with the central people and events of the Old Testament, God's original covenant.

Of course, the New Testament is central to our understanding of God's saving work through Jesus Christ. Jesus and the beginnings of the early Church are the focus in all twenty-seven of its books. And in the New Testament, the Gospels have a privileged position. They are "the heart of all the Scriptures 'because they are our principal source for the life and teaching of the Incarnate Word, our Savior'"[2] (*CCC*, number 125). In other words, the

Gospels are at the heart of all Scripture because Jesus Christ is at the heart of the Gospels. Future courses in this series will explore more deeply Jesus Christ's life and saving work found as proclaimed in the books of the New Testament. ✳

To fully understand Jesus Christ, we need to read and understand the New Testament as well as have an understanding of the Old Testament.

HMMMMM. . . Give two examples of how the New Testament is a fulfillment of the Old Testament.

1. Describe the process of how many of the books of the Bible came to be written.

2. How might the description of events written about in the Bible also reflect the human authors' current historical situation?

3. What criteria were used to select the books worthy to be included in the Bible?

4. Describe the difficulties involved in translating a Bible. Use an example to illustrate your point.

5. Why do we call the first section of the Bible the "Old" Testament, and the second section the "New" Testament?

6. Why do Christians include the Old Testament in their Sacred Scripture?

7. How is the New Testament a fulfillment of the Old Testament?

8. Why do we say the Gospels are the heart of all the Scriptures?

UNIT 1

THE OLD TESTAMENT'S RELATIONSHIP TO THE NEW TESTAMENT

This stained-glass window depicts four events from the Pentateuch (Genesis 22:1–19; Exodus 24:3–8; Numbers 13:1–24, 20:2–13). All four of these events are related to Jesus' saving death.

1. What events from the Old Testament are depicted in the outer four sections?

2. How are these events related to the image of Jesus in the center?

CHAPTER 4
Interpreting the Bible

HOW DO I MAKE SENSE OF ALL THOSE OLD STORIES IN THE BIBLE?

SNAPSHOT

Article 15   Page 85
Reliable Guides: The Magisterium and the Holy Spirit

Article 16   Page 88
Exegesis: What Does It Mean?

Article 17   Page 91
Making Sense of the Bible

Article 18   Page 94
The Literature of the Bible

Article 19   Page 98
Biblical Archaeology: Digging for Answers

Article 15

Reliable Guides: The Magisterium and the Holy Spirit

When you confront a problem or task, and you lack the knowledge and skill required to complete it, it is always smart to do your research before proceeding. For example, if your car breaks down, it would not be wise to take out a hammer and just start banging on the engine. Today's cars are a complicated mix of mechanical and computerized parts that require specialized knowledge to repair. With minor issues, you might be able to find some help on the internet, but it is important to remember that anyone can post on social media and call themselves an expert without actually being one. Things always turn out better when we use reliable and credible sources when doing any kind of research.

The same is true when it comes to understanding the Bible. Many parts of the Bible are pretty straightforward and easy to understand, but some complicated passages require certain knowledge and skills to accurately understand what is being revealed. Like car repair, seeking reliable and credible sources is essential to grasping what God wants to reveal through Scripture. Fortunately, God did not leave us to figure out the Bible's meaning without any guidance. This chapter explores the guidance God provides.

The Magisterium

The **Magisterium**, the Church's living teaching office, is that reliable and credible guide. The Magisterium consists of all the bishops in the world, in communion with the Pope, the bishop of Rome. God has given the Magisterium the responsibility and the gifts required to interpret Sacred Scripture correctly. The Magisterium does not have authority over the Bible, though. It is "not superior to the Word of God, but is its

Images like this one, of the Pope gathered with the bishops of the Church, give us a glimpse into the fullness of the Magisterium.

Magisterium ➤ The Church's living teaching office, which consists of all bishops, in communion with the Pope, the bishop of Rome.

servant"[1] (*CCC*, number 86), acting under the guidance of the Holy Spirit to faithfully teach the message that God revealed to the original Apostles. This is not merely an intellectual process of study and explanation. It requires the Pope and bishops to prayerfully listen to the Holy Spirit and be open to the truths God wants us to know.

The bishops and the Pope are not alone in their efforts. In their work of guiding our interpretation of the Bible, the Magisterium works with many biblical scholars. These experts work in various fields of study including theology, history, language, and archaeology.

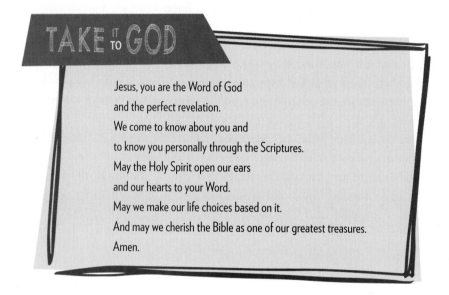

TAKE IT TO GOD

Jesus, you are the Word of God
and the perfect revelation.
We come to know about you and
to know you personally through the Scriptures.
May the Holy Spirit open our ears
and our hearts to your Word.
May we make our life choices based on it.
And may we cherish the Bible as one of our greatest treasures.
Amen.

Notable Moments

As scholars have developed new techniques for studying the Bible over the last one hundred years, the Magisterium has developed guidelines for how to best use those techniques. Here are descriptions of several notable Church documents that guide our interpretation of Scripture.

"Inspired by the Holy Spirit" ("*Divino Afflante Spiritu,*" 1943)

Written by Pope Pius XII, this **encyclical** calls for new translations of the Bible into modern languages and permits a limited use of modern methods of studying the Bible. This includes examining the various literary techniques used by its human authors.

---

encyclical ➤ A teaching letter from the Pope to the members of the Church on topics of social justice, human rights, and peace.

UNIT 1

Dogmatic Constitution on Divine Revelation (Dei Verbum, 1965)

Written during the **Second Vatican Council**, this document addresses the ways in which God reveals himself to us. It encourages scholars to recognize the different genres or types of biblical literature. "For truth is set forth and expressed differently in texts which are variously historical, prophetic, poetic, or of other forms" (number 12). The Council also supports studying the cultures in which the various books of the Bible were written. Understanding the cultural background and literary intentions of the human authors better enables us to comprehend God's Word.

Interpretation of the Bible in the Church (1993)

In this document, the Vatican's Pontifical Biblical Commission (a committee of biblical scholars) offers more specific directions and guidelines for interpreting the Bible. It examines how using historical and literary methods can help in understanding Scripture. It also provides interpreters with standards to guide them, including the importance of using other theological disciplines and **Sacred Tradition** in the work of biblical interpretation.

The participants in the Second Vatican Council consisted of the Pope and all Roman Catholic bishops worldwide. Why is it important that the Magisterium periodically gather together?

HMMMMM. . .   What kind of knowledge and skills would help you better understand the Bible?

Second Vatican Council ➤ The Ecumenical or General Council of the Roman Catholic Church that Pope Saint John XXIII convened as Pope in 1962 and that continued under Pope Saint Paul VI until 1965. Also called Vatican Council II.

Sacred Tradition ➤ The process of passing on the Gospel message. Sacred Tradition, which began with the oral communication of the Gospel by the Apostles, was written down in Sacred Scripture, is handed down and lived out in the life of the Church, and is interpreted by the Magisterium under the guidance of the Holy Spirit. Both Sacred Tradition and Sacred Scripture have their common source in the Revelation of Jesus Christ and must be equally honored.

Article 16

Exegesis: What Does It Mean?

Sebas, a foreign exchange student from Chile, is so excited to be in America. He likes his host family, his new high school, and his new friends. One day at school, just as students and faculty are arriving in the parking lot, it starts pouring rain. Everyone starts running for the school's main entrance. As Sebas approaches the doors, Mr. Bowler, one of the math teachers, shouts: "Students, hurry up and open that door! It is raining cats and dogs out here! I'm soaked!" *What? Raining cats and dogs? That doesn't make any sense. What is Mr. Bowler talking about?*

Of course, you know that when someone says it is raining cats and dogs it doesn't mean that dogs and cats are falling from the sky! It just means that it is raining hard. Expressions like this tend to be limited to a specific language, and sometimes even a particular place and time. A thousand years from now, if people read that phrase, they might have to do some research to figure out its true meaning.

This is kind of our situation when we read the Bible. The human authors who wrote down its words thousands of years ago sometimes used phrases, analogies, and even ways of thinking that are foreign to us. To truly understand the writings of the Bible, we must do some work to grasp what the human authors were trying to express. This is called **biblical exegesis**, the critical interpretation and explanation of Sacred Scripture. Used in this context, *critical* does not mean "disapproving or insulting," but rather "analytical or methodical." Good biblical exegesis requires that we pay attention to certain things so that we can better understand a text's true meaning.

Can you think of an expression you heard when you were younger, or that was translated from another language, that didn't make any sense to you?

© Igor Zakowski / Shutterstock.com

---

biblical exegesis ➤ The critical interpretation and explanation of Sacred Scripture.

Pay Attention to This!

The Church provides some specific guidance on what we need to pay attention to when we interpret the Bible. The Second Vatican Council issued a document called *Dogmatic Constitution on Divine Revelation* (*Dei Verbum*, 1965). In this document, they laid out a two-step process for biblical exegesis. For the first step, the document states that we "should carefully investigate what meaning the sacred [human] authors really intended" (number 12). To understand what the human author was trying to say, the document goes on to say that we should pay particular attention to the following:

- **The literary genres used by the author.** For example, was the author using poetry, religious history, prophetical oracles, debate, or symbolic stories?
- **The characteristic ways people spoke and wrote in their time.** For example, Hebrew poetry is quite different from the way we write poetry today.
- **The cultural ways people interacted with one another at the time.** For example, the roles of women and men were much more defined and separated at the time most of the Bible was written.

Years from now, you may not feel the pain from the physical injuries you received in your youth. But it's quite likely that many of the painful words aimed at you will still sting. Words mean something. They can build up and encourage others. They can also cause some serious emotional damage. Be mindful of how you speak to others. Do not underestimate the power your words can have to uplift or tear down.

For the second step, the document states that we must carefully investigate "what God wanted to manifest by means of their [the human authors'] words" (number 12). To understand what God wants to reveal to us, the document goes on to say that we should pay particular attention to the following:

- **"The content and unity of the whole Scripture"** (number 12). Any particular passage must be examined in light of the big picture that includes both the Old and New Testaments, keeping in mind most importantly the Passion, death, and Resurrection of Jesus Christ.
- **The living Tradition and teachings of the whole Church.** The Church continues to be guided by the Holy Spirit in its teachings and in the interpretation of Sacred Scripture.
- **The analogy of faith.** The **analogy of faith** is the unity of Church teachings within the whole of God's Revelation. Each truth God reveals is connected and united with all of the other truths of faith. Understanding one truth helps us grasp and appreciate the others more easily.

We must remember that the task of interpreting Sacred Scripture is not merely an intellectual activity. This job requires a prayerful openness to the Holy Spirit, similar to the openness the Gospel writers themselves had. "Sacred Scripture must be read and interpreted in the light of the same Spirit by whom it was written"[2] (*CCC*, number 111).

© Zvonimir Atletic / Shutterstock.com

Many parts of the Bible can only be fully understood in connection to the events in Jesus' life, particularly the Resurrection.

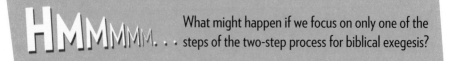

HMMMMM. . . What might happen if we focus on only one of the steps of the two-step process for biblical exegesis?

---

analogy of faith ▶ The coherence of individual doctrines with the whole of Revelation. In other words, as each doctrine is connected with Revelation, each doctrine is also connected with all other doctrines.

Article 17

Making Sense of the Bible

"That's the truth!" "How do you know that's true?" "The truth shall set you free." "Do you swear to tell the truth, the whole truth, and nothing but the truth?" "That's not true!" "True dat!"

When it comes to truth, what is your approach? Are you a person who doesn't believe in anything unless you can see it, touch it, or prove it by science and logic? Or do you believe there are many ways to know and experience truth, including some that go beyond the physical senses? For instance, you may feel a deep love for another person and know it is true even though there is no way to explain it or sometimes even to show it?

If you are more like the first person, you may be challenged to fully understand the Bible. This is because in order to fully understand the Bible, we need to be open to two different kinds of truth: literal truth and spiritual truth. The Church calls these two ways of approaching truth in the Bible the *literal sense* and the *spiritual sense*.

Why is the study of ancient biblical scrolls important to biblical interpretation?

Literal, Not "Literally"

The **literal sense** is a form of biblical interpretation that considers the plain meaning of the text. This does not mean reading the text "literally," that is, as if every story was meant to be historically and scientifically accurate. Actually, it means quite the opposite. The literal sense is the meaning intended by the human author. Because the human authors often used poetry, symbolism, metaphors, and even exaggeration, understanding the literal sense requires study and interpretation.

Let's look again at the phrase "raining cats and dogs." Reading it literally would lead you to the conclusion that dogs and cats were falling from the sky. However, the literal sense of this phrase is the meaning intended by the author: it's raining hard. Accurately understanding the literal sense lays the foundation for all other senses of Sacred Scripture. Once you understand it, you can move on to the spiritual sense.

literal sense ➤ A form of biblical interpretation that considers the explicit meaning of the text. It lays the foundation for all other senses of Sacred Scripture.

© Kobby Dagan / Shutterstock.com

When it comes to naming Jesus' profession, he is often called a carpenter. The actual Greek word used in the Bible for Jesus' profession is *tektōn*. This ancient Greek word meant something closer to "craftsman." This would have included work with wood, but also things like iron and stone masonry. This makes sense given that most of the homes and buildings at Jesus' time were made of stone. And maybe why Jesus said to Peter, "You are Peter, and upon this rock I will build my church" (Matthew 16:18).

So What?

After figuring out what the human author intended to say, we come to the next step in which we ask: "So what? What does this have to do with our lives?" This is an important question to ask when reading the Bible. God speaks through the words of the human authors, and often the literal sense makes clear what we are to believe and how we are to live. However, Scripture has many layers of meaning. Examining the spiritual sense of the text allows us to understand further aspects of God's Revelation and perhaps understand them even more deeply. The **spiritual sense** is interpretation that builds on the literal sense, considering what the realities and events of Scripture signify and mean for salvation. The spiritual sense can be broken into three categories or sub-senses: the allegorical sense, the moral sense, and the anagogical sense.

- **Allegorical sense.** An allegory is a literary device in which characters, events, and other elements represent abstract or spiritual truths. When we examine the allegorical sense of a biblical text, we look at how it points in some way to the mystery of Christ. For example, consider the biblical account of the Israelites' finding freedom from slavery by passing through the waters of the Red Sea. Allegorically, this represents the freedom we find from the slavery of sin by passing through the waters of Christ's Baptism.

---

spiritual sense ➤ A form of biblical interpretation that builds on the literal sense to consider what the realities and events of Sacred Scripture signify and mean for salvation.

UNIT 1

- **Moral sense.** When looking at a biblical passage from the moral sense, we ask what the text has to teach us about living a good, just, and moral life. We find answers to questions like these: How should we treat one another? What are good values to live by? How should we react when someone mistreats us?

  For example, from the cross, Jesus said, "Father, forgive them [the people who crucified him], they know not what they do" (Luke 23:34). Looking at the moral sense of this passage leads us to ask: "What does Jesus' forgiveness of the people who crucified him teach us? How should we treat people who have committed sins against us?" When applying the moral sense, remember that most people in the Bible were not perfect people—not even some of its greatest heroes. Just because David committed adultery does not mean it is okay for us to do so.

- **Anagogical sense.** Anagogical comes from a Greek word meaning "leading." This way of examining the Bible addresses the text's eternal significance. How are the people, events, and other elements in a passage leading us toward our heavenly home? For example, Jesus said: "Whoever wishes to come after me must deny himself, take up his cross, and follow me. For whoever wishes to save his life will lose it, but whoever loses his life for my sake and that of the gospel will save it" (Mark 8:34–35). Applying the anagogical sense to this passage points to the importance of selfless service in preparing us for eternal salvation.

"Father, forgive them, they know not what they do" (Luke 23:34).

Considering these three senses when reading a biblical passage allows us to answer the question "So what?" and to thus discover the truths God wants to understand.

HMMMMM... Pick a passage from the Bible and describe it using the literal sense of the text. Then determine all three elements of the spiritual sense of that same text.

Article 18

The Literature of the Bible

Picture this scenario: You are in your English class reading a poem, and you come across this line: "A bullet went through his skin, and a rose instantly blossomed from the wound." Would it surprise you to read this? Probably not. Why? Because you're reading poetry, and in poetry you would expect the use of imaginative metaphors that captivate your emotions, however illogical they might be.

Now let's say you are in your social studies class reading a historical account of the invasion of Normandy. In your textbook, you read the same line: "A bullet went through his skin, and a rose instantly blossomed from the wound." Would it surprise you to read this? Most likely. Why? Because you're reading from a history textbook based on objective facts. You would expect facts, and it is not a fact that roses bloom from wounded human flesh! History and poetry are two different literary genres. Each one has its own set of expectations and rules for grasping its meaning.

Biblical Literary Forms

Let's recall that the Bible is a collection of books, written by many different people over many centuries. These books use numerous **literary forms** or genres: religious history, prayer, song, poetry, proverbs, parables, letters, and gospels among others. Sometimes you can even find a diverse collection of literary forms within a single book.

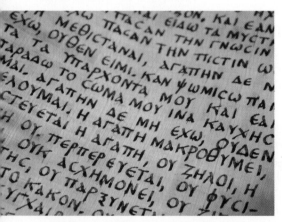

A Greek manuscript of Paul's Corinthians, chapter 13 on papyrus.

Just as you would have different expectations going from poetry to a history textbook, you must adjust your expectations when reading different genres found in biblical texts. For example, let's say you have been assigned to read Matthew 5:27–37, and you come across this sentence: "If your right eye causes you to sin, tear it out and

---

literary forms (genres) ➤ Different kinds of writing determined by their literary technique, content, tone, and purpose.

throw it away" (verse 29). You might be tempted to think: "No way! Jesus did not just say that!" Then you remember your teacher saying that in this passage Jesus sometimes uses hyperbole, or exaggeration, as a way to emphasize certain points. Building on the human author's use of hyperbole, you realize that the moral sense of this passage is to do everything we can (short of self-mutilation) to avoid the temptations that lead us to sin.

If you want to understand the text accurately, knowing the type of literature you are reading is essential. Here is a list of some of the literary forms used in the Bible, with some examples, and what you might expect from this type of writing.

Literary Form	Examples	What You Can Expect
Prayer	• Psalms • Our Father (Matthew 6:9–15)	emotional and poetic expressions of connection with God, requests for guidance, strength, comfort, and so on
Parable	• Parable of the Lost Son (Luke 15:11–32) • Parable of the Sower (Matthew 13:1–9)	teaching stories used to impart understanding, wisdom, guidance, and so on
Letter	• Letter to the Romans • First and Second Letters to the Corinthians • The Letter of James	advice and reprimands to the early churches on Christian living
Apocalyptic literature	• The Book of Revelation • Daniel, chapters 7–12	writing using symbolic imagery regarding the end-times; written to offer hope to persecuted communities
Religious History	• First and Second Books of Samuel • First and Second Books of Kings	narratives of past events infused with theological truths about the meaning of those events
Proverbs	• The Book of Proverbs • The Book of Ecclesiastes	short, wise sayings on living a life that is pleasing to God
Law	• The Ten Commandments (Exodus 20:1–16) • The Greatest Commandment (Matthew 22:34–40)	instructions on living in right relationship with God and other people

Going Deeper

Knowing the literary genre helps scholars gain a better understanding of Sacred Scripture. They do not stop there though. Scholars employ various forms of biblical criticism to deepen their understanding of how the human authors expressed God's Word. Remember that the word *criticism* does not refer to a negative viewpoint, like a bad movie review. It refers to an analysis or evaluation. There are numerous types of biblical criticism. Below are some examples and descriptions.

Type of Biblical Criticism	Description
Textual Criticism	We often have more than one ancient copy of a text. This type of criticism attempts to make sure that the text handed down from ancient times is the best and most accurate possible. Occasionally, there are slightly different versions of a text. Part of the textual critic's job is to figure out which one is the most original wording.
Source Criticism	Some of the writings of the Bible seem to have been borrowed from other sources—both oral traditions and earlier writings. This type of criticism tries to identify the sources that the biblical authors used to compose their texts.
Literary Criticism	This type of criticism examines the style, structure, and language of the text.
Form Criticism	This type of criticism identifies the literary form, or genre, of the text (poetry, history, law, prayer, and so on).
Historical Criticism	This field identifies and describes the historical situation *when a text was written* (not the time period the content addresses). It examines how that historical situation affected the human authors' viewpoints on the content subject matter.
Redaction Criticism	This field of study looks at how and why texts were edited and combined to create the final version of a biblical book.

Though each area of study seems to focus on a narrow and separate field, in reality they are very connected. Because all of them seek the same goal, they cannot work in isolation from one another. They rely on and often blend into one another.

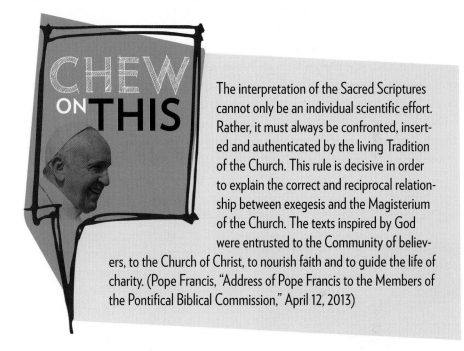

The interpretation of the Sacred Scriptures cannot only be an individual scientific effort. Rather, it must always be confronted, inserted and authenticated by the living Tradition of the Church. This rule is decisive in order to explain the correct and reciprocal relationship between exegesis and the Magisterium of the Church. The texts inspired by God were entrusted to the Community of believers, to the Church of Christ, to nourish faith and to guide the life of charity. (Pope Francis, "Address of Pope Francis to the Members of the Pontifical Biblical Commission," April 12, 2013)

How does knowing the type of literature used by a biblical author help in understanding a text's meaning?

Article 19

Biblical Archaeology: Digging for Answers

If you've ever been to a science museum or museum of natural history to see an exhibit on an ancient civilization, mummies, dinosaurs, and other unique and interesting displays, then you know and can appreciate the importance of **archaeology**.

Archaeology is the study of human activity and history by means of excavating and analyzing the artifacts and other physical materials. These artifacts include prehistoric tools, household items, writings, objects used in religious worship, and even the humans themselves. Archaeology is an essential tool in helping us understand the culture and history of past human societies. By digging, sifting through, and analyzing countless piles of earth, we are able to "travel" back in time to learn about our ancestors and their way of life.

Tzipori (Sepphoris) archaeological site in Israel.

© LevT / Shutterstock.com

If you ever get the chance to travel to the Holy Land, you will certainly have the opportunity to see a number of archaeological "digs," or excavation sites. Israel is a popular place for archaeological work because the world's three major religions—Christianity, Judaism, and Islam—all find their origins there.

A Town and a Tomb

Our understanding of the Bible has greatly benefited from the work of archaeology. As a matter of fact, some biblical scholars are also archaeologists. Their discoveries have led to a greater appreciation of how people lived in biblical times.

---

archaeology ➤ The study of human activity and history by means of excavating and analyzing the artifacts and other physical materials.

For example, archaeologists recently uncovered the city of Sepphoris, rebuilt by Rome at about the same time Jesus was born. It was a wealthy city at the center of trade for the area. Tradesmen like Jesus and his foster father, Joseph, were probably in great demand there. Because it was located just a few miles from Nazareth, it is quite possible that as a young man, Jesus took this hour-long walk to get work. The knowledge gained about the culture and history of Sepphoris offers us a glimpse into the world in which Jesus lived.

Another example is a discovery made in the late 1960s. Archaeologists found the remains of a man named Jehohanan in a burial site just north of Jerusalem. They estimated that he died sometime in the early to mid-first century—the same time as Jesus. Even more remarkable is something else he had in common with Jesus: he also was killed by crucifixion. The nail that had gone through his foot remained imbedded in the bone. What the archaeologists found so interesting was the placement of the nail. In most of the paintings and statues of Jesus, we usually see the nails going through his hands and the front of his feet. This was not the case for Jehohanan. The nail went through the side of his heel bone.

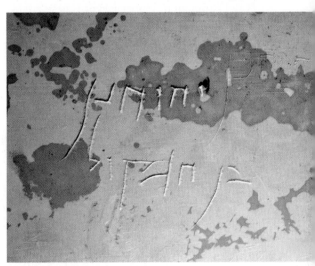

A stone ossuary found in a Jewish tomb near Jerusalem. The Hebrew inscription on the ossuary reads, "Jehohanan the son of Hgqwl," and dates to the first century AD.

Digging Up the Words

Another important type of archeological find is the discovery of ancient written texts. Though we do not have the original versions of any of the biblical books, we have older copies and more copies of the books of the Bible than for any other ancient text! Every ancient copy found has reinforced biblical scholars' certainty in the reliability of biblical text. Scholars are interested in nonbiblical writings as well, as these help us to understand the customs and beliefs of other peoples during biblical times.

One of the most important finds in the past century was the discovery of the Dead Sea Scrolls. In 1947, two young shepherds were grazing their flocks near some caves close to the northwestern shore of the Dead Sea. After one of the boys threw a stone into one of the caves, they heard something shatter. When they entered the cave, they found a few jars containing ancient scrolls, which possibly belonged to the **Essenes**, a group of pious, conservative Jews who left the Temple of Jerusalem and began a community called Qumran. Hundreds of scrolls were discovered around Qumran over the next few years. Included in these scrolls are some of the oldest copies of Old Testament books ever discovered. Other scrolls describe the Essenes, religious practices and their contemptuous relationship with the Jewish authorities. These discoveries are important because the Essenes lived at the same time as Jesus. Their writings offer insight into Jesus' world.

Another important discovery was the **Nag Hammadi manuscripts**. These are fourth-century, nonbiblical writings discovered in 1945 near the village of Nag Hammadi in Upper Egypt. These are invaluable sources of information regarding Gnostic beliefs, practices, and lifestyle. Gnosticism was an early Church heresy claiming that Christ's humanity was an illusion and that the human body is evil.

CATHOLICS **MAKING** A **DIFFERENCE**

How many priests do you know who like to go spelunking in search of cave paintings? Fr. Henri Breuil, SJ (1877–1961), was a Jesuit priest from France and a notable archaeologist. Breuil's most significant works are his studies and artistic reproductions of prehistoric cave paintings in Europe and Africa. His findings led the way for scientific discoveries of the Paleolithic world for decades afterward. He later became known as the Pope of Prehistory.

© Tarker/Bridgeman Images

Essenes ➤ A group of pious, ultraconservative Jews who left the Temple of Jerusalem and began a community by the Dead Sea, known as Qumran.

Nag Hammadi manuscripts ➤ Fourth-century writings, discovered in 1945 near the village of Nag Hammadi in Upper Egypt, that are invaluable sources of information regarding Gnostic beliefs, practices, and lifestyle. Gnosticism was an early Church heresy claiming that Christ's humanity was an illusion and the human body is evil.

UNIT 1

Pulling It All Together

So, how do you make sense of all those old stories in the Bible? As you have made your way through this chapter, you have discovered many ways to make sense of biblical accounts:

- First, look for the literal sense of what you are reading. What is the message the human author was trying to convey?
- Consider the literary genre in which the text was written to better understand the human author's intent.
- Investigate the culture in which the account took place to understand better the examples and symbols used by the author.
- Consider what biblical archaeologists have discovered and the implications of these discoveries for understanding the biblical accounts.
- Consider the three spiritual senses—allegorical, moral, and anagogical—to discover the religious truth God is revealing through the text.
- Look to the teachings of Church Tradition and the Magisterium for guidance on interpreting Scripture passages.
- Seek the guidance of the Holy Spirit. ✳

Qumran cave 4, one of the caves in which the Dead Sea Scrolls were found at the ruins of Khirbet Qumran in the desert of Israel.

Do some research online for recent discoveries in biblical archaeology. Write a three- to five-sentence paragraph summarizing what you find.

UNIT 1

1. Why do we rely on the Magisterium for interpretation of Sacred Scripture?

2. What is biblical exegesis, and why is it important?

3. What are the two main things we must consider when interpreting the Bible?

4. Explain the difference between the literal sense and the spiritual sense of a biblical text.

5. Why is knowing the literary form important to understanding a biblical text?

6. How do textual criticism and historical criticism rely on each other when interpreting a text?

7. What are the three things we should take into account when assessing what the human authors of the Bible were communicating?

8. What three things should we pay attention to when trying to understand what God intended to reveal in Scripture?

9. Why is archaeology an important tool for biblical scholarship?

Tools for Understanding the Bible

Understanding and interpreting the Bible correctly can be tricky. Fortunately, the Church provides tools and methods to help us.

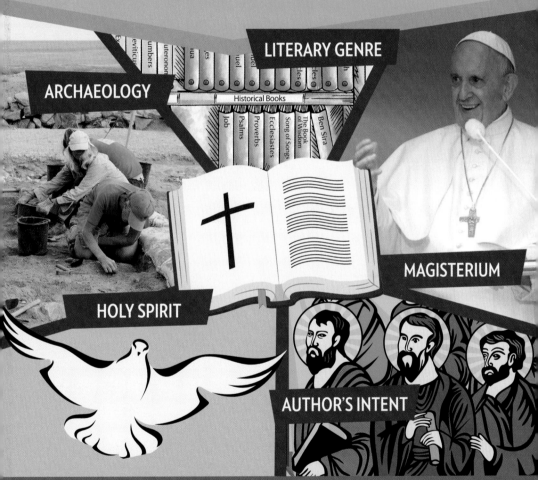

LITERARY GENRE

ARCHAEOLOGY

Historical Books

Job Psalms Proverbs Ecclesiastes Song of Songs The Book of Wisdom Ben Sira

MAGISTERIUM

HOLY SPIRIT

AUTHOR'S INTENT

1. Which of these tools helps you to understand Scripture the most?

2. What other tools can help you to better understand the Bible?

UNIT 1 HIGHLIGHTS

CHAPTER 1 God's Original Plan

Event 1
Creation: Original Holiness

God creates the universe and everything in it. It is all very good. God created humans in his own image.

Genesis, chapters 1–2

Event 2
The Fall

Humans are separated from God and one another as a result of Original Sin. Our original holiness was lost.

Genesis, chapter 3

Event 3
Sin's Ripple Effect

Sin brings about pain, suffering, death, and a loss of unity.

Its effect impacts others, leading to further sinful behavior.

Genesis, chapters 4–11

Two Kinds of Truth

Science (reason)   **Religion (faith)**

- deals with scientific truth and natural world

- focuses on the how

- based on objectively measurable phenomena

- conclusions discovered by observation

- deals with religious truth and spiritual realities

- focuses on the why

- cannot be measured objectively

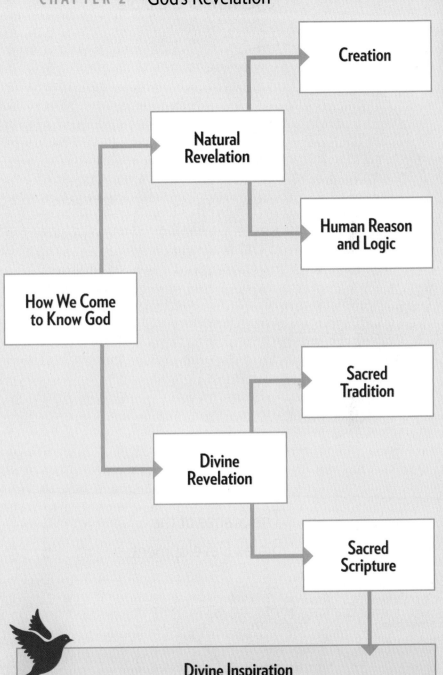

Creation

Natural Revelation

Human Reason and Logic

How We Come to Know God

Sacred Tradition

Divine Revelation

Sacred Scripture

Divine Inspiration

The Holy Spirit inspired the human authors to communicate through human words the divine message of salvation that God wishes to reveal.

UNIT 1

CHAPTER 3

Overview of the Bible

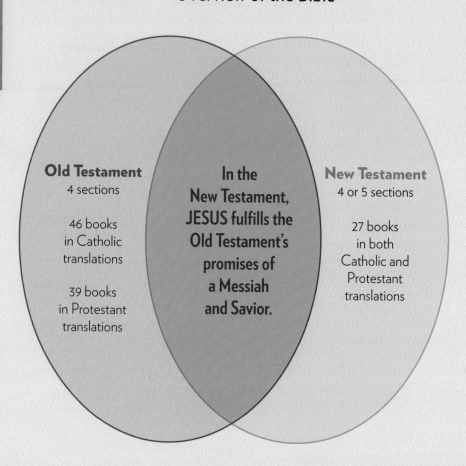

Old Testament
4 sections

46 books
in Catholic
translations

39 books
in Protestant
translations

In the
New Testament,
JESUS fulfills the
Old Testament's
promises of
a Messiah
and Savior.

New Testament
4 or 5 sections

27 books
in both
Catholic and
Protestant
translations

The Stages of the Bible's Development

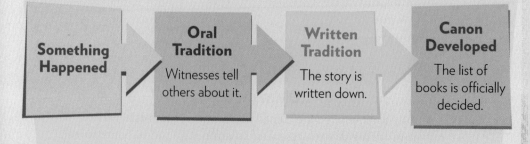

Something Happened

Oral Tradition
Witnesses tell others about it.

Written Tradition
The story is written down.

Canon Developed
The list of books is officially decided.

CHAPTER 4   Interpreting the Bible

Tools for Helping Us Understand and Interpret Scripture

Reliable Guide	Biblical Exegesis	Two Ways of Understanding Biblical Truth	Biblical Archaeology
1. The Holy Spirit 2. The Magisterium • The Church's living teaching office, acting under the guidance of the Holy Spirit to teach and interpret the message God revealed to the original Apostles	Exegesis is the critical interpretation and explanation of Scripture. Exegesis helps us pay attention to certain things so that we can better understand a text's true meaning. Some of those things include the following: • Literary genres, such as poetry, letters, parables, laws • The style, structure, and language of the text • The influence of culture, such as the roles of men and women	1. Literal Sense • The basic meaning of the text, what the human author wanted to convey 2. Spiritual Sense • The spiritual truths conveyed in the human author's words • Three categories: ◦ Allegorical sense ◦ Moral sense ◦ Anagogical sense	Excavating ancient sites helps us understand the culture, customs, beliefs, and history of the people who lived during biblical times.

UNIT 1
BRING IT HOME

HOW DOES THE BIBLE HELP ME KNOW GOD?

FOCUS QUESTIONS

CHAPTER 1	Why is there evil in the world? Was that part of God's plan?
CHAPTER 2	How do I know God exists?
CHAPTER 3	Why is the Bible so complicated?
CHAPTER 4	How do I make sense of all those old stories in the Bible?

UNIT 1

VIVA
Cotter High School

I think one of the most important truths that the Bible communicates is that we are not alone. Having our sisters and brothers to lean on is invaluable in helping us continue our journey. God is always with us. He is present in the Catholic community, he is present in every person, he is present in creation, and he is present in us.

REFLECT

Take some time to read and reflect on the unit and chapter focus questions listed on the facing page.

- What question or section did you identify most closely with?

- What did you find within the unit that was comforting or challenging?

UNIT 2
God Revealed
to His Chosen People

HOW DO
I KEEP
MY FOCUS
ON GOD?

LOOKING AHEAD

CHAPTER 5   Page 112

The Patriarchs: God Reveals Himself to a Chosen Family

CHAPTER 6   Page 132

The Pentateuch: God Reveals Himself to His Chosen People

CHAPTER 7   Page 160

Joshua and Judges

CHAPTER 8   Page 190

The Rise of the Monarchy

UNIT 2

Keeping my focus on God has been a struggle for me because I get so distracted. If I'm not using my phone, I'm using either my laptop or my iPad or watching TV. Sometimes I even let my worries prevent me from talking to God. I get so occupied thinking of everything that could go wrong instead of having faith that everything will work itself out with God by my side.

CAROLINA
Providence Catholic High School

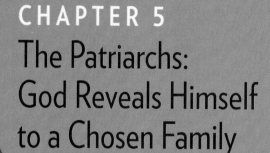

UNIT 2

CHAPTER 5
The Patriarchs: God Reveals Himself to a Chosen Family

HOW DO I FIND GOD WHEN MY LIFE CAN BE SUCH A MESS?

SNAPSHOT

Article 20   Page 113
Abraham and Sarah
- Pre-read: Genesis 12:1–20, 15:1–17:27, 21:1–22:19

Article 21   Page 120
Isaac and Jacob
- Pre-read: Genesis 24:1–66 (Isaac and Rebekah)
- Pre-read: Genesis 25:19–34, 27:1–45, 33:1–20 (Jacob and Esau)
- Pre-read: Genesis, chapter 32 (Jacob's new name)

Article 22   Page 126
Joseph
- Pre-read: Genesis, chapters 37–50 (Joseph and his brothers in Egypt)

Article 20
Abraham and Sarah

So far, we have covered these essential points:

- how God has revealed himself through natural revelation and Divine Revelation
- how the first eleven chapters of Genesis reveal God's original plan for humanity and how our first parents' sin sent that plan off course
- what the Bible is and how it came to be
- how to interpret the Bible so we correctly understand what God is revealing through its words

Now let's get back to the Bible and look at what the rest of Genesis and the other four books of the Pentateuch have to reveal to us.

You've probably come across a few miracle stories featured in social media. A teenager with incurable brain cancer is somehow healed, and the doctors have no explanation. A toddler is ripped from her mother's arms during a tornado, only to be found hundreds of feet away, alive with only minor scratches. Or maybe you have experienced something less dramatic, like a friend driving by just when you need a ride because you are late for practice. Some people will say these are just coincidences, but a person of faith sees the hand of God involved.

In Genesis, chapters 12–50, we have the accounts of a family that started with one couple, Abraham and Sarah. Their family is chosen for a special purpose by God, and their lives are filled with many adventures—some ordinary and some quite extraordinary. Along the way, they experience miraculous events as God intervenes to keep the promises he made to them.

A person who has survived an improbable, even life-threatening, situation might attribute their survival to the hand of God. Name a time when you felt God was watching over you as you faced a challenging situation.

© palidachan / Shutterstock.com

UNIT 2

Old as Dirt, Barren as the Desert

The history of our faith starts with God's relationship with Abraham and his wife, Sarah. Abraham is the first of the patriarchs. In common usage, a **patriarch** is the father or leader of a tribe, clan, or tradition. However, when used in the Bible, *patriarch* refers to the fathers of our faith: Abraham and his son Isaac, and Isaac's son Jacob.

We first meet Abraham and Sarah under their original names: Abram and Sarai—a childless husband and wife living in Haran, probably between 2000 and 1700 BC. In ancient cultures, being childless was not a good thing; having children was a sign that you were richly blessed. In fact, whenever God bestowed a blessing on the people of Israel, it often included fertility: "I will look with favor upon you, and make you fruitful and numerous, as I carry out my covenant with you" (Leviticus 26:9). Being elderly, Abram and Sarai no longer had any hopes of becoming parents, a situation many would call cursed. Why would God choose such a couple to start his plan of salvation?

Sarah overhears the three travelers confirm that Abram will be given the land of Canaan and that he will have an heir.

This is a common theme in the Bible: God does not always choose the most obvious and able-bodied candidates for the job. Why is this? Perhaps it is like that teenager whose cancer disappeared, or the baby who survived the tornado. Without any other natural explanations, we look to God. By choosing the least suitable person for the position, God turns our attention toward himself. Abram and Sarai are old and barren. They could not have done this on their own. God must have had a hand in it.

This is good news for you too. No matter how incapable, unattractive, or unqualified you think you are, you have a role in God's work. You are here for a reason—actually, for many reasons. Every moment of every day, you are

---

patriarch ➤ The father or leader of a tribe, clan, or tradition. Abraham, Isaac, and Jacob were the patriarchs of the Israelites.

TAKE IT TO GOD

Good and gracious God,

Abraham and Sarah had great faith.

They listened and followed you in their hearts, leaving everything they knew.

I feel many things in my heart from day to day,

But I do find it hard to figure out if any of it is actually from you.

Please help me sort through my inner thoughts

So that I, like Abraham and Sarah, may recognize your voice in my life

And have the faith and courage to do your will.

Amen.

UNIT 2

called to speak and act on behalf of God. God might even use your weaknesses. If you are academically inadequate, God can use your failures. If you are vertically challenged, God can use your shortness. If you are gravitationally gifted, God can use your weight. If you are athletically awkward, God can use your two left feet. God once told Saint Paul, "My grace is sufficient for you, for power is made perfect in weakness" (2 Corinthians 12:9). Reaching out to God in our weakness is what makes us strong. No talent is needed, and only one thing is required: faith.

Pack Up and Move Out

Imagine God telling you to pack up your things, move to a place you had never been, and live with people you do not know. You have no job, no connections, and perhaps you do not even know the language. Amidst all this, God promises you something that seems impossible or even ridiculous. In Abram's case, God tells him, "Go forth from your land, your relatives, and from your father's house to a land that I will show you" (Genesis 12:1). Would you go?

Moving can involve many emotions. How do you think Abraham and Sarah felt about leaving their home and families without being certain of their destination?

Abram is a childless old man who has the one thing that makes him an ideal candidate for God's mission: **faith**. Faith is the gift of God by which one freely accepts God's full Revelation. When God reveals himself and asks Abram to move to a new land, Abram does not question it (see Genesis 12:4). He trusts God's plan for him, so he acts accordingly and does what God asks. Some other examples of his faith and trust in God include these:

- When foreign kings capture Abraham's nephew, Lot, Abraham goes to battle to save him, evidently confident that God will protect him (see Genesis 14:1–16).
- When God tells Abraham that the sign of their covenant is male circumcision, Abraham and all the males of his household are circumcised—a rather painful experience (see Genesis, chapter 17).
- Abraham trusts God enough to confront God about the destruction of Sodom (see Genesis 18:16–32).
- When God asks Abraham to sacrifice his son Isaac, Abraham proves his willingness to do so. (This is discussed in the next article.)

This isn't to say that Abraham has perfect faith. He shows doubts several times. For example, when he and Sarah have to travel to Egypt to survive a famine, his trust in God's promise wavers a bit as he worries about the **pharaoh's** interest in his wife (see Genesis 12:10–20). Abraham tells Sarah to pretend she is his sister! God has to send plagues to Pharaoh's household to keep Sarah from becoming another one of Pharaoh's many wives. What's worse is that Abraham does this again (see Genesis 20:1–13).

Great faith does not mean sinless perfection. Despite our flaws, God still loves and desires a relationship with us.

Covenants: Promises Kept

God establishes a covenant with Abram. Three times in Genesis, the specifics of this covenant are spelled out: 12:1–7, 15:1–21, and 17:1–22. Recall that a covenant is a solemn agreement between human beings or between God and a human being in which mutual commitments are made. Covenants bind the parties together in a special relationship. One way to help understand covenants is to contrast them with contracts.

---

faith ▶ From the Latin *fides*, meaning "trust" or "belief," faith is the gift of God by which one freely accepts God's full Revelation in Jesus Christ. It is a matter of both the head (acceptance of God's revealed truth) and the heart (love of God and neighbor as a response to God's first loving us). Also, one of the three Theological Virtues.

pharaoh ▶ A ruler of ancient Egypt.

A contract	A covenant
focuses on things or events	focuses on relationships
is conditional (I will do this if you will do that.)	is unconditional; promises are meant to be kept whether or not the other party keeps their promise
ends once the commitments are fulfilled	is a lifelong commitment

UNIT 2

Marriage is a good example of a covenant and is often used in the Bible as a symbol for God's relationship with his people. In marriage, the bride and groom promise to be faithful in good times and in bad, in sickness and in health, and to love and honor each other for the rest of their lives. Marriage establishes a relationship: the two are now husband and wife. The wedding vows are unconditional promises. The groom does not promise to love and honor his wife *only if* she does the same. Instead, they make unconditional vows to love each other. Period. There are no conditions or requirements that need to be met. Finally, the marriage is lifelong. The wedding vows often include the phrase "until death do us part."

Similarly, God's covenant with Abraham establishes a relationship: "I will maintain my covenant between me and you and your descendants after you throughout the ages as an everlasting covenant, to be your God and the God of your descendants after you" (Genesis 17:7). God promises to be faithful to Abraham and his descendants, and Abraham promises to be faithful to God. God also promises to give Abraham land and a great nation (his descendants). It is also an "everlasting covenant" (verse 13) that extends down through Abraham's descendants.

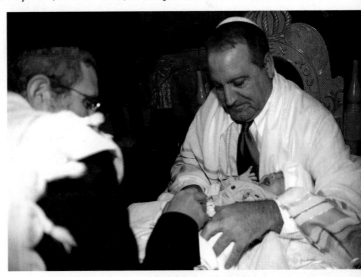

© Chameleons Eye / Shutterstock.com

A Jewish infant during his circumcision ceremony in Jerusalem, Israel.

Covenants are also marked with signs. A **sign** is an object, event, action, or outward mark that conveys a meaning or represents something else. Just as a ring worn on the left hands of spouses is a sign of their marriage, other covenants have signs too. When God promises not to destroy the Earth, he offers the sign of a rainbow (see Genesis 9:13). In his covenant with Abram, there are two signs. God changes their names from Abram and Sarai to Abraham ("the father is exalted") and Sarah ("princess"). The other sign is **circumcision**, the removal of the foreskin of the penis, to be performed on every male child eight days after he is born. Circumcision was an outward sign that emphasized the permanency of their intimate relationship with God. Jesus, being part of a faithful Jewish family, was circumcised (see Luke 2:21). This ritual is still performed by Jewish people today as a sign of their faithfulness to God's covenant.

Covenants are a very important part of salvation history. We will see God's covenant with Abraham renewed and expanded as we continue our study of the Old Testament.

God Is Always Faithful, but Us? Well, We Try!

Even in the best marriages, there are days when husbands and wives do not fully uphold their vows to love and honor each other, in sickness and in health, and in good times and in bad. Think about a mom and dad at the end of a hard day at work. They are tired and cranky, and then their kid shows up with a bad report card. The dog just vomited on the living room carpet, and then they find out the water bill has skyrocketed because someone left the water hose on all night. The stress mounts, and their vows of loving and

© Monkey Business Images / Shutterstock.com

When does the stress of life cause conflict in your family? What helps you to restore your covenant of love with one another?

---

sign ▶ An object, event, or action that conveys a meaning or represents something else.

circumcision ▶ The act, required by Jewish Law, of removing the foreskin of the penis. Since the time of Abraham, it has been a sign of God's covenant relationship with the Jewish People.

honoring each other are momentarily forgotten. They lash out at each other and say things that they later regret. This happens in the best of marriages. Later they calm down, apologize, and forgive each other. Because they did not live up perfectly to the promises they made to each other, does this mean their marriage is over? Of course not! Though spouses slip and fall in how they treat each other, their marriage covenant allows them to get back up and keep walking forward together.

In a similar way, this happens in our relationship with God, except God is not the one who slips and falls, because . . . well, he's God! We're the ones who are not always faithful. In times of stress or weakness, we try to control things ourselves, or we place our trust in something that provides only temporary satisfaction. On the other hand, God's faithfulness "will stand as long as the heavens" (Psalm 89:3). Like in any good marriage, we must realize when we have done wrong, apologize, and reconcile. The covenant keeps our relationship with God strong. ✳

UNIT 2

In what way is a covenant a much stronger bond and commitment than a verbal agreement? Give three reasons.

Article 21

Isaac and Jacob

Jordan tried to keep his problems to himself, but one night his need to talk to someone finally outweighed his embarrassment. Jordan showed up at his best friend's house, saying: "I just can't take being at my house anymore! Can I stay here tonight?" Jordan's oldest brother was on drugs, and no one else in the family would acknowledge it. His parents were hardly home, and when they were, they argued most of the time. His younger brother was totally spoiled, and their parents let him do whatever he wanted. Jordan's grandmother even quit coming to their house on holidays because it was all too crazy for her. Jordan sat on his friend's couch, covered his face with his hands and asked, "Why is my family so messed up?"

Who would you talk to if things at home became so frustrating or upsetting that you just couldn't take it anymore?

No matter how good and well-intentioned, every family has its variety of messy business to address. Reading the Bible, we learn that families from centuries ago were no different. The Book of Genesis recounts the lives of our ancestors in faith who struggled with these same issues. Beginning with Abraham's son Isaac, the competition and misunderstandings between family members threatens God's plan. What will help them overcome the separation that these family issues cause? The answer to this question is the grace of God, which helps them to forgive and reconcile with one another.

Everyone Needs a Good Laugh

Abraham is seventy-five years old when God first promises to give a child to him and his wife, Sarah (see Genesis 18:9–15). Over the next twenty-five years, Abraham has a child, Ishmael, with the maidservant, Hagar, but still no child with Sarah. When Abraham is ninety-nine years old, the Lord appears to him and Sarah as three visitors. Abraham invites them to dine with them, but Sarah remains in the tent:

"Where is your wife Sarah?" they asked him. "There in the tent," he replied. One of them said, "I will return to you about this time next year, and Sarah will then have a son." Sarah was listening at the entrance of the tent, just behind him. Now Abraham and Sarah were old, advanced in years, and Sarah had stopped having her menstrual periods. So Sarah laughed to herself and said, "Now that I am worn out and my husband is old, am I still to have sexual pleasure?" (Genesis 18:9–12)

© mountainpix / Shutterstock.com

Abraham offers a gift of bread to three mysterious strangers, who predict that he will be a father again.

God gives Sarah a good laugh, in more ways than she really expected. Sarah is soon pregnant. When she gives birth, she and Abraham name their son Isaac, which is derived from a Hebrew word meaning "laughter" (21:1–7).

Abraham faces some difficult times ahead. Because of Sarah's jealousy, Ishmael and Hagar are forced out of his life (see Genesis 21:9–21). Abraham also faces a test when God asks him to sacrifice Isaac, as in killing Isaac as a sacrifice to God. Before Abraham can actually finish the deed, God's angel stops him (see 22:1–18). Looking at this the wrong way, it might seem like a sick joke from God. God promises a son to an old childless couple, waits twenty-five years, and after the son is finally born, God demands his death, and then changes his mind at the last minute. Why would God do that? Why does he need to test Abraham? Doesn't God already know everything?

A "test" in this sense of the word is not the kind of test that you take in school. Your teacher gives a test to measure how much of the material you have grasped. This kind of test is different. This test is for the test-taker to discover what he already knows. God already knows what is deepest in Abraham's heart. He does not need to figure it out. Through this event, it is Abraham who discovers how much he is willing to trust God and follow his will. The test is Abraham's discovery of the faith he holds in his heart.

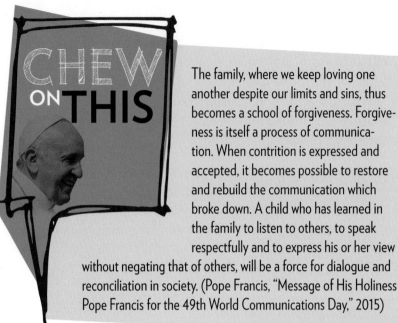

The family, where we keep loving one another despite our limits and sins, thus becomes a school of forgiveness. Forgiveness is itself a process of communication. When contrition is expressed and accepted, it becomes possible to restore and rebuild the communication which broke down. A child who has learned in the family to listen to others, to speak respectfully and to express his or her view without negating that of others, will be a force for dialogue and reconciliation in society. (Pope Francis, "Message of His Holiness Pope Francis for the 49th World Communications Day," 2015)

Some biblical scholars believe that this account also served as a teaching moment for the ancient Israelites, who lived beside people who sometimes practiced child sacrifice (see 2 Chronicles 28:1–3). By having God step in to stop Abraham from sacrificing Isaac, the account reinforces that Yahweh is a God of life. We have a God who wants us to respect every human being from conception until natural death. This narrative also prefigures God the Father's willingness to allow the sacrifice of his only Son, Jesus Christ. When Isaac asks his father what they would sacrifice, Abraham answers, "God will provide the sheep" (Genesis 22:8). If we fast-forward many centuries to New Testament times, we see that Jesus becomes the Lamb of God whose sacrifice saves us from sin and death.

© Artepics / Alamy Stock Photo

An angel of God stops Abraham from sacrificing his son Isaac, reinforcing the belief that Yahweh is a God of life. What other accounts in the Bible provide examples of God as a God of life?

Sibling Rivalry

God's covenant with Abraham is not meant for only Abraham. "I will maintain my covenant between me and you and your descendants after you throughout the ages as an everlasting covenant, to be your God and the God of your descendants after you" (Genesis 17:7). So God's covenant with Abraham continues with Abraham's son Isaac. We really don't hear much about Isaac. After Sarah's death, Abraham arranges for Isaac to be married to Rebekah, a woman from his homeland. In a continuation of the theme started with Sarah, Rebekah is also unable to bear children. With the help of the Lord, she becomes pregnant with twins, Jacob and Esau.

The accounts of Jacob and Esau's relationship really make the story interesting. You may have heard that the Bible is full of characters who are not worthy of being role models. It is true that you rarely find a perfect and blameless person within its pages. Isn't it interesting though that the Bible acknowledges their imperfections, while at the same time showing that these people still serve God's plan? Jacob and his twin, Esau, are prime examples of this.

Esau is the firstborn, which is important even though he and Jacob are twins. Tradition held that it was the birthright of the firstborn son to inherit his father's belongings and the leadership of his clan. However, there is one problem—Rebekah (the mom) favors Jacob and encourages him to use trickery to take away Esau's birthright and steal his aging father's blessing. Esau discovers what his brother has done, and it leaves him tearful, bitter, and ready for vengeance. Fearing that Esau might kill Jacob, Rebekah convinces Isaac to send Jacob away to find a wife (see Genesis 27:1–45).

Have you ever heard of someone trying to steal someone else's inheritance? It sometimes makes tabloid news, and it is known to cause irreparable damage to families. This is what could have easily happened to Jacob and Esau, but after they finally meet again, over fourteen

Jacob pretends to be his older twin, Esau, and tricks their blind father into giving him the family blessing. How do you feel when someone else receives recognition and praise for something you did?

years later, things are quite different. Jacob returns to his homeland, ready to apologize and make amends to Esau, but at the same time afraid of what Esau might do (see Genesis, chapter 32). He is prepared to face an angry foe ready to exact his vengeance, but instead he finds his brother, Esau, who "ran to meet him, embraced him, and flinging himself on his neck, kissed him as he wept" (33:4). Much like the father in Jesus' Parable of the Lost Son (see Luke 15:11–32), Esau is the model expression of God's love and forgiveness. Jacob even tells his brother, "To see your face is for me like seeing the face of God" (Genesis 33:10). God's grace has softened the brothers' hearts, overcoming past hurts and renewing their love for each other.

© Monkey Business Images / Shutterstock.com

Life with your siblings can be challenging at times. You can't control the actions of others, but you do have the power to conduct your own behavior. Consider this:

- Help a sibling with homework, even if you'd rather do something else.

- When a sibling has been thoughtless and rude, call them on it respectfully, forgive, and move on.

- If you're wrong, admit it. Take responsibility for your actions rather than blame someone else.

- Parents aren't perfect. When you disagree, discuss it respectfully and don't let anger get control.

No Pain, No Gain

The night before Jacob confronts Esau, he has an unusual, close encounter of a divine nature (see Genesis 32:23–33). In this highly symbolic story, Jacob wrestles with a divine being throughout the night. The being blesses Jacob and gives him a new name: Israel. This will also become the name of the nation consisting of the Twelve Tribes, descendants of Jacob's twelve sons. It also leaves Jacob limping away in pain.

People tend to want to avoid painful experiences, but as any athlete will tell you, no pain, no gain. Muscle grows when it is damaged. After you exercise, your body gets sore because the small fibers in your muscles have torn. When you rest, a cycle of repair and growth occurs, and more muscle develops. The only way muscle can grow is through a painful process.

This also applies to your emotional and spiritual life. Painful experiences in our relationships with God and other people encourage us to grow up and see life in a new light. This is just as true for fourteen-year-olds starting high school as it is for sixty-five-year-olds starting retirement. Jacob's confrontation with God is a painful and life-changing experience that leads him to a reconciliation with his brother, Esau. His new name is a sign of a new life as well. ✳

Have you ever experienced personal growth that came after a painful experience?

UNIT 2

© Brenda Carson / Shutterstock.com

HMMMMM. . . How had Jacob changed between the time he left his family and the time he returned?

Israel ➤ This name comes from Jacob's experience of "wrestling with God" (see Genesis 32:28) and is used to refer to several different things: (1) the Twelve Tribes of Israel as descendants of the twelve sons of Jacob, (2) the Chosen People or Jewish People as a whole, (3) the northern kingdom (Israel) in contrast to the southern kingdom (Judah), and (4) the modern nation of Israel.

Article 22

Joseph

The last thirteen chapters of Genesis cover the incredible adventure of Joseph, one of the youngest of Jacob's twelve sons. Joseph's story of triumph over tragedy strikes a universal chord, which might explain why it has been brought to life in movies and a popular Broadway musical. This account also sets the stage for the next major chapter in the history of our ancestors in faith: the ancient Israelites in Egypt.

Joseph tells his fantastic dreams and their meanings to his brothers. Have you ever had a dream with an important meaning?

Dream a Little Dream

Jacob has two wives: Leah and her sister, Rachel, who is his favorite. Between Leah and their two maidservants, Jacob has ten sons and one daughter, but Rachel (like Sarah and Rebekah before her) has not yet had any children. Then finally "God remembered Rachel" (Genesis 30:22), and she gives birth to Joseph, who becomes Jacob's favorite son. Being the favorite might have its perks, but it is not always such a great experience. Consider how a teacher's pet gets treated by his or her classmates. Add to the mix that Joseph was a dreamer and interpreter of dreams, and you have a recipe for disaster among brothers who do not appreciate his dreams at all.

The ancient world often believed that dreams and visions were ways that their gods communicated with them. In the Old Testament, dreams guided and helped the people to be more faithful to the covenant. Although Joseph is the youngest in his family, his dreams point to his future role as a leader and savior to his family. As you might imagine, these dreams don't go over well with his older brothers; they take Joseph's dreams as an insult. Resentful of their father's special love for Joseph, the brothers conspire to have him taken as a slave to Egypt. When the deed is done, they tell their father, Jacob, that Joseph is dead (see Genesis 37:1–35). Meanwhile, back in Egypt, Joseph's talent for dreaming and interpreting others' dreams eventually land him the job of being in charge of the pharaoh's household and the whole land of Egypt. Joseph has become the second most powerful man in Egypt next to Pharaoh (see 41:1–46).

The Key to Healing

One of the most remarkable events of Joseph's life occurs sometime after he becomes the pharaoh's right hand man. During a great famine, his brothers travel to Egypt to buy grain in order to survive. As governor of the country, Joseph is responsible for the sale of grain (see Genesis 42:1–46:34). When his brothers come to him, Joseph can easily turn them away, have them locked up forever, or take his vengeance out on them in some other way. Who could deny his anger at them? Yet despite his brothers' previous hatred for him, their jealous behavior, their forcing him into slavery, and the loss of so many years with his family, Joseph forgives his brothers!

Despite the fact that Joseph's brothers sold him into slavery, he ultimately forgives them. How challenging is it for you to forgive someone who has done you wrong?

How is one able to conjure up the strength to forgive after having been so harshly and cruelly treated by others? Perhaps Malala Yousafzai, the young Pakistani woman who survived an attempted assassination, can help us understand. Malala followed in her father's footsteps as an anti-Taliban activist when she was just a teenager. A death threat was placed on her after she publicly

I DIDN'T KNOW THAT!

Not only did Joseph rise to power in Egypt, he rose to fame on Broadway too! The account of Joseph and his family's journey to Egypt was developed into a musical, and later as a movie. *Joseph and the Amazing Technicolor Dreamcoat* was first staged in the early 1970s in London. In 1982, it came to Broadway, where it was nominated for six Tony Awards. It continues to win audiences all over the world with its humorous but heartfelt interpretation of Joseph's difficult family relationships, as well as his roller-coaster ride to become the Pharaoh's right-hand man.

UNIT 2

spoke out against the Taliban's prohibition of education for girls. In 2012, while riding the school bus home, fifteen-year-old Malala was shot in the head by a Taliban gunman. She survived.

Malala forgave her would-be assassin. Malala is deeply rooted in her Muslim faith and tries to live its teachings of compassion, peace, mercy, and forgiveness. To this day, she does not hold any anger toward her would-be assassin.

You might think, "I could never forgive someone who did that," but inside each one of us is a source of unending mercy that is not our own. God dwells not only beyond

Malala Yousafzai attends the Glamour Woman of the Year Awards at Carnegie Hall on November 11, 2013, in New York.

us in Heaven but also deep within us. We are made in God's image and likeness. God loved us into being. Love is at the core of every human person and therefore cannot be lost. It's there; we just have to be open to accessing its power.

Consider also the alternative: instead of living a life of anger and resentment, forgiveness of others is the key that opens the door to our own healing. This, in turn, allows us to move forward toward a happier life.

CATHOLICS MAKING A DIFFERENCE

Forgive the man who killed your husband? Who could do that? Saint Jane Frances de Chantal (1572–1641) is known primarily as the founder of a religious order, but long before she was a nun, she was the wife of a wealthy French baron. When she was twenty-eight, her husband was killed in a hunting accident, leaving her a widow with four children. It took a long time before she was able to forgive the man who killed her husband. Eventually, they reconciled and she even became the godmother to one of his children. Years later, after numerous hardships and with the guidance of Saint Francis de Sales (1567–1622), Jane founded the Congregation of the Visitation, a religious order for women who are rejected by other orders because of poor health or age. She was canonized a saint in 1767 and is a model of patience and humility.

S•F•A CHANTAL

UNIT 2

Finding the Good by Going through the Bad

Before Jacob's death, the brothers worry that Joseph is still nursing a grudge against them and is holding it back until their father passes away. When they beg for his forgiveness again, Joseph responds: "Do not fear. Can I take the place of God? Even though you meant harm to me, God meant it for good, to achieve this present end, the survival of many people" (Genesis 50:19–20). Like Malala, Joseph is empowered by God's grace to seek reconciliation over vengeance. Rather than focusing on his own small and limited viewpoint, Joseph looks at the bigger picture and sees his role in the grand scheme of things. If his brothers would not have sold him into slavery, not only his entire family but probably most of Egypt would have died in the famine.

When we are in the midst of a difficult, devastating life event, it is often impossible to see the bigger picture. For example, when someone we know and love gets cancer, we sometimes ask God why he would let it happen. Finding an answer is difficult at best. But we must remember that God is not a heartless puppet master who decides on who gets hurt and who doesn't. These painful events are not intentionally planned by God in order to achieve some greater good. Rather, when we remain trusting and open to God's grace, he can work through these events to bring about some good in our life and the lives of others.

Joseph, sold into slavery by his jealous brothers, rose to become vizier— the second most powerful man in Egypt next to Pharaoh.

As we go through life, let's remember that God has loved us into being. Like Abraham and Sarah, let's recognize that God's love is at our very core, giving us the strength to do what we may think is impossible. Like Isaac, Rebekah, Jacob, and Esau, let's love one another despite our flaws and hurtful behavior, and draw upon God's grace to forgive those who have hurt us, just as Joseph did. Let's let go of anger and resentment and move toward healing, remembering that through all of this, God is with us, helping us work through our hardships, forever remaining faithful to us no matter what our circumstances. ✳

HMMMMM. . .

How is offering forgiveness to someone who has wronged you a sign of strength, rather than weakness?

UNIT 2

1. The Bible often recounts the lives of people who seem incapable of doing the jobs God is asking of them. What seems to be the point of this?

2. Describe what a covenant is, using God's covenant with Abraham as an example.

3. How is our relationship with God similar to a marriage?

4. The patriarchs were faithful but imperfect human beings. Explain this statement using one of the patriarchs as an example.

5. Whose name was changed to Israel and what does he have to do with the Twelve Tribes?

6. Using Joseph and his brothers in your response, explain why forgiveness is important.

7. How can good come out of evil events?

JACOB WRESTLES WITH A MYSTERIOUS ADVERSARY (Genesis 32:23-33)

Jacob and the mysterious opponent wrestle all night. In the end, Jacob receives a blessing and a new name.

1. What do you see in the painting that indicates the importance of this wrestling match?

2. After wrestling all night, Jacob receives a new name from his opponent. What do you think this signifies?

CHAPTER 6
The Pentateuch: God Reveals Himself to His Chosen People

HOW DOES GOD FREE ME FROM THE THINGS THAT KEEP ME DOWN?

SNAPSHOT

Article 23 Page 133
Exodus: Free at Last!
• Pre-read: Exodus, chapters 1–16

Article 24 Page 140
Covenant: The Ties That Bind
• Pre-read: Exodus, chapters 19–20, 32–33, 36–39

Article 25 Page 145
Leviticus and Numbers: Being Holy
• Pre-read: Leviticus, chapters 1–7, 16, 23, 25
• Pre-read: Numbers 10:11–36; 11:1–6; chapter 12 13:1–14:38
• Pre-read: Deuteronomy, chapters 5–6

Article 26 Page 152
Numbers and Deuteronomy: The Promised Land
• Pre-read: Deuteronomy, chapter 34

Article 23

Exodus: Free at Last!

If the Book of Exodus were made into a movie (and it has been, several times), it would be an action adventure film (and it is). It comes complete with a powerful and dangerous villain, suspense, narrow escapes from impossible situations, and a humble hero who is willing to risk it all for the greater good.

Stories about heroes are very popular. *Heroes* can be defined as "people who give their lives to something greater than themselves." You can probably name a number of heroes: your local firefighters, perhaps your parents, or even a friend who takes the time to listen to your problems or help you with your homework. A hero is one who has a vision that goes beyond their own little world, who sees a greater purpose, who knows that the value of their life is found in serving others. In the Book of Exodus, our hero is Moses.

From Small Beginnings

The Book of Exodus picks up where Genesis left off. The sons of Jacob (Israel) and the generations that follow remain in Egypt for centuries. Over time, the Israelites have multiplied in number, surpassing the Egyptian population. To maintain power, Pharaoh, the ruler of Egypt, has enslaved the Israelites (see Exodus 1:1– 7). Worse yet, Pharaoh has ordered the Israelite midwives to kill all newborn baby boys to control the Israelite (also known as Hebrew) population (see verses 15–22)! Through a series of fortunate circumstances, Moses has escaped this fate and has been raised as an Egyptian in the house of the Pharaoh (see 2:1–10).

Despite growing up in the Egyptian royal family, Moses still identifies with the plight of the Israelites. After standing up for a fellow Israelite, Moses once again narrowly escapes death and flees to the land of Midian, where he marries, settles down as a shepherd, and has children (see Exodus 2:11–22). Life is good, life is easy . . . for now.

Firefighters are willing to sacrifice their lives to save the lives of others. Who is a modern-day hero for you?

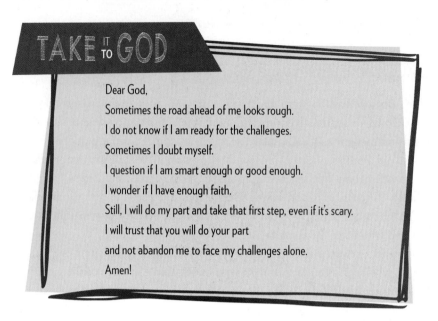

TAKE IT TO GOD

Dear God,

Sometimes the road ahead of me looks rough.

I do not know if I am ready for the challenges.

Sometimes I doubt myself.

I question if I am smart enough or good enough.

I wonder if I have enough faith.

Still, I will do my part and take that first step, even if it's scary.

I will trust that you will do your part

and not abandon me to face my challenges alone.

Amen!

Fire!

While out in the wilderness with his flock, Moses encounters God in a most unusual form—a bush that is on fire but is "not being consumed" (Exodus 3:2). This kind of appearance is called a **theophany**, God's manifestation of himself in a visible form to enrich human understanding of him. Fire is the element that God sometimes uses to appear to his people. There are many examples of this throughout the Bible:

- **Exodus 13:21–22:** Fire leads the Israelites to freedom.
- **Leviticus 6:2:** Fire is the means by which people offer their sacrifices to God.
- **Deuteronomy 4:11–12:** God descends on Mount Sinai.
- **Acts 2:3:** The Holy Spirit comes upon Jesus' disciples at Pentecost in tongues of fire.
- **2 Thessalonians 1:7–8:** Paul describes the second coming of Christ.

© modera76101 / Shutterstock.com

This painting, *God in the Burning Bush*, portrays God's miraculous appearance to Moses. Why do you think the artist portrayed the fire as a circle?

---

theophany ➤ God's manifestation of himself in a visible form to enrich human understanding of him. An example is God's appearance to Moses in the form of a burning bush.

Scripture tells us that God's fire is one that burns, but never consumes. It is an eternal flame, a light in the darkness, and our source for life.

God eases Moses' initial fear first by telling him that he is the God of his ancestors Abraham, Isaac, and Jacob. Later and most important, God reveals his name to Moses: **Yahweh**, which means something like "I am who am." In the ancient world, a person's name was more than an identifying label; a person's name also disclosed the character, traits, and very nature of that person. The name Yahweh reveals that God is eternal, the one who has been and will always be, the one who is the source of all things and all life. Like the ancient Israelites, Jewish people today do not say the name aloud out of reverence for God. Instead, they substitute it with the word *Adonai*, which means "Lord."

© emka74 / Shutterstock.com

UNIT 2

Mission Impossible

In 1936, after just eleven months as King of England, Edward VIII abdicated the throne, forcing his reluctant younger brother to take the throne as King George VI. To suddenly and unexpectedly be made king was a real challenge, especially because Europe was on the brink of World War II. But there was another challenge. King George VI stuttered. His struggle with public speaking was portrayed in the award-winning movie *The King's Speech* (2010). King George VI was terrified to speak in public due to his lack of confidence and his speech impediment. How could he possibly offer words of encouragement to thousands of English citizens?

Moses would have sympathized with King George VI. When Yahweh sends Moses on a mission to return to Egypt, confront the new Pharaoh, and demand the release of the Israelites from slavery, Moses immediately objects. Certainly, the mission is daunting, but there is another problem that fuels his reluctance: Moses is "slow of speech and tongue" (Exodus 4:10). His hesitancy leads some scholars to believe that Moses might have had a speech impediment. Regardless, God understands his predicament and offers a solution (see 4:10–16).

Despite having speech impediments, King George VI and Moses spoke to huge crowds. Have you ever had to speak in public? What was that experience like for you?

Yahweh ➤ The most sacred of the Old Testament names for God, which he revealed to Moses. It is frequently translated as "I AM" or "I am who am."

In the biblical account of Moses, we find another example of God choosing the least likely person to accomplish a major task. In acknowledging this, we should note a few things:

- Moses resists God's request because he thinks the task ridiculously impossible, and he feels incapable of carrying it out.
- God meets Moses halfway: If Moses does his part, God will do his share as well.
- God does not leave Moses to do his work alone; he includes Moses' brother, Aaron, to support him.
- Unlike the movie versions of this account, Moses is not outwardly bold and confrontational. His leadership and bravery are more understated, allowing others to take center stage.

Like Moses, we too might want to run away or offer excuses such as "I'm not good enough" or "I just can't do it" when facing a difficult task. The good news is that you do not have to be good enough. You only have to do your part and trust that God will do his part. For example, maybe your part is to reach out to people in your life, such as friends, family, teachers, and coaches, for help. In turn, the Spirit of God does his part by working through the people to help you.

When God tells Moses to go to Pharaoh and demand that Pharaoh free the Israelites, he doesn't leave Moses to do his work alone. He includes Moses' brother, Aaron, to support him. Name a time when a friend has supported you through a challenge.

Roadblocks

Doing God's will seems like it would be the ultimate hall pass. We can do what we want, wherever and whenever we want. If we are doing what God asks, then everything should go smoothly, right? Wrong. Moses and Aaron soon find this out when they confront Pharaoh with Yahweh's demand to free the Israelites. Pharaoh answers: "Who is the LORD, that I should obey him and let Israel go? I do not know the LORD, and I will not let Israel go" (Exodus 5:2). Then, to add more fuel to the fire, Pharaoh doubles the Israelites' workload. The Israelites are furious and complain to Moses. Moses, in turn, complains to God: "Why did you send me? From the time I went to Pharaoh to speak in your name, he has treated this people badly, and you have done nothing to rescue your people" (verses 22–23). As you might imagine, the dynamic between Moses and the Israelites is pretty fragile at this point. Things now seem worse than they were before!

Following God's will does not mean that life will go easily for you. You might think that someone blessed by God would have few difficulties in life, but that simply is not true. Comfort and ease are not a sign of God's approval. Jesus reminds us, "Blessed are you when they insult you and persecute you and utter every kind of evil against you" (Matthew 5:11).

MAKE IT SO

© Creativa Images / Shutterstock.com

Slavery was officially abolished in the United States over 150 years ago, but that does not mean slavery ended here. Human trafficking is a form of modern slavery in which people are forced into labor or sexual acts against their will. Some experts estimate that there are around twenty-one million victims worldwide, including in the United States. What can you do? Educate yourself so you can recognize the signs of human trafficking. Talk to others and spread the word about the severity of the problem. Contact your legislators to make sure they are acting on behalf of the silent victims all over the world. Be a modern Moses and demand freedom for people who are enslaved.

Freedom! (And Complaining!)

As promised, God does not abandon Moses at this crucial moment. To convince Pharaoh to let the Israelites go, God brings a series of plagues on the Egyptians. But it is not until the tenth and final plague, a plague causing the death of the firstborn of every household in the land of Egypt, that Pharaoh finally agrees to free the Israelites.

In preparation for this last plague, God instructs the Israelites to sacrifice an unblemished lamb and mark their homes with its blood so that "when the LORD goes by to strike down the Egyptians, seeing the blood [of the lamb] on the lintel and the two doorposts, the LORD will pass over that door," thus sparing the Israelites (Exodus 12:23). The sacrificial lamb is eaten in a special meal called the **Seder** during the religious feast called the Passover (described in Exodus, chapter 12). To this day, the **Passover** is one of Judaism's most important religious festivals. The blood of the sacrificial lamb, also known as the **Paschal Lamb**, plays a key role in the Israelites' freedom from slavery. We call Jesus the Lamb of God, because it is his sacrifice on the cross that saves us from the slavery of sin.

© BibleArtLibrary / iStock.com

"Seeing the blood [of the lamb] on the lintel and the two doorposts, the Lord will pass over that door, thus sparing the Israelites" (Exodus 12:23).

Seder ➤ This Hebrew word (meaning "order" or "procedure") refers to a Jewish ceremonial meal, usually celebrated at home during Passover, in commemoration of the Exodus of the Chosen People from Egypt.

Passover ➤ The night the Lord passed over the houses of the Israelites marked by the blood of the lamb, and spared the firstborn sons from death. It also is the feast that celebrates the deliverance of the Chosen People from bondage in Egypt and the Exodus from Egypt to the Promised Land.

Paschal Lamb ➤ In the Old Testament, the sacrificial lamb shared at the Seder meal of the Passover on the night the Israelites escaped from Egypt; in the New Testament, the Paschal Lamb is Jesus, the Incarnate Son of God who dies on a cross to take away "the sin of the world" (John 1:29).

As the Israelites make their way to freedom, Pharaoh changes his mind and sends his armies after them, chasing them toward the Red Sea. When the people look back to find Pharaoh and his army in close pursuit, they complain to Moses that they are all going to die. With Pharaoh and his army behind them and the Red Sea before them, they are trapped.

But Moses lifts up his staff, and the Lord sends a wind that pushes back the Red Sea, allowing the Israelites to escape on the dry land between the parted waters. When they safely make it through, the wind ceases, and the waters return, drowning Pharaoh's army (see Exodus 14:10–31). The Israelites celebrate, but only a few weeks later when faced with a lack of food and water in the wilderness, they complain yet again: "If only we had died at the LORD's hand in the land of Egypt, as we sat by our kettles of meat and ate our fill of bread! But you have led us into this wilderness to make this whole assembly die of famine!" (16:3). Poor Moses never seems to catch a break! ✳

UNIT 2

OVERVIEW of the Book of Exodus

- **Reason for writing:** To recount the Israelites' escape from slavery in Egypt and their time at Mount Sinai on the way to the Promised Land.
- **Time period:** Sometime between 1500 and 1250 BC.
- **Themes:** God liberates his people from slavery and oppression; God's covenant with Moses provides laws to guide us; God feeds and sustains us in difficult times.

HMMMMM. . . What things point to Moses's consistent trust in God despite facing many obstacles? What events show that God does not abandon Moses?

UNIT 2

Article 24
Covenant: The Ties That Bind

Have you ever witnessed a couple renew their wedding vows? People sometimes renew their wedding vows to mark a special anniversary—perhaps after twenty-five, thirty, or even fifty years of marriage. The renewal does not take the place of the old vows; rather, it expresses the couple's commitment to the covenant they made a long time ago.

Throughout salvation history, and especially in the books of the Pentateuch, God renews the covenant with his people a number of times. The covenant is the tie that binds God with his people. Each new covenant does not nullify the old one, but strengthens it and allows God's people to better understand and follow his will.

Can you think of any rules or boundaries at home or at school that might be annoying or restrictive to you, but are in place for your safety?

Laying Down the Law

Rules. Laws. Boundaries. Do this. Don't do that. No swimming. No skateboarding. No dogs allowed. No admission under age sixteen. No shoes, no service, no kidding!

Sometimes rules and regulations can feel like an annoying imposition on our freedom, keeping us from doing or getting what we want. As human beings, we value our independence, and as a teen, you want to exercise your growing independence. The thought of being free to do whatever you want, whenever you want, is liberating—no rules, no laws, no limits.

It's quite possible that the Israelites felt like this when they first set up camp at Sinai. After their slavery and lack of freedom in Egypt, they are free for the first time in their lives. The feeling must have been invigorating! There are no rules to follow, no schedules to keep. The possibilities are endless; they can do whatever, whenever they please.

All of this sounds wonderful, but what would the world really be like without rules? Think about it. Life would be pretty dangerous and chaotic. Rules and laws serve a significant purpose. They aren't meant to be a burden. For example, is a mother who forces her son to look both ways before he crosses the street doing this to keep him from having fun? Of course not. Her rule is a sign of her love for her son and her desire for him to be safe.

In order for the Israelites to live as a harmonious, safe, and just society, they need a set of rules too. So God calls Moses to the top of Mount Sinai and reestablishes the covenant he made with Abraham, Isaac, Jacob, and the Twelve Tribes of Israel, affirming the Israelites as his Chosen People.

Then God gives Moses a list of laws, including the **Ten Commandments**. In total, God gives Moses 613 laws to guide the Israelites in all aspects of their lives. Some of these laws are found in the Book of Exodus, but a majority of the 613 are in the remaining books of the Torah: Leviticus, Numbers, and Deuteronomy. The Ten Commandments are at the heart of this Law, summarizing our essential duties toward God and toward one another. Just as the mother's rule to look both ways before crossing the street is a sign of love for her son, the Ten Commandments are a sign of God's love for us and his desire for our happiness.

This renewal of God's covenant and the Laws that go with that renewal is called the Mosaic Covenant or the **Sinai Covenant**. The Laws by themselves are called the Mosaic Law, the Old Law, or the **Law of Moses**.

The Ten Commandments are at the heart of the Law, but are a tangible sign of God's love for us and desire for our happiness.

UNIT 2

Ten Commandments ➤ Sometimes called the Decalogue, the list of ten norms, or rules of moral behavior, that God gave Moses and that are the basis of ethical conduct.

Sinai Covenant (also called Mosaic Covenant) ➤ The covenant established with the Israelites at Mount Sinai that renewed God's covenant with Abraham's descendants. The Sinai Covenant establishes the Israelites as God's Chosen People.

Law of Moses (also called the Mosaic Law) ➤ The first five books of the Old Testament, which are also called the books of the law or the Torah. God gave Moses the tablets summarizing the Law (see Exodus 31:18), which is why it is also called the Law of Moses, or the Mosaic Law.

God's Portable House

The action-adventure movie *Raiders of the Lost Ark* (1981) is purely fiction, but it is based on the search for one of the most important and sacred objects in the Bible: the **Ark of the Covenant**. The Ark of the Covenant was the sacred chest in which the tablets containing the Ten Commandments were kept. The Book of Exodus goes into elaborate detail describing the construction of the Ark as well as the tent, or **Tabernacle**, that housed the Ark (see Exodus, chapters 36–38). Here is an interior view of the Tabernacle:

A model of the Ark of the Covenant.

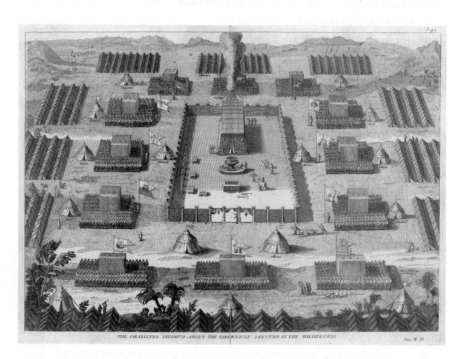

THE ISRAELITES INCAMP'D ABOUT THE TABERNACLE ERECTED IN THE WILDERNESS

Ark of the Covenant ➤ A sacred chest that housed the tablets of the Ten Commandments, placed within the sanctuary where God would come and dwell.

Tabernacle ➤ In the Old Testament, the portable tent that was used as a sanctuary for the Ark of the Covenant during the Israelite's migration in the desert.

A model of the tabernacle where the Ark of the Covenant was stored.

The Ark was the symbol of God's saving presence among the Israelites. To be in the presence of the Ark was to be in the presence of God. In the rear of the Tabernacle, the Ark of the Covenant was kept in an area called the **Holy of Holies**. This is where Moses would meet with the Lord, who often appeared there in the form of a cloud (see Exodus 40:34–38).

The Tabernacle, or tent, where the Ark of the Covenant resides is different from the tabernacle we would find in a Catholic church. However, the purpose of both is the same: to provide a sacred space for the presence of God.

The tabernacle in a Catholic church is not a tent but a sacred container. This sacred container houses the consecrated bread—the **Eucharist**, the Body of Christ, the real presence of God. The consecrated bread is reserved in the tabernacle so it can be distributed to the sick and those unable to attend Mass.

A Catholic church tabernacle.

Holy of Holies ➤ The most holy place in the Tabernacle and later the Temple in Jerusalem, where the Ark of the Covenant was kept. Only the High Priest could enter, and only once a year.

Eucharist ➤ The celebration of the entire Mass. The term can also refer specifically to the consecrated bread and wine that have become the Body and Blood of Christ.

In the beginning of the Gospel of John in the New Testament, it says that the Son of God "made his dwelling" among us (1:14). The word *dwelling* comes from a Greek word meaning "tent." So, in the Gospel, the author is saying that the Son of God "pitched his tent" among us—a reference to the tent or Tabernacle that housed the Ark of the Covenant. In essence, this verse from the Gospel of John is telling us that Jesus is our human Tabernacle, the true presence of God.

One Step Forward, Two Steps Back

While Moses is up on the mountain with God, the Israelites are waiting for him back at their camp. Moses is gone for a long time, and the Israelites begin worrying that God has abandoned them. So they take matters into their own hands and build a golden calf—a symbol of the Canaanite god Baal—to worship. When Moses returns and finds them adoring this false idol, he angrily smashes the two tablets containing God's Law, then orders that many of the idolaters be killed (see Exodus, chapter 32).

Sound familiar? Like the Israelites, we want things to happen on our time, and when God does not come through in the way that we expect, we can be tempted to give up on him and focus our lives elsewhere. Perhaps we are not worshipping golden calves, but there are subtler false gods to whom we bow our heads and offer our precious gifts of time and attention.

The good news we can gather from this story is that broken promises do not mean the covenant is ended. In a marriage, when one spouse acts in an unloving way, the two are still no less married. However, broken commitments must be reconciled. First, we must acknowledge our wrongdoing. Moses has an interesting take on this. He burns the golden calf, grinds it into powder, and then scatters the powder in the water for the Israelites to drink (see Exodus 32:20). He makes the Israelites taste and drink their own sin!

Reconciling a covenant calls for repentance and atonement as well (see Exodus 32:30–35). Finally, Moses renews the covenant by bringing down two more tablets of the covenant from the mountain (34:1–9), a symbol of the reconciliation between God and the Israelites. Sin separates us from God and one another, but the covenant is eternal. We are graced with God's forgiveness, and the covenant strengthens our relationship with him. 🌸

HMMMMMM. . . Why are laws or some kind of behavior agreements a crucial part of covenants?

Article 25
Leviticus and Numbers: Being Holy

What does the word *holy* mean to you? American culture often uses the word *holy* in a nonreligious way. Someone says, "Holy . . ." followed by a noun (sometimes a not-so-nice one) to express astonishment, disbelief, or shock, as in "Holy moly!" "Holy cow!" "Holy mac-n-cheese!" You have most likely heard the word used (and perhaps even used it yourself) in that context.

However, even when used in a religious way, the word *holy* can sometimes carry unwanted baggage with it. For some people, the word can carry a sense of purity that is stained by even the slightest impure thought. That kind of holiness feels like an impossible goal for mere mortals. Sometimes holy can even have a negative connotation, as if it were just the abbreviated version of "holier than thou." In this sense, being called "holy" is like someone slapping a label on you that says "religious snob." Sadly, these are not the true meanings of the word *holy*.

Being holy is simply about being your true self. God made you to be holy. When we sin, our true self diminishes, and we move away from the person God calls us to be. We become less holy. But we can regain our holiness by seeking forgiveness, making reparation, and once again committing to being faithful to God and his Law. The religious Laws of the Pentateuch, especially in the Books of Exodus and Leviticus, guided the Israelites in this struggle to be God's holy people.

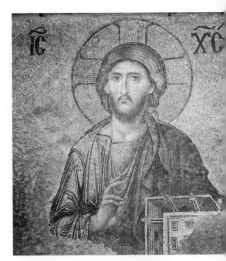

A halo, or crown of light, has been used for centuries in Christian art to indicate a holy person. The earliest figure to be seen with a halo is Christ, starting in the fourth century.

Don't Be Like Everyone Else

All of the Laws that guide the Israelites' lives center on one idea that God conveys through Moses: "Be holy, for I, the LORD your God, am holy" (Leviticus 19:2). For the Israelites, being holy means two things: first, it means living in right relationship with God and with

UNIT 2

---

holy ➤ To be dedicated to God; to reflect some aspect of God's being.

UNIT 2

one another, and second, it means being set apart or distinct. God tells the Israelites: "Do not conform, therefore, to the customs of the nations whom I am driving out of your way. . . . . I, the LORD, am your God, who have set you apart from other peoples" (20:23–24). This call to holiness—being good and different— influences the Laws that guide every aspect of the Israelites' lives from their religious rituals to the food they eat. These Laws can be found in the Pentateuch, the Bible's first five books, also called the **Torah**.

The Hebrew word *Torah* literally translates as "law" or "teaching," and it has several meanings. Depending on its context, *Torah* can refer to

- all of Jewish Scripture
- the first five books of the Old Testament
- the 613 Laws found mainly in the Books of Exodus, Leviticus, Numbers, and Deuteronomy

© Aleksandar Todorovic / Shutterstock.com

This modern Torah scroll is used in Jewish religious services. What do you notice in the photo that indicates the respect the people have for this sacred word?

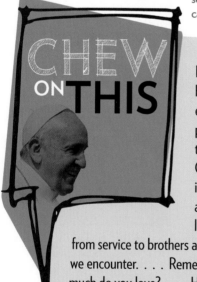

CHEW ON THIS

In the Old Testament, the requirement to be holy, in the image of God who is holy, included the duty to care for the most vulnerable people, such as the stranger, the orphan and the widow (cf. Ex 22:20–26). Jesus brings this Covenant law to fulfillment; He who unites in himself, in his flesh, divinity and humanity, a single mystery of love. . . . We can no longer separate a religious life, a pious life, from service to brothers and sisters, to the real brothers and sisters that we encounter. . . . Remember this: love is the measure of faith. How much do you love? . . . How is your faith? My faith is as I love. And faith is the soul of love. (Pope Francis, *Angelus*, October 26, 2014)

Torah ➤ A Hebrew word meaning "law," referring to the first five books of the Old Testament. It can also refer to the Law of Moses.

I DIDN'T KNOW THAT!

The Book of Leviticus has a number of laws that perhaps might seem a little pointless to our modern understanding. Here are a few: "Do not put on a garment woven with two different kinds of thread" (19:19). So I guess God is not cool with our polyblend T-shirts? "You may eat the following: whatever in the seas or in river waters that has both fins and scales you may eat" (11:9). No shrimp? "Do not clip your hair at the temples, nor spoil the edges of your beard" (19:27). Why does God care about hairstyles? Scholars do have explanations for some of the more peculiar rules in Leviticus, but not all of them. Some laws may have been just reminders to incorporate obedience to God in all parts of their lives, including haircuts!

Most of these Laws are found in the Book of Leviticus. This book gets its name from one of Jacob's sons, Levi, who is the patriarch of one of the Twelve Tribes of Israel. From the tribe of Levi comes the Israelite priests, called Levites, who lead the people's religious observances. Leviticus is sometimes referred to as the Torah (Law) of the Priests.

Give It Up to God

The first seven chapters of Leviticus cover instructions for the Israelites' various ritual sacrifices. These sacrifices include both burnt offerings of animals (holocausts) and grain. The occasions for these sacrifices include daily offerings and purifications for sins. The Laws include directions for communal and individual offerings. Special considerations are made based on a person's status within the community, and for those who cannot financially afford to make the normally expected sacrifice (see Leviticus 5:7).

The notion of sacrificing animals as an offering to God might seem strange, even barbaric to us. But during that time period and within that culture, sacrificing animals to the gods was not unusual. Some of the Israelites' neighbors even sacrifice their own children to their gods! The Israelites do not do this because, as God said, they are different and set apart from other tribes.

So then, why do the ancient Israelites deem it necessary to sacrifice animals? There are several reasons:

- The animal acts as a substitute for a human (see Genesis 22:9–13).
- The smoke from the holocaust connects them to God, who lives in the heavens above.
- Their livelihood depends on animals. Animals are very valuable, so offering the best of their animals to God shows their great devotion to him.
- While understanding that God transcends all human characteristics, the Israelites see this as a way to symbolically share their food with God, who is sometimes portrayed as enjoying the smell of the sacrifices (see Genesis 8:20–21).

Please Pass the Fried Grasshoppers!

The call to holiness also influences the Israelites' choice of food and how that food is prepared (see Leviticus 11:1–7). The **kosher laws** are a set of dietary restrictions that govern the foods they can eat (clean), and those they cannot eat (unclean). Many Jewish people still follow these laws.

For a water creature to be considered clean, it must have both fins and scales. For a land animal to be considered clean, it must have hooves, be cloven (split) footed, and chew its cud. Some animals have a digestive system in which they regurgitate part of the food that is swallowed, called the "cud," which is then chewed again. When chewing their cud, you can see their lower jaws making a side-to-side grinding motion.

Pigs are not considered kosher because they don't have hooves and do not chew their cud.

As an example of laws governing food preparation, consider this law from the Book of Exodus: "You shall not boil a young goat in its mother's milk" (34:26). The Israelites interpret this to mean not to mix meat and dairy products together when cooking. Jewish people who follow the kosher laws today will not cook meat and dairy together. They will even designate certain pots, pans, and utensils for cooking meat, and others for cooking dairy.

© MediaProduction / iStock.com

---

kosher laws ➤ A set of dietary and food preparation restrictions that govern the foods Jewish people can and cannot eat.

Clean ≠ Not Dirty

Have you ever heard someone say, "Cleanliness is next to godliness"? It's not a direct quote from Scripture, but it is certainly implied in the Laws addressing cleanliness (see Leviticus, chapters 11–15). In these Laws, "unclean" has nothing to do with being physically dirty. In the ancient, Israelite culture, "clean" is a person's ordinary, uncorrupted state, as God created us to be. However, after Adam and Eve's Original Sin, it is no longer possible for human beings to perfectly maintain that state. So the Laws in Leviticus help identify the ways that a person becomes corrupted, or unclean (often with no choice on their part). Eating unclean food isn't the only way. Here are some others, according to the Laws in Leviticus:

- touching blood and some other bodily fluids
- contracting skin diseases, including leprosy
- touching a dead body

You can see each of these things has to do with death and decay, which are not part of God's original plan for human beings.

By today's standards, "unclean" people in ancient Israel are not treated very well: they can't be touched, they cannot participate in worship, and they have to physically distance themselves from the community. Lepers in particular have to cry out, "Unclean, unclean!" (Leviticus 13:45) so that others can avoid them. However, keep in mind that these Laws are intended to protect other people from becoming unclean, and more important, they provide a way for people who have become unclean to be purified and return to the community.

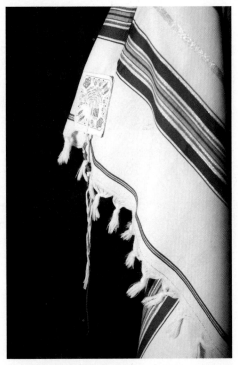

A tallit (prayer shawl). Through some symbolic Hebrew math, the fringes have a numerical value of 613, corresponding to the number of laws in the Book of Leviticus.

UNIT 2

Despite the positive intent of these Laws, being unclean could be physically painful, emotionally painful, or both. It causes distress not only for the afflicted person but for their family and friends as well. Perhaps this is why Jesus spends much of his time with these outcasts.

Holy Days

The Lord set apart one day to be a holy day (see Leviticus 23:3). The seventh day of the week (Saturday) is called the Sabbath. It is a day of rest; no work is to be done. A number of other days during the year are also designated as holy (see Leviticus, chapters 16 and 23). This chart shows each of those holy days:

Name	Hebrew name	What is celebrated	Found in the Bible
Day of Atonement	Yom Kippur	Reparation for wrongdoing or sin and reconciliation with God	Leviticus 16:1–34
Passover	Pesach	The Israelites' escape from slavery in Egypt	Leviticus 23:4–14
Pentecost	Shavuot	The harvest of the firstfruits of the Lord. During Jesus' time, this feast commemorated the giving of the Torah to Moses.	Leviticus 23:15–22
New Year's Day	Rosh Hashanah	The new year	Leviticus 23:23–25
Feast of Booths	Sukkot	Historically, it recalls the Israelites' years of wandering in the desert living in tents (booths); agriculturally, Sukkot is a harvest festival.	Leviticus 23:33–44

The Poor and the Outcast

The Torah also has laws that specifically deal with fairness and how to treat the *anawim*, the Hebrew word for the poor and marginalized. The *anawim* are the people who are most vulnerable in a society. In biblical times, this is usually orphans, widows, foreigners, and poor people. Here are some of those laws:

- Leave the edges of the crops unharvested so that passing foreigners and the poor can easily get food (see Leviticus 19:9–10).
- Be compassionate to those who cannot afford to pay back their loans (see Exodus 22:24–26).
- Take care of foreigners in your land (see Exodus 22:20).
- On the Sabbath year (every seventh year), forgive debts (see Deuteronomy 15:1–2).

For the Jewish People, all of the laws focus on one thing: being holy, just as God is holy. Being holy means that they need to be in loving and just relationships with God and with all people, both Israelites and non-Israelites. By following God's Law, they will also be different, or set apart, from the people of other cultures and nations. Their practices and celebrations regularly remind them that obedience to God's Law is a fundamental part of their lives. ✳

OVERVIEW of Leviticus

- **Time period:** After the Exodus, during the Israelites, encampment at Mount Sinai.
- **Time written:** Most likely after the Babylonian Exile.
- **Theme:** To teach the way of holiness through observance of the Law and religious rituals.

HMMMMM. . . The laws on cleanliness may seem harsh and restrictive to us. Why are these laws so important to the Israelites?

anawim ➤ A Hebrew word for the poor and marginalized.

UNIT 2

Article 26
Numbers and Deuteronomy: The Promised Land

Ari has played soccer since she was in fifth grade. She went to every practice, worked hard at her soccer skills, and in eighth grade, she won the trophy for most valuable player. Her soccer coach recommended that she try out for the high school varsity team, and her mom encouraged her to do so.

Soccer tryouts took place right after school ended for the summer. The weeks leading up to them were tortuous for Ari; it was all she could think about. The more she thought about trying out, the worse her anxiety became. She started complaining to her parents: "I can't do it. I'm not good enough. The older girls will crush me! I want to go back to the fun of playing with my old soccer team!"

Can you think of a time when you have been willing to push aside your doubts and fears to try and accomplish your dream or goal?

Sometimes when we are called to tackle a new challenge, we can experience doubt and confusion. It is easier to stay in a place we are comfortable than to take the risk of failing at something new. This was certainly true for the Israelites who followed Moses out of Egypt.

Run Away

The Book of Numbers has several accounts of the obstacles the Israelites encountered on their way to the Promised Land. Many of these obstacles were of their own making. After a little over a year in the wilderness camped near Mount Sinai, Moses and the Israelites break camp and head out for the Promised Land: Canaan (see Numbers 10:11–36). Then the complaining begins:

- Even though God has been feeding them with manna, they complain: "If only we had meat for food! We remember the fish we used to eat without cost in Egypt, and the cucumbers, the melons, the leeks, the onions, and the garlic. But now we are famished; we have nothing to look forward to but this manna" (11:4–6).
- Aaron and Miriam start some jealous complaining against their brother, Moses. The Lord doesn't put up with this (see chapter 12).

This culminates in one event that illustrates a serious lack of faith in God's power. Because Canaan is not far from them, Moses sends in twelve men to scout out the situation. After forty days, they return with descriptions of a very large and powerful people. They report, "We cannot attack these people; they are too strong for us" (Numbers 13:31), so the people complained and threatened to revolt against Moses and return to Egypt. Because of this lack of faith in God's promises to them, God sentences them to wander in the desert until all the adults die off! The result of this punishment was that none of the adults who left Egypt would actually see the Promised Land except for the two men who never lost faith in God: Caleb and Joshua (see 13:1–14:38).

But as for you, your bodies shall fall here in the wilderness, while your children will wander for forty years, suffering for your infidelity, till the last of you lies dead in the wilderness. Corresponding to the number of days you spent reconnoitering the land—forty days—you shall bear your punishment one year for each day: forty years. Thus you will realize what it means to oppose me. I, the Lord, have spoken; and I will surely do this to the entire wicked community that conspired against me: here in the wilderness they shall come to their end and there they will die (14:32-35).

Pilgrims hiking down from the top of Mount Sinai in Egypt, a site that is sacred to Muslims, Christians, and Jews.

UNIT 2

Remember that in the Bible, the number four or forty is also a symbolic number. The author of Numbers is indicating that this punishment from God was perfect given the seriousness of the Israelites' lack of faith. The result of this punishment was that none of the adults who left Egypt would actually see the Promised Land except for the two men who never lost faith in God: Caleb and Joshua. (see 13:1–14:38).

Confronting a seemingly sure defeat can be a difficult and trying experience. Whether it is as simple as facing a dominant team in a sporting event, or as complicated as a drug addiction, our first response is often to run away. We logically try to convince ourselves that retreat is surely better than defeat. Yet there are times in our lives when we have to face what we fear, and we must remember that when God calls us to move forward, he does not ask us to do it alone. We must trust that there are unseen resources for us. We have no guarantee of smooth sailing, but a land of milk and honey awaits us.

Don't Forget

"Remember, you have a test on Wednesday!" "Don't forget to feed the dog!" "Turn the lights off when you leave!" How often have you heard these or similar reminders from your parents? Maybe they do it so often that you do not need to remember—they will recall it for you! The truth is that everyone

Can you imagine traveling through this land on foot?

sometimes needs a reminder, including the Israelites.

The Book of Deuteronomy is sort of like Moses's final reminders to the Israelites, his last will and testament. Moses knows that he won't be crossing over into the Promised Land with his people, so he reviews with them the Laws they received from God at Mount Sinai (also called Mount Horeb). This is why the Book of Deuteronomy has so many of the same stories and Laws that are in Exodus, Leviticus, and Numbers.

Deuteronomy is a Greek word, meaning "second law." The key theme of Deuteronomy is that Moses calls the Israelites to totally commit themselves to the God who has revealed himself to them. In his restatement of the Law, Moses offers what Jewish people today call the Shema:

I DIDN'T KNOW THAT!

How would you feel about putting a written prayer in a box and then tying that box to your head and arm? Though it might seem quite foreign to us, this holy practice is taken straight from the pages of the Bible. The Shema (see Deuteronomy 6:4–5) is the closest thing the Jewish People have to a **creed**. Deuteronomy instructs its readers to "bind them on your arm as a sign and let them be as a pendant on your forehead" (6:8). Orthodox Jews take this commandment literally by putting copies of the Shema in containers called tefillin. These are then placed on their heads and arms for prayer. In this way, they honor God's most holy Law, with both an inward intention and an outward sign.

UNIT 2

"Hear, O Israel! The Lord is our God, the Lord alone! Therefore, you shall love the Lord, your God, with your whole heart, and with your whole being, and with your whole strength" (Deuteronomy 6:4–5). When asked what is the greatest Law (see Matthew 22:34–40), Jesus offers this same Commandment as his response, but then adds another Law from the Book of Leviticus: "You shall love your neighbor as yourself" (19:18).

So Close, But Just Out of Reach

Being committed to God and his Law is at the heart of our faith, and we certainly need reminders of its importance for living happy and holy lives. Sometimes the Promised Land—a wonderful symbol for those times and places where everything is as God means it to be—feels so distant and we do not feel like we will ever make it there. Other times it feels so close, but just out of reach. We might feel like Moses, who went to the mountaintop and could see the land of Canaan that God promised to the descendants of Abraham but never made it there. Before he died in the wilderness, Moses turned his leadership over to his longtime aide, Joshua (see Deuteronomy 34:1–12).

---

creed ➤ A short summary statement or profession of faith. The Nicene and Apostles' Creeds are the Church's most familiar and important creeds.

Dr. Martin Luther King Jr., a Baptist minister and civil rights leader, sometimes compared the African-American movement for equal rights with the Israelites' struggle for freedom from slavery. Like Moses's confrontation with Pharaoh, Dr. King went to the leaders of this country and demanded equal treatment for African Americans.

Martin Luther King Jr Memorial in West Potomac Park, Washington, DC.

Sadly, Dr. King, like Moses, was not able to see it all the way through to the end. On April 3, 1968, he was in Memphis, Tennessee, where he spoke at a church to support the sanitation workers' strike. He closed this famous speech, known by the popular name "I've Been to the Mountaintop," with the following words:

> Like anybody, I would like to live a long life. Longevity has its place. But I'm not concerned about that now. I just want to do God's will. And He's allowed me to go up to the mountain. And I've looked over. And I've seen the Promised Land. I may not get there with you. But I want you to know tonight, that we, as a people, will get to the promised land. And I'm happy, tonight. I'm not worried about anything. I'm not fearing any man. Mine eyes have seen the glory of the coming of the Lord.

These were the last words he said to a public audience. The next day, he was assassinated.

Why is it that people so faithful to God do not find the happy ending we all so much desire? It seems unfair if we only consider it through a worldly perspective. With the eyes of faith, though, we see the longer view. Our lives are not over when our physical life on Earth is finished. We believe that those who do God's will are rewarded in the next life. Their faith is rooted in a trust in God that is not dependent on their own personal satisfaction. They seek to do only what pleases God, relying on him to take care of everything else. ✳

OVERVIEW of Numbers

- **Title:** Called the Book of Numbers because of the two censuses in it; the Hebrew title means "in the desert."
- **Time period:** Picks up where Exodus ends and covers the remaining thirty-eight years of wandering in the desert.
- **Time written:** Most likely after the Babylonian Exile ended (538 BC).
- **Themes:** Entering the Promised Land, faithfulness and gratefulness to God are needed.

OVERVIEW of Deuteronomy

- **Time period:** Right before the Israelites enter the Promised Land.
- **Time written:** Most likely in the eighth century BC.
- **Themes:** Importance of the Covenant, commitment to God's Law.

HMMMMM. . . The Israelites had Moses to remind them of God's Law. Who do we have to remind us of God's Law today? Give several examples of how this is done.

UNIT 2

1. What name does God reveal to Moses? What does that name literally mean?

2. Describe the events of Passover and what they mean for the Israelites.

3. What is the Sinai Covenant?

4. Explain the connection between the Mosaic Covenant and the Mosaic Law.

5. What significance does the Ark of the Covenant hold for the Israelites?

6. What does it mean to the Israelites to be "holy"?

7. What does being "clean" versus "unclean" mean to the Israelites? Offer two examples in your response.

8. What does Moses tell the Israelites shortly before they enter the Promised Land?

Images © 2019 www.theglorystory.com (top left, middle left), Shutterstock.com (lower left), Trikosko, Marion S. / Library of Congress Prints and Photographs Division (upper right), Public Domain (middle and lower right)

THE CIVIL RIGHTS MOVEMENT:
A Modern-Day Exodus

The civil rights leader and Baptist minister Dr. Martin Luther King Jr. recognized the similarities between the struggle of the Israelites and the Civil Rights Movement.

Some parallels between the Civil Rights Movement and the Exodus.

UNIT 2

OPPRESSION

A LEADER COMES FORTH

LIBERATION

1. How would you describe the connections between the pairs of images?

2. What other leaders have you studied who have spoken out for people's freedom and justice, as Moses did?

CHAPTER 7
Joshua and Judges

DOES GOD GET TIRED OF US MAKING THE SAME MISTAKES OVER AND OVER?

SNAPSHOT

Article 27   Page 161
What Goes Around Comes Around . . . Or Does It?

Article 28   Page 168
Joshua: The New Moses
• Pre-read: Joshua, chapters 1–7, 24

Article 29   Page 172
The Judges: New Authority Figures
• Pre-read: Judges, chapters 1–5, 13–16

Article 30   Page 178
Samuel: Reluctant Kingmaker
• Pre-read: 1 Samuel, chapters 1–4, 8–10

Article 31   Page 184
Ruth: An Unexpected Hero
• Pre-read: Book of Ruth

Article 27

What Goes Around Comes Around . . . Or Does It?

 "What goes around, comes around" is a common saying in American culture, referring to the law of cause and effect. Some people call this karma. The phrase basically means that our actions, whether good or bad, have consequences: if you do not study for a test, you will most likely fail; if you eat poorly and do not exercise, your health will almost certainly suffer; if you lead a life of crime, you will probably end up in jail; if you treat others badly, eventually you will be treated badly in turn.

Some even attribute the pain that one suffers to God's punishment for their poor behavior. Plenty of passages in the Bible might seem to support this viewpoint, but does God actually punish us? And perhaps more troubling, does God actually seek the destruction of people who stand in the way of his divine plan?

Our actions, whether good or bad, have consequences. For example, if you eat well and exercise, you can improve your health.

UNIT 2

Reward and Punishment

In the Old Testament, our ancestors in faith saw God's handiwork in all parts of their lives. When good things happened, they believed it was God's reward for their good behavior, specifically, for obeying the covenant and Divine Law. Health, wealth, and happiness were signs that God was pleased with them: "Fear the LORD and turn away from evil; / This will mean health for your flesh / and vigor for your bones" (Proverbs 3:7–8).

They also saw the opposite to be true. When they went through difficulties or painful experiences, they believed God was unhappy with them. For example, the Book of Leviticus records God telling the Israelites, "If you reject my statutes and loathe my decrees, refusing to obey all my commandments and breaking my covenant, then I, in turn, will do this to you: I will bring terror upon you—with consumption and fever to dim the eyes and sap the life" (26:15–16). Breaking God's Law leads to suffering.

The belief that God rewards and punishes people based on their behavior in this lifetime is called **divine retributive justice**—*divine* meaning "from God," *retributive* meaning "payback or vengeance," and *justice* meaning "fair, rightful, or morally good."

Recall that one of the principles for interpreting the Bible is that we must consider the cultural beliefs of the human authors. Many of the human authors of the Old Testament were influenced by the cultural belief in divine retributive justice. This belief made sense to them for two reasons:

1. At this point in their history, the Israelites did not have a clear belief in life after death. Therefore, any reward or punishment that was coming to people had to happen in this life.
2. The Israelites also had a deeply held belief that God was in charge of everything. Therefore, God had his hand in everything that happened in life. (In contrast, today we give more emphasis to human free will. Therefore, we believe that bad things happen as the consequence of our sinful choices, not because God wanted them to happen.)

When we read the Old Testament, it's important to keep in mind that this belief in divine retributive justice must be balanced by Jesus Christ's teaching on the love and mercy of God. By itself, divine retributive justice is an incomplete understanding of the nature of God.

---

divine retributive justice ➤ The belief that God punishes people for their sins during this lifetime.

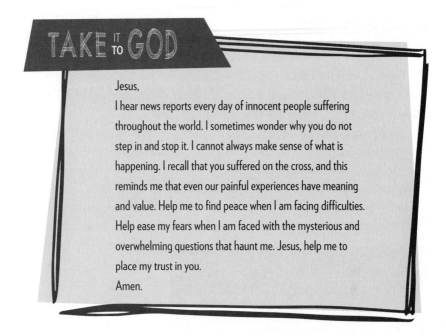

TAKE IT TO GOD

Jesus,

I hear news reports every day of innocent people suffering throughout the world. I sometimes wonder why you do not step in and stop it. I cannot always make sense of what is happening. I recall that you suffered on the cross, and this reminds me that even our painful experiences have meaning and value. Help me to find peace when I am facing difficulties. Help ease my fears when I am faced with the mysterious and overwhelming questions that haunt me. Jesus, help me to place my trust in you.

Amen.

UNIT 2

A Violent God?

"Okay," you might be saying, "I can see why many of the Old Testament authors believed in divine retributive justice, but why does God seem to order the destruction of entire groups of people?" This is a good question and one that we should not ignore.

Like many of their neighboring tribes, the Israelites believed that their God was a warrior who led them into battles. You have already seen an example of this in the Book of Exodus when Yahweh faced off with Pharaoh and used his power to free the Israelites from slavery. It might be difficult for us to imagine our God as a warrior, especially in light of Jesus' teaching to love our enemies (see Luke 6:27), but God was teaching our ancestors in faith that God fights for his Chosen People. God's fighting for his people expresses his love for them. Through the teachings of Jesus Christ and the guidance of the Holy Spirit in the early Church, God will fully reveal that he loves all people.

Let's look more closely at a biblical narrative like this one, in which the prophet Samuel tells King Saul: "Thus says the LORD of hosts: I will punish what Amalek did to the Israelites when he barred their way as they came up from Egypt. Go, now, attack Amalek, and put under the ban everything he has. Do not spare him; kill men and women, children and infants, oxen and sheep, camels and donkeys" (1 Samuel 15:2–3).

This passage is an example of the Israelites' belief in divine retributive justice. This belief touched all areas of their lives, including their interaction with other nations. They believed that if God was not pleased with their behavior, he would allow their enemies to defeat them in battle. If God was happy with their behavior, he would help them defeat their enemies. But even beyond that, if God was extremely happy with them, he would allow them to annihilate their foes. This brings us to what is called "the ban" (1 Samuel 15:3).

The **ban** is the practice of destroying everyone—men and women, old and young, including babies—and everything—livestock, goods, belongings—in a defeated city and then burning it as a sacrificial offering to God. From our twenty-first-century perspective, this is a cruel, pointless, devastating, and even sinful act. Why would God ask for the annihilation of an entire city and its inhabitants as a sign of his happiness and glowing approval of the Israelites? It doesn't make

© 360b / Shutterstock.com

The Babylonian creation myth, the Enuma Elish, is an example of the ban as told by another culture. In the story, the dragon Marduk annihilates several gods, in particular the goddess of chaos, and makes himself the chief god of Babylon.

---

ban ➤ The practice of destroying everyone and everything in a defeated town and burning it as a sacrificial offering to God.

sense to us. But for the Israelites, it made perfect sense. To them, the ban was
the following:

- a sign that God was pleased with them
- a way of placing their trust in God alone
- God's punishment for the wicked
- a sacrificial offering to God

Thankfully, with God's Revelation through Jesus Christ, we have moved
away from the belief that God is a violent warrior. We know that God is a
God of love and endless mercy. We know that the ban is a horrific and terrible
act to carry out. The murder of innocent people is never God's will. In some
sense, we can say that God is a warrior who battles against injustice and false
religious beliefs; however, Jesus refused to use violence in his courageous battle
against these things. His "weapon" was love, expressed through nonviolent
words and actions.

Growing Pains

The Bible recounts that in some cases, God did not punish the sinner alone.
One could do something so evil that God would punish the children of the
sinner too! "For I, the LORD, your God, am a jealous God, inflicting punishment for their ancestors' wickedness on the children of those who hate me,
down to the third and fourth generation" (Exodus 20:5). Passages like this can
be hard to swallow! How can God punish innocent people for things their
parents did?

Recall that the Bible is a collection of books, written by different human
authors who expressed God's message from a particular perspective and understanding. Sometimes it seems that the books are saying conflicting things.
In one book of the Bible, you might read that God punishes the children of
sinners. In another book, written later in Israelite history, you will come across
a passage in which God says: "Only the one who sins shall die. The son shall
not be charged with the guilt of his father, nor shall the father be charged with
the guilt of his son" (Ezekiel 18:20).

On the surface, these appear to be conflicting statements. The Church
gives us this guidance in interpreting such passages: "God communicates
himself to man gradually. He prepares him to welcome by stages the supernat-
ural Revelation that is to culminate in the person and mission of the incarnate
Word, Jesus Christ" (CCC, number 53).

UNIT 2

Consider this: Schools do not teach algebra in first grade. They start with addition and work their way up , learning mathematical principles gradually and in stages. Similarly, God has revealed himself gradually and in stages throughout salvation history.

Jesus made it clear that blindness and other diseases were not punishments from God (*The Miracle of Christ Healing the Blind,* by Antonio Trevisan).

© Renata Sedmakova / Shutterstock.com

Blossoming

Jesus was once asked about divine retributive justice (it was not worded quite like that, but it was the same nonetheless): "As he passed by he saw a man blind from birth. His disciples asked him, 'Rabbi, who sinned, this man or his parents, that he was born blind?' Jesus answered, 'Neither he nor his parents sinned; it is so that the works of God might be made visible through him'" (John 9:1–3). Here we see the next step in the growth of understanding of God's Revelation in Jesus Christ. Jesus answers both of the disciples' questions with an unexpected response: God is not the source of our pain in this world. In this brief statement, he unveils a few important truths:

- Children are not punished for the sins of their parents.
- The suffering we experience in this lifetime is not a result of God's punishment for our sins.
- Our pain can actually be a way in which we reveal and participate in the work of God.

This last point would have been quite startling to many of Jesus' listeners. He was talking to people who, for the most part, believed that their suffering was a result of God's punishment. Jesus told them the complete opposite! God is not the source of our pain in this world. Like Jesus' agony on the cross, our suffering can be **redemptive**; that is, it can participate in God's saving work. It certainly is not easy, but if we allow it, there can be grace-filled moments in which we grow closer to God and one another.

The ancient Israelites believed that God's rewards and punishments came during this lifetime. It is important to understand the limits of their cultural viewpoint so we do not misinterpret God's Word, especially in the Old Testament. God's Revelation in Jesus Christ has given us a deeper understanding of the suffering we experience. The rewards for our faithful service are found in the actions themselves, and they also wait for us in our heavenly home.

UNIT 2

Looking Back and Finding God

Our faith rests on confident belief that God acts in human history. The human authors of the Bible witnessed God's saving work and recorded it in the Historical Books of the Old Testament. Most modern historians attempt to offer an objective analysis of past events based on the available historical information without any reference to God. In the Historical Books of the Bible, we find something different. They reveal the hand of God at work in human history.

This is something we are still called to do. It is important to spend time reflecting on our lives to see the hand of God at work. People and events in our past hold special meaning for us. Through both difficulties and good fortune, we can identify the influence God has had in our lives. That is a good thing! ✳

HMMMMMM...

Explain why it made sense for the ancient Israelites to believe in divine retributive justice. What is the problem with this belief?

---

redemption, redemptive ➤ From the Latin *redemptio*, meaning "a buying back," referring, in the Old Testament, to Yahweh's deliverance of Israel and, in the New Testament, to Christ's deliverance of all Christians from the forces of sin.

Article 28

Joshua: The New Moses

Imagine that you have been watching a miniseries on television. The main character is on the verge of accomplishing a goal set generations ago by his ancestors. He's so close! But then he is wounded. His life is about to end before he completes his task, and he knows it. As he struggles to take his final breaths, he turns the mission over to his second in command. Then the TV screen fades to black. You are left in suspense . . . until the next episode.

This scenario closely describes where we currently stand in the great history of God's plan for our salvation as recorded in the Bible. Before proceeding, let's briefly recall what happened before.

Abraham establishes a covenant with God in which he is promised land and many descendants. His descendants become the Israelites (who later become the Jews). Generations later, Moses helps free the Israelites from slavery and takes them just to the border of the Promised Land. Knowing he is about to die, Moses turns the leadership over to his second in command, Joshua (see Deuteronomy 34:9). Now the Book of Joshua picks up the account.

© Anthony VanArsdale / Saint Mary's Press

Joshua preparing to cross the Jordan River to the Promised Land (Joshua 1:1–3). Illustration, *African American Catholic Youth Bible* (Saint Mary's Press, 2015).

Same Job, New Leader

In the Book of Joshua, parallels are made between Joshua and Moses. God makes it clear to Joshua, early in the book, that he is the new Moses. God says to him, "As I was with Moses, I will be with you" (Joshua 1:5). The similarities between these two are relatively easy to spot. The first and most obvious is that they are both leaders of the Israelites. Both are commissioned by God to lead his people to the land Canaan. Here are two more examples:

- Just as Moses follows God in the form of clouds and fire in the Israelites' escape from Egypt (see Exodus 13:21), Joshua follows God's presence in the Ark of the Covenant into the Promised Land (see Joshua 3:6).
- As Moses guides the Israelites through the parted Red Sea, the waters similarly part for Joshua as he leads the Israelites through the Jordan River to their new home (see Joshua 3:14–17).

Joshua reminds the Israelites that through these miracles "you will know that there is a living God in your midst" (3:10).

UNIT 2

© CSLD / Shutterstock.com

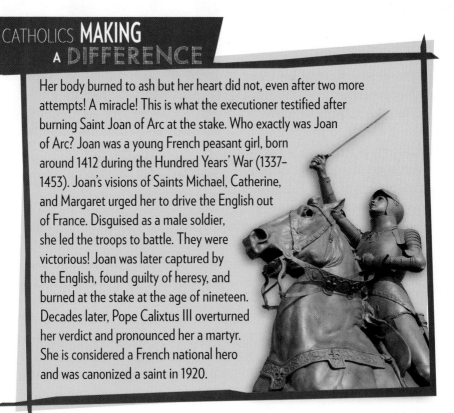

CATHOLICS **MAKING** A **DIFFERENCE**

Her body burned to ash but her heart did not, even after two more attempts! A miracle! This is what the executioner testified after burning Saint Joan of Arc at the stake. Who exactly was Joan of Arc? Joan was a young French peasant girl, born around 1412 during the Hundred Years' War (1337–1453). Joan's visions of Saints Michael, Catherine, and Margaret urged her to drive the English out of France. Disguised as a male soldier, she led the troops to battle. They were victorious! Joan was later captured by the English, found guilty of heresy, and burned at the stake at the age of nineteen. Decades later, Pope Calixtus III overturned her verdict and pronounced her a martyr. She is considered a French national hero and was canonized a saint in 1920.

Though the mission is not over, the Israelites have finally made it into the Promised Land. As soon as they enter, they celebrate two rituals that are fundamental to their faith: the circumcision of the men (an event that seems to have inspired the most interesting name for a town in the Bible) and the celebration of Passover, the event that started their amazing journey (see Joshua 5:1–12). Now begins the task of actually conquering the land.

Tear Down Those Walls

The *haka* is a traditional war dance performed by the Maori people who were indigenous to New Zealand. The *haka's* use of menacing postures, feet-stomping, thunderous screams, and frightening facial expressions was meant to threaten and possibly scare off their enemies. You can find numerous videos on the internet of New Zealand rugby teams performing this intimidating ritual before matches. It is quite a menacing sight to behold, and its effects are almost certainly felt by their opponents.

New Zealand rugby team players, the All Blacks, perform the haka, the Maori traditional war dance, before their match with Italy in Rome.

In the first battle for the conquest of the Promised Land, the inhabitants of Jericho must have felt a similar dread in the approaching attack of the Israelites. The noise, the synchronized shouting, and the choreographed marches were stretched out over seven days. This alone may have defeated Jericho's spirit to fight before the Israelites even pulled out their swords. When the Israelites finally did take the city, they observed the ban ordered by God, with the exception of honoring the promises made to Rahab (see Joshua 6:1–27).

Eventually Joshua and the Israelites conquered all of Canaan, the land the Lord had promised to Abraham. The second half of the Book of Joshua details how the land was divided among the Twelve Tribes and reports the last days of Joshua. After calling all the Tribes of Israel together, Joshua recalls all that God has done for them from the time of Abraham to their conquering the

Promised Land. He then encourages them to rededicate their faith in the Lord as they renew their covenant with God. Joshua dies soon afterward (see Joshua 24:1–33).

The Book of Joshua recounts the Israelites' swift and solid defeat of the city of Jericho and the reclaiming of the Promised Land. It offers its earliest audiences a model of strong, bold, and courageous leadership in times when they need encouragement. In Joshua, we can find someone who strove to follow God's will and guided others to do the same.

For our part, Joshua's call to the Israelites to renew their faith in God is a good reminder for us to do the same: "If it is displeasing to you to serve the LORD, choose today whom you will serve, the gods your ancestors served beyond the River or the gods of the Amorites in whose country you are dwelling. As for me and my household, we will serve the LORD" (Joshua 24:15). ✳

This painting, *The Battle of Jericho*, illustrates a miraculous victory the Israelites attributed to the power of God. How do you experience God's power?

UNIT 2

OVERVIEW of Joshua

- **Time period:** Around 1250–1200 BC.
- **Intended audience:** The Jewish People of the seventh or sixth century BC.
- **Themes:** God rewards the good and punishes the evil; Israel's conquest of the Promised Land (see Joshua, chapters 1–12); the division of the land among the tribes (see chapters 13–19).

HMMMMM. . .

How would you compare Joshua's leadership to Moses's leadership?

Article 29
The Judges: New Authority Figures

It's not unusual to hear high school students complain every so often about the teachers at their school. Teachers can be a pain to deal with sometimes. But imagine what school would be like if they were not there to address discipline issues. You can argue about the effectiveness of some teachers, but there is no denying their necessity when it comes to keeping young people on track.

For the Israelites, the period of time after settling into the Promised Land could be called their adolescent phase. They are still trying to figure out who they are as a people and how to be faithful to their covenant with God. The Twelve Tribes are fighting with other nations, and the people are fighting with one another too. They need a strong hand to guide them, and God provides it for them in the judges.

A stamp printed in Israel c. 1956 honoring the Twelve Tribes of Israel shows the tribe of Judah represented as a lion.

Cycle and Repeat

The Book of Judges opens with a short jump back in time with a slightly different explanation of the Israelites' conquest of the Promised Land. The first chapter of Judges tells how only the tribe of Judah drove all the Canaanites out of their territory. Israel's other tribes allowed Canaanites to live within their borders for various reasons. The author of Joshua sees the Israelites' failure to drive these people out of the land as the reason for their future troubles.

We don't know who wrote the Book of Judges. Scholars call him the Deuteronomist, which is the name given to the person (or group of people) who wrote and organized all of the books from Deuteronomy through Second Kings. One of the themes in these books is called the **deuteronomic cycle.** This cycle is a pattern of sin and repentance that the Israelites repeat time and time again, usually going through these stages:

1. The Israelites sin by worshiping other gods or some other form of disobeying God.
2. The Lord punishes the Israelites, typically by allowing them to be defeated and oppressed by another nation.
3. The Israelites repent and cry out to God for mercy.
4. God sends a leader to deliver them. They triumph over their enemies and find peace and prosperity.
5. The Israelites grow complacent and fall into sinful practices, and then the cycle starts all over again.

UNIT 2

The call of Gideon (Judges 6:11–14). Illustration, *African American Catholic Youth Bible* (Saint Mary's Press, 2015).

deuteronomic cycle ➤ The pattern repeated by the Israelites found in the writings of the Deuteronomist. The pattern was (1) the Israelites forget their covenant commitments and fall into sin; (2) God's punishes them, allowing them to be conquered by their enemies; (3) the people repent and cry for God's mercy; and (4) God hears their cry and sends a leader to deliver them.

Twelve Leadership Lessons from Pope Francis

1. Lead with humility,
2. Smell like your flock.
3. Who am I to judge?
4. Don't change—reinvent.
5. Make inclusivity a top priority.
6. Avoid insularity.
7. Choose pragmatism over ideology.
8. The optics of decision making.
9. Run your organization like a field hospital.
10. Live on the frontier.
11. Overcoming vs. sidestepping adversity.
12. Pay attention to non-customers.

(Homily at Casa Santa Marta, January 19, 2016)

Heroes and Warriors

The leaders God sends in the Book of Judges to deliver the Israelites are called **judges**. These are not the kind of judges we think of today. The judges in the Historical Books of the Bible are elders, heroes, and military leaders. They were sent by God to deliver the Israelites from the oppression they brought on themselves by their infidelity to God. The judges ruled Israel for about two hundred years, from the time of Joshua until the time of Israel's kings. The Book of Judges presents the accounts of twelve of these judges.

The twelve judges described in the Book of Judges were quite diverse, both in character and in what was recorded about them. Some of them barely even get a mention. For example, everything said about the judge Shamgar is

---

judges ➤ The eleven men and one woman who served the Hebrew people as tribal leaders, military commanders, arbiters of disputes, and enliveners of faith.

included in a single verse: "After him there was Shamgar, son of Anath, who slew six hundred Philistines with an oxgoad. He, too, was a savior for Israel" (Judges 3:31). Other judges get a lot of attention, like Gideon and Deborah.

Deborah has special distinction among the judges for several reasons:

- She is the only female judge among the twelve listed in the Book of Judges. She is also a prophetess.
- When the Israelites are under the reign of the Canaanite king, Deborah summons the Israelite military leader Barak to take ten thousand men to fight the Canaanite army. Deborah's fame as an inspirational leader is so great that Barak refuses to go into battle unless she accompanies the Israelite army (see Judges 4:8). There is an amazing written account about her leadership (see 4:1–24).
- Deborah is the only judge with a song recalling her feats (see chapter 5):

> When I, Deborah, arose,
> when I arose, a mother in Israel.
> My heart is with the leaders of Israel,
> with the dedicated ones of the people—bless the LORD;
> Those who ride on white donkeys,
> seated on saddle rugs,
> and those who travel the road,
> Sing of them
> to the sounds of musicians at the wells.
> There they recount the just deeds of the LORD,
> his just deeds bringing freedom to Israel.
> Awake, awake, Deborah!
> Awake, awake, strike up a song! . . .
> Then down went Israel against the mighty,
> the army of the LORD went down for him
> against the warriors.
>
> (Verses 7-13)

Reading the account of Deborah's time as a judge leaves no question about a woman's ability to be lead and rule a nation. She is held up as a model of wisdom, courage, and holiness.

Deborah calls the people to fight against their oppressors.

UNIT 2

Deborah was the fourth judge. After her time as a judge, a disturbing pattern begins to emerge among the judges that follow her. Some of these later judges become less and less admirable in their behavior. For example:

- Gideon, the fifth judge, has an amazing lack of faith in God's call. He puts God to the test several times before finally agreeing to do what God asks (see Judges, chapter 6). Then, after his victories in battle, he erects a golden idol (ephod) that all the people worship (see 8:24–27).
- Jephthah, the eight judge, makes a foolish and unnecessary vow and ends up sacrificing his own daughter (see 11:29–40).

This brings us to Samson, the twelfth and final judge in the Book of Judges. Samson was a strong man and that strength came from an unusual source: his long locks of hair, which had never been cut. Before he was born, an angel told his mother, "No razor shall touch his head, for the boy is to be a nazirite for God from the womb" (13:5). **Nazirites** were people who were consecrated to God through a vow to remain in a holy state. The vow required that they refrain from drinking alcohol; stay away from dead bodies; and keep their hair uncut.

Samson knew how to use his strength well, but he failed in keeping his vows before God. He touched the dead body of a lion in order to get a little honey (see Judges 14:5–9). He slept with a prostitute and a foreign woman

(see 16:1–4). He foolishly let his hair be cut, leading to him losing his strength (see 16:4–22). He was the poster boy of bad choices and failing to keep his commitments to God.

Samson's account is a cautionary tale of what happens when we forget

Samson defeats the Philistines, killing himself in the process (Judges 16:23–31)

---

nazirites ➤ People who were consecrated to God through a vow to remain in a holy state, which required that they refrain from drinking alcohol, stay away from dead bodies, and keep their hair uncut.

UNIT 2

that our true strength is found in our reliance on God. When we think we are in control and leave God out of the picture, sooner or later, things spin out of control. However, Samson also teaches us the power of repentance. In the end, Samson remembers the true source of his strength and humbly calls on God. God answers his call, and Samson defeats the Philistine kings, sacrificing himself in the process (see 16:23–31).

As you read through the Book of Judges, you will see the deuteronomic cycle being repeated after every judge. Rather than being a land filled with God's peace and justice, the Promised Land was becoming a land filled with chaos and violence. In the Book of Judges, this culminates in a horrible story about a woman being raped to death (see 19:22–30), followed by a civil war that ended in the near **genocide** of the tribe of Benjamin (see chapter 20). A future filled with so much promise now seems dismal and hopeless. The people's disobedience to their covenant obligations has brought about injustice, violence, and disunity. The very last sentence of the book summarizes the situation: "In those days there was no king in Israel; everyone did what was right in their own sight" (21:25). ✳

OVERVIEW of The Book of Judges

- **Time period:** Around 1220–1000 BC.
- **Inspired author:** An unknown person from the deuteronomic school, writing sometime during the Israelite monarchy.
- **Themes addressed:** When God's people are unfaithful, they experience injustice, violence, and chaos; when God's people are faithful, God provides leaders to save them.
- **Important people:** Twelve judges including Gideon, Deborah, and Samson.

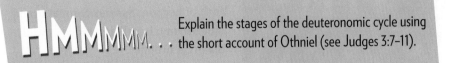

HMMMMMM. . . Explain the stages of the deuteronomic cycle using the short account of Othniel (see Judges 3:7–11).

---

genocide ➤ The systematic and planned extermination of a national, racial, ethnic, or cultural group.

UNIT 2

Article 30
Samuel: Reluctant Kingmaker

Theo and his parents were having a major disagreement. Theo wanted to spend the money he'd saved up from his summer job on a new gaming system, even though the system he already had was only a year old. His parents kept telling him his old gaming system was fine and that he'd find a better use for the money. Finally, Theo's dad gave in and took him to the store to buy the new system. Later, his mom and dad had a conversation. "Why did you give in to Theo?" his mom demanded. "Honey," his dad replied, "sometimes the best thing we can do for our kids is to let them learn from the consequences of making their own decisions."

Experience is a great teacher if we allow ourselves to learn from it. Our failures have as much to teach us as do our successes. This is true for the Israelites as they move from being ruled by judges to being ruled by kings. The person in the middle of it all is Samuel, the last judge and a reluctant kingmaker.

Hannah presenting her son
Samuel to the priest Eli.

© Zvonimir Atletic / Shutterstock.com

Hannah: A Familiar Story

At the beginning of the First Book of Samuel, we meet a woman named Hannah, who has a familiar problem: she is barren, which means she is unable to have children. Hannah joins Sarah, Rebekah, and Rachel, all of whom you've met in the Book of Genesis, in experiencing the pain of not being able to have a child. And just as he answered the prayers of these faithful women, God answers Hannah's prayer. The blessing of God is made visible through Hannah's pregnancy and the birth of her son, Samuel. Samuel would later become Israel's last judge as well as a great prophet.

Hannah also prefigures the Virgin Mary, preparing us to better understand Mary's role as the mother of Jesus Christ. Both of these faithful women gave birth in miraculous circumstances, and both of their children became leaders who carried out God's will. There are striking similarities between the prayer Hannah said after she gave birth to Samuel and the prayer Mary offered shortly before Jesus' birth.

Hannah's Prayer (1 Samuel 2:1–10)	Mary's Prayer (Canticle of Mary) (Luke 1:46–55)
My heart exults in the LORD, my horn is exalted by my God. (Verse 1)	My soul proclaims the greatness of the Lord; my spirit rejoices in God my savior. (Verses 46–47)
There is no Holy One like the LORD. (Verse 2)	The Mighty One has done great things for me, and holy is his name. (Verse 49)
The well-fed hire themselves out for bread, while the hungry no longer have to toil. (Verse 5)	The hungry he has filled with good things; the rich he has sent away empty. (Verse 53)
The bows of the mighty are broken. (Verse 4) He raises the needy from the dust; from the ash heap lifts up the poor. (Verse 8)	He has thrown down the rulers from their thrones but lifted up the lowly. (Verse 52)
He guards the footsteps of his faithful ones, but the wicked shall perish in the darkness. (Verse 9)	His mercy is from age to age to those who fear him. He has shown might with his arm, dispersed the arrogant of mind and heart. (Verses 50–51)

UNIT 2

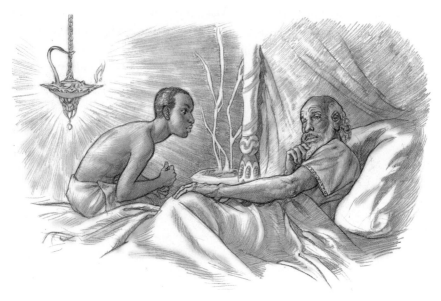

God calls the young Samuel (1 Samuel 3:9). Illustration, *African American Catholic Youth Bible* (Saint Mary's Press, 2015).

Samuel: Telling a Tough Truth

As a young boy, Samuel assisted Eli, a priest, prophet, and one of the last of the judges, with his religious duties in the Temple. One day, while Eli and Samuel were sleeping near the Ark of the Covenant, Samuel heard a voice call for him. He ran to Eli and said, "Here I am" (1 Samuel 3:4). Eli said he did not call him and sent him back to sleep. The voice repeated the call to Samuel, and again, Eli sent him back to sleep. When it happened the third time, Eli told him to respond, "Speak, Lord, for your servant is listening" (3:9). Samuel then heard God explain the fate of Eli and his family because of the wicked things Eli's sons had done. The next morning when Eli asked Samuel what God had said, Samuel held nothing back (see 3:11–18).

Samuel is a unique young man. It is no wonder God chose him to do his work. Even at his young age, Samuel models some important behaviors that can help strengthen our relationship with God:

- **Be persistent in listening to God's voice.** Though confused about whose voice he was hearing, Samuel was persistent and kept listening and responding to the voice he heard.
- **Seek out a faithful and more experienced person to be your spiritual guide.** Having a mentor is extremely valuable in discerning what God might be saying to you.
- **Tell the truth, no matter how hard it is.** Eli was Samuel's mentor, and God's message was a difficult one for Eli to hear. Samuel knew this, yet despite the pain it would cause, he chose to say it anyway because it was the truth.

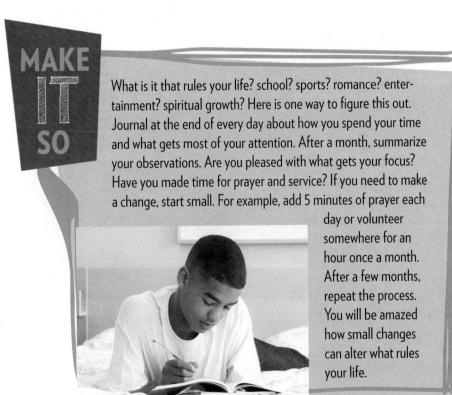

MAKE IT SO

What is it that rules your life? school? sports? romance? entertainment? spiritual growth? Here is one way to figure this out. Journal at the end of every day about how you spend your time and what gets most of your attention. After a month, summarize your observations. Are you pleased with what gets your focus? Have you made time for prayer and service? If you need to make a change, start small. For example, add 5 minutes of prayer each day or volunteer somewhere for an hour once a month. After a few months, repeat the process. You will be amazed how small changes can alter what rules your life.

Wanting a King in the Face of Fear

Fear is a powerful emotion. When people are afraid, they naturally react by seeking security. Often this is the security of a charismatic leader. Throughout history there are many examples of nations who sought powerful leaders to calm their fears and anxieties. Sometimes these charismatic leaders can be positive, such as people like Mahatma Gandhi and Dr. Martin Luther King Jr. And sometimes these leaders can be negative, such as Adolf Hitler. The Israelites have experienced both positive and negative leaders with the judges, and they think they need a change.

The wars with other nations throughout the time of the judges brings a healthy sense of fear to the Israelites. During Eli and Samuel's time, this fear is focused on one nation in particular: the Philistines (see 1 Samuel 4:1–3). The Philistines had captured the Ark of the Covenant, not once, but several times in many battles (see 1 Samuel, chapters 4–5). Remember that for the Israelites, the Ark of the Covenant is a visible sign of the presence of God. This is why losing the Ark to a foreign nation is seen as a sure sign that God is not pleased with the Israelites.

After Eli's death, Samuel becomes the last judge of Israel. He instructs the people to repent and give up their worship of foreign gods and goddesses to serve the Lord alone. The people obey, which leads to victory over the Philistines. For a short time, the Israelites find the peace they have desired (see 1 Samuel 7:2–17).

However, as Samuel enters old age, the Israelites are concerned about who will lead them next. They can see that Samuel's sons are not model citizens and would be poor replacements for their father. So the people want Samuel to "appoint a king over us, like all the nations, to rule us" (1 Samuel 8:5).

© Renata Sedmakova / Shutterstock.com

This statue of the prophet Samuel by Constantin Philipp Sartori, shows Samuel carrying a horn (of oil) and a crown. How are these objects connected to Samuel's life?

This desire to be like all the other nations is a problem for the Israelites. They have forgotten what it means to be holy: "To me, therefore, you shall be holy; for I, the LORD, am holy, and I have set you apart from other peoples to be my own" (Leviticus 20:26). The Israelites are not supposed to be like the other nations. God is their king. Their desire for a human to rule over them is a rejection of God, and Samuel knows this. After consulting God, Samuel follows God's advice to let the people know how displeased he is with their request, warning them of the consequences of being ruled by a king (see 1 Samuel 8:6–18).

Sometimes it seems the only way people learn is through their own mistakes. The pain of the consequences is the only evidence powerful enough to make them understand. This is the case with the Israelites. They ignore Samuel's warnings and continue begging him for a king. At last, God tells Samuel: "Listen to them! Appoint a king to rule over them" (1 Samuel 8:22).

The appointment of Saul as the first king is a monumental change in Israelite history. While there were some good kings, the human authors of First and Second Samuel and First and Second Kings see that the **monarchy** has ultimately failed to provide the security the Israelites hoped for. Remember that they are writing about these events years later with the benefit of knowing the end of the story. They see Israel's desire for a king as the cause for much of the suffering the nation has experienced. Human kings cannot replace God's leadership, especially if the kings and the people forget their covenant commitments to God. ✳

UNIT 2

HMMMMM... Explain why the Israelites' wanted a human king to rule them rather than continuing to be ruled by judges.

---

monarchy ➤ A government or a state headed by a single person, such as a king or queen. As a biblical term, it refers to the period when the Israelites existed as an independent nation.

Article 31

Ruth: An Unexpected Hero

James Earl Jones is a talented actor with one of the most recognizable voices of all time. You most likely know him as the voice of both Mufasa in *The Lion King* and Darth Vader in the Star Wars series. Would it surprise you to know that he kept his powerfully deep voice quiet for many years when he was growing up? Jones had a terrible stutter that rendered him almost silent as a youth. James Earl Jones defied all expectations, did the unexpected, and became one of the most well-respected actors of his generation.

A hero in salvation history also did the unexpected. This hero was not a military leader, was not a man (notable in a male-dominated society!), and most surprisingly was not even an Israelite! Her name was Ruth.

A Surprising Choice

The Book of Ruth recounts the life of its namesake, a Moabite woman who lived during the time of the judges. Ruth is the daughter-in-law of an Israelite woman named Naomi, a widow with two sons living in the land of Moab (see Ruth 1:1–3). Her other daughter-in-law is Orpah. After the husbands of both Ruth and Orpah die, the three women are left with nothing but each other (see 1:4). This can be a dangerous situation for a widow. Without any connection with a man—husband, brother, uncle, son—a woman is vulnerable in a male-dominated society. The smart thing for women in this situation to do is to return to their families for protection.

James Earl Jones had a severe stutter as a child. He defied all odds to go on to have a successful acting career.

Naomi plans to return to her family in Israel and urges her daughters-in-law to remain in Moab and return to their families. Orpah stays, but Ruth will not leave her elderly mother-in-law to fend for herself (see Ruth 1:6–14). Surprisingly, Ruth leaves her homeland and accompanies Naomi back to Bethlehem. In one of the book's most quoted passages, Ruth tells Naomi: "Wherever you go I will go, / wherever you lodge I will lodge. / Your people shall be my people / and your God, my God" (1:16). The rest of Ruth's story is a testament to faithful companionship and selflessness. She eventually marries another relative of Naomi's and becomes a happy wife and mother (see 4:13–17).

UNIT 2

Ruth's declaration to Naomi is a perfect example of faithfulness and love. Illustration, *African American Catholic Youth Bible* (Saint Mary's Press, 2015).

A Different Perspective

This account stands in contrast to the books that precede and follow the Book of Ruth. On one side, the Book of Judges recounts the Israelites' battles with their neighbors, including Ruth's people, the Moabites. On the other side, the First Book of Samuel tells the grand stories of Israel's first kings, including their internal struggles and wars with other nations. In between them is this short, sweet narrative about the kindness of a foreign woman who comes to believe in Yahweh as the one, true God.

UNIT 2

This is a good time to remind ourselves that the Bible is not a single work, but a collection of books that is inspired by the Holy Spirit. Though its human authors wrote from a particular viewpoint, God's viewpoint is much greater. The books of the Old Testament certainly agree that the Israelites were God's special people, but the Book of Ruth attempts to broaden this perspective. Ruth's story reminds the Israelites that God includes the people of other nations in his saving plan.

Ruth is not remembered merely as a kind lady in a sweet story. This Moabite woman has a significant role in salvation history. She is the great-grandmother of David, Israel's greatest king. The Book of Ruth points this out by listing her famous descendants at the end of the text (see 4:17–22). Ruth is also one of only four women recalled in Matthew's genealogy of Jesus (Matthew 1:1–17). In this way, Ruth foreshadows the New Covenant of Jesus Christ, extended to all people, of every race and nation.

Ruth reminds us that kindness and faithfulness can have far-reaching effects. People who are kind and faithful can break down negative stereotypes. In Ruth's case, the effects of her kindness and faithfulness can be traced for generations. The Book of Ruth reminds us that our actions are not judged by how grand and powerful they appear, but rather by the simple goodness and integrity that inspires them. ✳

Ruth wed Boaz and gave birth to Obed. She is the great-grandmother to David, Israel's greatest king.

UNIT 2

How would you like to be named "Not Pitied"? That's what God told the prophet Hosea to name one of his children (Hosea 1:6). In the Bible, people's names often carry symbolic meaning, revealing something about their character. Consider the meaning of the Hebrew words used as names in the Book of Ruth. Can you see their symbolic meaning?

- *Ruth* means "companion."
- *Naomi* means "pleasant."
- *Orpah* means "disloyal."
- *Boaz* means "strength."
- *Bethlehem* means "house of bread."

 of the Book of Ruth

- **Time period:** During the period of the judges, between 1200 and 1000 BC.
- **Inspired author:** Unknown but probably took its final form in the sixth century BC.
- **Themes:** God's saving plan includes non-Israelites; God works through ordinary people.
- **Important people:** Ruth, Naomi, and Boaz.

HMMMMM... What are the most significant and important elements of the Book of Ruth?

1. What is divine retributive justice?

2. What is the ban, and what did it mean to the Israelites? How do we view the ban today?

3. How is history presented differently in the Bible versus how historians present it today?

4. Explain why Joshua is considered the "new Moses."

5. Explain how the deuteronomic cycle is repeated in the Book of Judges.

6. How does Hannah prefigure the Virgin Mary?

7. Why was it a bad idea for the Israelites to request a king?

8. In what ways was Ruth an unusual hero in the Old Testament?

What R U doing?

HW

Wut ya gotta do?

Read 3 chs of the Bk of Joshua.

Isn't that where God tells the Israelites to kill innocent people, like babies and old people?

Uh...well, yeah. It does kind of imply that in some places.

So, you believe that God wants us to kill innocent people?

SMH. Of course not!

Well I guess you just don't believe what the Bible says.

Of course I do! It's just that Catholics don't read the Bible literally.

You don't make any sense.

Listen. Over time, God reveals himself more & more to the people in the Bible. Their understanding of God developed. So our understanding of God developed too.

READING BIBLICAL TEXTS

1. How do these two friends differ in the way they interpret the Bible?

2. What other examples can you think of that show the importance of interpreting the Bible correctly?

CHAPTER 8
The Rise of the Monarchy

WHAT TEMPTS ME TO STRAY FROM GOD'S CALL?

SNAPSHOT

Article 32   Page 191
King Saul: A Disappointing Start
- Pre-read: 1 Samuel, chapters 13–19, 21–22, 26, 31

Article 33   Page 196
David: A New King Emerges
- Pre-read: 2 Samuel 1:1–2:7
- Pre-read: 2 Samuel, chapters 5–7

Article 34   Page 201
King David's Downfall
- Pre-read: 2 Samuel 11:1–12:12
- Pre-read: 2 Samuel, chapter 13
- Pre-read: 2 Samuel 17:1–19:1

Article 35   Page 205
King Solomon: The Last of the Good Old Days
- Pre-read: 1 Kings, chapters 1–3

Article 36   Page 210
The End of One Nation
- Pre-read: 1 Kings, chapters 9–11

Article 32

King Saul: A Disappointing Start

Brandon was a junior in high school and had hopes of going to college on a baseball scholarship. He and his dad were very close. During the baseball season, Brandon's dad never missed a game. When Brandon's parents divorced that year, he was heartbroken. His dad moved out of the house and started dating another woman a few months later. Brandon hardly saw his dad after that. Their relationship grew strained, and by Brandon's senior year, his dad rarely came to his baseball games. When Brandon would visit his father's house on the weekends, he mainly hid out in his room.

UNIT 2

© vm / iStock.com

We've all been disappointed by people we care about, whether family members or close friends. Perhaps someone promised to attend an extremely important occasion with you but then did not show up. Maybe you were going through a difficult time and needed support, but they were too busy to listen.

When the Israelites asked for a king, Samuel—the last of the judges—reminded them that God was their king. But the Israelites were stubborn. They wanted to be like the other nations who had monarchies, so God gave them what they asked for. Samuel helped mediate the process, and Saul was chosen as the first king of Israel, but not without a warning. Samuel said: "Now here is the king you chose. See! The Lord has given you a king. . . . But if you do not listen to the voice of the Lord and if you rebel against the Lord's command, the hand of the Lord will be against you and your king" (1 Samuel 12:13,15).

How do you cope with disappointment? Do you confront it head-on or do you try to avoid it?

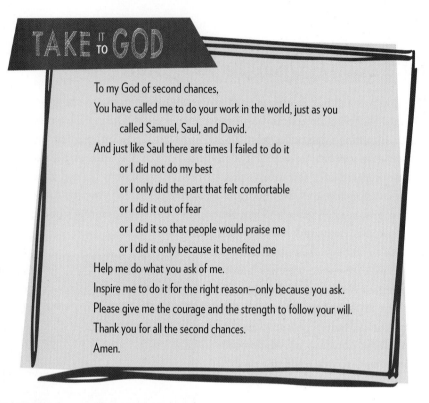

TAKE IT TO GOD

To my God of second chances,

You have called me to do your work in the world, just as you
     called Samuel, Saul, and David.

And just like Saul there are times I failed to do it

     or I did not do my best

     or I only did the part that felt comfortable

     or I did it out of fear

     or I did it so that people would praise me

     or I did it only because it benefited me

Help me do what you ask of me.

Inspire me to do it for the right reason—only because you ask.

Please give me the courage and the strength to follow your will.

Thank you for all the second chances.

Amen.

God's Way versus Our Way

Though Saul had some military successes as the new king, his lack of faith in God's commands would prove him a disappointment and an unfit leader for the Israelites. When Saul failed to complete the ban placed on the Amalekites, Samuel stepped in and told him, "You rejected the word of the LORD and the LORD has rejected you as king of Israel" (1 Samuel 15:26). Then Samuel went to Agag, the king of the Amalekites, and finished the job Saul should have done (see verses 32–34). Samuel never saw Saul again.

In this painting of Saul, what do you think the artist was trying to communicate about this failed king?

God now sends Samuel to Bethlehem in search of a new king. Samuel visits a man named Jesse, who has eight sons. Upon seeing the oldest of Jesse's sons, Samuel believes he has found Israel's next king. God has other ideas and tells Samuel: "Do not judge from his appearance or from his lofty stature. . . . God does not see as a mortal, who sees the appearance. The LORD looks into the heart" (1 Samuel 16:7). Following God's lead, Samuel rejects Jesse's seven oldest sons as candidates. When Samuel sees the youngest son, a mere boy named David who is tending to the sheep, the Lord tells Samuel that David will be the next king.

Choosing a young shepherd boy like David to be the next king does not seem like a smart decision. David is simply too young for anyone to know whether he has the qualities necessary to be king. Samuel, however, seems to be in touch with a similar deeper sense of knowing. We may find this idea to be a little too far-fetched. But remember, Samuel's profound perception comes from his close relationship with God. Through prayer, we too can establish a deeper relationship with God and a more profound way of knowing.

Fighting Goliath

Undoubtedly, the most popular event included in children's books of Bible stories is David's fight with the Philistine, Goliath (see 1 Samuel 17:1–54). You may have even seen cartoons in which talking vegetables humorously act out this narrative. Because of this, it might be tempting to write this off as a story meant for kids. Not so! It has a powerful message for everyone, regardless of age.

David was a boy who accepted a one-on-one battle with an experienced Philistine soldier who was so big that none of the Israelite soldiers would fight him. *Any* person who is relying on common sense would never accept a challenge that would most certainly lead to his own death. However, David's trust is in God, not his own power, and despite these seemingly overwhelming odds, he wins the battle. Like so many stories in the Bible, David's story shows us the surprising power of absolute faith in God.

This sculpture of David, by Gian Lorenzo Bernini, portrays David's strength and determination for doing God's will.

UNIT 2

© wjarek / Shutterstock.com

Many people today face similar, seemingly impossible battles: drug addictions, depression, physical handicaps, living in places ravaged by war, aging, and so on. If we face these challenges relying on only our own power, it is quite possible that we will lose. David went into battle with Goliath with the confidence that God was with him (see 1 Samuel 17:37). Though faith does not necessarily guarantee a "win," it does change the nature of our battles. No longer are we alone; God is with us, and there is never a loss in that. Jesus echoed the confidence of David when he said, "For God all things are possible" (Matthew 19:26).

The Green-Eyed Monster

Have you ever been overcome by feelings of hurt, insecurity, or anger because someone's affections for you have drifted? If so, you have been bitten by what Shakespeare called the green-eyed monster: jealousy. As David's fame and popularity rose among the people, Saul could feel his own revered status slipping away from him. Even Saul's son Jonathan sides with David. Saul is so consumed with jealousy that he persecutes and even tries to kill David (see 1 Samuel, chapters 18–19).

© BibleArtLibrary / iStock.com

The jealous King Saul seeks his younger rival, David, in a cave. When has jealousy negatively affected your judgment?

David now becomes a fugitive, seeking help from other nations. Saul has no problem punishing those who have been helpful to David. The jealous king even puts the entire city of Nob to death for assisting him. David is partly to blame for this. He needed help, and in order to get it, he lied to the priest of Nob (see 1 Samuel, chapters 21–22). Even the heroes in God's plan of salvation are not without fault (and this is just a preview).

David could have reasoned that since he was anointed by Samuel to be the next king, he should kill Saul and take over. He even has two chances to do that, yet he refuses to do so, saying, "But the LORD forbid that I lay a hand on the LORD's anointed!" (1 Samuel 26:11). Again, David shows that he trusts God to take care of the situation.

When Saul finds out that David has spared his life, guilt seizes him and he expresses his sorrow to David. But because of Saul's previous actions, David still doesn't trust him. David stays with Israel's enemies, the Philistines, for over a year. He attacks numerous distant towns and brings back what he's plundered. David gains the trust of the Philistines through lies, telling them that he has attacked Israelite towns (see 1 Samuel 26:17–27:12).

The First Book of Samuel comes to a dramatic ending with the death of Saul and his sons. Severely wounded by the Philistines, Saul decides to take his own life rather than face the abuse from his enemies (see chapter 31). Saul's dishonorable death stands as a reminder to the readers that disobedience to God's Commandments brings on a heavy debt to pay, while surrendering oneself to God's will brings happiness and joy to your life.

OVERVIEW of the Book of First Samuel

- **Time period:** Around 1080–1000 BC.
- **Author:** Unknown, from the Deuteronomic tradition, which gathered accounts probably taken from court documents and hero narratives; First and Second Samuel were originally written as one book.
- **Themes:** Tension between the need for a king and the Israelites' reliance on God.
- **Important people:** Samuel, Saul, and David.

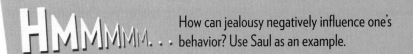

HMMMMMM. . . How can jealousy negatively influence one's behavior? Use Saul as an example.

UNIT 2

UNIT 2

Article 33
David: A New King Emerges

Chris was a good student in junior high, getting all A's and B's without exerting much effort. Math, his best subject, came to him very easily. He'd finish his math homework quickly, and he barely studied for his tests. When he reached high school, he was placed in an advanced math class, and the teacher moved through the material much faster than his teachers in junior high. Chris soon found himself falling behind. Even though his grade in math was plummeting, he did not change how he studied. By the end of the semester, he was failing the class. Only after this humiliating experience did he realize that he needed to make some changes.

Have you ever struggled in academics or extracurricular activities and felt at a loss for how to improve your situation or performance?

Growth requires change, and change can often be painful—which is why we tend to avoid it. Growth does not come easily, and when it does come, it usually makes life a little chaotic. When change is required on a nationwide scale, the chaos affects many people. We find this situation at the beginning of the Second Book of Samuel. After King Saul's death, his followers battle with David for the throne and chaos ensues.

© Lisa F. Young / Shutterstock.com

A Painful Change

The Second Book of Samuel picks up right where First Samuel leaves off. In chapter 1, David mourns the death of Saul and his friend Jonathan, Saul's son. In chapter 2, David prays for guidance, and God sends him to the city of Hebron, where the people anoint him king of Israel. Now David faces the monumental task of bringing order to the pandemonium and disorder that resulted after Saul's death, which included battles against Saul's general, Abner, and Saul's son, Ishbaal; battles against the Philistines; assassination attempts on David; quarreling; and murders (see 2 Samuel, chapters 2–5).

Finally, the chaos subsides, and David has united all of the tribes and become king over a united Israel. He has also captured **Jerusalem** (see 2 Samuel, chapter 5). Jerusalem, from the Hebrew meaning "foundation of peace," is the name of the city that becomes Israel's capital and is the future location of the Temple. This city is also known as the City of David or **Zion**. Zion originally referred to the mountain on which stood the Canaanite fortress that was captured by David. It was later used to designate the Temple and the entire city of Jerusalem.

UNIT 2

CATHOLICS **MAKING** A **DIFFERENCE**

A pope who liked to tell jokes? A pope who had the nickname of "Johnny Walker" because he liked to sneak out of the Vatican late at night to walk the streets of Rome? This was Pope Saint John XXIII.

When Cardinal Angelo Roncalli became Pope John XXIII in 1958, few imagined that he would make major changes. He was an older man who many expected would steer the Catholic Church in the same direction it had been going for centuries. However, Pope John recognized that the Church needed some changes. He stunned the world by calling an ecumenical council—only the second one convened in about four hundred years. The Second Vatican Council (1962–1965) brought a number of changes. Though there were some growing pains, the wisdom and humor of Pope John eased the Church into a renewed life.

Jerusalem ➤ From the Hebrew meaning "foundation of peace," the name of the city in Palestine that was Israel's capital where Solomon built the Temple and where Jesus was crucified.

Zion (also Sion) ➤ This word originally referred to the mountain on which stood the Canaanite fortress that was captured by David. It was later used to designate the Temple built on that location, and then eventually it referred to the whole city of Jerusalem, Israel's capital; the term is also used to refer to the New Jerusalem, the heavenly city of the future.

Jerusalem is a sacred and holy site for Jews, Muslims, and Christians. Later in the Bible, the city takes on a symbolic, spiritual meaning, as the dwelling place for God: "Blessed be the Lord from Zion, / who dwells in Jerusalem! / Hallelujah!" (Psalm 135:21). The Book of Revelation in the New Testament takes this symbolic meaning one step farther. It calls our heavenly home the **New Jerusalem** where God "will wipe every tear from their eyes, and there shall be no more death or mourning, wailing or pain" (Revelation 21:4).

"Then David came dancing before the Lord with abandon" (2 Samuel 6:14). *David Dancing Before the Ark,* by J. James Tissot.

Building the House

Nothing symbolizes David's accomplishments better than the day he brings the Ark of the Covenant to Jerusalem (see 2 Samuel, chapter 6). It is a sign of both his deep faith in God and his success as a warrior and leader. After one botched attempt, David brings the Ark into Jerusalem with sacrifices, dancing, and a big party! His joy is so great that he himself dances with great abandon, something that his wife, Michal, is offended by, thinking that such actions are beneath the king. David replies to her: "I was dancing before the Lord. As the Lord lives, who . . . appointed me ruler over the Lord's people, Israel, not only will I make merry before the Lord, but I will demean myself even more" (verses 21–22).

New Jerusalem ➤ In the Book of Revelation, a symbol of a renewed society in which God dwells; a symbol of the Church, the "holy city," the assembly of the People of God called together from "the ends of the earth"; also, in other settings, a symbol of Heaven.

Since their days in the desert with Moses, the Israelites had been sheltering the Ark in a tent. But David wants something better (see 2 Samuel, chapter 7). He suggests to the prophet Nathan that he should build a house for the Ark. Nathan responds with a message from the Lord, which basically says: "Do not build me a house. Your son will do that. Instead, I will build you a house." The house to which God refers is not a building, but rather the House of David—a **dynasty**, or a line of descendants whose "throne shall be firmly established forever" (verse 16).

The House of David has special meaning to Christians. God's promise to David is fulfilled in the person of Jesus Christ. We find this in the first chapter of Luke's Gospel: "The angel Gabriel was sent from God to a town of Galilee called Nazareth, to a virgin betrothed to a man named Joseph, of the house of David" (verses 26–27). The angel tells Mary that God will give Jesus "the throne of David his father, and he will rule over the house of Jacob forever, and of his kingdom there will be no end" (verses 32–33). Jesus is the eternal king of the House of David whose reign endures forever.

© alefbet / Shutterstock.com

Statue of King David playing the harp near the entrance to his tomb on Mount Zion in Jerusalem, Israel.

---

dynasty ➤ Any sequence of powerful leaders of the same family.

Good Times

David's role as the military leader of Israel is well noted in Second Samuel. The Deuteronomist author viewed the victorious battles against the Philistines, and numerous other foes, as a sign of God's approval of David: "Thus the LORD brought David victory in all his undertakings. David was king over all Israel; he dispensed justice and right to all his people" (2 Samuel 8:14–15). David's good fortune was extended to others and he even showed kindness to Saul's family (see 9:1–13).

This is the high point of Israelite history. What was previously a group of tribes held as slaves in Egypt is now unified as a single nation under a good king. They have conquered most of their enemies and are living peacefully in the land that God promised to Abraham. As long as they are faithful to the covenant and Law, things will go well for David and the Israelites. Unfortunately, these good times do not last long. ✳

OVERVIEW of the Book of Second Samuel

- **Time period:** Around 1000–960 BC.

- **Author:** Same as First Samuel, an author from the Deuteronomic tradition; First and Second Samuel were originally written as one book.

- **Themes addressed:** David's rise as the king and his fall into sin.

- **Important people:** David, Nathan, Bathsheba, and Absalom.

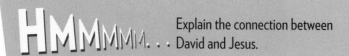

HMMMMMM. . . Explain the connection between David and Jesus.

Article 34
King David's Downfall

We often, we hear or read in the news stories of politicians, athletes, movie stars, and even religious leaders involved in some sort of scandal. In the public eye, these people may be admired and held up as role models—perhaps even as heroes—but behind closed doors, something much less flattering is going on. Only later when their wrongdoing catches up to them do we find out that they are guilty of crimes such as abuse, theft, or even murder. Our images of them are shattered. In the Second Book of Samuel, we find that a similar fate falls on King David.

UNIT 2

Another Man's Wife

By now, you've probably noticed that like many of the men you've met in the Bible, David is not a one-woman man. Though monogamy was the ideal, it was a common practice for kings to have multiple wives. After settling in Jerusalem, "David took more concubines and wives" (2 Samuel 5:13). Sadly, his desire for new female companions, in particular a certain married woman, leads to his downfall.

The account of David's relationship with Bathsheba, the wife of Uriah, a soldier in David's army, reveals two aspects of David's

© Oleg Golovnev / Shutterstock.com

In this painting, *David and Uriah,* what feeling was the famous artist Rembrandt trying to convey?

nature. The first is the depth of his character flaws. Comparing David and Uriah's roles and actions in Second Samuel emphasizes how much David has become corrupted by power and lust. Take a look at this chart:

David's Roles and Actions	Uriah's Roles and Actions
King (2 Samuel 2:1–4)	Soldier (2 Samuel 11:3)
Adulterer (11:1–5)	Husband (11:3)
Murderer (11:6–17)	Murder victim (11:17)
Stayed away from the battle (11:1)	Would not leave the battle (11:8–11)
Actions guided by lust and self-interest (11:14–17)	Actions guided by concern for others (11:8–11)
Far away from the Ark (God) (11:1)	Remained with the Ark (God) when tempted to leave it (11:11)

The prophet Nathan knows David is guilty of this terrible act. He calls David out by telling him a story about a rich man abusing a poor man, symbolizing the whole sad event (see 12:1–4). When David tells Nathan that the rich man deserves death, Nathan cries out dramatically, "You are the man!" (verse 7). Busted. Nathan then speaks for God, foretelling the disturbing consequences of David's sin (see verses 7–12).

The aftermath of David's sin reveals the second aspect of David's character: his ability to admit his sin and repent. The Deuteronomist author is quick to point out that despite David's repentance, his actions will not go unpunished. David marries Bathsheba and their child dies soon after birth. Other consequences are yet to come.

The portrayal of King David in Second Samuel is certainly not idealized. We meet a man who, like the rest of us, is merely a human being with strengths and weaknesses. He can be selfish and arrogant, and he can accept the criticism of others. He is capable of both carrying out the will of God and committing terrible offenses. He is both a sinner and God's chosen one. But most important, he is another reminder that God can accomplish great things even through our flaws and weaknesses.

Suffering the Consequences

The negative consequences of David's sin have only just begun. Nathan prophesies that "the sword shall never depart from your house, because you have despised me and have taken the wife of Uriah the Hittite to be your wife. Thus says the LORD: I will bring evil upon you out of your own house" (2 Samuel 12:10–11). And so it goes. David's own children rape and murder one another. For his part, David ignores these tragedies. He loves

Look closely at this image of the prophet Nathan confronting King David. What is the mood of this artwork, and how did the artist create that mood?

his children, forgives them too easily, and provides little punishment. So they continue their poor behavior (see chapter 13).

The family feud doesn't stop here. Things are about to get worse. David's beloved son Absalom rebels against David and declares himself king (see 2 Samuel 15:1–6). As Absalom's rebellion gathers popularity, David is forced out of Jerusalem. Despite this, David still loves Absalom. Just before his army is about to battle Absalom's rebels, David calls for his men to "be gentle with young Absalom for my sake" (18:5). His men are victorious, but they do not heed David's request, and Absalom is killed. Upon seeing the men return with news of the battle, David does not ask who won. His only concern is the well-being of Absalom. After being told of his death, David weeps and cries: "My son Absalom! My son, my son Absalom! If only I had died instead of you, Absalom, my son, my son!" (19:1).

The same flaw that allows David to overlook his children's faults also allows him to play favorites within the kingdom. This only fuels dissension among the people. By the end of the Second Book of Samuel, David's popularity has diminished and Israel's peace is no more.

© WPWittman.com

MAKE IT SO

Okay, come on, fess up! Everyone sins. Some sins are worse than others, some people sin more often than others, but everyone sins. What makes a saint though, is what someone does after their sin. Unrepentant people try to cover it up or lie about it and then end up digging themselves into a deeper hole. Great saints, like David, admit and take responsibility for their actions. So just do it. Fess up. Admit your sins. Celebrate the Sacrament of Penance and Reconciliation. Make amends. Ask for forgiveness. It is the right thing to do.

The accounts of the first two kings of Israel, Saul and David, remind us that looking to the leadership of a king (or of any human person in a leadership position) can be likened to riding a roller coaster—there will be lots of ups and downs. The temptations that come with power can be a corruptive influence. Because of the flawed humanity of any earthly leader, reliance on earthly powers will never lead us to our heavenly home, the New Jerusalem. This goal can only be attained by following the guidance of our one true king: God. ✳

HMMMMM. . .
How would you compare David and Saul? How would you contrast David and Saul?

Article 35
King Solomon:
The Last of the Good Old Days

Don't you hate it when your parents, grandparents, or some other group of older adults sit around and talk about the "good old days" when they were young? They go on and on about how great life was back then, as if nothing good has happened since they were twenty years old! The truth is that they probably complained when their parents talked about the "good old days" too, and your kids will do the same when you reminisce about your own childhood.

In the First Book of Kings, the Deuteronomist author shines a light on what could be considered Israel's good old days. In the first half of the book, Solomon addresses the troubled situation left by his father's reign, unites the people, and builds a marvelous Temple for the Lord. Israel is once again a single, prosperous, united nation with its own land and its own king. These are the good old days of Israel!

But before all of these good things happen, David is still alive and the family feud is still brewing. The First Book of Kings picks up the story here.

A Greek orthodox icon depicting King Solomon, son of David.

Unfinished Business

The First Book of Kings begins with a short story about the aging King David. His servants could not keep him warm and sought out an unmarried woman to sleep with him to warm him. Though this seems highly sexual (the author takes pains to make it clear that it is not), the point is that David is nearing death. We are at another one of those times of growth and potential chaos.

Trouble begins to stir. Adonijah, one of David's remaining sons, decides that he should be the new king, so he gathers the support of some important people and declares himself king. Word of this news spreads, and another potential candidate comes forward: Bathsheba's son, Solomon. With the encouragement of the prophet Nathan and Bathsheba, David decides to pass his reign on to Solomon (see 1 Kings, chapter 1). In fear for his life, Adonijah acknowledges Solomon as king.

Before David dies, he offers Solomon some final instructions that seem to be hard-earned lessons from his time as the leader of Israel: "Keep the mandate of the Lord, your God, walking in his ways and keeping his statutes, commands, ordinances, and decrees as they are written in the law of Moses, that you may succeed in whatever you do, and wherever you turn" (1 Kings 2:3). After forty years of being the king of Israel, David dies. Solomon then

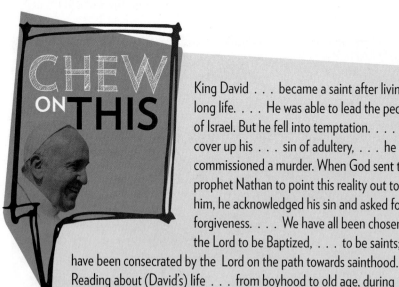

King David . . . became a saint after living a long life. . . . He was able to lead the people of Israel. But he fell into temptation. . . . To cover up his . . . sin of adultery, . . . he commissioned a murder. When God sent the prophet Nathan to point this reality out to him, he acknowledged his sin and asked for forgiveness. . . . We have all been chosen by the Lord to be Baptized, . . . to be saints; we have been consecrated by the Lord on the path towards sainthood. Reading about (David's) life . . . from boyhood to old age, during which he did many good things and others that were not so good, . . . makes me think that during the Christian journey, . . . there is no saint without a past and no sinner without a future. (Pope Francis, radio address at Casa Santa Marta, January 19, 2016)

cleans house, eliminating any potential enemies that might be ready to pounce on him as he establishes his power (see 1 Kings, chapter 2).

A Listening Heart

One of Solomon's most famous characteristics was his wisdom. Several of the wisdom books of the Bible are attributed to him. (We will explore those in chapter 14.) In First Kings, Solomon has a dream in which God tells him that God will give him whatever he requests (see 3:4–15).

> In Gibeon the LORD appeared to Solomon in a dream at night. God said: Whatever you ask I shall give you. Solomon answered: "You have shown great kindness to your servant, David my father, because he walked before you with fidelity, justice, and an upright heart; and you have continued this great kindness toward him today, giving him a son to sit upon his throne. . . .

Solomon's request for wisdom and knowledge (2 Chronicles 1:7–10). Illustration, *African American Catholic Youth Bible* (Saint Mary's Press, 2015).

> I am a mere youth, not knowing at all how to act— I, your servant, among the people you have chosen, a people so vast that it cannot be numbered or counted. Give your servant, therefore, a listening heart to judge your people and to distinguish between good and evil. (3:5–9)

© Anthony VanArsdale / Saint Mary's Press

UNIT 2

Solomon's response is extraordinarily beautiful and humble. He does not ask for riches or great power. His request centers on servanthood and doing what is best for his people. God rewards this answer by giving Solomon this gift and more.

Notice that Solomon asks for the wisdom of a "listening heart." In contrast, we tend to understand the functioning of good judgment as part of the logical workings of our brain. We often make decisions based on lists of pros and cons that point us in the right direction. That is not what Solomon wants. He requests a listening heart—the wisdom that comes from deep within all of us to know goodness and to allow God to act through us.

Solomon demonstrates his wisdom in the famous account of the two arguing prostitutes. After the death of one child, both of the women claim to be the surviving child's mother. The shocking decision Solomon renders in the case certainly inspires the audience's awe and amazement over his wisdom (see 3:16–28).

© Renata Sedmakova / Shutterstock.com

Solomon demonstrates his wisdom in the account of the two arguing prostitutes.

A Sign of God's Approval

Recall the Deuteronomic writer's belief in divine retributive justice: God rewards the good and punishes the evil in this lifetime. Considering this, First Kings provides bold and lengthy statements of Solomon's successes, which are meant to point to God's initial approval of Solomon. The officials who are at his service are named, the lands over which he rules are identified, his riches are listed; he is at peace with the nations on Israel's borders, and his wisdom and knowledge are admired (see 1 Kings, chapters 4–5). The author leaves little doubt that God is pleased with Solomon.

The centerpiece of Solomon's accomplishments is found in the construction of the Temple. Recall that Solomon's father, King David, first suggests a permanent dwelling for the Ark of the Covenant, but God promises that David's offspring will accomplish this task (see 2 Samuel 7:13). The author devotes over three chapters to detailing the preparations for building, the description of the various items and rooms, and the dedication of the Temple. (We will explore the details of the Temple in chapter 13.)

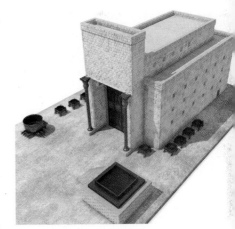

The First Book of Kings was written hundreds of years after the Temple was constructed . . . and perhaps not too long after it was destroyed. This detailed description was intended to inspire and remind its readers that good comes to those who follow God's Commandments. ✱

King Solomon's Temple with large basin, called Brazen Sea, and bronze altar.

 **OVERVIEW** of the Book of First Kings

- **Period covered:** 960–850 BC.

- **Author:** Unknown, from the Deuteronomic tradition.

- **Themes:** The reign of Solomon, building the Temple, the split in the kingdom, the history of Israel's and Judah's kings, and the works of the prophet Elijah.

- **Important people:** Solomon, Elijah, Ahab, and Jezebel.

HMMMMM. . .

How does the First Book of Kings make the point that the Israelites believed that God approved of Solomon?

Article 36

The End of One Nation

Sonja was so excited to start ninth grade. She loved her junior high school but was definitely ready for a change. She had heard all about how great her new school would be. The teachers were laid back and not too hard. When school started that fall, that is exactly what Sonja found. She loved it! It was all so much better than junior high. But as time went by, she discovered that her new teachers were not as wonderful as she had first thought. Their assignments got a little tougher, and their flaws became a little easier to see. Some of them took a long time to return graded tests. Others could be moody. Sonja realized that even the best teachers were not perfect.

Can you think of a time when you've realized that a person or experience isn't everything you hoped they would be?

© stockfour / Shutterstock.com

With every beginning comes the hopeful promises of a new start. This is how the Israelites felt when their new king, Solomon, seceded the throne. Solomon was greatly admired for his wisdom and leadership, but his flaws became apparent after a while. These flaws had consequences. For Solomon, these consequences included a disappointing end to his reign as king, as well as the end of Israel's united kingdom.

A Dark Future Ahead

At the start of the First Book of Kings, Solomon hears a warning from his father, David, to take heed and follow God's Commandments. After the Temple's construction is complete, Solomon receives similar, but far more ominous, advice from God: "If ever you and your descendants turn from following me, fail to keep my commandments and statutes which I set before you, and proceed to serve other gods and bow down to them, I will cut off Israel from the land I gave them. . . . And this house shall become a heap of ruins" (1 Kings 9:6–8).

God's warning seems to point to a dark future for Solomon and all of Israel. And that's exactly what happens because of King Solomon's two major

UNIT 2

sinful behaviors. His first sinful behavior is a failure to treat people justly. In his desire to be like other nations, Solomon embarks on a massive building program to create a world-class capital. He can pay for this only by heavily taxing his people and drafting people into forced labor. This leads to poverty and slavery for many Israelites and non-Israelites. Just compare the description of Solomon's "conscript labor force" in 1 Kings 9:15–23 with Samuel's warning about kings in 1 Samuel 8:10–18. The oppression Samuel had foretold has come true under King Solomon.

Solomon's second sinful behavior allows idolatry, the worship of foreign gods and goddesses, to creep back into the kingdom. King Solomon creates alliances with other nations by marrying numerous foreign wives, violating God's command to be different from the other nations. These wives want to have places to worship the gods and goddesses of their homelands (see 1 Kings 11:1–13). So the author of First Kings tells us, "When Solomon was old his wives had turned his heart to follow other gods" (verse 4). These two sinful behaviors lead to Solomon's downfall and the splitting of the kingdom (more on this in chapter 9).

Just as Solomon probably thought, we would like to think that we are independent thinkers and capable of protecting ourselves from the negative influences around us, but no one is immune. Though we might not be literally bowing down to worship false gods, we have our own modern versions of idolatry—things that shift our intentions away from what is good and right become our gods. The people with whom we choose to surround ourselves have an influence on us. That's why it is so important to have a group of people around you who encourage and applaud your positive choices, versus a crowd who leads you down the wrong path.

In this painting, *The Idolatry of King Solomon*, how is the artist depicting Solomon's worship of foreign gods?

Split in Two

After the death of Solomon around 922 BC, Israel splits into two separate kingdoms: Israel in the north, and Judah in the south. What happens at this point in the Bible is similar to a feature some televisions have: the split screen. Made especially for sports fanatics, the split screen allows people to watch two games on two different channels at the same time.

The narrative in First and Second Kings alternates back and forth between the accounts of the succeeding kings of Israel in the north and Judah in the south. In order to keep his people from going to Jerusalem to worship, Jeroboam, the first king of Israel, creates golden idols for the people to worship (see 1 Kings 12:28–29). The succeeding kings of Israel follow suit and continue to worship false gods. This and the unjust treatment of the poor eventually lead to Israel's conquest by the Assyrians in 721 BC.

The kings of Judah are all descendants of David. They too fall into idolatry and injustice, but the kingdom of Judah will also have some faithful kings that prolong the kingdom's survival. But this isn't enough. The Babylonians will eventually conquer Judah in 587 BC.

Remember, God established a covenant with Abraham. He promised that his descendants would become a nation with a land of its own. God fulfilled his promises, but the Israelites failed to be faithful to the covenant. We will see the consequences of their unfaithfulness in chapter 9. ✳

I DIDN'T KNOW THAT!

The Bible records that King Solomon had seven hundred wives and three hundred concubines! His wives were foreign princesses from different nations. Besides his lustful tendencies, he also breaks God's Law that states not to intermarry with foreign women. God warns that "they would turn your sons from following me to serving other gods" (Deuteronomy 7:4). And this is exactly what happens to Solomon. In the Bible, the number seven is sometimes a symbol for completion or fullness. Multiplying it times one hundred emphasizes its meaning. So, having seven hundred foreign wives tells us how terribly Solomon is engaging in idolatry (see 1 Kings 11:1–3).

The Empire of David and Solomon

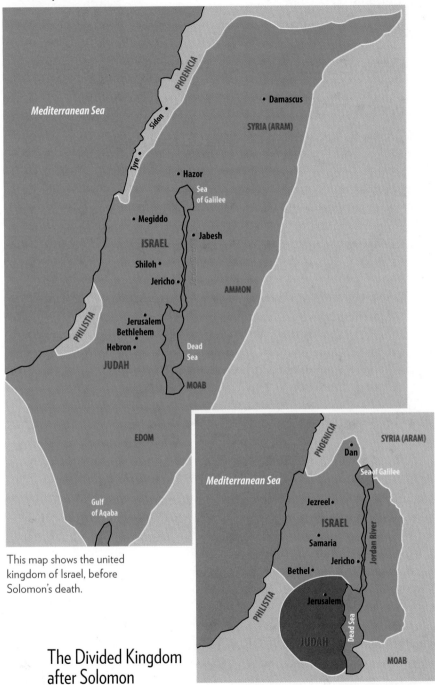

This map shows the united kingdom of Israel, before Solomon's death.

The Divided Kingdom after Solomon

This map shows the split of the kingdom after Solomon's death, with Israel to the north and Judah to the south.

1. How is David, the least likely son of Jesse, chosen to be the next king?

2. Why does Saul become jealous of David?

3. Why is Jerusalem a significant city?

4. What is the high point of the Israelite monarchy?

5. Explain how the Bible presents a balanced portrayal of King David's positive and negative characteristics.

6. What are some of King David's flaws?

7. Offer an example of Solomon's wisdom.

8. What are some signs that God is approving of Solomon's reign?

9. What triggers Solomon's downfall, and what splits the kingdom of Israel?

UNIT 2

KING DAVID: SAINT AND SINNER

These paintings depict the young David anointed as king and an older David watching Bathsheba bathe.

1. Where is David in both of these paintings?

2. How does each artist use light in their respective painting?

3. What do each of these paintings express about David's character?

UNIT 2 HIGHLIGHTS

CHAPTER 5 The Patriarchs: God Reveals Himself to a Chosen Family

Yahweh Establishes a Covenant with Abraham and Sarah and Their Descendants

Abraham and Sarah

- God's relationship with Abraham and Sarah is the foundation of the Jewish, Christian, and Muslim faiths.
- Abraham is the first patriarch.
- God makes a covenant with Abraham, promising him land and many descendants who will be a light for the nations.
- Sarah gives birth to Isaac in her old age.

Isaac and Rebekah

- God continues his covenant with Isaac.
- Rebekah gives birth to twins, Esau and Jacob.
- Jacob uses trickery to steal Esau's birthright and Isaac's blessing.
- Jacob and Esau eventually reconcile.

Joseph

- Joseph receives a special coat from his father.
- Out of jealousy, Joseph's brothers sell him as a slave to Egypt.
- After interpreting Pharaoh's dreams, Joseph becomes an important official.
- Joseph reconciles with his brothers, continuing the covenant.

Jacob and Rachel

- The covenant continues with Jacob.
- Jacob is tricked into marrying two sisters, Leah and Rachel.
- Jacob has ten sons and one daughter with Leah and Rachel and their maidservants.
- Rachel gives birth to Joseph, Jacob's favorite son.

CHAPTER 6 The Pentateuch: God Reveals Himself to His Chosen People

Exodus to Deuteronomy: Liberation, Covenant, and Law

Exodus	Leviticus	Numbers	Deuteronomy
• The book begins with the Israelites enslaved in Egypt. • Moses is called by God (Yahweh) to free the Israelites. • God sends ten plagues to convince Pharaoh to free the Israelites. • The Israelites share the Passover meal, escape Egypt, and cross the Red Sea to freedom. • The Israelites receive the Ten Commandments and enter into a covenant with God. • The Ark of the Covenant houses the Ten Commandments.	• Most of the religious laws are found in this book. • The book teaches that the way of holiness is through observance of the Law and religious rituals. • Being holy means being in right relationship and being good and different. • These laws guide the Israelites in their unique role as God's Chosen People.	• This book picks up where the Exodus ends and covers the years before the Israelites entered the Holy Land. • This book name refers to the two censuses. • This book gives several accounts of the obstacles the Israelites encountered on their way to the Promised Land. • Because of their lack of faith, the Israelites must wander in the desert for forty years.	• *Deuteronomy* (Greek) means "second law." • The book describes events just before the Israelites enter the Promised Land. • Moses reviews the Israelites' history and the Laws they received from God. • Moses reminds the Israelites to commit themselves completely to God. • Moses offers the Shema, the great summary of the Law.

CHAPTER 7 Joshua and Judges

Before he dies, Moses passes on his leadership to Joshua. Joshua's first task is to regain the Promised Land, which is now occupied by the Canaanites.

The Israelites' belief in divine retributive justice fuels their confidence, as they know that their warrior, God, is with them.

Joshua and the Israelites enact the ban, conquer the Canaanites, and take back the Promised Land.

The Promised Land is divided among the Twelve Tribes, who fight with other nations and among themselves.

Joshua dies. Twelve judges, charismatic leaders such as Deborah and Samson, lead the Israelites for the next two hundred years.

The Israelites don't want a judge; they want a king to rule them so they can be like other nations.

Samuel, the last judge and great prophet, reminds the Israelites that God is their king. He reluctantly anoints Saul as the first king of Israel.

CHAPTER 8 The Rise of the Monarchy

3

2

1

Saul

- Has some military successes
- Lacks faith in God and doesn't follow God's commands
- Is driven by jealousy of the younger, more popular David
- Is plagued by mental instability
- Takes his own life on the battlefield after being severely wounded

David

- Anointed by Samuel when he was still a young shepherd boy
- Has deep faith and complete trust in God
- Defeats the giant Philistine, Goliath, in a one-on-one battle
- Unifies the separate Israelite tribes
- Becomes king of a united Israel with Jerusalem as its capital
- Brings the Ark of the Covenant to Jerusalem
- Is capable of both carrying out God's will and committing terrible offenses

Solomon

- Son of David and Bathsheba
- Asks God for the gift of wisdom
- Has several Wisdom books, such as Proverbs and Ecclesiastes, attributed to himself
- Builds the Temple
- Later begins treating people unjustly and starts worshipping other gods
- After his death, the nation of Israel splits into two kingdoms.

UNIT 2
BRING IT HOME

HOW DO I KEEP
MY FOCUS ON GOD?

FOCUS QUESTIONS

CHAPTER 5   How do I find God when my life can be such a mess?

CHAPTER 6   How does God free me from the things that keep me down?

CHAPTER 7   Does God get tired of us making the same mistakes over and over?

CHAPTER 8   What tempts me to stray from God's call?

CAROLINA
Providence Catholic High School

I learned different ways to not only focus on God but also to find God. God accomplishes things through our weaknesses and strengths, but we must have faith in him. We can find God in others and in ourselves because God loved us into being. Throughout the Bible, God uses people with imperfections to show us that we don't have to be perfect to participate in God's plan.

REFLECT

Take some time to read and reflect on the unit and chapter focus questions listed on the facing page.

- What question or section did you identify most closely with?

- What did you find within the unit that was comforting or challenging?

UNIT 3
God Revealed
through Kings and Prophets

WHY DO
THE KINGS
AND
PROPHETS
MATTER?

LOOKING AHEAD

CHAPTER 9   Page 224

The Kings and Prophets
of the Northern Kingdom

CHAPTER 10   Page 258

The Kings and Prophets
of the Southern Kingdom

CHAPTER 11   Page 288

The Messianic Prophecies

UNIT 3

I've heard about the kings and prophets in my religion classes and at Mass, but they are not an integral part of my life. I think the kings and prophets are very important though. They teach many lessons about the way God wants us to live. They show how power can change a person for better or worse.

CASEY
Mater Dei High School

CHAPTER 9
The Kings and Prophets of the Northern Kingdom

HOW DID THE KINGS AND PROPHETS GET ALONG?

SNAPSHOT

Article 37 Page 225
Divided We Fall: The Kingdom Splits
- Pre-read: 1 Kings, chapters 11–12, 15–16

Article 38 Page 230
Prophets: God's Messengers
- Pre-read: Jeremiah 1:1–19

Article 39 Page 238
Elijah and Elisha: Hard-Core Prophets
- Pre-read: 1 Kings, chapters 17–22
- Pre-read: 2 Kings, chapters 1–5

Article 40 Page 245
Sex and Money: Hosea and Amos
- Pre-read: Hosea, chapters 1–3, 6
- Pre-read: Amos 1:1–2
- Pre-read: Amos, chapter 5

Article 41 Page 251
Jonah: Laughter Is the Best Medicine
- Pre-read: Book of Jonah

Article 37

Divided We Fall: The Kingdom Splits

There's a well-known adage that people sometimes use to describe ineffective behavior: "The definition of *insanity* is doing the same thing over and over and expecting a different result." Although this is not the actual definition of *insanity*, it still makes a good point: We sometimes repeat the same mistakes over and over again, even though the negative consequences of our actions are consistently the same.

This is the nature of sin. The more we do it, the less we consider its harmful effects. After a while, the sin becomes the "new norm," and then change requires a lot of effort. Sometimes it may take an earth-shattering moment to wake us up and realize the insanity we are living. The Israelites experience this throughout the time they are ruled by kings. They keep returning to their worship of false gods and unjust treatment of others, until it becomes their new norm. Unfortunately, even the warnings God sends through the prophets are not enough to wake them up to their wrongdoing, and in the end, they pay for it with dire consequences.

UNIT 3

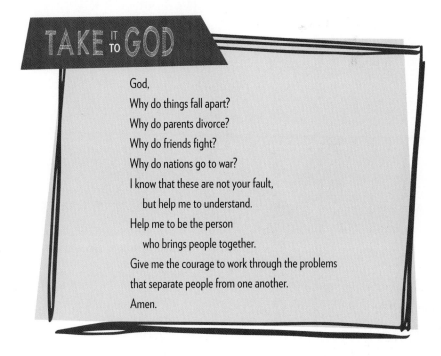

TAKE IT TO GOD

God,
Why do things fall apart?
Why do parents divorce?
Why do friends fight?
Why do nations go to war?
I know that these are not your fault,
      but help me to understand.
Help me to be the person
      who brings people together.
Give me the courage to work through the problems
that separate people from one another.
Amen.

Painful Split

Solomon's reign as the king of Israel does not come to a gentle close. Recall that he has numerous wives from other nations who influence him to introduce the worship of false gods, and he imposes forced labor and heavy taxes on the people. The author of the First Book of Kings reminds the audience that Solomon's descendants will experience terrible consequences due to his actions:

> So the LORD said to Solomon: . . . I will surely tear the kingdom away from you and give it to your servant. But I will not do this during your lifetime, for the sake of David your father; I will tear it away from your son's hand. Nor will I tear away the whole kingdom. I will give your son one tribe for the sake of David my servant and for the sake of Jerusalem, which I have chosen. (1 Kings 11:11–13)

Solomon's worship of false gods, imposed labor, and heavy taxes on the people led to his downfall as king.

UNIT 3

So, after forty years as the king of Israel, Solomon dies, leaving a dark cloud over Israel. His son Rehoboam succeeds him as king (see 11:26–43).

Inspired by a prophet's message from the Lord, Jeroboam, a former servant in King Solomon's court, confronts Rehoboam. Speaking on behalf of all the Israelites living north of Jerusalem, Jeroboam promises their support, but only if Rehoboam ends the oppression started by his father. Before responding, Rehoboam seeks advice from two groups: the elders and the youth. The elders suggest that "if today you become the servant of this people and serve them, and give them a favorable answer, they will be your servants forever" (1 Kings 12:7). On the other hand, the young men have more of a "get tough" approach in mind, and recommend he tell them, "My father beat you with whips, but I will beat you with scorpions" (verse 14).

The difference between the two groups that Rehoboam consults comes down to one thing: experience.

UNIT 3

The Elders	The Youth
• have been around long enough to see the more long-term consequences • know that harsh treatment leads to unhappy people, and possibly even rebellion • see the sins of Solomon and the punishment that follows • know that kindness and compassion have the power to unite and strengthen a group of people	• do not have enough experience to foresee how continued oppression would affect the future • fail to acknowledge the inherent dignity of every Israelite and that their poor treatment of them is sinful • are easily impressed by tough talk and macho behavior, which clouds their judgment

Rehoboam's decision to go with the youthful response to the Israelites' complaints only affirms what Jeroboam has heard from the prophet: that Israel will split into two separate kingdoms and that God will give Jeroboam kingship over the larger of the two. The ten tribes of the north become Israel, led by Jeroboam. The remaining two tribes in the south stay with Rehoboam and become the kingdom of Judah. Jerusalem continues to be their capital (see 1 Kings 12:1–25).

Without the Temple

The northern kingdom, Israel, has an immediate problem. The focal point of the Israelites' worship is the Temple, which is in Jerusalem, in the southern kingdom. If Jeroboam allows his people to go to Jerusalem, their allegiance to him could be easily turned. His response to this dilemma is to build golden calves for the Israelites to worship (see 1 Kings 12:26–33). Encouraging the Israelites to worship these false gods leads to Jeroboam's downfall.

Jeroboam confronts Rehoboam. Speaking on behalf of the Israelites, Jeroboam promises to support King Rehoboam, but only if he ends the oppression started by his father, Solomon.

Following Jeroboam is a succession of kings in the north who engage in a variety of wicked behaviors and idolatry. Some of the kings are sons who inherit their royal power and sinful traits from their fathers. Some are rebel leaders who gain power by murdering their predecessors. Things go from bad to worse. Israel fights not only against the southern kingdom of Judah but also against themselves in a civil war. They establish a terrible tradition of sinful violence (see 1 Kings, chapters 15–16).

As the Israelites continue to sin and fall further and further into disorder and distress, God sends his holy messengers, the prophets, to guide them back to the covenant. Men like Elijah, Elisha, Amos, and Hosea give voice to God's warnings, but the people do not listen. (For more on these prophets, see articles 39 and 40.)

UNIT 3

The northern kingdom of Israel ultimately falls to the Assyrians in 721 BC. Hoshea, the king of Israel, is forced into paying **tributes** (an arrangement to avoid being attacked) to the king of the Assyrians. But Shalmaneser, the king of Assyria, considers Hoshea guilty of conspiracy and failure to pay the tribute. As a result, he attacks and conquers the northern kingdom. By detailing a list of Israel's sins, the Deuteronomist leaves no doubt for the causes of the northern kingdom's downfall: failure to follow God's Commandments, making golden calves as idols, worshipping false gods, and even offering their children as burnt sacrifices. "Finally, the LORD removed Israel from his presence, just as he had declared through all his servants, the prophets. Thus Israel went into exile from their native soil to Assyria until this very day" (2 Kings 17:23). The Israelites are spread throughout the surrounding lands, never to return as a kingdom again. ✳

UNIT 3

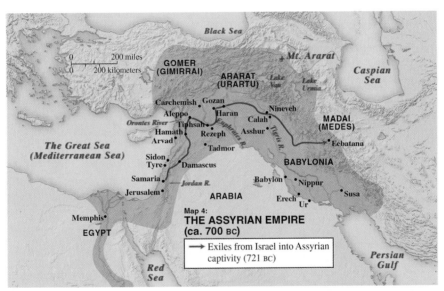

Assyria was one of the most powerful nations on Earth. At its height, it encompassed 540,543 square miles (1.4 million square kilometers) of land.

HMMMMM. . . Why did Israel split into two kingdoms? What decisions could have been made differently to keep the split from occurring?

tribute ▶ A payment by one ruler or state to another, usually as an acknowledgment of submission.

Article 38

Prophets: God's Messengers

On their way to school, Davion and his friend Victor stopped the car at a light where a homeless person held up a sign asking for a job or spare change. Davion pulled out his wallet and gave a dollar bill to the man. Victor asked: "Man, why did you do that? He's only going buy drugs with that money. These people need to get a job." Davion pulled the car over into an empty parking lot, cut the engine off, and turned to speak to Victor.

Years later, Victor recalled this event with a smile on his face. "I remember Davion had this look in his eyes. It was like calm and fiery all at the same time. He just said, 'Victor, you're right. Some of these homeless people are drug addicts. And some of them, for whatever reason, can't work or find a job. But you don't know if *that* person is a drug addict. You don't know if *that* person is able to work or not, so you cannot judge. We just have to care for those in need, not decide who is worthy of our help.' And then he drove off. It was like

Sometimes, our family members and friends are the messengers God sends to remind us of our call to be loving and merciful!

a slap in my face—but a good one! That moment changed the way I looked at people for the rest of my life. It felt like Davion was God's messenger sent directly to me."

God does send us holy messengers who remind us of our call to be loving and merciful. It's true! These people are called **prophets**, and the Bible has numerous records of their works. God does not quit sending prophets at the end of the biblical era. He keeps sending people like Davion to speak his truth.

---

prophet ➤ A person God chooses to speak his message of salvation. In the Bible, primarily a communicator of a divine message of repentance to the Chosen People, not necessarily a person who predicted the future.

A Prophet Is Not . . .

There are many misconceptions as to what a prophet is. But before addressing what a prophet *is*, let's first take a brief look at what a prophet *is not*. When hearing the word *prophet*, many people often think of someone who can foretell the future. They might even have an image of a fortune-teller looking into a crystal ball. This is not what the biblical prophets were. The prophets were just normal human beings, and though they did some-

A prophet is not a fortune-teller who peers into a crystal ball.

times accurately predict the future, it was not due to any superhuman powers. They were simply pointing to the obvious consequences of people's actions, or just sharing the message God had given them.

Ten Characteristics of a Prophet

Prophets are people chosen by God to speak his message of salvation. In the Bible, their primary role was to call the Chosen People to be faithful to the covenant and the Law. Because of their role, prophets embody certain quali-ties, do particular things, and experience certain situations. Following are ten general characteristics of prophets.

1. **Prophets are regular people.** They do not have superhuman powers or strengths. They experience fear, joy, anger, despair, confidence, and all the other human emotions.
2. **Prophets "hear" a call from God.** At some point, each prophet some-how becomes aware of their role as God's messenger. Many times in the Bible, this is recorded as a conversation between God and the prophet, but not all of the prophets actually hear a voice. Other people come to a knowledge of their vocation through different means.
3. **Some resist the call.** Quite often prophets will refuse their role, attempt to talk God out of it, or even try to run away from God. God asks them to do things that are not easy. The weight of a prophet's burden is heavy and undesirable, to say the least.

4. **Prophets often go through some sort of initiation.** There is occasionally some sort of ritual act, gesture, and words involved when prophets takes on their new role. This marks the beginning of their journey as God's messengers.

5. **Prophets speak on behalf of the oppressed.** They cry out for justice on behalf of people who do not have the power to change or improve their circumstances. They speak for those to whom no one listens.

6. **Prophets use shock tactics to get their message across.** The biblical prophets occasionally take extreme measures to wake up God's people. Some of their tactics would still shock people today!

7. **The prophets' messages challenge people, making the prophets unpopular.** They usually call people to repent for their sin, confronting people's failure to follow God's Law and encouraging them to change their lives. People do not like being told that their behavior is sinful, so the prophets are often shunned and mistreated.

8. **Prophets go through periods of discouragement.** This is a natural consequence of being unpopular. Some prophets are plagued by depression and anxiety.

9. **Prophets are dedicated to doing God's work.** Despite the hardships they face, they continue to do their work as God's messengers. Nothing in their lives is more important.

10. **Prophets sometimes die because of their message.** They often oppose powerful religious and governmental leaders, exposing the wrongdoings of those in charge. Consequently, they are considered dangerous threats. This sometimes leads to their execution.

Remember that these are simply general characteristics. If you were to look at one particular prophet's life, you might not find all of these qualities.

WWW.ANSAFRICA.ORG

TISTS FOR A SOUTH AFRICA   STS FOR A OUTH AFRICA

For decades, South African Anglican cleric and theologian Archbishop Desmond Tutu has spoken out strongly and nonviolently against apartheid and other human rights abuses, at the risk of his own life.

© Tinseltown / Shutterstock.com

Prophets in the Bible

Several prophets have books of the Bible named after them. They are sometimes called the writing prophets. There are also a number of nonwriting prophets, such as Samuel and Nathan, whose stories are told in other books.

Moses is one of the most prominent of the prophets in the Old Testament. Take a look at this chart to see how well he fits the characteristics of a prophet.

Characteristic	Moses
They are regular people.	Moses was born to a regular family from the tribe of Levi (see Exodus 2:1–2). Moses is not perfect. He has flaws (see 4:10).
They "hear" a call from God.	"God called out to him from the bush: Moses! Moses! He answered, 'Here I am.' . . . I am the God of your father, he continued, the God of Abraham, the God of Isaac, and the God of Jacob" (Exodus 3:4,6).
They sometimes resist the call.	"Moses, however, said to the LORD, 'If you please, my Lord, I have never been eloquent, neither in the past nor now that you have spoken to your servant; but I am slow of speech and tongue.' . . . 'If you please, my Lord, send someone else!'" (Exodus 4:10,13).
They speak on behalf of the oppressed.	God told Moses, "Now indeed the outcry of the Israelites has reached me, and I have seen how the Egyptians are oppressing them. Now, go! I am sending you to Pharaoh to bring my people, the Israelites, out of Egypt" (Exodus 3:9–10).
They use shock tactics.	The Ten Plagues (see Exodus, chapters 7–12)
Their message challenges people, which makes the prophet unpopular.	"Here in the wilderness the whole Israelite community grumbled against Moses and Aaron. . . . But you have led us into this wilderness to make this whole assembly die of famine!" (Exodus 16:2–3).
They experience periods of discouragement.	Moses complained to God, "I cannot carry all this people by myself, for they are too heavy for me. If this is the way you will deal with me, then please do me the favor of killing me at once, so that I need no longer face my distress" (Numbers 11:14–15).
They are dedicated to doing God's work.	"Since then no prophet has arisen in Israel like Moses, whom the LORD knew face to face, in all the signs and wonders the LORD sent him to perform in the land of Egypt against Pharaoh and all his servants and against all his land, and all the great might and the awesome power that Moses displayed in the sight of all Israel" (Deuteronomy 34:10–12).

UNIT 3

The New Testament has its share of prophets too. John the Baptist was a prophet, crying out against the sins of King Herod and pointing the way toward Christ. Jesus is also considered a prophet, but in a unique way. As the Word Made Flesh, his whole life is Divine Revelation. Jesus' words and actions are the fulfillment of all the prophecies in the Bible.

Jesus drove out of the Temple all who were engaged in buying and selling. "My house shall be a house of prayer, / but you are making it a den of thieves" (Matthew 21:13).

Some of Jesus' words and actions are very similar to those of the prophets of the Old Testament. Consider his actions in the Temple:

> Jesus entered the temple area and drove out all those engaged in selling and buying there. He overturned the tables of the money changers and the seats of those who were selling doves. And he said to them, "It is written:
> 'My house shall be a house of prayer,'
> but you are making it a den of thieves."
>
> (Matthew 21:12–13)

At first glance, one might wrongly misinterpret this as Jesus throwing a temper tantrum. However, Jesus is continuing a long tradition of prophetic works. This is a shock tactic aimed at grabbing the people's attention and shining a light on sin. And like many Old Testament prophets, John the Baptist and Jesus, with their words and actions, anger those in authority, which leads to their deaths.

UNIT 3

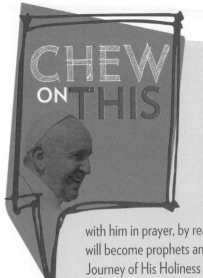

CHEW ON THIS

Young friends, you also have a decisive role to play in confronting the challenges of our times: certainly material challenges, but more so those which concern the vision of the human person. Together with Christ, you young men and women are the vitality of the Church and society. If you let Christ form you, if you are open to dialogue with him in prayer, by reading and meditating upon the Gospel, you will become prophets and witnesses to hope! (Pope Francis, "Apostolic Journey of His Holiness Pope Francis to Sarajevo," June 6, 2015)

UNIT 3

Prophets All Around

Sin thrives in the darkness. People are usually ashamed of their sins and want to hide them, or better yet, deny that they even exist. As long as sin remains in the dark, we can ignore it, which just allows it to grow out of control. Metaphorically speaking, a prophet shines a spotlight on the sin, so that everyone—including the sinner—can see it. Change can come only after the sin is seen and acknowledged. Sin has not left us, so God still sends prophets to guide us toward goodness.

Dorothy Day was an American writer and social activist. She led a rather turbulent life as a young adult. She found herself attracted more and more to the Catholic Church and was baptized at the age of thirty, not long after the birth of her only daughter. She spent the rest of her life shining a light on the plight of the poor. She started the Catholic Worker Movement in 1933, creating houses of hospitality called Catholic Worker Houses. These houses provided shelter as well as food and clothing without charge to those in need. Dorothy herself lived in one and spent the rest of her life in service to homeless and hungry people. She also published a regular newspaper (still in production to this day), marched with farmworkers, protested against injustices of the nuclear arms race and the war in Vietnam, and participated in many other protest activities.

© Milwaukee Journal photo, courtesy of the Department of Special Collections and University Archives, Marquette University Libraries. The photo was taken in Milwaukee in February 1968.

Like the prophets of the Old Testament, Dorothy suffered for her fight for justice. She was arrested multiple times for her protest activities, though it never hindered her desire or her work for justice. She wrote, "The mystery of the poor is this: That they are Jesus, and what you do for them you do for Him." Today there are nearly 250 Catholic Worker Houses of Hospitality worldwide. In 2000, Pope Saint John Paul II declared her to be a servant of God and opened the way for her canonization.

American social activist Dorothy Day (1897–1980), founder of the Catholic Worker Movement, addresses a demonstration in Union Square, New York, where five men burned draft cards to protest against the Vietnam War (c. 1969).

Another person who is considered a modern-day prophet is Saint Óscar Romero. In 1977 Romero became the Archbishop of San Salvador in El Salvador. At that time, many people in El Salvador were suffering from numerous violations of their human rights at the hands of the Salvadoran regime. Romero spoke up for workers' rights and condemned abuses such as government-sponsored terrorism, torture, and political assassinations. Though many of his fellow priests who voiced their opposition were murdered, it did not quiet Romero's voice. He criticized countries like the United States for giving military assistance that only increased the injustices the people suffered. He preached that God wanted his people free from oppression. Because he shined a light on the sins of the leaders in his country, he was seen as an enemy. Romero was murdered by a gunman while celebrating Mass in 1980. He was canonized in 2018.

Prophets are not limited to people in the Bible and famous religious people. At our Baptism, all Christians are anointed to share in Christ's ministry as priest, prophet, and king. You are called to be God's messenger in your own place and time. This does not mean that you should walk around pointing fingers at other people's sins. First and foremost, prophets live the message they preach. We can live that message by doing the following:

- bringing the Good News of Jesus Christ into the daily lives of others
- encouraging people to be faithful to God
- making ourselves aware of the suffering of others and trying to ease their pain
- speaking on behalf of those who are oppressed or in need, and working to "do justice and to love goodness, / and to walk humbly with [our] God" (Micah 6:8).

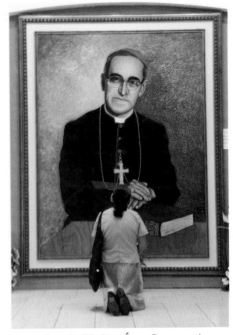

Saint Archbishop Óscar Romero, who spoke up for human rights in El Salvador, is considered a modern-day prophet.

UNIT 3

HMMMMMM. . .

Read Jeremiah 1:1–19 and identify at least four of the characteristics of a prophet from the reading.

Article 39

Elijah and Elisha: Hard-Core Prophets

If you made a movie about these next couple of prophets, it would probably be an action film. You would need a couple of highly paid actors—the ones who can play tough heroes with a soft heart. You would also need a good budget for computer graphics to depict all the amazing miracles these prophets performed.

The First and Second Books of Kings are not just about the kings of Israel and Judah. These books also contain accounts of several prophets, especially Elijah and Elisha. The narratives about Elijah and his successor, Elisha, point backward in time to the prophet Moses, and also point forward in time, giving a hint of what is to come in the New Testament: the fulfillment of all Old Testament prophecy, Jesus Christ.

Turn to God

Elijah appears during the reign of King Ahab, who is the leader of the northern kingdom of Israel in the ninth century BC. Ahab is married to the not-so-nice Jezebel, who has quite an influence on him. Jezebel is not an Israelite, and like many of King Solomon's wives, King Ahab's wife wants to worship her own gods. This is unfortunate for all of Israel because she convinces Ahab to worship her false gods, Baal and Asherah. Worse yet, she persecutes the prophets of Israel and has many of them slaughtered (see 1 Kings 18:1–20).

Elijah chastises King Ahab about his worship of false gods. Then, to prove that Yahweh is the one true God, Elijah challenges all the prophets of Baal and Asherah (850 in total) in a head-to-head battle of the prophets! Not only that, Elijah has the king gather all the Israelites to watch as he mercilessly taunts and

Like Moses, Elijah is considered a major prophet called to serve God during a critical point in Israelite history.

defeats the prophets of Baal and Asherah. This amazing spectacle is not meant for Elijah to show off, but rather is an opportunity for him to proclaim:

> Lord, God of Abraham, Isaac, and Israel, let it be known this day that you are God in Israel and that I am your servant and have done all these things at your command. Answer me, Lord! Answer me, that this people may know that you, Lord, are God and that you have turned their hearts back to you.
>
> (1 Kings 18:36–37)

God did answer, and the hearts of the Israelites turned back toward God (see verses 21–39).

This painting contrasts the court of Queen Jezebel (on the left) with the prophet Elijah in the wilderness (on the right). Who do you think is hearing the voice of God?

UNIT 3

God's Inside Voice

What does God sound like? Many people might suggest that the actor Morgan Freeman comes closest to representing the voice of God. If we were to actually hear God speak to us, what would it sound like? The Book of Job reports that God's voice is loud and thunderous: "Listen to his angry voice / and the rumble that comes forth from his mouth! / . . . Again his voice roars, / his majestic voice thunders; / he does not restrain them when his voice is heard" (37:2,4). This is not the only way the prophets hear the voice of God, however.

After wiping out the prophets of Baal and Asherah, Elijah flees from Jezebel, who threatens to kill him. With God's assistance, he travels for forty days and nights to Mount Horeb (another name for Mount Sinai), where God gave the Law to Moses. As he is hiding in a cave, God tells him to go up the mountain where he will reveal himself to Elijah:

> There he came to a cave, where he took shelter. But the word of the LORD came to him: Why are you here, Elijah? He answered: "I have been most zealous for the LORD, the God of hosts, but the Israelites have forsaken your covenant. They have destroyed your altars and murdered your prophets by the sword. I alone remain, and they seek to take my life." Then the LORD said: Go out and stand on the mountain before the LORD; the LORD will pass by. There was a strong and violent wind rending the mountains and crushing rocks before the LORD—but the LORD was not in the wind; after the wind, an earthquake—but the LORD was not in the earthquake; after the earthquake, fire—but the LORD was not in the fire; after the fire, a light silent sound. (1 Kings 19:9–12)

Elijah does not experience God in thunderous blasts or earthquakes, like Moses and Job did, but rather in "a light silent sound." God has many ways of making himself known to us.

Hearing God's voice requires one thing: a listening heart. Though prayer certainly includes talking to God, too often the other side of the conversation is missing. Taking quiet time to listen to God's voice is admittedly difficult when you live in a culture that is saturated with noise, technology, and various forms of media. How often do we see people pulling out their phones every free moment they get? It can be hard to avoid that temptation, but it's not impossible.

© sedmak / iStock.com

Elijah doesn't hear God's voice in thunderous blasts or earthquakes, but in a "light silent sound" (1 Kings 19:12).

When you wake up in the morning or before you go to bed, close your eyes, lie quietly, ask God to be with you, and listen with the "ear of the heart," as Saint Benedict said, for God's "inside voice." Then you will be better able to hear his voice within yourself, or through the events and people in your life.

Moving Backward in Time: Moses and Joshua Rebooted

Before Elijah turns his job over to Elisha, we get another peek into the future, as well as a reminder of the past. In the first chapter of Second Kings, someone describes Elijah to King Ahaziah as wearing "a hairy garment with a leather belt around his waist" (1:8). Fast-forward to the New Testament, and we find that both Matthew's and Mark's Gospels use this same description for the clothing of John the Baptist (see Matthew 3:4, Mark 1:6). This tells their audiences that John the Baptist is a great prophet like Elijah.

This connection between Elijah and John the Baptist is another example of an Old Testament person foreshadowing a New Testament person. Having read a portion of this text and the Bible, you know that these parallels are common. Let's compare the similarities between Moses and Joshua, and Elijah and Elisha.

UNIT 3

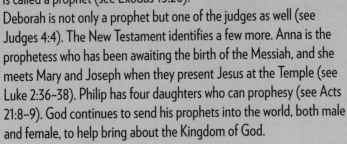

Female prophets in the Bible? Absolutely! The Bible mentions a number of female prophets, or prophetesses. Miriam, Moses's sister, is called a prophet (see Exodus 15:20). Deborah is not only a prophet but one of the judges as well (see Judges 4:4). The New Testament identifies a few more. Anna is the prophetess who has been awaiting the birth of the Messiah, and she meets Mary and Joseph when they present Jesus at the Temple (see Luke 2:36–38). Philip has four daughters who can prophesy (see Acts 21:8–9). God continues to send his prophets into the world, both male and female, to help bring about the Kingdom of God.

Moses and Joshua	Elijah and Elisha
Joshua crosses the Jordan River and then goes to Jericho and Bethel (see Joshua 3:14–17).	Elijah and Elisha go from Bethel to Jericho and then to the Jordan River (a sort of backwards version of Joshua and the Israelites' entrance into the Promised Land) (see 2 Kings 2:1–6).
Joshua splits the waters of the Jordan (see Joshua 3:7–13), and Moses splits the Red Sea (see Exodus 14:26–27).	Elijah and Elisha split the waters of the Jordan (see 2 Kings 2:8,14).
Moses gives the leadership to Joshua (see Deuteronomy 31:7–8).	Elijah gives his prophetic leadership to Elisha (see 2 Kings 2:9–10).
Moses dies on the other side of the Jordan, just outside the Promised Land (see Deuteronomy 34:1–8).	Elijah is taken to Heaven on the other side of the Jordan, just outside the Promised Land (see 2 Kings 2:11–12).

UNIT 3

Why does the Bible contain these parallels? By emphasizing the similarities that Moses and Joshua shared with Elijah and Elisha, the human author highlights how they carried out similar roles. These commonalities emphasize the importance of Elijah and Elisha in Israelite history. Elijah and Elisha, like their predecessors Moses and Joshua, defend the covenant and encourage the people to be faithful to God's Law.

Moving Forward in Time: Elijah, John, Elisha, Jesus

At the end of Elijah's life, Elisha asks for a "double portion" of Elijah's spirit. Elijah says that if he is "taken up" from Elisha, then Elisha's wish will be granted. Just then, a fiery chariot with horses comes between them to take Elijah up to Heaven. Elisha then picks up the mantle, or cloak, that Elijah left behind (see 2 Kings 2:8–14). The mantle is the symbol of Elijah's prophetic leadership being handed on to Elisha. The chariot and horses point to the greatness of Elijah and the respect God's People have for him. His mysterious disappearance leads to the Jewish people's expectation that Elijah will return again to proclaim the coming of the Messiah.

Fast-forward to the New Testament, and we can find the connection between Elijah and John the Baptist. Elijah prefigures John the Baptist in several ways:

- He is cast in the role of the prophet Elijah who is sent to announce the coming of the Messiah "in the spirit and power of Elijah" (Luke 1:17).
- There are similarities of dress and lifestyle between Elijah and John (see Mark 1:6).
- Jesus himself recognizes John as Elijah (see Matthew 11:11–14).

For his part, Elisha prefigures Jesus in many ways:

- They are both prophets who speak on behalf of God.
- They are both preceded by other prophets (Elijah and John the Baptist) who turn their mission over to them.
- Elisha's miracles also foreshadow the work of God accomplished through Jesus Christ. Here is a comparison of these miracles:

Elisha	Jesus
Elisha fills the empty vessels with oil (see 2 Kings 4:1–7).	Jesus turns the jars of water into wine (see John 2:1–10).
Elisha brings the Shunammite's son back to life (see 2 Kings 4:31–37).	Jesus brings the widow's son back to life (see Luke 7:11–17).
Elisha feeds a hundred men with twenty barley loaves and has some left over (see 2 Kings 4:42–44).	Jesus feeds four thousand with a few loaves and fishes and has some left over (see Matthew 14:13–21).
Elisha cures Naaman of leprosy (2 Kings 5:1–14).	Jesus cures ten lepers (see Luke 17:11–19).
Elisha makes the blade of an ax float on the water (see 2 Kings 6:1–7).	Jesus walks on water (see Matthew 14:22–33).

UNIT 3

UNIT 3

A fiery chariot and fiery horses came between the two of them, and Elijah went up to heaven in a whirlwind, and Elisha saw it happen" (2 Kings 2:11–12).

Elijah and Elisha were prophets who did not hold back. They could show extreme kindness to those in need, yet their vengeance could be deadly. Elijah is considered to be the prophet "par excellence," the prophet above all others until Jesus. In the New Testament, Elijah is often portrayed as a representative of all the prophets. At Jesus' Transfiguration, he appears with Moses, who represents the Law. Jesus identifies John the Baptist as the new Elijah: "'Elijah will indeed come and restore all things; but I tell you that Elijah has already come, and they did not recognize him but did to him whatever they pleased. So also will the Son of Man suffer at their hands.' Then the disciples understood that he was speaking to them of John the Baptist" (Matthew 17:11–13). ✳

OVERVIEW of the Book of Second Kings

- **Time period:** 850–587 BC.

- **Author:** Unknown, from the Deuteronomic tradition.

- **Themes:** Accounts of the prophet Elisha; the history of Israel's and Judah's kings until the fall of Jerusalem.

- **Important people:** Elijah and Elisha.

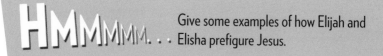

HMMMMM... Give some examples of how Elijah and Elisha prefigure Jesus.

Article 40

Sex and Money: Hosea and Amos

Did the title of this article get your attention? It most likely did because it touches on two aspects of our lives that are connected to strong emotions. Sex and money are fundamental concerns that all humans have: love, power, family, career, lust, greed, hope, survival, companionship, and many others.

This is just as true today as it was thousands of years ago. The prophets Hosea and Amos cleverly use these intense and complex topics to address how the Israelites have failed to keep God's Law. Both live in the northern kingdom of Israel in the years before Assyria's defeat of Israel in 721 BC.

The Prophet Hosea, mosaic detail, twelfth century.

UNIT 3

Hosea: Go Marry a Prostitute?

Why would God tell his prophet Hosea to marry a prostitute and have children with her? It's an unusual assignment, to say the least. As a prophet, Hosea is committed to God and does what the Lord asks. Likewise, he is committed to his wife, Gomer, even though she is a prostitute who strays from him. Hosea uses his marriage to Gomer as a metaphor to describe God's relationship with Israel. As Gomer is unfaithful to Hosea, the Israelites are unfaithful to God (see Hosea, chapters 1–2).

Hosea = God = faithful to his people
Gomer = Israelites = unfaithful to God
Hosea and Gomer's marriage = the covenant

Hosea and Gomer's children represent the results of Israel's infidelity to God and the current state of his relationship with Israel. This broken relationship is revealed in the names of their son and daughter: "Not pitied" and "Not my people." Israel is no longer God's people, and God does not pity them (see Hosea 1:6–8).

Gomer is unfaithful to Hosea; she wanders off to be with other men. The Israelites are unfaithful to God; they wander off to worship other gods, in particular the god Baal. "Go, love a woman / who is loved by her spouse but commits adultery; / Just as the LORD loves the Israelites, / though they turn to other gods" (Hosea 3:1).

The word *baal* means "lord or master." This is what women called their husbands in biblical times. It is also the name of the main Canaanite god. Speaking through Hosea, the Lord says to the Israelites, "You shall call me 'My husband,' / and you shall never again call me 'My baal'" (Hosea 2:18). The temple of Baal was known for its use of temple prostitutes. It seems that Gomer may have been one of them, for God tells Hosea to go and pay to get her back (see 3:2–5).

The name *Hosea* means "salvation," and this is what God offers to Israel over and over again. Just as Hosea never stops loving Gomer, no matter how much she hurts him, so God never stops loving Israel. Despite the Israelites' unfaithfulness, God is always willing to bring his people back to himself.

CATHOLICS MAKING A DIFFERENCE

Womanizer. Father of an illegitimate child. Party animal. Meet Thomas Merton, one of the most influential Catholic authors of the twentieth century. As a young man, he searched for meaning and connection, sometimes in the wrong ways and wrong places. His search ultimately led him to become a Trappist monk, priest, and writer, whom many consider to be a modern-day prophet. In his writings, he cries out against the injustices of poverty, racism, and war, and calls for Christians to live up to the standards set by Christ. Pope Francis, in his address to the United States Congress on September 24, 2015, called Merton "a man of prayer, a thinker who challenged the certitudes of his time and opened new horizons for souls and for the Church . . . a promoter of peace between peoples and religions."

An ancient temple of Baal in Palmyra, Syria. Destroyed by ISIS in 2015, the temple of Baal was known for its use of temple prostitutes. Gomer may have been one of them.

© Homo Cosmicos / Shutterstock.com

UNIT 3

Know the Lord

The Hebrew word *yada* means "knowledge" or "to know," but it has layers of meaning that go beyond what we usually associate with those words. For example, *yada* is used to refer to a sexual relationship. Some translations of the Bible talk about Adam and Eve's sexual relationship like this: "Now the man knew his wife Eve, and she conceived and bore Cain" (Genesis 4:1, *NRSV*). In this sense, "knowing" is more than just "knowing about" someone. It refers to the complete knowledge of another person—physically, emotionally, spiritually—that should characterize the intimate relationship of a husband and wife.

This is why Hosea uses these words to call the Israelites to renew their intimate relationship with God: "Come, let us return to the LORD . . . / Let us know, let us strive to know the LORD" (Hosea 6:1,3). Without such a relationship, the consequences are dire: "There is no fidelity, no loyalty, / no knowledge of God in the land. / Swearing, lying, murder, / stealing and adultery break out; / bloodshed follows bloodshed" (4:1–2).

Amos: The Wealthy Must Care for the Vulnerable

Amos is a shepherd and tree trimmer from the southern kingdom of Judah. When he becomes a prophet, he preaches in the northern kingdom, Israel, making him an outsider. But being an outsider has its perks. It gives him the freedom to say whatever he wants, as he has no allegiances other than to God. Amos offers a bleak picture for Israel's future, speaking of the destruction they will surely face because of their lack of faithfulness to the covenant.

The Mosaic Law requires special care for the *anawim*—the poor, widows, orphans, aliens (foreigners), those who are most vulnerable. Specific laws ensure that food is available for them (see Deuteronomy 24:17–22), that widows are supported after the deaths of their husbands (see 25:5), that foreigners are treated no differently than their fellow Israelites (see Leviticus 19:33–34), and that the poor can afford to make sacrifices to God (see 27:8). These are the people for whom Amos is fighting.

The prophet Amos was a farmer. What does this say about the kind of people God calls to speak his message?

Amos does not hold anything back in his poetic rant condemning the Israelites for their numerous sins. The wealthy people's abuse of the poor is at the top of his list. "They trample the heads of the destitute / into the dust of the earth, / and force the lowly out of the way" (Amos 2:7). He calls the pampered women in Samaria "cows" (4:1). Among the abuses of power, he lists "oppressing the just, accepting bribes, / turning away the needy at the gate" (5:12).

Fake Faith

Imagine worshipping, praying, and singing in church, just as you normally do on Sunday morning. Suddenly you hear the voice of God boom down to say that your prayers are whiny and annoying, that your noisy songs hurt his ears, and that your worship means nothing to him. Ouch! That would be pretty awful, right? This is God's message that Amos prophesies to the Israelites: "I hate, I despise your feasts, / I take no pleasure in your solemnities. / . . . Take away from me / your noisy songs; / The melodies of your harps, / I will not listen to them" (Amos 5:21,23).

Why would God say such things? The problem is not the Israelites' worship, but rather their hypocrisy. Their worship follows the ritual laws of the covenant, but that's all it does. Their daily lives do not reflect faithfulness to the covenant. For example, wealthy people spend lots of money to have the best animals to sacrifice (see Amos 5:22), yet abuse and oppress poor people (see 2:6–7). If the Israelites want their worship to be acceptable to God, this is what God tells them to do through Amos: "Rather let justice surge like waters, / and righteousness like an unfailing stream" (5:24).

UNIT 3

© Leah-Anne Thompson

Rather let justice surge like waters, / and righteousness like an unfailing stream" (Amos 5:24).

Amos's words should remind you of the words and actions of Jesus Christ. Like Amos, Jesus does not have kind words for religious hypocrites. In the Gospel of Matthew, Jesus quotes the prophet Isaiah to describe the Pharisees and scribes: "This people honors me with their lips, / but their hearts are far from me; / in vain do they worship me, / teaching as doctrines human precepts" (15:8–9). For a shocking condemnation of the hypocrisy of the religious leaders of his time, read Jesus' speech in Matthew, chapter 23.

Through Amos, God reveals to us that true faith is not something that is practiced for only one hour on Sunday mornings. It is something that pervades all parts of our life. God is most pleased when our sincere worship reflects our faithfulness to his Law, including care for the most vulnerable in our society. ✳

OVERVIEW of the Book of Hosea

- **Time period:** 750 to after 732 BC.
- **Author:** Compiled by Hosea or his disciples.
- **Themes:** God's faithful love for Israel, the image of God as a loving parent.

OVERVIEW of the Book of Amos

- **Time period:** 760 to after 750 BC.
- **Author:** Compiled by Amos or his disciples.
- **Theme:** The destruction of Israel is caused by the injustice and hypocrisy of the wealthy and ruling classes.

 HMMMMMM. . . Given the focus of Amos and Hosea's prophecy, what things would they speak out against in today's world?

Article 41

Jonah: Laughter Is the Best Medicine

A comedian has the ability to examine daily observations from a different point of view and creatively expresses those observations in a way that makes us laugh. Sometimes those observations poke fun of us humans, revealing our flaws and shortcomings. Through humor, a comedian can help us to confront certain realities or truths that we might prefer to ignore. Humor and laughter make it easier for us to take criticism. In this way, good comedy has the power to be prophetic, because it shines a light on the dark places in life. Laughter can be good medicine for change.

Good comedians have the power to be prophetic, because their humor shines a light on the dark places in life. Similarly, the Book of Jonah uses humor to make its points.

Jesus sometimes uses humor, especially in his parables. For example, his listeners would have been chuckling over the thought of a rich, pampered young man ending up feeding pigs. The authors of the Old Testament sometimes use humor too. The Book of Jonah is one of the best examples. When we interpret the Bible, one of the important things to consider is the literary style the human author is using, and Jonah's literary style is satire, or extended parable, which uses humor to make its points.

UNIT 3

© Fer Gregory / Shutterstock.com

To understand the point that Jonah is making, we also need to consider the historical situation at the time. The book most likely was written after the people of Judah returned from their captivity in Babylon. Understandably, there was a great deal of fear and distrust of foreign nations and foreign people. Taken too far, this distrust resulted in an unfortunate and ungodly prejudice: that non-Jews were beyond God's saving power. God worked through the author of the Book of Jonah to counter this narrow viewpoint with a little humor.

Initially, Jonah rejects God's call to be a prophet. Jonah soon finds out that he can run, but he can't hide from God, and ends up in the belly of a fish for three days.

Three Days in the Belly

Like many before him, Jonah rejects God's call to be a prophet, but he never actually says no. He just starts comically running away, as if there is somewhere to hide where God will not find him! He makes his way to another town and sails off on a ship. When the sailors find out that Jonah is running from God, they toss him overboard, practically into the jaws of a giant fish.

Jonah spends three days and three nights inside the fish, until finally he offers a prayer to God and the fish spits him out (see Jonah 2:1–11). In the New Testament, this will be seen to prefigure Jesus' Resurrection, occurring three days after being in the "belly" of the Earth. A number of times in the Gospels, Jesus is confronted by religious leaders and asked to prove himself with a sign. Jesus' response on one occasion includes a reference to Jonah: "Just as Jonah was in the belly of the whale three days and three nights, so will the Son of Man be in the heart of the earth three days and three nights" (Matthew 12:40).

After finally resigning himself to his role as a prophet, Jonah takes on God's mission to preach in Nineveh. The Ninevites are Israel's sworn enemies, and the original audience certainly expects that Jonah will either be laughed out of town or, more likely, killed. Jonah seems ready for a great confrontation as well, but when he preaches, an unexpected turn of events—with a bit of comic timing—happens. The people report it to the king, who puts on a sackcloth and sits in ashes! Fasting, sitting in ashes, and wearing sackcloth (clothing made from uncomfortable material) are all signs of repentance. The funny thing is that not only are the king and the people fasting and wearing sackcloth, the animals are too (see Jonah 3:1–10)!

UNIT 3

Jonah is angry over a dead gourd plant and tells God he would rather die than live without its shade (Jonah 4:6).

The Book of Jonah is a reminder to the original audience that all people are God's children. Consider how your life can reflect this belief. Is there anyone in your school or neighborhood who is considered an outcast? You can do simple things to end their exclusion: say hello to them, smile at them, have lunch with them occasionally, let them know they are needed by asking them for help, or just talk to them before or after class. Remember that you do not have to agree with someone to be kind to them. Differences never excuse you from your call to be Christlike.

UNIT 3

God Loves All

The absurdity continues when Jonah becomes frustrated. He is ready for an all-out battle in which the wrath of God will strike down these heathens! Instead, God accepts the Ninevites' repentance. This is not what Jonah signed up for. At the end of the book, Jonah is angry over a dead gourd plant and tells God he would rather die than live without its shade. We are no longer laughing at Jonah but shaking our heads at his pettiness. God tells Jonah:

> You are concerned over the gourd plant which cost you no effort and which you did not grow; it came up in one night and in one night it perished. And should I not be concerned over the great city of Nineveh, in which there are more than a hundred and twenty thousand persons? (Jonah 4:10–11)

This is a good question for us too. Do we want to see our enemies change for the good? Or are we more like Jonah, who would rather see them punished?

The people of Nineveh are "the others," enemies from a different nation who worship other gods. When we, like Jonah, isolate groups of people and distance ourselves from them, it becomes easier to see them as "less than" us. History has shown that this can lead to a kind of dehumanization, which can have horrendous consequences. God loves all people no matter their race, religion, nationality, or any other categories used to divide us. The story of Jonah is a humorous reminder to abandon the prejudices that divide us and to see one another as God does. ✳

OVERVIEW of the Book of Jonah

- **Time period:** Eighth century BC.
- **Author:** Unknown, probably writing in the fifth century.
- **Theme:** God's care for all people, including Israel's enemies.

UNIT 3

HMMMMM. . . What details from the Book of Jonah could you use to explain its religious message?

1. What reasons does the author of the First Book of Kings give to explain the split of the kingdom?

2. How does Rehoboam respond to Jeroboam's request to ease the oppression of the Israelites? Explain why he responds this way.

3. Explain what a prophet is and how people often misunderstand the role of the biblical prophets.

4. Offer two or three examples of how Jesus is a prophet.

5. How does Elijah prefigure Jesus?

6. Describe John the Baptist's clothing. What does his clothing tell the audience about his role?

7. Why does Hosea marry a prostitute?

8. Why does the prophet Amos deem the Israelites hypocritical?

9. What is the main point of the Book of Jonah?

Ten Characteristics of a Prophet

1. Prophets are regular people like you and me.

2. They "hear" a call from God.

3. They do not want the call!

4. They go through an initiation of some sort.

5. They speak on behalf of the oppressed.

6. Prophets use shock tactics to get their message across.

7. Their message challenges people, which makes them unpopular.

8. Prophets go through periods of discouragement.

9. They are dedicated to doing God's work.

10. Prophets often die as a result of proclaiming their message.

1. Which of these characteristics did you see in your study of Jeremiah, Elijah, Elisha, Hosea, Amos, and Jonah?

2. Which of these characteristics do you most identify with? Which would be the hardest for you to accept?

CHAPTER 10
The Kings and Prophets of the Southern Kingdom

HOW DOES GOD REACT WHEN WE SCREW UP?

UNIT 3

SNAPSHOT

Article 42   Page 259
Good Kings: Shining Stars on a Dark Horizon
- Pre-read: 2 Kings, chapters 18–20, 22–23

Article 43   Page 264
Isaiah Part 1: Hope for the Hopeless
- Pre-read: Isaiah, chapters 1–5, 6:1–7:16, 9:1–6, 11:1–9

Article 44   Page 268
Jeremiah: Outrageous Heart
- Pre-read: Jeremiah 1:1–10; 7:1–15; 13:1–11; chapter 19; 20:7–18, 27

Article 45   Page 274
Ezekiel: Actions Speak Louder Than Words
- Pre-read: Ezekiel, chapters 1–5, chapter 12, 36:16–37:14

Article 46   Page 279
The Babylonian Exile: Far Away from Home
- Pre-read: Psalm 137; Lamentations, chapter 5

Article 47   Page 283
Isaiah Parts 2 and 3: A Light in the Darkness
- Pre-read: Isaiah 40:1–11, 44:24–45:13, chapter 55

Article 42

Good Kings: Shining Stars on a Dark Horizon

When the united kingdom of Israel splits in the tenth century BC, after Solomon's death, the kingdom of Judah is on its own in the south. Like Israel, the northern kingdom, the kingdom of Judah has strings of bad kings, but they also have a couple of good ones. These kings are shining stars in an otherwise dismal run of royal losers. They are able to turn Judah back to a people who are faithful to the covenant . . . but only for a while.

Meanwhile, Back in the South . . .

The northern kingdom of Israel goes through violent changes of leadership that ultimately end with Assyria's conquest of that kingdom in 721 BC. Meanwhile, back in Judah, things have not been going so well either. With Israel gone, "Only the tribe of Judah was left. Even the people of Judah did not keep the commandments of the Lord, their God, but followed the rites practiced by Israel" (2 Kings 17:18–19). Not all of the kings of Judah are as bad as their counterparts in the north. Many allow the worship of false gods, and some kings are just downright awful. One of them burns his own child as a sacrificial offering (see 16:3). Another repeats that sin and also set up altars to other gods in the Temple (see 21:3–6).

The Kingdom of Judah has a couple of redeeming qualities. First, as God promises David, the royal leadership of Judah remains within a single family line—the descendants of King David. Second, two good kings make important religious reforms. These kings bring the Chosen People in the kingdom back into right relationship with God, at least for a short time.

The lion is the symbol of the Jewish tribe of Judah. The symbol dates back to the tribe's patriarch, Jacob, who referred to his son Judah as "the young lion" (Genesis 49:9).

The Good Guys

The first of the good kings is Hezekiah, who rules Judah from approximately 726 to 697 BC. He is fortunate that when the Assyrians conquer Israel, they do not continue south and attack Judah. But this relative peace is short lived.

About ten years later, Assyria returns in a second effort to conquer Judah. Sennacherib, king of Assyria, succeeds in defeating most of the cities in the kingdom, saving Jerusalem for last. He sends a commander to Jerusalem who taunts the king's assistants, makes fun of Hezekiah's trust in the Lord, and tells them that surrendering is the only thing that will save them (see 18:13–37). The Assyrians have left a trail of defeated enemies behind them, so there is good reason for Hezekiah to be worried. But his trust in God does not waver. He prays to the Lord, and God responds by sending a new and important Old Testament figure: the prophet Isaiah. Through Isaiah's prophecies, God assures Hezekiah that Sennacherib will not conquer Jerusalem. Sure enough, the Lord does as he promised. Second Kings describes Jerusalem's rescue through a death-dealing angel and a hasty withdrawal by the Assyrians (see chapter 19).

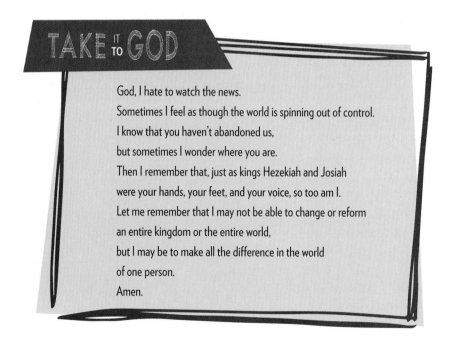

TAKE IT TO GOD

God, I hate to watch the news.
Sometimes I feel as though the world is spinning out of control.
I know that you haven't abandoned us,
but sometimes I wonder where you are.
Then I remember that, just as kings Hezekiah and Josiah
were your hands, your feet, and your voice, so too am I.
Let me remember that I may not be able to change or reform
an entire kingdom or the entire world,
but I may be to make all the difference in the world
of one person.
Amen.

UNIT 3

The Assyrian army was an aggressive, murderous regime. They were the first to use iron weaponry, which could be mass produced, allowing a very large army to be fully equipped in no time.

Why is Judah successful in surviving the Assyrian attack while the kingdom of Israel is unsuccessful? Second Kings provides this theological answer: Hezekiah "put his trust in the LORD, the God of Israel; . . . and never turned away from following him, but observed the commandments the LORD had given Moses" (18:5–6).

Later on, Hezekiah becomes terribly ill and is near death, but Isaiah communicates a shadowy prophecy that reassures the king that he will live. Soon afterward, Hezekiah receives a visit from a group sent by the Babylonian king to wish him well on his recovery. After Hezekiah makes a grave mistake, Isaiah warns that the Babylonians will return, and when they do, Judah will lose everything to them (see 2 Kings 20:12–19). After Hezekiah's death, Judah endures two more rounds of bad kings separated by one more shining star, King Josiah.

Josiah, the Boy King

By the time Josiah becomes king, things have gotten so bad that the Israel-ites do not even seem to be aware of the Law of the Covenant. Josiah is only eight years old, but even as a youth "he did what was right in the LORD's sight, walking in the way of David his father, not turning right or left" (2 Kings 22:2). Only by chance does Josiah discover a book of the Law during a Temple ren-ovation. After having it read to him, he realizes Judah's great sins and tears his garments in shame. He then reads it to the people and begins a great reform in which they remove the idols from the Temple, tear down the altars built to other gods, and abandon all of the practices they have taken on from other religions (see chapter 23). Then he leads the people in celebrating a special Passover: "No Passover such as this had been observed during the period when the judges ruled Israel, or during the entire period of the kings of Israel and the kings of Judah" (23:22).

Even though "before him there had been no king who turned to the LORD as he did," Josiah is killed by the Egyptian army, and "the LORD did not turn from his fiercely burning anger against Judah" (2 Kings 23:25–26). Follow-ing Josiah's death, Judah suffers the reign of a few more bad kings before the kingdom falls.

King Nebuchadnezzar II was the greatest king of Babylon, known for his military might, the splendor of Babylon, and his significant part in Jewish history.

As Isaiah prophesied to King Hezekiah, God will ultimately punish Judah for its sins, and the punishment will come through the hands of the Babylonians. Nebuchadnezzar, king of Babylon, directs his army to conquer the city of Jerusalem. By 587 BC, Judah has been captured and its citizens taken into captivity in Babylon.

Taken

Celestino was arrested for conspiracy to commit murder. When his boss decided he wanted someone killed, Celestino agreed to act as a translator between his boss and the hitmen. The victim survived the attack, and everyone involved was arrested. Celestino soon realized the depths to which he had fallen. Waiting in jail for trial, he faced losing his marriage, family, friends, job, home, and everything else he cared about in this world. He realized that his faith in God had just slowly drifted away. Celestino pled guilty, apologized to his victim, and worked for the prosecution as a witness in the other trials. He vowed to spend the rest of his time in prison reviving his relationship with God and making some serious life changes. Years later, Celestino said that because he had hit the lowest depths of his life, he was ready to reach out to God and change his life for the better.

Celestino's traumatic experience can be likened to that of God's people after Jerusalem falls. There is hardly a darker time in their history than the era of the divided kingdom. The list of what they experience on the way to their downfall is overwhelming: worship of false gods, unjust treatment of their citizens, a steady stream of bad royal leadership, the conquest of Israel, then finally the capture of the people of Judah and the destruction of the Temple (see 2 Kings, chapters 17 and 25). Almost everything they know and love is taken away. Unfortunately, it sometimes takes these dark times for us to truly realize our need for God. ✳

Sometimes it takes the darkest of times for us to truly realize our need for God.

UNIT 3

© sakhorn / Shutterstock.com

HMMMMMM. . .

Even though Judah ultimately falls into captivity, what good comes from the changes Hezekiah and Josiah make?

Article 43

Isaiah Part 1: Hope for the Hopeless

The prophets often warn God's people that they are heading in the wrong direction. They advise people to be faithful to God and to practice justice, or else life will not go well for them. In the Book of Isaiah, we come across three prophets who, each in their own way, point the people in the right direction. But, the people often ignore the prophets' guidance and suffer the consequences.

The Three Isaiahs

There is a famous spy movie called *Casino Royale*, in which the Soviet Union is the bad guy. This movie came out in 1967, at the height of the Cold War, when tensions between the Soviet Union and the United States were high. The movie was remade in 2006, but in that film, the bad guys were Sudanese terrorists. Why the difference? When the remake was produced, the Cold War had ended and the United States and the Soviet Union were on much better terms. The audience would more readily accept Sudanese terrorists than Soviet terrorists because the Sudanese were more of a threat at the time.

The Book of Isaiah has a similar history. Almost two centuries after First Isaiah wrote his prophecies, the authors of Second Isaiah and Third Isaiah write theirs. They address similar themes as their predecessor, but because so much time has passed, these last two authors adapt their messages to make them relatable to their current audience. You might ask, "Why do they pretend to be Isaiah?" The answer is that they aren't pretending; rather, they are honoring the prophet who provides their inspiration. Today, writing under someone else's name would be considered fraud. Back then, it was a way of honoring and giving credit to the original source. This chart shows the three different authors, the chapters attributed to them, and when they prophesied.

Author	Chapters Written	Time Period Written
First Isaiah	1–39	Approximately 740–700 BC
Second Isaiah	40–55	During the Babylonian Exile (586–537 BC) or shortly afterward
Third Isaiah	56–66	After the Babylonian Exile

A Dark Future

We first learn of Isaiah in the account of King Hezekiah in the Second Book of Kings, where he advises the king and prophesies about the coming of the Babylonians (see chapter 19). But we do not actually "meet" him until chapter 6 in the Book of Isaiah, when he is called by God (see 6:1–8). The Book of Isaiah begins in the days of King Ahaz, sometime around 735 BC. Assyria has already conquered the Northern Kingdom of Israel. Now it is threatening to conquer the Southern Kingdom, Judah, so there is plenty for the king to fear.

Isaiah advises King Hezekiah and prophesies about the coming of the Babylonians (Isaiah, chapter 19).

© BibleArtLibrary / iStock.com

UNIT 3

Though Second and Third Isaiah offer a hopeful future for Judah after the return from the Babylonian Exile, First Isaiah paints a gloomy outlook before the Exile:

- He denounces the hypocrisy of the leaders who practice empty religious rituals while oppressing the weaker members of their society (see 1:10–23).
- He alerts Judah of their impending punishment due to their worship of "their idols of silver and their idols of gold" (2:20) and for mistreatment of the poor (see 3:15). He specifically takes aim at the "daughters of Zion," the wealthy women of Jerusalem, whose jewelry is paid for at the expense of the poor (see 3:13–26).
- He warns Judah that they will face the wrath of God through an invasion by another nation and that their corpses shall be like refuse in the streets" (5:25). This would be fulfilled when Babylon conquers Judah over a century later.

First Isaiah extends the Lord's condemnation to other countries as well. Isaiah denounces Babylon because it "made the world a wilderness, / razed its cities, / and gave captives no release" (14:17). He accuses Damascus—the capital of Babylon—of worshipping false gods (see 17:7–8.) Isaiah ultimately prophesies doom for the entire world: "The earth shall be utterly laid waste, utterly stripped, / for the Lᴏʀᴅ has decreed this word. . . . / The earth is polluted because of its inhabitants, / for they have transgressed laws, violated statutes, / broken the ancient covenant" (24:3,5).

CATHOLICS MAKING A DIFFERENCE

After being married for thirteen years, Mark and Louise Zwick opened Casa Juan Diego in 1980. Casa Juan Diego is a Catholic Worker House in Houston, Texas, providing emergency food, clothing, and shelter to the city's predominantly Hispanic immigrants. The Zwicks live with those escaping poverty and violence in their homeland. They freely took on a life of poverty together and do not receive paychecks. Mark said: "We are faith people. And we believe that the Lord gives us strength to survive this work and these challenges." In 1997, Pope John Paul II recognized the Zwicks' ministry with the *Pro Ecclesia et Pontifice* award. Mark passed away in 2016, and Louise continues her work at Casa Juan Diego.

Not All Gloom and Doom

According to Isaiah's prophesy, the future isn't looking bright for the People of God. Despite this apparently dark future, Isaiah encourages the king to have faith, reassuring him that the Lord will give a sign: "The young woman, pregnant and about to bear a son, shall name him **Emmanuel**" (Isaiah 7:14). *Emmanuel* is a Hebrew word meaning "God is with us." Later, in chapter 9, Isaiah describes an ideal king—perhaps the child from chapter 7 grown up. "The people who walked in darkness / have seen a great light; . . . / They name him Wonder-Counselor, God-Hero, / Father-Forever, Prince of Peace. / His dominion is vast / and forever peaceful, / Upon David's throne, and over his kingdom" (9:1,5–6).

The ideal king, as described by Isaiah, is exactly the kind of leader Judah needs at this time. In looking toward the future, it is easy to see how Jesus Christ fulfills that description; he is both a descendent of King David, and **Emmanuel**, who will bring salvation to his people. In that light, there is nothing to fear; the future doesn't look so dim. ✳

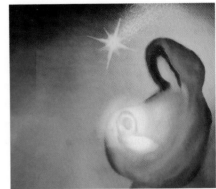

"The young woman, pregnant and about to bear a son, shall name him Emmanuel" (Isaiah 7:14).

UNIT 3

OVERVIEW of the Book of Isaiah

- **Time period:** Between 742 and 500 BC.
- **Author:** The three Isaiahs or their followers.
- **Themes:** Faithfulness to God, justice for the poor, hope for the future, messianic prophecies, God as lord over all nations.
- **Important persons:** Isaiah, and the last kings of Judah: Uzziah, Jotham, Ahaz, and Hezekiah.

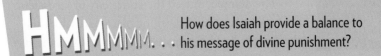

HMMMMM. . . How does Isaiah provide a balance to his message of divine punishment?

Emmanuel ➤ A Hebrew word meaning "God is with us."

Article 44

Jeremiah: Outrageous Heart

Like the prophets before him, Jeremiah resisted God's call. In response he says: "I do not know how to speak. I am too young" (Jeremiah 1:6). The Lord quickly dismissed that excuse and moved on with Jeremiah's directions. "To whomever I send you, you shall go; / whatever I command you, you shall speak" (1:7). It's almost as if God were saying to Jeremiah: "Trust me. Don't worry about what's in the future. Just take each situation as it comes, and rely on me for help."

Hearing that God has a purpose and a mission for each of us is not really that earth shattering. Yet some young people think they are in a spiritual holding pattern and will discover their true calling later on in life. God has given you a purpose and a mission to complete *right now*. Answering God's call is not something to put off until later. You already know that God's call means being kind and forgiving to friends, family, and classmates. It means serving those most in need by collecting food for a homeless shelter, or volunteering at a children's hospital, or raising money for refugees. Your call might not make the evening news, but your mission is no less important. You are never too young to do God's work.

Shock Treatment

Jeremiah's ministry begins around 626 BC, during the reign of one of the good kings of Judah, King Josiah. Unfortunately, the kings who follow Josiah are not so good, and the people once again lose sight of their covenant commitments to God. They have forgotten the reforms of King Hezekiah and are falling into patterns of injustice and idolatry. To shake them out of their apathy, Jeremiah not only uses words but eventually also does some crazy things to get their attention.

The Temple, indeed the entire city of Jerusalem, is God's home, God's dwelling place. Jerusalem and the Temple had been spared from the Assyrian invasion in 721. Because of this, the people have grown a false sense of safety. They think, "Of course, nothing bad will happen to us, for the Temple is here and the

Like the prophet Jeremiah, when have you felt too young to do God's work?

Temple is God's home." Jeremiah boldly stands in front of the Temple and calls them out on this, hoping his words will shock them into changing. He warns the people of Judah that they will only be able to remain in the land God has given them if they stop oppressing those in need and worshipping false gods. Otherwise God will allow the one thing the people find incomprehensible: the destruction of the Temple (see Jeremiah 7:1–15).

The Temple and the entire city of Jerusalem are God's dwelling place, God's home. How do you think the people felt when Jeremiah prophesied that the Temple would be destroyed?

At first, Jeremiah's words fall on deaf ears, so he kicks his strategy up a few notches, following God's lead. Jeremiah takes a dirty loincloth—basically a pair of underwear—stuffs it into a rock, and weeks later retrieves it. Then he boldly stands in front of the Temple, holds up the dirty, rotting loincloth, and says, "This wicked people who refuse to obey my words, who walk in the stubbornness of their hearts and follow other gods, serving and worshiping them, will be like this loincloth, good for nothing" (Jeremiah 13:10) and rotting from sin and corruption! How would you like being told that God thinks you are like old, rotten, dirty underwear?

Jeremiah's flair for the dramatic does not stop there. In chapter 16, he warns the people not to get married and have kids, because their children will just end up dead: "Of deadly disease they shall die. Unlamented and unburied they will lie like dung on the ground. Sword and famine will make an end of them" (verse 4). He takes the elders and priests out to the places where Judah's kings had previously sacrificed their own children. He warns them that they will soon "eat the flesh of their sons and daughters; they shall eat one another's flesh during the harsh siege" of the Babylonians (19:9). Then he smashes a potter's flask and tells them that their sinful behavior has done irreparable harm, and like the flask, it cannot be fixed (see 19:10–11).

By the reign of King Zedekiah in 597 BC, it becomes clear that Babylon is going to overtake Judah. However, numerous false prophets encourage the people to fight, promising that they will be victorious. Jeremiah is convinced that because of their lack of faith, they are doomed and should just give up. In chapter 27, he makes his point by putting a yoke around his neck. A yoke is a wooden beam that is put over the necks of animals and attached to a plow or cart so the animals can pull it. The yoke symbolizes the slavery and bondage the Babylonians will inflict upon them. He walks around with the yoke, telling the people not to listen to the false prophets but rather to give up and "serve the king of Babylon that you may live" (Jeremiah 27:17). As you might imagine, this does not go over well with his fellow citizens!

UNIT 3

Oxen wear a yoke attached to a plow. Jeremiah puts a yoke around his neck to symbolize the slavery the Babylonians will inflict on the Israelites if they don't turn from their sinful behavior.

Heart on His Sleeve

Jeremiah's passion as a prophet and his faithfulness to God's mission does not win him many friends: he points out their sins; he tells them about God's disapproval; he foretells their bleak future; and his attention-getting tactics are, at times, grotesque and lurid. Jeremiah is not a popular guy! As a result, he is put in jail (see Jeremiah 20:2), mocked and ridiculed (see 20:7–8), and even threatened with death (see 26:11).

You might think this is no big deal, that Jeremiah must have been a pretty tough guy in order to be God's prophet. Thankfully, we have Jeremiah's own words to help us understand the sensitive heart of this prophet (see Jeremiah 15:10–18). He is someone who wears his heart on his sleeve; whatever thought comes into his mind comes right out of his mouth, as we see in several passages expressing his loneliness and distress. In these passages, Jeremiah freely questions and complains to the Lord (see 11:18–19, 18:19–23, 20:7–18).

In these famous crisis moments, Jeremiah is like someone with a split personality. On one hand, his anger at God is blazing: "You seduced me LORD. . . . / The word of the LORD has brought me / reproach and derision all day long" (Jeremiah 20:7–8). On the other hand, he cannot deny his love for God: "But the LORD is with me, like a mighty champion" (verse 11). Then he slips right back into a dark depression: "Cursed be the day / on which I was born!" (verse 14). Jeremiah expresses his emotions, both his highs and lows to God, with complete abandon. These passages can be reassuring to us—even great prophets and holy people like Jeremiah had their moments of doubt.

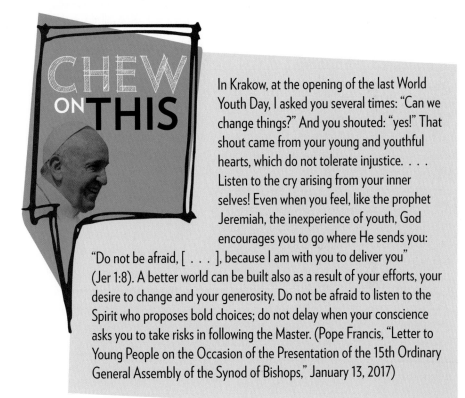

CHEW ON THIS

In Krakow, at the opening of the last World Youth Day, I asked you several times: "Can we change things?" And you shouted: "yes!" That shout came from your young and youthful hearts, which do not tolerate injustice. . . . Listen to the cry arising from your inner selves! Even when you feel, like the prophet Jeremiah, the inexperience of youth, God encourages you to go where He sends you: "Do not be afraid, [. . .], because I am with you to deliver you" (Jer 1:8). A better world can be built also as a result of your efforts, your desire to change and your generosity. Do not be afraid to listen to the Spirit who proposes bold choices; do not delay when your conscience asks you to take risks in following the Master. (Pope Francis, "Letter to Young People on the Occasion of the Presentation of the 15th Ordinary General Assembly of the Synod of Bishops," January 13, 2017)

UNIT 3

Pointing to Christ

The prophets of the Old Testament clearly pointed toward the coming of Christ, both with their words and their lives. Like Jesus, Jeremiah calls the people to return to the Lord and to be faithful to him and his laws. The resemblance is strong enough that when Jesus asks his disciples who the people think he is, they respond, "Some say John the Baptist, others Elijah, still others

Jeremiah or one of the prophets" (Matthew 16:14). The comparison of Jesus and Jeremiah is not surprising because there are a number of interesting similarities between the two.

WAYS JEREMIAH POINTS TO JESUS	
Jeremiah	**Jesus**
"Before I formed you in the womb I knew you, / before you were born I dedicated you, / a prophet to the nations I appointed you." (Jeremiah 1:5)	"Behold, you will conceive in your womb and bear a son, and you shall name him Jesus. He will be great and will be called Son of the Most High, and the Lord God will give him the throne of David his father." (Luke 1:31-32)
"Your kindred and your father's house, even they betray you; they have recruited a force against you." (Jeremiah 12:6)	"And [Jesus] said, 'Amen, I say to you, no prophet is accepted in his own native place.' . . . They rose up, drove him out of the town, and led him to the brow of the hill on which their town had been built, to hurl him down headlong." (Luke 4:24,29)
"Oh, that my head were a spring of water, / my eyes a fountain of tears, / That I might weep day and night / over the slain from the daughter of my people!" (Jeremiah 8:23)	"As he drew near, [Jesus] saw the city and wept over it." (Luke 19:41)
"I will have them eat the flesh of their sons and daughters; they shall eat one another's flesh during the harsh siege under which their enemies and those who seek their lives will confine them." (Jeremiah 19:9)	"For the days are coming upon you when your enemies will raise a palisade against you; they will encircle you and hem you in on all sides. They will smash you to the ground and your children within you" (Luke 19:43-44)
"Has this house which bears my name become in your eyes a den of thieves?" (Jeremiah 7:11)	"And he said to them, 'It is written: / "My house shall be a house of prayer," / but you are making it a den of thieves.'" (Matthew 21:13)
"See, days are coming—oracle of the LORD— when I will make a new covenant with the house of Israel and the house of Judah." (Jeremiah 31:31)	"This cup is the new covenant in my blood, which will be shed for you." (Luke 22:20)

Exiled

Jeremiah was passionate about getting the people to be faithful to God. His tactics were bold and outrageous; his heart was devout and sometimes broken; and despite the feelings of hopelessness he sometimes experienced, his dedication to God was unwavering. He was a man who practiced what he preached, but his cries for God's people to change came too little, too late for Judah.

In 587 BC, the Babylonians finally conquer Jerusalem, destroy the city and the Temple, and take most of its inhabitants to Babylon (see article 52). Jeremiah stays behind in Judah with those

In this painting by Rembrandt, Jeremiah sits outdoors with a golden bowl, carpet, and books, apparently objects saved from the ruined Temple. In the left background, burning Jerusalem falls to the Babylonian army in the sixth century BC.

who remain in the ruined city, but eventually they flee to Egypt (see Jeremiah 43:1–13). Jeremiah continues to prophesy there, but he soon disappears. No one knows what happened to him, but his legacy as a passionate and devoted messenger of God continues to deeply inspire to this day. ✳

UNIT 3

OVERVIEW of Jeremiah

- **Time period:** 626–583 BC.
- **Author:** Jeremiah and his disciples, including Baruch.
- **Audience:** The people of the Kingdom of Judah just prior to the Babylonian Exile.
- **Themes:** Israel's need for repentance, Jeremiah's struggles, the New Covenant.

How do Jeremiah's shocking acts help to emphasize his verbal message? Use one of his examples to explain.

Article 45

Ezekiel: Actions Speak Louder Than Words

In October of 1968, the United States was still reeling from the assassination of Martin Luther King Jr. The last civil rights act was passed in April, but race relations were still tense. The Black Power Movement sought to improve the standing of African Americans. It was against this backdrop that John Carlos and Tommie Smith, two African American track and field athletes representing the United States, went to the podium to receive their Olympic medals.

As "The Star-Spangled Banner" played, they silently raised their gloved fists and bowed their heads to bring attention to the racial inequality in their home country. This simple, but powerful, gesture was not intended as a sign of disrespect for their country, but it nonetheless caused an uproar that led to their expulsion from the Olympic Games. They went home to face a public outcry and numerous death threats. Only years later were they honored for this silent and moving protest against injustice.

Tommie Smith (C) and John Carlos (R) raise their gloved fists in the Black Power salute to express their opposition to racism in the United States during the US national anthem after receiving their medals on October 17, 1968.

The prophet Ezekiel also uses symbolic acts to protest the behavior of his fellow citizens. He attempts to shake up the people of Judah and convince them to be faithful to God and treat one another justly. His dramatic and sometimes bizarre, symbolic demonstrations disturb his audience, bringing Ezekiel disdain and ridicule. Yet years (and centuries) later, Jews and Christians honor him for his courage and insights.

The prophet Ezekiel used interesting and clever symbolic actions to convince the people to be faithful God.

Warnings

Like his fellow prophet Jeremiah, Ezekiel prophesies in the last years before the Babylonians conquered Judah. However, he is already in Babylon at the time, having been captured during an earlier attack on Jerusalem (597 BC). He receives God's call in an elaborate vision that includes strange creatures and a hand that feeds him God's words. Oddly enough, Ezekiel is initially struck mute by God, so for a time he is forced to prophesy without using words as God had instructed him (see Ezekiel, chapters 1–3).

His first act warns of the upcoming clash with the Babylonians. This elaborate act takes Ezekiel over a year to accomplish. God instructs him to do the following:

1. Build a model of Jerusalem.
2. Put all the instruments used for a siege upon a city, such as battering rams, ramps, campsites, and so on, around the model.
3. Place an iron pan between the model city and himself, sit silently, and watch it for about fourteen months.

What did it mean? Ezekiel's model represents God doing nothing as Jerusalem is conquered, and the iron pan stands for the separation between God and his people. Also during this time, God instructs Ezekiel to cook his food on human excrement to represent the depths to which people would go to ease their starvation during the siege. Ezekiel just cannot handle that, so God kindly lets him use cow dung instead! He cuts off his hair, using it to represent what will happen to the people of Jerusalem if they don't turn back to God (see Ezekiel, chapters 4–5). But wait, there's more!

Ezekiel does a number of other symbolic acts. He packs his bags and walks around town as if he is ready to be taken away (see Ezekiel, chapter 12). When Ezekiel's wife dies, God tells him not to mourn her, just as the people of Jerusalem will not be able to mourn their loved ones as they head off into exile (see 24:15–24). These actions are intended as a wake-up call, reminding the people to follow God's Law, and when the events Ezekiel foretold occur, the people "shall know that I am the Lord God" (24:24).

Being Molded

God calls the prophet Ezekiel **Son of Man** over ninety times in the Book of Ezekiel, and this phrase is also found in the Book of Daniel (see 7:13–14). Not only is "Son of Man" the title Jesus most often chose for himself, it is the only messianic title he used (see Luke 21:27). Recall that *man* is the translation for the Hebrew term *adam*. Being called a "Son of Man" is a reference to Ezekiel's humanity—that he is made of flesh and bones by his Creator. The Book of Genesis describes how God formed Adam from the ground, like a craftsman molding pottery (see 2:7). Ezekiel prefigures how Jesus would place himself in God's hands, conforming himself to his Father's will (see Matthew 26:39).

Sometimes we compare our humanity to God's divinity. In doing so, we perceive our human nature as a less than good thing. Certainly, none of us is perfect, but this term *Son of Man* is intended to heighten the respect we have for ourselves as human beings. Jesus Christ is true God and true man, and he assumed his human nature at his conception. If God became human, then being human must be a good thing! Jesus is the "New Adam" (see 1 Corinthians 15:36-49) and a role model for our own humanity. Like Jesus, we are called to put ourselves into God's hands and let him mold our lives and direct our actions.

Son of Man ➤ A messianic title from the Book of Daniel, used to describe a figure who receives authority over other nations from God; the only messianic title in the Gospels used by Jesus to describe himself.

A Spirit of Hope

Like his counterpart Jeremiah, Ezekiel is not all gloom and doom. He gives the people a vision for a hopeful future that will come after the turmoil and grief they will experience in exile. His prophetic vision includes three beautiful images.

In the first image, he expresses God's willingness to forgive and his desire to make things new: "I will give you a new heart, and a new spirit I will put within you. I will remove the heart of stone from your flesh and give you a heart of flesh" (Ezekiel 36:26). Consider the differences between the two: a heart of stone is inflexible and difficult to move. It is rigid and cannot be hurt. When a stone is struck hard, it will either crack and fall apart, or it will break the thing that hit it. A heart of flesh is living and breathing. Flesh is soft and sensitive to another's touch. It can be bruised somewhat easily, but it can also heal.

The second image is Ezekiel's vision of the dry bones coming to life (see Ezekiel 37:1–14). The Bible uses the words *breath*, *wind*, and *spirit* to describe what gives life to these dead bones, but in the original Hebrew, only one word was needed: *ruah*. Ruah is the wind that split the waters of the Red Sea for Moses and the Israelites (see Exodus 14:21), the breath that gave Adam life (see Genesis 2:7), and the spirit that allows Ezekiel to hear God's voice (see Ezekiel 2:2).

This vision of the dry bones is a powerful metaphor. It implies a future "resurrection" of the people in exile: "I will make you come up out of your graves, my people, and bring you back to the land of Israel" (Ezekiel 37:12), offering the exiles a hope of escaping their "death" in captivity and eventually returning home.

The third image is most important: the reestablishment of the Temple. Recall that for the people of Judah, the primary experience of God's presence is found in the Temple. However, Ezekiel sees God's presence leave the Temple before the Babylonians conquer Judah and destroy the city of Jerusalem and the Temple. Now, with the survivors living as slaves in Babylon,

"I will make you come up out of your graves, my people, and bring you back to the land of Israel" (Ezekiel 37:12).

UNIT 3

God expresses his forgiveness for their sins and tells Ezekiel, "I will no longer hide my face from them once I pour out my spirit upon the house of Israel" (Ezekiel 39:29). Ezekiel delivers this hopeful prophecy to the exiles: a new Temple will be built when they return from exile (see chapters 41–42), and God's presence will return once more to Jerusalem.

Ezekiel's second and third images also point to a significant event and a glorious vision found in the New Testament. First, the image of the bones coming to life prefigures Jesus' Resurrection from the dead. Second, the author of the Book of Revelation borrows some of Ezekiel's imagery of the New Jerusalem to describe Heaven itself (see Revelation 21:9-27). ✳

Ezekiel's vision of the bones coming to life prefigures Jesus' resurrection of the dead.

OVERVIEW of the Book of Ezekiel

- **Time period:** 593–573 BC.
- **Author:** Ezekiel and the scribes recorded Ezekiel's words and actions.
- **Audience:** The Jewish People shortly before, during, and slightly after the Babylonian Exile.
- **Themes:** Jerusalem will be destroyed because of the Israelites' sin. God's glory will be known to all the nations. God will restore the Israelites to their land, and the Temple will be rebuilt.

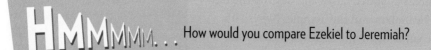

HMMMMM. . . How would you compare Ezekiel to Jeremiah?

Article 46

The Babylonian Exile: Far Away from Home

Far away from home, miserable, homesick. That is exactly what the people of Judah are experiencing. The Babylonian king, Nebuchadnezzar, and his army have conquered Jerusalem, destroyed the Temple, killed thousands of people, and taken most of the survivors back to Babylon as captives. This period of captivity, called the Babylonian Exile, lasts from about 587 to 539 BC. It is a dark and sad period of salvation history, but it also motivates the Israelites to reflect on their past and their relationship with God.

Held Captive

Recall King Josiah's discovery of the Book of the Law and his religious reforms that direct the people back to the covenant in the Second Book of Kings (see chapters 22–23). Josiah's reign ends in 609 BC and is followed by a few more bad kings. In 597 BC, the Babylonians first attack and conquer Jerusalem. They capture King Jehoiachin, his officers, the army and all the treasures of the

The fall of Jerusalem and the exile to Babylon mark the beginning of one of the darkest periods in Jewish history.

Temple. They take Jehoiachin and many Israelites back to Babylon and make King Jehoiachin's uncle, Zedekiah, the king.

A few years later, Zedekiah rebels against the Babylonians. His rebellion leads to the another Babylonian attack on Jerusalem, laying siege to the city. With their access to food cut off, the people within the walls of Jerusalem begin to starve. The Babylonians eventually capture the city, kill Zedekiah's children in front of him, and then poke out his eyes. After Nebuchadnezzar's army destroys the Temple, King Zedekiah and most of the rest of the people still in Judah are sent to Babylon in chains (see 2 Kings, chapters 24–25).

© North Wind Picture Archives / Alamy Stock Photo

UNIT 3

By the rivers of Babylon
there we sat weeping
when we remembered Zion.
On the poplars in its midst
we hung up our harps.
For there our captors asked us
for the words of a song;
Our tormentors, for joy:
"Sing for us a song of Zion!"
But how could we sing
    a song of the LORD
    in a foreign land?
              (Psalm 137:1–4)

"By the rivers of Babylon / there we sat weeping when we remembered Zion" (Psalm 137:1).

This psalm recalls the time of the Babylonian Exile when the people of Judah are mockingly asked to sing about their home, Zion (another name for Jerusalem). The sadness is painfully evident in this song, but their time in Babylon is not as bad as one might think. They are not slaves or held in prison camps; rather, they are free to make a living and settle down in their own homes. On the other hand, they are not allowed to return home and cannot perform any of their religious practices in public.

A Time to Reflect

Without being able to practice their faith in public, the exiled Israelites have to create a new religious identity that is not centered on sacrificial offerings and Temple worship. They focus on their oral tradition and the need to record it. It is at this point that the majority of the Old Testament is written.

Guided by the Holy Spirit, the Israelites begin to reflect on their past and see more clearly God at work in their history. Through their writings, God reveals that when they are faithful to the Covenant and the Law, he blesses them, but when they fail to be faithful, eventually there are negative consequences! The Deuteronomic history, which includes the Books of Deuteronomy through Second Kings (except for Ruth), reflects these truths in its explanation of why the kingdom failed and how God's people ended up in

UNIT 3

exile. Worshipping false gods, the unjust treatment of those in need, and the failure to follow the Law are listed as the prominent causes for their eventual downfall as a nation (see 2 Kings, chapter 17). As you read the Deuteronomic history, you will also see the emphasis on Israel and Judah's leaders, such as judges, prophets, and kings. Notice that the only important quality by which these leaders are judged is their faithfulness to God. These books reveal God as the Israelites' true leader and king, and whenever God's people fail to recognize his kingship and follow his Law, bad things happen.

The people in exile are also inspired to create new works, such as the Book of Lamentations. This book is a collection of highly emotional poems grieving the destruction of Jerusalem and the difficulties the people face in Babylon. Parts of this book graphically describe the starvation that resulted from the siege (see Lamentations 4:8–10), yet there are also glimmers of hope in their God whose mercy is unending (see 3:31–33). The end of the Book of Lamentations expresses the heartbreak of rejection the people feel, as well as a deep trust in God and hope for the future. "Bring us back to you, LORD, that we may return: / renew our days as of old. / For now, you have indeed rejected us / and utterly turned your wrath against us" (5:21–22).

UNIT 3

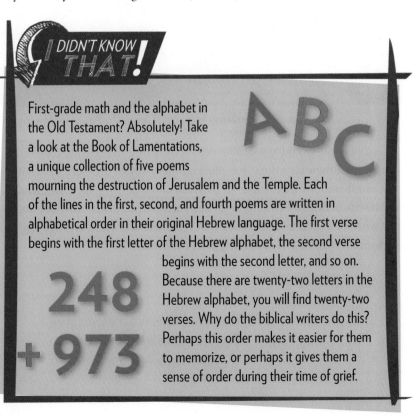

I DIDN'T KNOW THAT!

First-grade math and the alphabet in the Old Testament? Absolutely! Take a look at the Book of Lamentations, a unique collection of five poems mourning the destruction of Jerusalem and the Temple. Each of the lines in the first, second, and fourth poems are written in alphabetical order in their original Hebrew language. The first verse begins with the first letter of the Hebrew alphabet, the second verse begins with the second letter, and so on. Because there are twenty-two letters in the Hebrew alphabet, you will find twenty-two verses. Why do the biblical writers do this? Perhaps this order makes it easier for them to memorize, or perhaps it gives them a sense of order during their time of grief.

$$248$$
$$+973$$

ABC

A New Beginning Ahead

Endings are the birthplaces of beginnings. The end of junior high leads to the beginning of high school. Breaking up with a romantic interest can open the door to a new love. Life is full of endings and beginnings, but in the midst of an ending, it is hard to have an optimistic attitude toward the future. Overwhelmed by the sadness that comes with loss, it is hard to see how any good can come of our misery.

Endings, like a graduation from school, are the birthplace for new beginnings.

God's people would agree. The deaths of family and friends—as well as destruction of their city, their Temple, and their way of life—are devastating. God's people mourn their losses in Babylon and wonder what it all means. Jesus' disciples experience similar feelings after his Crucifixion. They are like sheep without a shepherd, unaware that Jesus will rise again in three days. Yet, even with these losses, God's saving plan continues. ✳

 How do the tragic circumstances of the Babylonian Exile bring about positive change for the people of Judah?

Article 47

Isaiah Parts 2 and 3: A Light in the Darkness

Steven sat on the floor of his bedroom bouncing the tennis ball off his wall over and over. His computer and phone privileges had been taken away due to his recent bad grades. His girlfriend had dumped him a few weeks before when she found out he'd gone on a date with someone else. Steven had made a mess of things. Bouncing the ball was the only way he could distract himself. His annoyed father walked in to tell him to stop it, but he could tell his son was stressed. As Steven's dad sat down on the floor next to him, Steven said he wanted to be left alone, but his dad did not budge.

His dad knew what was wrong. He told Steven a story about a girl he dated a couple of times when he was in college, but he also went out with someone else. When the first girl found out about it, she wanted nothing to do with him anymore. It was only then that he realized how much he really liked her, but it was too late. He was depressed and he ached for her. A year later, he had finally moved on. One day he went to a friend's party and she was there. They talked. He apologized. They talked some more. They started laughing, and then he told Steven, "The rest is history." Steven said: "Huh? What happened with the girl?" His dad answered, "She's your mom."

In the midst of great darkness, when things aren't going well, and you are sad, life can seem unbearable. It's during times like these that we need someone to be with us who can shine a little light of hope. Steven's father told a story that encouraged his son to trust and hope that things will work out. "For in hope we were saved" (Romans 8:24). Toward the end of the Babylonian Exile (587–539 BC), it is Second Isaiah who offers the light of hope to the captives who are far away from home.

When things aren't going well and we're sad, sometimes we just need someone to be with us to give us a little glimmer of hope.

UNIT 3

© CREATISTA / Stock.com

Isaiah Parts 2 and 3: Offering Comfort

The Book of Isaiah was most likely written over a period of two centuries. Chapters 1–39 were written in the eighth century by First Isaiah. Chapters 40–55 were written over a century later, when the anonymous author, Second Isaiah, along with most of the people of Judah, were held in captivity in Babylon. God commanded Second Isaiah, "Comfort, give comfort to my people, / says your God" (Isaiah 40:1). When things are going badly, simply knowing that there is a way out can be the only thing that will give you hope. Second Isaiah gives hope to the people of Judah by identifying two kinds of servants who would carry out God's will:

1. **The Suffering Servant.** This was the description of their ideal leader who, instead of being served like a king, was a servant to his people. This description can be found in what is now called "The Servant Songs." (See article 49 for more on Second Isaiah's prophecies of the Suffering Servant.)

2. **The King of Persia.** Someone who was not a member of their nation, nor even a descendant of Abraham, made for quite an unusual servant! "Thus says the LORD to his anointed, Cyrus, / whose right hand I grasp. . . . / I am the LORD, there is no other, / there is no God besides me. / It is I who arm you, / though you do not know me" (45:1,5). Led by King Cyrus, the Persians would conquer the Babylonians in 539 BC and allow the captive Israelites to return to Jerusalem and begin rebuilding.

© Joel Carillet / iStock.com

MAKE IT SO

In numerous places in the Bible, God commands us to help the alien, that is, the migrant, the immigrant, or the refugee. God orders the Israelites, "You shall love the alien as yourself; for you too were once aliens in the land of Egypt" (Leviticus 19:34). Refugees should have a special place in our hearts because they are forced from their home countries by war, poverty, natural disaster, or persecution. Jesus was once a refugee (see Matthew 2:13–23). In 2017 there were over 20 million refugees worldwide. You can help refugees by doing the following:

- donating to or fund-raising for Catholic Relief Services
- educating yourself (Go to *crs.org* to learn more.)
- using social media to spread the word and to educate others
- writing to your local politicians
- praying

Second Isaiah identifies Cyrus as an agent of God, even though Cyrus does not acknowledge the Lord as God. Why does God choose him? In numerous places, the Bible points out that the Holy Spirit "blows where it wills" (John 3:8) and that God's work can be accomplished through anyone, regardless of their religion, or even their past sinful life. Along with Ruth and Rahab, King Cyrus is another Gentile through whom God accomplishes his work of salvation.

Hope in Christ

The hope of Second Isaiah is echoed in the New Testament. John the Baptist points toward our Savior, Jesus Christ, for those held in the captivity of sin. In

Cyrus II, King of Persia, was known as Cyrus the Great. He ruled over the largest empire of his time. A brilliant military leader, he was even more revered for being a wise and tolerant ruler.

UNIT 3

fact, all four Gospel writers (see Matthew 3:3, Mark 1:3, Luke 3:4, and John 1:23) include John the Baptist's quotation of Second Isaiah's prophecy: "A voice proclaims: / In the wilderness prepare the way of the LORD! / Make straight in the wasteland a highway for our God!" (Isaiah 40:3).

Saint Paul teaches us to "rejoice in hope" (Romans 12:12). Even though we might be burdened with academic failures, drug addiction, family problems, depression, or whatever darkness fills our lives, we can have hope that with God's grace we can find fulfillment and happiness. Because of our faith in Jesus Christ, we have a reason to hope, and therefore a reason to rejoice. Because of his Resurrection, we know that there is light after darkness, forgiveness after sin, and life after death. That is why we too can rejoice! ✳

HMMMMM. . .

Isaiah speaks of a suffering servant in the Servant Songs. Why is it significant that the servant is suffering?

1. What are the differences between the kings of Israel and the kings of Judah?

2. Describe the reigns of King Hezekiah and King Josiah.

3. Explain the difference between the three Isaiahs.

4. What significance does First Isaiah's writings on Emmanuel have for Christians?

5. Describe two tactics Jeremiah uses to get the people's attention.

6. Describe two tactics Ezekiel uses to get the people's attention.

7. Describe and explain Ezekiel's vision of the dry bones.

8. How does the Babylonian Exile play a role in the development of the captives' faith?

9. What are the similarities between Second Isaiah and John the Baptist's messages?

KINGS AND PROPHETS
A Unique Relationship
The Last Kings and Prophets of Judah

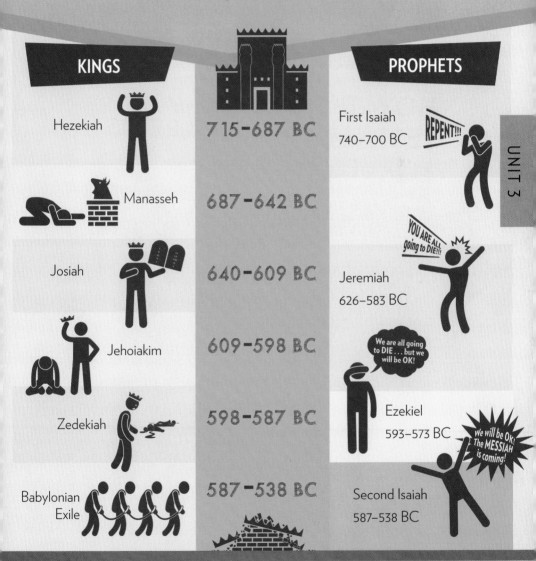

1. What does the infographic illustrate about the kings of Judah (the southern kingdom)?

2. How did the message of the prophets change emphasis as the historical situation of the Israelites changed?

UNIT 3

CHAPTER 11
The Messianic Prophecies

HOW DOES THE OLD TESTAMENT PREPARE US FOR JESUS?

SNAPSHOT

Article 48   Page 289
Old Testament, New Testament: Woven Together

Article 49   Page 292
Messianic Prophecies: Pointing toward the Light
- Pre-read: Isaiah 42:1–7, 49:1–6, 50:4–9, 52:13–53:12
- Pre-read: Matthew 2:1–3:3
- Pre-read: Luke 1:1–3:6

Article 50   Page 298
Psalms: Guided by Poetry
- Pre-read: Psalm 2, 22, 110, 118:19–25
- Pre-read: Wisdom 2:12–20

Article 51   Page 303
Previews: Moses, Joshua, David
- Pre-read: Matthew 5:17–48
- Pre-read: Exodus 20:1–17
- Pre-read: Leviticus 19:1–17, 24:17–22

Article 48

Old Testament, New Testament: Woven Together

One summer day, Max was bored, so he started looking through old family albums and found some black-and-white photos of his great-grandfather in his Army uniform. He asked his mother about them. She reminded Max that his grandfather was a soldier in World War II, in a division that had liberated the Buchenwald concentration camp in Germany in 1945. Max's mom said that the stories she had heard from her grandfather had a big impact on her life and this is why she volunteers at the local Holocaust museum. It's also why she read Max all those Jewish folktales that he loved so much when he was younger.

Max felt a strong sense of pride, as well as a deeper connection to his family's history. He realized how one significant event in his great-grandfather's life had impacted his life and his mom's life, forming both of them into the people they are today. Max understood how the past and the present are woven together and cannot be separated.

Understanding our past and learning about our ancestors can shed light on who we are.

UNIT 3

© zmenow / iStock.com   © Everett Historical / Shutterstock.com   © marlenka / iStock.com

TAKE IT TO GOD

Dear God, weaver of past, present, and future,

Thank you for everything that allowed me to be here today:

My parents, grandparents, great-grandparents, and all the
countless ancestors upon whom my very existence depends;

The friends, family, acquaintances, and random strangers who
have helped me—some in ways that I will never know.

Let all that has been given to me by the people of my past and
present be an inspiration to extend your blessings to others.

Amen!

Two Testaments, One Bible

This interweaving of past and present is also part of our faith life. Understanding our religious past and our spiritual ancestors helps shed light on who we are now. This is why the Old Testament is an integral part of the Christian Bible. It is never to be discarded or ignored just because, as Christians, we have a New Testament. All salvation history recorded in the Old Testament still has—and will always have—inherent value and importance.

Christians read the Old Testament in light of Christ's death and Resurrection. Think of it this way: if you've ever watched a movie or read a novel a second time, you know that you are better able to see how people and events introduced early in the story provided hints about the final outcome. That's kind of what it's like when we read the Old Testament—we can see how certain types of people and events point toward what happens in the New Testament. The study of how God's work in the Old Testament points to what he later accomplished through Jesus Christ in the New Testament is called **typology**. Typology illuminates the unity of God's plan in the two testaments but does not devalue the Old Covenant or its ongoing relevance and value for the Jewish people. For example, because Moses helped free the Israelites from slavery, he is an Old Testament person who points toward Jesus' saving acts that free us from sin.

---

typology ➤ The discernment of God's work in the Old Testament as a prefiguration of what he accomplished through Jesus Christ in the fullness of time. Typology illuminates the unity of God's plan in the two Testaments but does not devalue the Old Covenant or its ongoing relevance and value for the Jewish people.

Reading and studying the Old Testament can help us see how certain people and events point toward what happens in the New Testament.

UNIT 3

We need the Old Testament so that we can understand the life and mission of Jesus Christ. The New Covenant is founded upon the Old, and the Old Covenant prepares the way to the New. Both the Old and New Testaments are therefore vital to help us see the big picture of God's gift of grace and redemption. The Church reminds us of the unity of the Old and New Testaments: "The New Testament lies hidden in the Old and the Old Testament is unveiled in the New"[1] (*Catechism of the Catholic Church [CCC]*, number 129). For this reason, Christians understand that "the Old Testament prepares for the New and the New Testament fulfills the Old; the two shed light on each other; both are true Word of God" (number 140). ✳

HMMMMM. . .

Give two examples that show how the Old Testament and New Testament are interwoven.

Article 49

Messianic Prophecies: Pointing toward the Light

In the late 1970s, El Salvador was a country on the verge of a civil war. Salvadorans were suffering from human rights abuse and violence at the hands of their own government. Óscar Romero (1917–1980), the Archbishop of El Salvador, called his country's leaders out and demanded an end to their oppression. On the radio, he would often list the names of those who were tortured, murdered, or who had disappeared. He would demand that El Salvador's leaders practice justice and be faithful to God. "Either we serve the life of Salvadorans or we are accomplices in their death. And here is what is most fundamental about the faith given expression in history: either we believe in a God of life or we serve the idols of death." In March of 1980, just a few weeks after saying these words, Romero was murdered by a gunman while saying Mass. Saint Óscar Romero was canonized in 2018.

Romero followed in the footsteps of the prophets of the Old Testament. They called people to be faithful to the ideals of God's covenant. They demanded that people practice justice and be faithful to God. They not only preached it but lived it as well. To give people hope, the Old Testament prophets sometimes point toward the future when a messiah would arrive and bring

Like the prophets of the Old Testament, Saint Óscar Romero called his country's leaders out and demanded an end to their oppression.

about the peace and justice they sought. *Messiah* is a Hebrew word meaning "anointed one." The Greek equivalent of this Hebrew word is *christos*, from which we get Jesus' title, "Christ." Throughout the Old Testament, there were many anointed ones. Kings, prophets, and priests were all anointed to begin their ministries. These messiahs (lowercase *m*) give glimpses into the character of the one true Messiah (capital *M*) to come: Jesus Christ.

The city of Bethlehem today. The prophet Micah points to Bethlehem as the place of King David's birth, and the expectation that the Messiah is to be from the family of David.

Messianic prophecies are the visionary descriptions spoken by some of the prophets in the Old Testament, which point to the coming of the ideal Messiah, Jesus Christ. These prophecies expressed comfort to those in darkness and despair, people who longed for peace and justice to reign again. Sometimes the messianic prophecies fit Jesus so well it's almost like peeking through a portal to the time of Jesus Christ. The messianic prophecies were inspired by the Holy Spirit, allowing the prophets to describe the type of person the Messiah would be. The messianic prophecies are almost like a job description, outlining the life and mission of Jesus Christ.

Messiah ➤ Hebrew word for "anointed one." The equivalent Greek term is *christos*. We call Jesus the Christ and the Messiah because he is the Anointed One who brings salvation through his life, death, and Resurrection.

messianic prophecy ➤ A message communicated on behalf of God by his messengers, that points toward the coming of the Savior, Jesus Christ. These were often expressed as words of hope and comfort to those living in times of darkness and despair.

UNIT 3

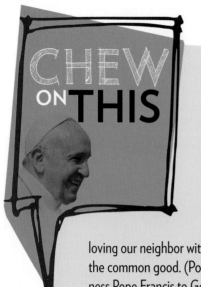

And so, we are not called to serve merely in order to receive a reward, but rather to imitate God, who made himself a servant for our love. Nor are we called to serve only now and again, but to live in serving. Service is thus a way of life; indeed it recapitulates the entire Christian way of life: serving God in adoration and prayer; being open and available; loving our neighbor with practical deeds; passionately working for the common good. (Pope Francis, "Apostolic Journey of His Holiness Pope Francis to Georgia and Azerbaijan," October 2, 2016)

God with Us

Many of the messianic prophecies focus on the family tree and the birth of the Messiah. The prophet Micah reminds his readers of King David's birthplace, Bethlehem, and the expectation of the Messiah to be from the family of David (see Micah 5:1). Jeremiah's prophecy echoes a similar image: "I will raise up a righteous branch for David; / As king he shall reign and govern wisely" (Jeremiah 23:5).

First Isaiah points to the birth of Emmanuel, a name meaning "God with us" (see Isaiah 7:14). He later adds, "For a child is born to us, a son is given to us; / upon his shoulder dominion rests. / They name him Wonder-Counselor, God-Hero, / Father-Forever, Prince of Peace" (9:5). Second Isaiah implies that the Messiah will have someone to blaze the trail before he arrives: "A voice proclaims: / In the wilderness prepare the way of the Lord!" (40:3). The prophet Malachi does the same (see Malachi 3:1). Third Isaiah joins in with a prophecy about people "bearing gold and frankincense, / and heralding the praises of the Lord" (60:6).

The Gospel writers were among the first to understand these messianic prophecies and how they were fulfilled in Jesus. The Gospels of Matthew and Luke outline Jesus' family tree and have stories about his birth, showing the connections to the messianic prophecies. They quote the Old Testament prophets, and the author of Matthew even says, "Thus it has been written through the prophet" (Matthew 2:5). Here is a chart showing some Old Testament prophecies and how they were fulfilled in Jesus.

PROPHETIC IMAGES OF THE MESSIAH		
Prophecy	Old Testament	New Testament
The Son of Man	The son of man, the Bar Nasa, came on the clouds of heaven, was ministered to by heavenly beings, and was given by God an everlasting kingdom (Daniel 7:9–28).	Jesus used the divine title "Son of Man" to refer to himself and his Passion (see Matthew 8:20, 12:34; Luke 9:58, 18:8; John 8:28, 9:31–32); was fully human (Luke 7:34); came from heaven (John 3:13) to save the lost (Luke 19:10); was honored as Lord (Acts 2:36); was ministered to and honored by angels (Luke 24:23, John 20:12); returned to the heavens (Acts 1:10–11); and will return to earth amid wondrous signs (Matthew 24:27–31,37,39,44; Mark 14:62; Luke 7:19–22, 12:40; John 6:62).
Miracle Worker	On the day of the Lord, the blind will see, the deaf will hear, the mute will sing, and the lame will leap (Isaiah 29:18, 35:5–6).	Jesus heals the deaf and the mute (Mark 7:31–37), the blind (Matthew 20:29–34; Mark 8:22–26, 9:32; John 9:1–41), and the lame (John 5:1–9).
Savior King of the Jews	The savior king enters Jerusalem on a donkey (Zechariah 9:9).	Jesus enters Jerusalem on a donkey amid palms and chants (Matthew 21:5–11, John 12:12–16).
Thirty Pieces of Silver	A shepherd whose service was valued at thirty pieces of silver, which were thrown into the treasury of the Temple (Zechariah 11:12–13).	Judas betrayed Jesus for thirty pieces of silver, which he later threw into the treasury (Matthew 27:3–10).

UNIT 3

MAKE IT SO

Run for student council? Me? Sure, why not? But it isn't necessary to be a servant leader. To be a servant leader like Jesus, you do not have to be an officially recognized head of some group. You just have to lead *by serving*. This kind of leadership does not require popularity, public speaking skills, or a magnetic personality. It requires a faithful heart, care for others, and your time and effort. Being a servant leader means stocking food on the shelves at your local food bank, tutoring fellow students needing academic help, or visiting a friend in the hospital. By serving those in need, you are setting an example for others and leading them toward Christian discipleship.

The Suffering Servant

The work of Second Isaiah (see chapters 40–55) contains the most notable Old Testament writings that point to Jesus. Composed during, or just after, the Babylonian Exile, Second Isaiah addresses a community in need of comfort and hope. In four passages called "The Servant Songs" (see 42:1–7, 49:1–6, 50:4–9, 52:13–53:12), the prophet offers ideal descriptions of someone who models **servant leadership**—a type of leadership based on humble service to all God's people:

> Yet it was our pain that he bore,
> our sufferings he endured.
> We thought of him as stricken,
> struck down by God and afflicted,
> But he was pierced for our sins,
> crushed for our iniquity.
> He bore the punishment that makes us whole,
> by his wounds we were healed.
> We had all gone astray like sheep,
> all following our own way;
> But the LORD laid upon him
> the guilt of us all.
>
> (53:4–6)

---

servant leadership ➤ A type of leadership based on humble service to all God's people.

The early Christians see the obvious connections between Jesus and Second Isaiah's "Suffering Servant." Isaiah is quoted in the New Testament sixty-eight times, more than any other prophet, and ten of these quotations are from the Servant Songs. The final Servant Song illuminates the meaning of Jesus' Passion and death. It describes a servant who is "seized and condemned . . . though he had done no wrong" (Isaiah 53:8–9). This description of the ideal servant leader is fulfilled by Jesus Christ, who "was pierced for our sins," but "by his wounds we were healed" (53:5). ✳

Tutoring a student in need of academic assistance is an excellent example of what it means to be a servant leader.

HMMMMM. . . How are some of the messianic prophecies like a job description?

UNIT 3

Article 50

Psalms: Guided by Poetry

Adrian listened to music whenever he could, whether it was in the hallway between classes with his headphones on or after school in his car with his tunes blaring out the window. He loved all kinds of music. He appreciated the poetry of rap, the energy of speed metal, the freeform soloing in jazz, and just the fun found in a lot of pop music. For Adrian, music expressed what words alone could not say. His favorite songs were the ones that guided him and gave him a direction in life. In those songs, Adrian found common experiences with the songwriters, which gave him hope and inspired him to be a better person.

The Book of Psalms is part of the wisdom books section of the Bible. The Psalms are songs used for group and personal prayer. Many were originally sung during Israelite worship. Christians and Jews still sing them today. Like some music today, the symbolic language used in the Psalms is intended to inspire and connect with one's heart on a deeper level. In them, we can also find poetic hints of the coming Messiah. The Book of Psalms is quoted in the New Testament more than any other Old Testament book. It is obvious that the early Christians were guided by its heartfelt poetry, which offered insight into their understanding of Jesus Christ.

Almost all of the presidents of the United States have taken their oath of office with their hand placed on a Bible. Some have even opened the Bible to a particular verse that is their favorite. Presidents have placed their hand on passages from the Book of Psalms more than any other book in the Bible.

President-elect Woodrow Wilson (center right) takes the oath of office, March 5, 1913.

UNIT 3

The King

Despite living with the Gospel message for over two thousand years, some of us are still stuck on the idea that God will reward us if we are good. Put another way, we sometimes assume that when life is difficult and painful, God is punishing us for our sins, despite the fact that Jesus said the exact opposite (see John 9:1–3, Mark 8:34–35, Matthew 16:21–23). The prophetic wisdom of the Psalms reassures us that our suffering can be the path to holiness. It also reveals that suffering and rejection were the path of the coming Messiah, Jesus Christ.

Some psalms foreshadow the coming of the Messiah. These prophetic portrayals of the Christ sometimes describe a king who will be glorified but first will be rejected (see Psalm 2:1–2). Psalm 2 was used for the coronations of kings, and it refers to the Lord's "anointed one," or Messiah, as God's Son (verse 7). The early Christians saw this psalm as a messianic prophecy pointing toward Christ: "We ourselves are proclaiming this good news to you that what God promised our ancestors he has brought to fulfillment for us, [their] children, by raising up Jesus, as it is written in the second psalm, 'You are my son; this day I have begotten you'" (Acts 13:32–33).

The early Christians saw Psalm 2 as a messianic prophecy pointing toward Jesus Christ, "the anointed one." In Mark's Gospel, an unnamed woman anoints Jesus.

Psalm 110 also addresses a royal coronation, but the king is initiated as a priest "in the manner of Melchizedek" (verse 4). Melchizedek was the ancient king of Salem (Jerusalem), who also performed the priestly duty of blessing Abraham (see Genesis 14:18–20). The name Melchizedek means "king of righteousness," and Salem means "peace." The early Christians read this psalm and understood that this union of priest and righteous king of peace could only point to Jesus Christ. The Book of Hebrews refers to Jesus Christ as the high priest whose sacrifice atoned for the sins of "all when he offered himself" (7:27).

UNIT 3

Rejected and Suffering

"Oh, how foolish you are! How slow of heart to believe all that the prophets spoke! Was it not necessary that the Messiah should suffer these things and enter into his glory?" (Luke 24:25–26). Jesus does not make it any clearer than this. Though most kings are lifted up and honored, the Book of Psalms describes a Messiah who will suffer and be rejected.

Psalm 118 is a good example of this: "The stone the builders rejected / has become the cornerstone" (verse 22). A cornerstone refers to the first stone laid in the construction of a building or house. It is the most important one because all of the other stones are set in relation to that one. Great care was taken in choosing one. Jesus quotes this psalm when he tells a story symbolizing how he will be put to death (see Matthew 21:33–46). Psalm 118 prophesies that the most important foundation of our faith, Jesus, our cornerstone and Messiah, will first be rejected.

The cornerstone is critical in constructing a building. Jesus, the foundation on which our faith sits, compares himself to a rejected cornerstone when he quotes Psalm 118.

UNIT 3

Jesus is not like any other king. The crown he wears is a crown of thorns. Psalm 22 describes the pain the Messiah will suffer. Jesus even quotes this psalm while he is dying on the cross: "My God, my God, why have you abandoned me?" (Psalm 22:2, Mark 15:34). For the Israelites, reciting the first line of a psalm is an easy way of referencing its entirety. It is kind of like someone saying, "Four score and seven years ago." That one phrase can help recall the greater meaning of Abraham Lincoln's Gettysburg Address. The same goes for Jesus' recitation of that one verse on the cross. At first glance, it might seem like Jesus' moment of doubt. But for us to fully and correctly grasp the meaning of that one line, we have to read the entire psalm.

Psalm 22 is the prayer of an innocent person who feels abandoned by God, as he is despised and mocked by others (see verses 7–8). His hands and feet have been pierced and the "evildoers" are casting lots (gambling) for his garments (see verses 17–19). Yet despite his feeling of abandonment, his faith in God does not waver. "But you, Lord, do not stay far off; /my strength, come quickly to help me. / Deliver my soul from the sword" (verses 20–21). The next eleven verses echo this confidence in God. Rather than a sign of doubt, Jesus' quotation of the first line of Psalm 22 actually points to his ultimate trust in God despite his present suffering.

A Murderous Plot

The messianic prophecy in the Book of Wisdom (see 2:12–20) takes an interesting twist. It is told from the perspective of the "evildoers" responsible for the Messiah's death. It begins, "Let us lie in wait for the righteous one" (verse 12) and then lists the reasons they despise him. They find this messianic figure annoying because he criticizes their behavior (see verses 12, 16), and he is different from them (see verse 15). They plot to kill this "son of God" (verse 18) and find out how gentle and patient he really is. Though there are no cited references to this passage in the New Testament, its obvious connections to Jesus' Passion and death clearly mark it as a messianic prophecy.

Like the accounts of the kings and the prophets, the wisdom books of the Old Testament point toward the coming of Jesus Christ. The images of the king, high priest, and the suffering Messiah prefigure the saving work of the Son of God. The Psalms reflect the hope for a savior that is ultimately fulfilled in Jesus Christ. ✳

OVERVIEW of the Book of Psalms

- **Author:** Attributed to King David, but there were actually many authors, sometimes called psalmists.
- **Audience:** The Jewish People during or shortly after the Babylonian Exile.
- **Content:** A collection of hymns, or songs of prayer.
- **Themes:** A wide variety, including praise, thanksgiving, lament, and petition.

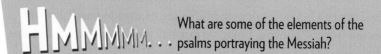

HMMMMM. . . What are some of the elements of the psalms portraying the Messiah?

Article 51
Previews: Moses, Joshua, David

On the inside jacket of a novel, or sometimes on its back cover, we find a brief synopsis of the story, giving us a hint of its plot. We are introduced to the characters in the book and the situation or crisis they are involved in. All of these build excitement and expectations, and a desire to read the story to find out what happens.

The journey through salvation history is kind of like that. Numerous people in the Old Testament give us a preview of what is to come in the New Testament. In different ways, these people embody some aspect of Jesus Christ, be it through the events that shaped their lives, their personal character traits, or their God-given mission. Notable Old Testament figures who accomplished this are Moses, Joshua, and King David.

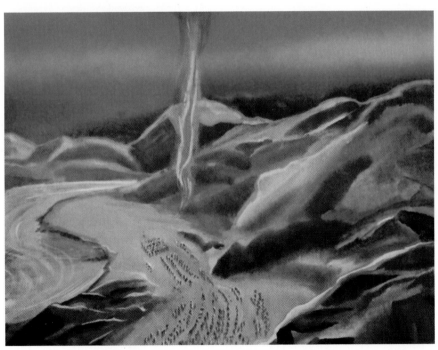

Moses's celebration of the Passover and the Israelites' escape from Egypt enables the Israelites' freedom from the bondage of slavery and prefigures Jesus' saving actions.

UNIT 3

Savior and Lawgiver

The four Gospels are directed to specific groups of people and address issues
that are important to their respective audiences. Matthew's audience is primarily Jewish Christians who want to understand better how Jesus fits into their
history and faith. Right from the start of the Gospel, the author of Matthew
addresses that concern. The account of Jesus' birth makes the connection between Jesus and Moses very clear for those familiar with Moses's story.

SIMILARITIES BETWEEN BIRTHS AND CHILDHOODS OF MOSES AND JESUS	
Moses	**Jesus**
Pharaoh fears losing his power (Exodus 1:7–10).	King Herod fears losing his power (Matthew 2:1–3).
Pharaoh orders the death of newborn boys (1:16).	King Herod orders the deaths of all boys under two years old (Matthew 2:16).
Moses is hidden from Pharaoh to save his life (2:2–4).	Jesus is hidden from King Herod to save his life (Matthew 2:13–15).
Moses leaves Egypt to preserve his life (2:15).	Jesus leaves Israel (to Egypt) to preserve his life (Matthew 2:13–15).
Moses and the Israelites come out of Egypt (chapter 14).	Jesus and his family come out of Egypt (2:13–21).
Long period of silence between childhood to adulthood.	Long period of silence between childhood to adulthood.

UNIT 3

Matthew's infancy narrative is just the beginning. Throughout the Gospel, the author of Matthew offers his Jewish audience a portrayal of Jesus as the New Moses. He highlights all the ways in which Moses prefigures Jesus, including his position as mediator between God and humanity, as well as his role as lawgiver and guide. For example, just as Moses delivers God's Law from Mount Sinai, Jesus delivers the New Law in the Sermon on the Mount (see Matthew 5:1). Just as Moses goes up Mount Sinai to meet God, Jesus goes to the mountaintop to meet his Father in prayer (see 14:23).

Moses's celebration of the Passover and the Israelites' escape from Egypt is another prefiguring of Jesus. Moses enables the Israelites' freedom from the bondage of slavery, and so prefigures Jesus' saving activities. Jesus' celebration of the Last Supper, a Passover meal, leads into his Passion, death, and Resurrection, which frees us from the bondage of sin.

© Adam Jan Figel / Shutterstock.com

Jesus' celebration of the Last Supper, a Passover meal, leads into his Passion, death, and Resurrection, which frees us from the bondage of sin.

A Guide for the Journey

Jesus is the Greek form of the Hebrew name Yeshua, or as we say it, Joshua. The name means "God saves." It should be no surprise then, that Joshua—the successor to Moses—also prefigures Jesus Christ. Both Joshua and Jesus are "filled with the spirit" (Deuteronomy 34:9, Luke 4:1). Joshua's leadership of the Twelve Tribes points toward Jesus' guidance of the Twelve Apostles. Joshua chooses twelve men to carry the Ark of the Covenant (the presence of God) across the Jordan River (see Joshua 3:12), while "Jesus sent out these twelve" to carry God's message as they preach and heal others (Matthew 10:5).

UNIT 3

When Moses is talking with God about who will act as his successor, he asks that the Israelites will "not be like sheep without a shepherd" (Numbers 27:17). God replies by offering Joshua to shepherd the Israelites, which prefigures Jesus' shepherding of God's people. "When [Jesus] disembarked and saw the vast crowd, his heart was moved with pity for them, for they were like sheep without a shepherd" (Mark 6:34). Though Moses sets the stage and prepares the people, it is actually Joshua who finally leads the Israelites into the Promised Land (see Joshua 3:14–17). This is a wonderful and significant event on its own terms, but it also hints at our own salvation and Christ's role as our Savior. Moses and the prophets have prepared for the Messiah, but it is Jesus who finally offers us salvation and entry into our heavenly Promised Land (see Hebrews 9:24).

CATHOLICS **MAKING** A DIFFERENCE

The Poor Man of the Forty Hours' Devotion. The Beggar of Rome. That's what people called Saint Benedict Joseph Labre (1748–1783), a quirky man and at first appearances, a most unlikely saint. Benedict was born in France. At the age of sixteen, after a failed attempt at becoming a priest, he settled on a life of poverty and pilgrimage, walking hundreds of miles to many Christian shrines in Europe. He wore rags, slept outdoors, begged for food, and shared what little he had with the poor. He was filled with love for God, for every person he met, and he had a special devotion to Mary and to the Eucharist. Unfortunately, his suffering and self-denial took a toll on his body. On the last day of his life, he collapsed on the steps of a church, was carried to a nearby house, and died. Within three months after his death, there were 136 certified, miraculous cures attributed to his intercession! Saint Benedict Joseph Labre was a familiar and well-liked figure in Rome and is the patron saint of the homeless.

Head Honcho

El numero uno. The top dog. The head honcho. Being king or queen is a powerful position that carries great responsibility in caring for God's people. King David's rule of Israel offers a hint as to Jesus' own leadership as the Messiah. Though he certainly was not perfect, David was faithful to God. His leadership of Israel gives a taste of what the Kingdom of God will be like with Jesus as king.

When we first meet David in the First Book of Samuel, he is a mere boy tending to his sheep (see 16:11), long before he shepherds the entire flock of Israel. Jesus is also a good shepherd who would lay "down his life for the sheep" (John 10:11). David's battle against the Philistine giant Goliath (see 1 Samuel 17:41–51) hints at the confrontations Jesus will face against the Temple leadership and the Roman authorities (see Matthew 26:57–27:26). David's trust in God prefigures Jesus' trust in his Father's will (see 26:39).

The kingdom that David governs includes land and a specific group of people, the Israelites. They are united by their faith and willingness to follow God. This is a wonderful moment in Israelite history, but it is just a small sign of the Messiah's Kingdom. The Kingdom of God is not a place at all, nor is Jesus' role as king an earthly authority. When the Roman governor asks Jesus if he is a king, Jesus responds, "My kingdom does not belong to this world" (John 18:36). Jesus' role as king is different because rather than being served, he is a servant to others (see 13:12–15). And he does not serve just one group of people; Jesus is the Servant King for *all* people, "a light" (Luke 2:32) for every race and every nation, in every time and place. Further, in his Kingdom there is a special concern for all the oppressed and the vulnerable (see 6:20–23; 9:11,46–48). ✳

UNIT 3

HMMMMM. . . . How can imperfect people like Moses and David prefigure Jesus Christ, the Son of God and Savior of the world?

1. If Jesus most fully reveals God, then why do we still need the Old Testament?

2. What are messianic prophecies?

3. What are the similarities between Second Isaiah's description of the "Suffering Servant" and Jesus?

4. In what ways do the Psalms point to the coming of Jesus as the Messiah?

5. Describe the messianic prophecy found in the Book of Wisdom.

6. How does Matthew's infancy narrative show that Moses prefigures Jesus?

7. How does Joshua prefigure Jesus?

© Krzysztof Slusarczyk / Shutterstock.com

UNIT 3

ISAIAH: PROPHET EXTRAORDINAIRE

This famous sculpture of the prophet Isaiah is found in Rome in a public square.

1. What moment in Isaiah's life has the sculptor captured?

2. What do you think Isaiah is looking at?

UNIT 3 HIGHLIGHTS

CHAPTER 9 The Kings and Prophets
of the Northern Kingdom

After Solomon's Death, Israel Splits into Two Kingdoms and the Prophets Attempt Rescue

Israel

- Northern kingdom
- King Jeroboam leads ten of Israel's tribes.
- Samaria is its capital.

Judah

- Southern kingdom
- King Rehoboam leads remaining two tribes.
- Jerusalem is its capital.

Israel: The Northern Kingdom

- Prophets of Israel (northern kingdom) rise up.
- Elijah, Elisha, Hosea, Amos, Jonah
- Prophets warn Israelites to turn back to God or face impending doom.

- Northern kingdom refuses to listen to prophets and is conquered by Assyria in 721 BC.

Prophets of the Northern Kingdom

Elijah	Elisha	Hosea	Amos	Jonah
• Chastises King Ahab about worshipping the false gods Baal and Asherah • Wipes out the prophets of Baal and Asherah • Is taken up to Heaven in a fiery chariot • Prefigures John the Baptist	• Succeeds Elijah's prophetic leadership • Prefigures Jesus • Brings a young man back to life • Cures a man of leprosy • Feeds a hundred men with twenty barley loaves	• Committed to God • Committed to his prostitute wife, Gomer • Uses his marriage to Gomer as a metaphor to describe God's relationship with Israel	• An outsider from Judah who preaches in Israel • Condemns the Israelites for their treatment of the *anawim* • Chastises the Israelites for their religious hypocrisy	• Runs from God's call to preach to the Ninevites • Ends up in belly of fish and resigns to preach • Is perplexed when God accepts the Ninevites' repentance • Reminds us to accept all as God's children

CHAPTER 10 The Kings and Prophets of the Southern Kingdom

Judah: The Southern Kingdom

- Judah has mostly bad kings.
- These kings allow the worship of false gods and mistreat the poor and oppressed.

- Prophets rise up, warning people to turn back to God.
- Key prophets: First Isaiah, Jeremiah, Ezekiel

- Hezekiah and Josiah are good kings who make reforms.
- Their reforms do not take hold, however.

- Babylonians sack Jerusalem, destroy the Temple, and conquer Judah (BC 587).

- Babylonians take people of Judah as captives back to Babylon.
- Israelites remain in Exile for about fifty years.

- During the Exile, Israelites reflect on their history and religious life.
- Majority of the Old Testament is written during this period.

Prophets of the Southern Kingdom

First Isaiah	Jeremiah	Ezekiel	Second and Third Isaiah
• Prophet to good King Hezekiah • Prophesies that Judah will not be defeated by Assyria. • After Hezekiah, bad kings follow and Judah falls into sin. • Prophesies Babylonian invasion	• Called by God at a young age • Points out Judah's many sins • Uses dramatic tactics to foretell Babylonian invasion	• Receives God's call in an elaborate vision • Uses a number of symbolic acts to prophesy • Gives the people visions of a hopeful future	• Comforts people of Judah during Babylonian Exile • Describes an ideal leader, the Suffering Servant • The hope of Isaiah's Suffering Servant points to Jesus.

CHAPTER 11   The Messianic Prophecies

Messianic Prophecies

"I will raise up a righteous branch for David; / As king he shall reign and govern wisely."
(Jeremiah 23:5)

"The young woman, pregnant and about to bear a son, shall name him Emmanuel."
(Isaiah 7:14)

"Yet it was our pain that he bore, / our sufferings he endured."
(Isaiah 53:4)

"But he was pierced for our sins. . . . / He bore the punishment that makes us whole / by his wounds we were healed."
(Isaiah 53:5)

"The stone the builders rejected / has become the cornerstone."
(Psalm 118:22)

Jesus Previews: Moses, Joshua, and David Prefigure Jesus

Moses

- Moses enables the Israelites' freedom from slavery; Jesus frees us from sin.
- Moses delivers the Old Law (Ten Commandments); Jesus delivers the New Law (Sermon on the Mount).

Joshua

- Joshua leads the Twelve Tribes; Jesus leads the Twelve Apostles.
- *Joshua* is the Hebrew form of *Jesus* (Greek).

David

- David starts as a shepherd as a boy and later shepherds Israel as a king; Jesus is the Good Shepherd for all people.
- David confronts Goliath; Jesus confronts Temple and Roman authorities.
- David and Jesus are both powerful leaders and lovers of God.

UNIT 3
BRING IT HOME

WHY DO THE KINGS AND PROPHETS MATTER?

FOCUS QUESTIONS

CHAPTER 9   How did the kings and prophets get along?

CHAPTER 10   How does God react when we screw up?

CHAPTER 11   How does the Old Testament prepare us for Jesus?

CASEY
Mater Dei High School

After reading about the Kings and prophets, I realized how important they really were. I always thought prophets were found only in the Bible. Now I realize that there are prophets even today. The Kings I can relate to the most. I often think that everyone in the Bible is perfect. But now I know that even the great Kings strayed from God's path. I am human, I make mistakes, and God still loves me no matter what, just like he did the Kings.

UNIT 3

REFLECT

Take some time to read and reflect on the unit and chapter focus questions listed on the facing page.

- What question or section did you identify most closely with?

- What did you find within the unit that was comforting or challenging?

UNIT 4
God Revealed through
Holy People and Worship

HOW DO
CHALLENGING
TIMES DEEPEN
OUR FAITH?

LOOKING AHEAD

CHAPTER 12 Page 318

Rebuilding Jerusalem and the Temple

CHAPTER 13 Page 340

Ordinary People Give Extraordinary Witness

CHAPTER 14 Page 364

The Wisdom Books

UNIT 4

When times get hard, I tend to ask myself, Why? Then, I think about the grand scheme of things: if today is really hard, tomorrow can't get any worse, and if I fail the test today, I can make it up with the next quiz. My faith is sort of a pulley system that digs deep and pulls up at the same time, using the good times and the hard times for support.

IFE
Mater Dei High School

CHAPTER 12
Rebuilding Jerusalem and the Temple

WHY WAS REBUILDING THE TEMPLE SO IMPORTANT?

SNAPSHOT

Article 52   Page 319
Leaving Babylon, Going Home

Article 53   Page 323
The Temple: Worship Central
- Pre-read: 1 Kings, chapters 6–7
- Pre-read: 1 Chronicles, chapter 22
- Pre-read: 2 Chronicles, chapters 3–4

Article 54   Page 327
Rebuilding Jerusalem
- Pre-read: Ezra 1:1–4, 3:1–4:5, chapters 9–10
- Pre-read: Nehemiah, chapters 1–2 and 5–6

Article 55   Page 332
Psalms: Songs for Every Occasion
- Pre-read: Psalms 23 and 42

Article 52
Leaving Babylon, Going Home

Right before her freshman year of high school, Damaris's family had to pack up and move. Her mom had been promoted, and her new job was in another state. During winter break, Damaris's mom let her fly back home to visit her friends. Even though she had only been gone a few months, things had changed a lot. People who used to be close with one another were not anymore. Many had new friends whom Damaris had never met. Some had become involved in activities she would have never guessed. When Damaris returned from her trip, she told her mom that she had a great time and was glad she went, but then she added, "Home had never felt so unfamiliar to me before."

After almost fifty years of exile in Babylon, most of the Israelites—now called **Jews**— returned home to Jerusalem. But most of them were born and raised in Babylon. Jerusalem felt foreign to them, despite the fact that it was the home of their ancestors. For those who could remember the days before the Exile, Jerusalem looked and felt very different. In many ways it was still a city in ruins. They had a lot of work ahead of them to make the beloved city their home again.

Have you ever gone back to the city you used to live in, or back to your former neighborhood, or even back to your old grade school? What seemed different to you?

UNIT 4

Jews ▶ The term used to refer to all of the physical and spiritual descendants of Jacob (Israel) as well as to the patriarchs Abraham and Isaac and their wives. Originally referred specifically to the members of the tribe of Judah.

UNIT 4

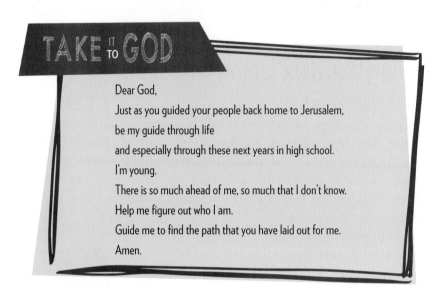

TAKE IT TO GOD

Dear God,

Just as you guided your people back home to Jerusalem,

be my guide through life

and especially through these next years in high school.

I'm young.

There is so much ahead of me, so much that I don't know.

Help me figure out who I am.

Guide me to find the path that you have laid out for me.

Amen.

Crisis Is Fertilizer for Humans

When people face crisis moments, they begin to question who they are and what they believe. When married couples have difficulties, they might question their relationship with each other and their role in the family. When the United States was attacked on 9-11, some questioned our country's policies on citizenship and border protection.

Growth often requires struggle, and struggle does not arrive until there is a crisis. In that regard, crises often act like fertilizer for human beings. These difficult moments are turning points that spur renewal and growth. Married couples who work through their troubles become stronger and closer. The Babylonian Exile is the crisis that triggered the Jewish People to examine their history and their relationship with God. This in turn brought about new writings and the formation of most of the Old Testament.

The Diaspora: An Unexpected Turn

The Lord said: "I say of Cyrus, My shepherd! / He carries out my every wish, / Saying of Jerusalem, 'Let it be rebuilt,' / and of the temple, 'Lay its foundations'" (Isaiah 44:28). Second Isaiah calls the Emperor Cyrus God's anointed one (see 45:1) because he freed the Israelite captives and allowed them to return to Jerusalem and rebuild. Cyrus is an unexpected savior because he is not Jewish, and because he is the king of another country: Persia. After Persia conquers the Babylonians in 537 BC and allows the Jewish People to return home, they see the hand of God guiding Cyrus.

After the Exile, most of the remaining Israelites live in the southern king-dom of Judah, so they become known as Judeans or Jews. This is where we also get the term for the religious faith of **Judaism**. Many of the exiled Jews return to Jerusalem, but not all of them. Some are already living in other thriving Jewish communities in cities surrounding the Mediterranean Sea. Some even remain in Babylon after the Exile, choosing not to return to Jerusalem.

All of these communities, called the Jews of the Dispersion (Diaspora), are no less Jewish than their counterparts in Jerusalem. Though they once sought unity by living together in a single homeland, the Jews take the unexpected turn of becoming a people who are no longer bound to a particular place. By the time of Christ's birth, Jewish communities are found all around the Medi-terranean Sea and beyond.

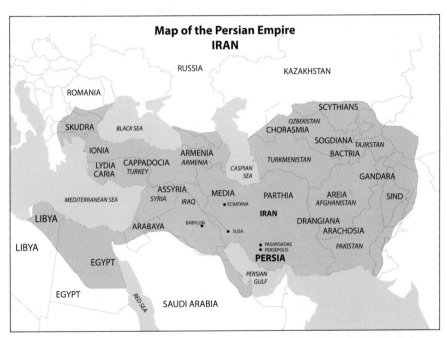

At its height, the ancient Persian Empire (in gray) controlled more than 29 million square miles of land in Asia, Africa, and Europe.

UNIT 4

Judaism ➤ This word (which has been traced to Judah, the fourth son of Jacob and the tribe descended from him) refers to the monotheistic religion of the Jewish People who trace their origin to Abraham and whose religious observance is based on the Torah and Talmud.

The **Diaspora** Jews do not have access to the Temple in Jerusalem, so they center their faith life around **synagogues**. A synagogue, at this time, was a building that served as the assembly place and center of worship for Jews. The New Testament records the important role the synagogue plays in the lives of Jesus, his followers, and the early Christian leaders.

Ruins of a synagogue at Capernaum in Israel. The word *synagogue* comes from the Greek word *synagōgē*, meaning "meeting" or "assembly."

Some Jews remain in Jerusalem during the Babylonian Exile. When their families return from Babylon, together they face the task of rebuilding the Temple and the ruined city. However, their biggest undertaking is to restore their identity as a faith community and to strengthen their relationship with God. ✳

HMMMMM...

What happens during the Babylonian Exile that greatly changes the way the Jews worship? Why is this so significant?

Diaspora ➤ For the Jewish People, the dispersion or scattering away from their homeland.

synagogue ➤ This word (from the Greek *synagōgē*, meaning "meeting" or "assembly") refers to the worship assemblies of Jews, to celebrate the Sabbath; Jesus is depicted in the Gospel of Luke (see 4:14–30) as beginning his Galilean ministry in the synagogue at Nazareth.

Article 53
The Temple: Worship Central

We all look at the world from a unique perspective, because our understanding is influenced by our cultural background and personal experience. This is also true for the biblical authors. After the Babylonian Exile, the Jewish People view their history and relationship with God a little differently than the Deuteronomists (who wrote the Historical Books we have covered so far). A person or group we call the Chronicler wrote the First and Second Books of Chronicles, covering much of the same history but from a different perspective. What's interesting is that the Bible includes both of their viewpoints!

The First and Second Books of Chronicles cover the history of Israel from Adam and Eve to the end of the Babylonian Exile. Nine chapters of genealogies—"so-and-so was the son of so-and-so" repeated many times!—provide a lot of this history. The interesting thing, though, is that the author of Chronicles hardly even mentions Moses or the Sinai Covenant. The Deuteronomist authors view their history through the lens of faithfulness to God's Law and the Covenant, while the Chronicler emphasizes the importance of proper worship in the Jerusalem Temple. The Chronicler sees this as the most important thing for sustaining their relationship with God.

UNIT 4

A scale model of the front of Solomon's Temple in Jerusalem. The Temple sat at the top of a hill. It must have been quite a site to behold!

The Temple: God's House

Recall that the Temple was originally a portable tent, or tabernacle, that housed the Ark of the Covenant, and the Ark of the Covenant housed the Ten Commandments (and other sacred objects). The Israelites considered the Ark most sacred because it was the dwelling place of God. To understand the history of the Temple, recall the story of Moses and the Israelites and the establishment of the Sinai Covenant. After God reveals the Ten Commandments at Mount Sinai, they keep the tablets in the Ark of the Covenant. For hundreds of years, the Ark of the Covenant is kept in a tent as it travels from place to place. Then King Solomon accomplishes the dream of his father, David, by building a real house for God, the Temple in Jerusalem. Now the Ark of the Covenant has a permanent home. The Temple is not like our church buildings where all people can go inside to worship. Only the priests are allowed inside the Temple building. The people offer sacrifices outside the Temple.

The Temple is truly an exquisite palace. Much of it is covered in gold. Inside the Temple is a room called the Holy of Holies. In this room, the cherubim (winged lions with human heads), the guardians and carriers of God's throne, shelter the Ark of the Covenant. No one except the high priest can enter the Holy of Holies, and he only once a year, on the Day of Atonement.

The front pillars of the Temple are named Jachin, meaning "he makes solid," and Boaz, meaning "strength," signifying the enduring power of Yahweh and Israel. In front is the Sea of Bronze, a tank that contains 12,000 gallons of water used for ritual washing. It rests on twelve statues of oxen, signifying the Twelve Tribes, and its waters represent the powers of chaos ruled over by Yahweh (see Genesis 1:1–2). First Kings offers a detailed description of the Temple (see chapters 6–7).

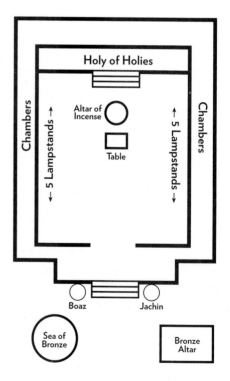

UNIT 4

The Ark of the Covenant inside the Holy of Holies.

Solomon's Temple with a large basin, called the Sea of Bronze (left), and bronze altar (right).

Interior of the Temple: the altar of incense and steps leading to the Holy of Holies.

UNIT 4

Rebuilding God's House

First and Second Chronicles covers a period from Adam to the end of the Babylonian Exile. Yet almost half the content focuses on King David and King Solomon and the building of the Temple. The Chronicler presents David and Solomon as the founders of Temple worship. In wanting to keep the images of these two kings pure, the Chronicler does not mention the sins of David and Solomon; rather, the Chronicler emphasizes King David setting the foundations for the Temple, directing its future liturgies, appointing its priests, and even drawing up the Temple designs (see 1 Chronicles, chapters 22–28). Solomon's role in building the Temple is also emphasized, his wealth highlighted in the descriptions of the building of the Temple (see 2 Chronicles, chapters 3–4).

The Chronicler believes that the future of the Jewish People after the Exile rests on proper Temple worship. By presenting a picture of David and Solomon as ideal leaders who are focused on the establishment of the Temple, the Chronicler hopes to inspire a new commitment to Temple worship. The importance of Temple worship is also emphasized in the Books of Ezra and Nehemiah. These books are about the exiles' return to Jerusalem and their restoration of the Temple and Jewish life. ✳

© ChameleonsEye / Shutterstock.com

If he wasn't sleeping at someone's house, Jesus would sleep outside on the grass or a mat, or in a tent. No big deal. Living in tents is not unusual; people have done so for thousands of years. Tents are portable, making travel easy. This is necessary for nomadic tribes and shepherds who move their herds to forage new pastures. In the Gospel of John, we read, "And the Word became flesh / and made his dwelling among us" (1:14). In Greek, the phrase "made his dwelling" means "pitched his tent." Just as the Israelites experience God's presence in the tent that is the original Tabernacle, and then later in the Tabernacle in the Temple, we experience the fullness of God revealed through Jesus Christ, the living Tabernacle. Through his Body and Blood, God is made fully present for us.

UNIT 4

OVERVIEW of the Books of First and Second Chronicles

- **Time period:** From Adam to the end of the Babylonian Exile.
- **Author:** Called the Chronicler, possibly a Levite cantor and scribe.
- **Audience:** The Jewish People after the Babylonian Exile, around 400 BC.
- **Themes:** Israel can secure its future by being united as one people worshipping at the Temple in Jerusalem.

HMMMMM. . . How does the Chronicler portray David and Solomon differently than the Deuteronomists?

Article 54

Rebuilding Jerusalem

Two months after Hurricane Katrina had devastated her hometown of New Orleans in 2005, Malia and her family went back to see what was left of their house. It was completely gone. Because so much in her neighborhood had been destroyed, it took Malia's family a while to even figure out where the house once stood. Almost every one of their friends and relatives were now spread out, many of them hundreds of miles away. Some would return; others would not. Malia's family had lived in New Orleans for generations, and her parents were committed to their community. There was nothing left, but Malia and her family were determined to rebuild.

When the exiled Jews returned from Babylon, they came home to face a similar devastation. The city of Jerusalem was not how the exiles remembered it: their homes were gone. The Temple had been destroyed. They faced the daunting task of rebuilding their homes, rebuilding the Temple, and rebuilding themselves as a faith community.

© vichinterlang / iStock.com

UNIT 4

What do you think it would be like if you had to leave home due to an impending hurricane, flood, or tornado, only to return days later to find your neighborhood in ruins?

© MindStorm / Shutterstock.com

Help families rebuild their lives? Yes, even if you are only fourteen years old! All over the country families are rebuilding their lives after some type of crisis: immigrants who have escaped from a war-torn homeland, people whose homes have been destroyed by natural disasters, or families struggling to rise above personal tragedies that had dire consequences. Habitat for Humanity, an organization that builds homes for those in need, encourages students to open campus chapters at their high schools. Catholic Charities and the St. Vincent de Paul Society need young people to help with fund-raising, food and clothing drives, and hands-on work. As Pope Francis said: "I ask you to be builders of the world, to work for a better world. Dear young people, please, don't be observers of life, but get involved." ("Apostolic Journey to Rio de Janeiro on the Occasion of the XXVIII World Youth Day," July 27, 2013)

Us and Them

It was tough enough to restore their homeland from the rubble, but the returning exiles also faced opposition. People from neighboring lands had occupied Judah in their absence. As the exiles arrive from Babylon in waves and start work on the Temple, their neighbors start to resent the newcomers. They ask the current king of Persia to stop them, which temporarily stalls their progress (see Ezra 4:6–6:22).

Others, however, want to join forces with the exiles: "Let us build with you, for we seek your God just as you do, and we have sacrificed to him since the days of Esarhaddon, king of Assyria, who brought us here" (Ezra 4:2). However, the returning exiles even turn down these people's assistance because of their different religious beliefs.

Recall that the Assyrians conquer the northern kingdom of Israel in 721 BC, and the Israelites are then scattered throughout the Assyrian Empire. Those who remain in the territory of Samaria in the north intermarry with foreigners from other religions. These Israelites become known as the

Samaritans. They reject the Jerusalem Temple and worship instead at Mount Gerizim. This leads to a great deal of hostility between the Samaritans and the Jews who are rebuilding the Temple in Jerusalem after the Exile. This hostility continues even to the time of Jesus (see the Parable of the Good Samaritan, Luke 10:29–37).

After the Temple is rebuilt, Ezra, a scribe and priest who is assigned by the Persian king to lead the Jews (see Ezra 7:25–26), arrives from Babylon. He immediately has to deal with an issue concerning the people who remained in Jerusalem during the Babylonian Exile. The returning leaders address Ezra: "Neither the Israelite laymen nor the priests nor the Levites have kept themselves separate from the peoples of the lands and their abominations . . . for they have taken some of their daughters as wives for themselves and their sons, thus intermingling the holy seed with the peoples of the lands" (9:1–2). In response, Ezra demands that those Jewish men who have married foreigners abandon their wives and children (see 10:2–3).

Two Samaritan men walking on Mount Gerizim in modern-day Samaria.

Yes, you heard that correctly. Ezra's response to this crisis of mixed marriages is quite shocking, and seems harsh by our standards. Certainly, women and children should never be abandoned. To understand this situation, we have to look at it from the perspective of their place and time. In their understanding, intermarriage watered down their faith and made it less likely that they and their offspring would be devoted to the authentic Jewish faith and practice. The severity of Ezra's command reflects the Jewish leaders' fear that their way

---

Samaritan ➤ An inhabitant of Samaria. The Samaritans rejected the Jerusalem Temple and worshipped instead at Mount Gerizim. The hostility between Jews and Samaritans is often recounted in the New Testament.

of life is unstable and its future is at stake. To maintain it, they need to secure the foundations of their authentic religious beliefs and practices. One way to do that is to remove the people whose influence has watered down these authentic beliefs and practices. Ezra's command is one example of this approach.

Nehemiah: Building Walls

For our ancient ancestors in faith, having a city wall was necessary. It not only marked the city boundaries but also kept the city safer from foreign attacks. Jerusalem's city walls have to be rebuilt, and Nehemiah is the man chosen to make it happen (see Nehemiah 2:1–6). Nehemiah is a Jewish leader who holds a privileged position in the court of the king of Persia but leaves this post to become the governor of Judah. He is a selfless leader and a model citizen who engages all of the Jewish People in rebuilding the city walls. They complete it in just fifty-two days (see 6:15).

Both Ezra and Nehemiah are dealing with a people in crisis. Though it is true that walls and rigid social barriers are sometimes necessary, there is the potential for them to become obstacles that separate us from one another.

Jesus often ignores the social barriers that keep people from one another. He spends much of his time with sinners who are normally shunned by religious figures (see Mark 2:13–17). He came as a savior, not only for his fellow Jews, but also as "a light for revelation to the Gentiles" (Luke 2:32). Today some of the walls between us are social, economic, political, and religious. Like Jesus, we are called to break down what divides us and follow his commandment: "Love one another. As I have loved you, so you also should love one another. This is how all will know that you are my disciples, if you have love for one another" (John 13:34–35). ✳

UNIT 4

CATHOLICS MAKING A DIFFERENCE

Nuns as construction workers? Since 2009, Catholic sisters from religious orders across North America have come to Louisiana to par-   ticipate in Nuns Build. Nuns Build is their yearly effort to rebuild homes destroyed by Hurricane Katrina. Sr. Mary Keefe, OP, came up with the idea after she heard of a similar group called Women Build. She thought, "We should do a Nuns Build!" Each year Nuns Build works with the St. Bernard Project to help rebuild homes in St. Bernard's Parish (just outside of New Orleans) for those who cannot afford the cost of rebuilding.

© Serhiy Kobyakov / Shutterstock.com

After the Temple is rebuilt in Jerusalem, Persian King Cyrus assigns Ezra to lead the Jews (see Ezra 7:25–26). If you were Ezra, what is one of the first things you'd do?

OVERVIEW of the Books of Ezra and Nehemiah

- **Time period:** From the Exiles return to Jerusalem through Nehemiah's tenure as governor of Judah, from 538 to about 400 BC.

- **Author:** Some scholars believe that these two books are a result of a "Chronistic school" influence, drawing on Ezra's and Nehemiah's memoirs and others sources. Some scholars believe the author to be the same writer (the Chronicler) who wrote the First and Second Books of Chronicles.

- **Audience:** The Jewish People after the Babylonian Exile, around 400 BC.

- **Themes:** The return of the Jews from captivity, the rebuilding of Jerusalem and the Temple.

HMMMMM. . .

During the rebuilding of Jerusalem and the Temple, why do Ezra and Nehemiah have such an "us (the returning exiles) versus them (everyone else)" mentality?

Article 55

Psalms: Songs for Every Occasion

What would a birthday party be like without everyone singing "Happy Birthday"? How would it feel to go to a professional baseball game and not sing "Take Me Out to the Ball Game" during the seventh-inning stretch? Or how about July 4th without the "Star-Spangled Banner"? Songs are one of the ways we express ideals, hopes, and dreams for ourselves or for others. For thousands of years, cultures all around the world have marked times and traditions with music. The Jewish People were no different.

In the Bible, that musical expression is found in the Book of Psalms, also known as the **Psalter**. Just as we sing hymns during Mass today, the Jewish People sang hymns in their Temple worship. The Hebrew name for this book is *Tehillim*, which means "praises" or "hymns of praise to God." These hymns of praise are emotional and poetic expressions to God during some of the most poignant times in our lives. Even Jesus turns to the Psalms for comfort when he is on the cross (see Matthew 27:46, Psalm 22).

Time for a Song!

Our culture has all sorts of songs: love songs, dance songs, patriotic songs, protest songs, and so on. Similarly, the Jewish psalms address different occasions. Some are specific to religious feast days. Others are emotional expressions that address the ups and downs of life and our relationship with God.

Songs like "Happy Birthday" are a way to express our hope and dreams for others or ourselves.

Psalter ➤ The Book of Psalms of the Old Testament, which contains 150 Psalms.

We sometimes group the Psalms into these categories:

- **Hymns of praise or thanksgiving**
(such as Psalms 8, 24, 47, 93, 95-99, 113–118, 136, 150)

> The LORD is my shepherd;
>> there is nothing I lack.
> In green pastures he makes me lie down;
>> to still waters he leads me;
>> he restores my soul.
>
>> (23:1-3)

- **Songs of lament (sorrow) or petition**
(such as Psalms 38, 51, 55, 58, 59, 74, 78, 105, 106)

> Deliver me, LORD, from the wicked;
>> preserve me from the violent,
> From those who plan evil in their hearts,
>> who stir up conflicts every day,
> Who sharpen their tongue like a serpent,
>> venom of asps upon their lips.
>
>> (140:2-4)

- **Wisdom hymns** (such as Psalms 1, 34, 37, 49, 73, 112, 128)

> Sin directs the heart of the wicked man;
>> his eyes are closed to the fear of God.
> For he lives with the delusion:
>> his guilt will not be known and hated.
> Empty and false are the words of his mouth;
>> he has ceased to be wise and do good.
>
>> (36:2-4)

- **Liturgical or worship psalms** (such as Psalms 15, 24, 134)

> Your procession comes into view, O God,
>> your procession into the holy place, my God and king.
> The singers go first, the harpists follow;
>> in their midst girls sound the timbrels.
> In your choirs, bless God;
>> LORD, Israel's fountain.
>
>> (68:25-27)

- **Historical psalms** (such as Psalms 78, 105, 106, 135, and 136)

> Our ancestors in Egypt
>> did not attend to your wonders.
> They did not remember your manifold mercy;
>> they defied the Most High at the Red Sea.
> Yet he saved them for his name's sake
>> to make his power known.
>
>> (106:7-8)

UNIT 4

Temple worship sometimes included weekly activities as well as special sacrifices at particular times of the year. Many of these services included animal or cereal (grain) offerings. Some psalms seem to have specific uses in these communal worship services. For example, the chanting of the following could have accompanied the sacrificial offering of an animal:

> I will bring burnt offerings to your house;
>> to you I will fulfill my vows,
> Which my lips pronounced
>> and my mouth spoke in my distress.
> Burnt offerings of fatlings I will offer you
>> and sacrificial smoke of rams;
>> I will sacrifice oxen and goats.
>
> (66:13-15)

We still sing or recite the Psalms today at every Mass.

UNIT 4

Songs for Today

The Psalms are not only the ancient songbook for Jewish worship but are also an important part of Catholic communal prayer. For example, a psalm is sung or recited in the **Liturgy of the Word** at every Mass. The chanting or recitation of the Psalms plays a major role in the Liturgy of the Hours too. The **Liturgy of the Hours** is the official public, daily prayer of the Catholic Church. It provides standard prayers, Scripture readings, and reflections to be prayed at regular times throughout the day.

Although the Psalms were written with communal activities in mind, they are also wonderful for private reflection and prayer. Read the following psalm of lament:

> Be gracious to me, LORD, for I am in distress;
>> affliction is wearing down my eyes,
>> my throat and my insides.
> My life is worn out by sorrow,
>> and my years by sighing.
> My strength fails in my affliction;
>> my bones are wearing down.
>
> . . . .
>
> But I trust in you, LORD;
>> I say, "You are my God."
>
> . . . .
>
> Let your face shine on your servant;
>> save me in your mercy.
> Do not let me be put to shame,
>> for I have called to you, LORD.
>> (Psalm 31:10–11,15,17–18)

Who has not felt like this at some point in their life?

UNIT 4

Liturgy of the Word ➤ This term refers to the first part of the Mass that includes the introductory rite, the readings from Scripture, the homily, and the prayers of the faithful.

Liturgy of the Hours ➤ Also known as the Divine Office, the official public, daily prayer of the Catholic Church. The Divine Office provides standard prayers, Scripture readings, and reflections at regular hours throughout the day.

Sometimes when we pray, it's difficult to express what we're feeling. The Psalms can provide words for us when we don't know what to say. When we are in need, we can look to the psalms of petition. When we're feeling down, perhaps a psalm of lament can speak our sadness and comfort us. When we have to make a difficult decision, the wisdom psalms can give us inspiration, strength, and courage. When we just want to give thanks and praise to our awesome and wonderful God, we can say: "Hallelujah! / Sing to the LORD a new song, / his praise in the assembly of the faithful" (Psalm 149:1). ✳

We can turn to the Psalms in prayer when we can't find our own words to express our feelings.

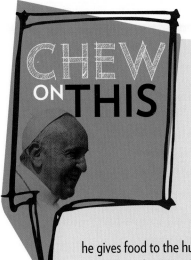

CHEW
ON THIS

In a special way the Psalms bring to the fore the grandeur of [God's] merciful action: "He forgives all your iniquity, he heals all your diseases, he redeems your life from the pit, he crowns you with steadfast love and mercy" (Psalm 103:3–4). Another psalm, in an even more explicit way, attests to the concrete signs of his mercy: "He executes justice for the oppressed; he gives food to the hungry. The Lord sets the prisoners free; the Lord opens the eyes of the blind. The Lord lifts up those who are bowed down; the Lord loves the righteous. The Lord watches over the sojourners, he upholds the widow and the fatherless; but the way of the wicked he brings to ruin" (Psalm 146:7–9). (Pope Francis, *Misericordiae Vultus,* number 6, April 11, 2015)

UNIT 4

HMMMMM. . . Why are there 150 Psalms in the Bible? Why not just twenty-five?

1. Who is Cyrus, and why is he an unexpected savior to the Jewish People?

2. What effects does the Babylonian Exile have on Judaism?

3. In what ways does the Chronicler view Israel's past history differently than the Deuteronomist writers?

4. What is the Ark of the Covenant, and why is it so important to the Jewish People?

5. Why do the Jewish People have such dislike for the Samaritans?

6. Why does Ezra demand that the men who have married foreign women abandon their wives and children?

7. What role do the Psalms play in the communal life of the Church today?

8. Describe some of the different types of psalms and how the ancient Israelites used them.

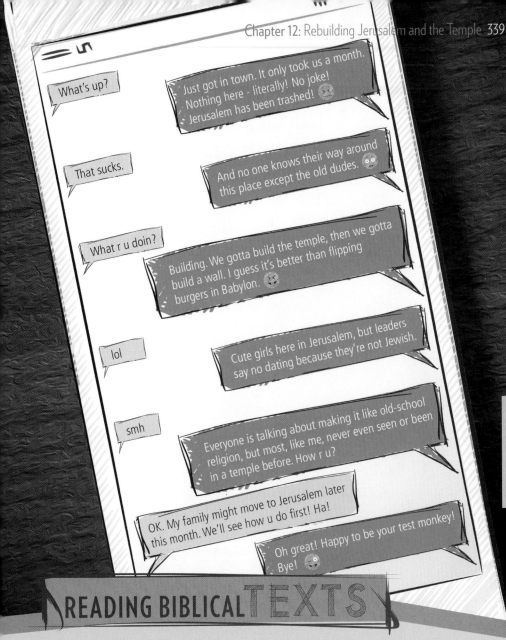

UNIT 4

READING BIBLICAL TEXTS

TEXTING FROM JERUSALEM TO BABYLON

The year is 537 BC. The exiles in Babylon are returning to Jerusalem to rebuild the city and the Temple. Imagine this text exchange between a teen returning from exile and a teen remaining in Babylon.

1. What would it be like to leave a place that felt familiar, but where your family members were servants or slaves, to go to a country where you would be free but had never seen before?

2. How do you keep your faith beliefs strong while also respecting the beliefs of others?

CHAPTER 13
Ordinary People Give Extraordinary Witness

HOW DO PEOPLE FACE BIG CHALLENGES IN BIBLICAL TIMES?

SNAPSHOT

Article 56   Page 341
Tobit, Judith, Esther: A Happy Ending
- Pre-read: The Book of Tobit, chapters 1–13
- Pre-read: The Book of Judith
- Pre-read: The Book of Esther (chapter A–chapter 9)

Article 57   Page 349
Maccabees Part 1: Fighting a Just War
- Pre-read: 1 Maccabees, chapters 2–5

Article 58   Page 353
Maccabees Part 2: Witness Testimony
- Pre-read: 1 Maccabees, chapter 7

Article 59   Page 357
Maccabees Part 3: Life after Death
- Pre-read: 2 Maccabees 12:38–46
- Pre-read: 2 Maccabees 15:6–20

Article 56
Tobit, Judith, Esther: A Happy Ending

Why is that we are so captivated and inspired by fictional heroes like Batman, Frodo Baggins, and Katniss Everdeen? They are merely imaginary people, right? Right, but their stories can teach us important truths about what it means to be a human being. These fictional heroes inspire us to fight back against injustice, to not let our shortcomings define us, and to be courageous and honest.

Frodo Baggins is the unlikely hero in the story *The Lord of the Rings*, by J. R. R. Tolkien.

The Bible has its own assortment of historical fiction. The canon of the Old Testament includes three short novels, or novellas: the Books of Tobit, Judith, and Esther. "While they may contain kernels of historical fact, these stories are told primarily to illustrate truths that transcend history" (*NABRE* introduction to the biblical novellas). Each of these books is inspired by the Holy Spirit to express religious truths that God wants us to know for our salvation. They emphasize the importance of prayer, courage in times of trouble, trust in God, and God's special care for the vulnerable.

UNIT 4

Tobit: A Classic Tale

The Book of Tobit is set in the eighth century BC, when the northern kingdom of Israel was conquered by the Assyrians. Many Israelites were taken from their country, including the hero of this story, Tobit, who found himself far from home in the Assyrian city of Nineveh. However, the book was written for Jewish People living five hundred years later, when another hostile group was governing them: the Greeks. Tobit's story of perseverance and trust in God is exactly what the Jewish People needed to hear during the period of Greek oppression.

The Book of Tobit begins with two people whose lives are so bad that they would rather be dead. First, we meet Tobit, a good and faithful Jewish man, oppressed by the Assyrians who have captured him and sent him to Nineveh. Blinded by a freak accident and completely frustrated, he begs God to end his life (see Tobit 1:16–3:6).

Next, we meet a young woman named Sarah, who is from another town. Like Tobit, Sarah is a good person who has experienced terrible misfortune. Every single one of her seven husbands died on their wedding night before the marriage could be consummated: "The wicked demon Asmodeus kept killing them off before they could have intercourse with her" (Tobit 3:8). And like Tobit, Sarah prays to God, asking for her death.

Do these two seemingly separate and unrelated characters ever meet? To find out, you have to read the rest of the Book of Tobit, but here's a quick introduction. Tobiah, the son of Tobit, is sent to Sarah's town to run an errand.

At the same time, the angel Raphael appears in human form and accompanies Tobiah on his journey. Tobiah and Raphael's journey is a classic tale of adventure, with heroes, villains, true love, and a happy ending.

The Book of Tobit addresses how God works mysteriously in the lives of those who are open and faithful to him in ways we cannot foresee. Its insistence on God's presence in our lives and God's concern for those who suffer is just as important for us today as it was for the Israelites.

The journey of Tobiah and the angel Raphael is a classic tale of adventure, with heroes, villains, true love, and a happy ending.

TAKE IT TO GOD

Dear God,

Thank you for the big and little heroes
  you have placed in my life.

The ones like Tobit,
  who are patient with me and ever faithful to you, no matter what.

The ones like Judith,
  whose courage inspires me to meet life challenges head on.

The ones like Esther,
  who put my needs ahead of their own to protect me.

The ones like the Maccabees
  whose devotion to their faith motivates me to be faithful.

Amen!

UNIT 4

Judith: An Unlikely Hero

The Book of Judith continues the biblical tradition of unlikely heroes as Judith, a woman and a widow, saves her city and the nation from destruction by the Assyrians. We know the Book of Judith is not a historically accurate account. There are several clues to alert us. In the first lines of the book (see 1:1–11), Nebuchadnezzar is inaccurately named as the ruler of the Assyrians. Historically, he was a ruler of the Babylonians who died about 160 years after the Assyrian invasion! Another clue is the main character of the book, Judith. In Hebrew, Judith isn't a proper name; it means "Jewish woman." Judith represents all Jewish women of the past who have served God through their faith, courage, and decisive action.

The first few chapters of the Book of Judith set the scene: King Nebuchadnezzer wants to wage war against the Persians, but his subject peoples, including the Israelites, refuse to join his campaign (see chapters 1 and 2). The king defeats the Persians but then sends his general, Holofernes, to destroy the nations who refused to fight (see chapter 4). Holofernes successfully demolishes all, except one—the nation of Israel. The Israelites are holed up in mountainous cities that are hard to access. Judith's town, Bethulia, is strategically located near the mountains at the entrance of the narrow corridor leading to Jerusalem. If Bethulia falls to an enemy, then all of Israel is in danger. Holofernes lays siege on the town and cuts off their water supply. After thirty-four days, the water supply in Bethulia is dry and the Israelite elders agree that if God does not intervene within five days, they will have to hand the city over to the Assyrians (see chapter 7).

This is when Judith steps in, now almost halfway through the book. She is a widow, a hard worker, and a good, beautiful woman. "No one had a bad word to say about her, for she feared God greatly" (Judith 8:8). She scolds the elders: "Do not impose conditions on the plans of the Lord our God. God is not like a human being to be moved by threats, nor like a mortal to be cajoled. So while we wait for the salvation that comes from him, let us call upon him to help us" (8:16–17).

Judith now takes control of the situation and comes up with a plan. Her prayer to God sums up the main point of this book:

Judith's secret weapon is her womanhood. She saves the Israelites in a way that no man could.

> Crush their arrogance by the hand of a female.
>
> Your strength is not in numbers, nor does your might depend upon the powerful.
> You are God of the lowly, helper of those of little account, supporter of the weak,
> protector of those in despair, savior of those without hope. (Judith 9:10–11)

Judith's plot to kill the Assyrian general, Holofernes, requires a shrewd use of her beauty and a lot of bravery (see chapters 10–13). The story is interesting not only because a woman is the hero but also because she is a hero by virtue of her womanhood. This Jewish woman is able to do something that a man cannot not do. It's quite an astonishing story considering that the Israelites were a patriarchal society in which men had all of the power.

In the end, Judith's actions allow the Israelites to drive away and plunder the Assyrians. Leaders from Jerusalem even come to Bethulia to congratulate Judith. Then the Israelites hold a victory celebration in which "at the head of all the people, [Judith] led the women in the dance, while the men of Israel followed" (Judith 15:13). It is a sign of Judith's humility that her song (see 16:1–17) praises God, whom she acknowledges as the true hero of this story.

Esther: The Right Person at the Right Time

Assassination attempts, secret identities, treason, and a genocidal maniac make the Book of Esther an interesting read. Though all of this is intriguing, the main point of the book is lost if we focus on these aspects alone. Ultimately this text points toward the goodness of God, while also explaining the origin of the Jewish feast of Purim. Like the Book of Judith, this novella features another unlikely female hero: Esther.

Navigating the Book of Esther requires some understanding of its origins. The original was written in Hebrew, probably in the third or second century BC. A later Greek version, which includes a number of additions and changes, was composed sometime between 116 to 48 BC. The chapters in the book are arranged differently depending on the translation. In some translations, the Greek additions and changes are seamlessly combined with the original Hebrew. In the *New American Bible, Revised Edition*, the Greek additions are labeled as chapters A through F.

The book is set in the years after the Babylonian Exile, when Persia reigns over Israel. Many Jews who did not return to Israel after the Exile are living in communities throughout Persia. Mordecai is one of these Jews. Serving in the court of the Persian King Ahasuerus, Mordecai thwarts a plot to assassinate the king and is rewarded for his actions (see Esther, chapter A). Later the king seeks a replacement for his queen (see chapter 1). Mordecai presents to the king his cousin Esther, who is "beautifully formed and lovely to behold" (2:7). He instructs Esther to keep her Jewish heritage a secret from the king. The king ultimately chooses Esther to be his queen.

The Book of Esther is the story of how Mordecai and his courageous cousin Esther prevented a genocidal plot against the Jews from being carried out.

UNIT 4

© BibleArtLibrary / iStock.com

Mordecai runs into a conflict with the evil Haman, the king's right-hand man. Haman seeks revenge, not only on Mordecai but the entire Jewish People. To convince King Ahasuerus to eliminate the Jewish People, Haman lies to him, saying: "Throughout the provinces of your kingdom, there is a certain people living apart. Their laws differ from those of every other people and they do not obey the laws of the king; so it is not proper for the king to tolerate them" (Esther 3:8). The king is convinced by this argument and orders the destruction of "all the Jews, young and old, including women and children" (3:13). Because they view this calamity as a sign of God's displeasure with them (see Esther's prayer, C:17–18), Mordecai, Esther, and all the Jews begin to fast in order to purify themselves of whatever sins they have committed (see chapter 4).

The Jewish People have been the victims of prejudice for centuries. Six million Jews and other groups deemed inferior by the Nazis were murdered in the **Holocaust** during the Second World War. The Holocaust actually began years before the first person was killed. It started with Nazi leaders spreading

© Everett Historical / Shutterstock.com

Rows of bodies at the Bergen-Belsen Concentration Camp, April 15, 1945. The bodies were among thousands of corpses that lay unburied on the camp grounds when the camp was liberated by the British Army in World War II.

Holocaust ▶ In the Old Testament, this refers to a sacrifice consumed by fire. In the twentieth century, *Holocaust* is the widely used term to designate the attempted extermination of the Jews by the Nazis during the Second World War (1939–1945).

lies about the Jewish People. Like Haman's lies to King Ahasuerus and his plan for genocide of the Jewish People, the Nazis wrongfully blamed all of their problems on the Jewish People. As most of German society started to accept the lies, the Nazi leaders dehumanized the Jewish People, calling them animals and saying they spread disease. After years of being fed these lies, a majority of German people were ready to inflict the persecution of the Jews through anti-Jewish legislation, boycotting Jewish businesses, seizing their homes, moving them into ghettoes, and many other atrocities. This ultimately led to the concentration camps and gas chambers where they were murdered. The few people who spread the initial lies started all of this horror.

Oppression and genocide are like diseases that must be stopped in the early stages before it is too late. To do this, we need people who are going to speak the truth even though it may have negative, perhaps even deadly, personal consequences. Esther is the truth-teller in this story. In an effort to save her people, she takes a chance that could end her life. Even as queen, she cannot approach the king unbidden. So she uses her power to host royal banquets to create an opportunity to tell the king the truth. In the end, she defeats Haman, and her people are saved from annihilation (see Esther, chapters 4–8).

After they defeated their enemies, "they rested, and made it a day of feasting and rejoicing" (Esther 9:17). This day is called Purim. What does it mean? When deciding on the day to kill the Jewish People, Haman has someone draw a lot (or a *pur*, as the Persians called it [see 3:7]). Jewish People all over the world still joyfully celebrate the Feast of Purim every year to commemorate the defeat of their enemies and honor the bravery of Esther.

UNIT 4

The story of Esther is the basis for the Jewish celebration of Purim.
Young people in Eliat Israel celebrate at a Purim Carnival.

Reward to the Faithful

The Jewish People of the second and first century BC suffer under the oppressive rule of the Greeks. The happy endings in the Books of Tobit, Judith, and Esther encourage the Jews to maintain their hope in God's power. The books encourage faithfulness to God's commandments (see Tobit 4:1–19); teach the value of marriage and family (see Tobit, chapters 7–8); show God's special care for the lowly (see Judith 9:10–11); and express the importance of prayer, fasting, and trust in God (see Esther, chapter 4). Despite the sufferings the Jewish People endure, their faithfulness to God will finally be rewarded and "the gates of Jerusalem will sing hymns of gladness, / and all its houses will cry out, Hallelujah!" (Tobit 13:18). ✴

OVERVIEW of the Book of Tobit

- **Time period:** The book reflects the historical situation of the Israelites deported from Israel to Nineveh in 721 BC.
- **Author:** Unknown, writing sometime in the second century BC when the Jewish People were governed by oppressive, Greek rulers.
- **Themes:** In time, God will aid the faithful who suffer. God always rewards the faithful, even if it doesn't happen right away.

OVERVIEW of the Book of Judith

- **Time period:** There is no clear historical setting.
- **Author:** Unknown, writing in the third or second century BC, when the Jewish People were governed by oppressive Greek rulers.
- **Themes:** A woman of faith, cleverness, and courage; trusting in God's saving power.

OVERVIEW of the Book of Esther

- **Setting:** Persia after the Babylonian Exile.
- **Authors:** *Hebrew version:* unknown, probably written in the third or second century BC. *Greek version:* unknown, written between 116 and 48 BC.
- **Themes:** God's love for the little ones; the origin of the feast of Purim.

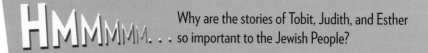

HMMMMM. . . Why are the stories of Tobit, Judith, and Esther so important to the Jewish People?

Article 57

Maccabees Part 1: Fighting a Just War

In July of 1863, around fifty thousand soldiers were either killed or wounded at the Battle of Gettysburg, the bloodiest days of the United States Civil War. A few months later, President Abraham Lincoln came to dedicate the Soldiers' National Cemetery "as a final resting place for those who here gave their lives that that nation might live." In his "Gettysburg Address," Lincoln encouraged the continued struggle to free people from the oppression of slavery. He also connected the lives of those remaining with those who died in battle: "From these honored dead we take increased devotion to that cause for which they gave the last full measure of devotion—that we here highly resolve that these dead shall not have died in vain."

Gettysburg battlefield. Like Lincoln's "Gettysburg Address," the writings of I and II Maccabees explore the purpose of the Jewish People's suffering.

In the second century BC, the Jewish People are ruled by an oppressive Greek general who does not respect their religious faith and traditions. Their successful struggle against the Greek army is recorded in the First and Second Books of Maccabees. Like Lincoln's "Gettysburg Address," these writings explore the purpose of their suffering, and draw a spiritual connection between the living and the dead.

UNIT 4

Another Madman in Charge

After Persia defeats the Babylonians, the Jewish People are allowed to return to Jerusalem and rebuild their personal and religious life. The Persians allow them to practice their faith and live in relative peace for almost two centuries. Then in 330 BC, Alexander the Great and his Greek army conquer the Persian Empire.

Now under the rule of the Greeks, the Jewish People are challenged by the culture of the Greek empire. Greek philosophy, science, and literature give more importance to reason rather than religious beliefs. Over time, Greek becomes the main language, so much so that some Jews never learn Hebrew; they speak and read only Greek. Some of the biblical books during this time are written in Greek because of this.

This Greek influence brings great tension in the Jewish community. Some Jews insist on keeping the Jewish religious traditions that have been handed down over the centuries. Others think that accommodating Greek religious practices might be the best way to survive in such a hostile environment (see 1 Maccabees 1:41–43). The Greek leaders use this conflict between pro-Greek and anti-Greek Jews to keep the Jews divided and to maintain control.

When the Greek King Antiochus IV comes into power in 175 BC, he gives himself another name: Epiphanes, meaning "God made visible" (1 Maccabees 1:10). To give you an idea of what kind of leader he is, his subjects give him the nickname Epimanes, meaning "madman." Antiochus's reign begins a period of harsh persecution of the faithful Jews: he forbids the practice of Jewish religion, forces the Jewish People to embrace the king's pagan religion, desecrates and robs the Temple, and murders the families who circumcise their children (see verses 16–62). Some Jews give into the pressure and abandon their faith, but many do not.

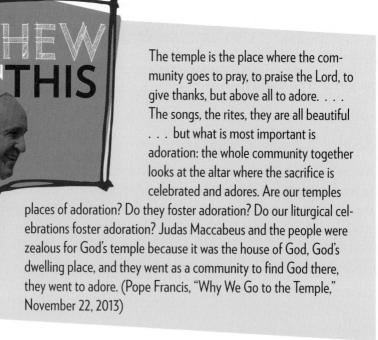

CHEW ON THIS

The temple is the place where the community goes to pray, to praise the Lord, to give thanks, but above all to adore. . . . The songs, the rites, they are all beautiful . . . but what is most important is adoration: the whole community together looks at the altar where the sacrifice is celebrated and adores. Are our temples places of adoration? Do they foster adoration? Do our liturgical celebrations foster adoration? Judas Maccabeus and the people were zealous for God's temple because it was the house of God, God's dwelling place, and they went as a community to find God there, they went to adore. (Pope Francis, "Why We Go to the Temple," November 22, 2013)

A Faithful Fighter

Mattathias is a faithful Jew who refuses to offer sacrifices to the king's gods during this time. After committing an intense act of rebellion, Mattathias, his five sons, and others escape to the hills to form a rebel army to fight their Greek oppressors (see 1 Maccabees 2:1–28). The word *Maccabee* comes from the Hebrew word for *hammer*. It is originally the nickname for Mattathias's son Judas, who becomes the leader of the Jewish revolt after Mattathias's death. Later the name was also adopted by his entire family and the followers who participated in this rebellion.

The accounts of Judas's successes clearly display his bravery, but the author of First Maccabees makes it clear that all of these victories come from God. Judas relies on the assistance of God in the face of apparent defeat (see 1 Maccabees 4:8–11) and prays before every battle (see verses 26–35). After a successful battle, King Antiochus's army retreats, allowing Judas to go to Jerusalem to purify and rededicate the Temple. The Jewish People joyfully celebrate for eight days (see verses 36–61). Since then, every year in the month of December, the Jewish People remember this event in the feast of Dedication, also known as Hanukkah.

On each night of this eight-day celebration, they light a candle to remember the rededication of the Temple by the Maccabees.

Judas has many successes fighting against the Greek oppressors. Sadly, he dies in battle. "All Israel wept for him with great lamentation. They mourn for him many days, and they say, 'How the mighty one has fallen, the savior of Israel!'" (1 Maccabees 9:20–21). Judas's brother Jonathan, a great warrior, succeeds him. After Antiochus

Judas Maccabeus led the Jews in a successful revolt (167–164 BC) against the Greek persecution. Israel remained free from foreign domination for the next hundred years.

IV dies, his son Alexander succeeds him as the Greek king. King Alexander has heard of the bravery of Jonathan and his brothers and is so impressed that he and Jonathan become friends. Alexander even makes him governor of the province (see 10:51–66). Therefore, Jonathan is able to gain some independence for the Jewish People. Without the Maccabee family's determination and self-sacrifice, it is very possible that Judaism would not have survived. ✳

OVERVIEW of the Book of First Maccabees

- **Period covered:** 175 to 134 BC.
- **Author:** Unknown, writing approximately 100 BC.
- **Theme:** God brings Israel to freedom through a faithful family and faithful people.
- **Of note:** First Maccabees is not considered canonical by Protestants or Jews.

HMMMMMM. . .

How does the influence of Greek culture cause a division among the Jewish People, and what effect does it have on them?

Article 58

Maccabees Part 2: Witness Testimony

Ragheed Ganni was a Chaldean Catholic born in Mosul, Iraq, in 1972. He entered the seminary in Iraq in 1996, and then studied in Rome for several years. He was ordained a priest just about a month after the 9-11 terrorist attacks. In 2003, the United States invaded Iraq, and the country became unstable and dangerous. Many Christians were being persecuted and killed by extremists. Nonetheless, Father Ganni asked to return to Mosul, where he became the pastor of a church. In 2007, terrorists demanded that his church close down. After serving Mass one day, he and three companions were confronted in their car by armed men. Asked why he had not closed the church, Father Ganni responded, "How can I close the house of God?" All four of them were shot and killed.

The Catholic Church recognizes Father Ganni as a **martyr**. A martyr is a person killed because of their beliefs. The word itself means *witness*—someone who sees, knows, and can testify to something. Martyrs, then, are witnesses to their unwavering faith in God, even to their death. The Iraqi Christians suffered similar circumstances experienced by the Jewish People in the Second Book of Maccabees. These Jewish martyrs, who also accepted death rather than denounce their faith, surely offered inspiration to the many Christian martyrs, such as Father Ganni, who followed later.

Fr. Ragheed Ganni, a Chaldean Catholic priest from Mosul, Iraq, was martyred when he refused to denounce his faith.

© JamiHuizenga / iStock.com

UNIT 4

---

martyr ➤ A person who suffers death because of his or her beliefs. The Church has canonized many Christian martyrs as saints.

A Life-and-Death Decision

The First Book of Maccabees offers a broad historical look at the Maccabees' victory over their Greek oppressors, which brings freedom for the Jewish People. The Second Book of Maccabees is a bit different than the first. These writings delve into the variety of ways the Jewish People face their persecution, and it explores the spiritual dimensions of that experience.

The Second Book of Maccabees emphasizes the importance of following God's Law, even if it means death. The faithful ones, who accept death rather than break the Law, are remembered and honored. Their memories encourage the readers to stay faithful, despite their continued oppression.

Recall that the influence of Greek culture is having a detrimental impact on the Jewish community. They have split into two camps: pro-Greek and anti-Greek. The Greeks take advantage of this rupture and attempt to force the Jewish People to abandon their religion. One of the repulsive methods they use to do this is to give people a choice: eat pork or be tortured and killed. Pork is not a kosher food. Jews are forbidden to eat it. If they eat it, they are breaking God's Law and therefore committing **apostasy**, the act of renouncing one's faith.

© Peter Horree / Alamy Stock Photo

One might think they should eat the pork just that one time for show and then continue their faith as it was before. Some do choose to do this. But what really is at stake is the faith of the entire community. If the anti-Greek Jews give in to the pressure, they know Judaism will come to an end. Enduring the torture and refusing to commit apostasy is their witness to keeping God's Law a non-negotiable, essential part of their lives.

Eleazar, a dignified, elderly scribe who has followed God his whole life, chose death rather than break God's commandment. He knows his example will influence younger people and give courage to others.

apostasy ➤ The act of renouncing one's faith.

CATHOLICS MAKING A DIFFERENCE

In the 1540s, many Catholic missionaries began spreading the Gospel in Japan, and over 100,000 Japanese people were baptized. Due to Japanese leaders' misunderstanding of the missionaries' work, Christianity was banned. The missionaries were expelled, and many who refused to leave were martyred. By the early 1600s, Kakure Kirishitans ("hidden Christians") were forced to practice their faith in secret. Sometimes, when Japanese officials suspected people of being Catholic, the suspects were given the option to either stomp on a "fumie" (an image of the Virgin Mary or Christ) or be tortured. Many chose torture and death over desecrating a holy image. The faith of these Japanese martyrs continues to inspire us to stay true to our faith, even in the most difficult times.

UNIT 4

An Example for Others

An old man named Eleazar is faced with this decision to eat pork or keep God's Law. An old acquaintance of his is a fellow Jew in charge of the test. He suggests that Eleazar bring some other meat so that it only appears that he's eaten pork, thus avoiding torture and death. Eleazar knows that young people will be watching, and he says, "If I dissemble to gain a brief moment of life, they would be led astray by me, while I would bring defilement and dishonor on my old age" (2 Maccabees 6:25). Eleazar chooses death, explaining that keeping his faith and devotion to God is what matters most to him. His martyrdom also affects many others by leaving "an unforgettable example of virtue not only for the young but for the whole nation" (verse 31).

The story of the martyrdom of a mother and her seven sons offers a graphic and painful example of the cruelty the Jewish People face (see 2 Maccabees, chapter 7). It also reflects a new revelation for Judaism: the belief in a life after death (see article 59 for more on this).

The Second Book of Maccabees is written around 100 BC. Its accounts encourage later generations of Jewish People to remain faithful in the face of oppression and even death. These martyrs give witness to an unwavering commitment to following God's Law. Their determined faith also inspires the early Christians to face their own hardships and persecution with the same trust in God. *

The dramatic story of the martyrdom of the Jewish mother and her seven sons (2 Maccabees, chapter 7) offers a graphic and painful example of the cruelty the Jewish People faced at the hands of the Greeks.

OVERVIEW of the Book of Second Maccabees

- **Period covered:** 180 to 161 BC.
- **Author:** Unknown, writing around 100 BC.
- **Themes:** Differing responses to persecution, the glorification of God's holy martyrs.
- **Of note:** Second Maccabees is not considered canonical by Protestants or Jews.

HMMMMM. . .

How does martyrdom lead the Jewish People to the belief in life after death?

UNIT 4

Article 59
Maccabees Part 3: Life after Death

What happens to us after we die? Where do we go? Death is mysterious, but God's Revelation in the New Testament offers us some glimpses into the afterlife (see 1 Corinthians 15:42–55, Romans 6:5–10). Christians have focused a considerable amount of attention on what happens to us after we die. Jewish People have had a less definite viewpoint on this. For most of the Old Testament, little is said about what happens after we die. One of the most striking aspects of the Second Book of Maccabees is the strong belief in the resurrection of the dead.

One of the most striking aspects of the Second Book of Maccabees is the strong belief in the resurrection of the dead. In his painting, *The Last Judgment*, Michelangelo gives his interpretation of the resurrection of the dead.

UNIT 4

The Next Life

The account of the martyrdom of the mother and her seven sons in chapter 7 of Second Maccabees, raises the question of unjust suffering to a new level. Job represents people who have no choice in their suffering. But the martyrs in Second Maccabees represent a people who do have a choice. They can break the Mosaic Law by eating pork; they can die a horrible death; or they can just cross their fingers, eat the pork, and live happily ever after. What would motivate them to make the choice to remain true to their faith and suffer the consequence of extreme torture and death?

The answer is their belief that there is a life after death. At this point in Jewish history, there is a growing belief and hope by some Jews in a future resurrection, an afterlife, when those who remained faithful to God would be rewarded. Listen to the response of the mother's fourth son to his torturers: "It is my choice to die at the hands of mortals with the hope that God will restore me to life; but for you, there will be no resurrection to life" (2 Maccabees 7:14).

The speech given by the mother of the seven martyrs states this belief even more clearly:

> I do not know how you came to be in my womb; it was not I who gave you breath and life. . . . Therefore, since it is the Creator of the universe who shaped the beginning of humankind and brought about the origin of everything, he, in his mercy, will give you back both breath and life, because you now disregard yourselves for the sake of his law.
>
> . . . . I beg you, child, to look at the heavens and the earth and see all that is in them; then you will know that God did not make them out of existing things. In the same way humankind came into existence. Do not be afraid of this executioner, but be worthy of your brothers and accept death, so that in the time of mercy I may receive you again with your brothers.
>
> (2 Maccabees 7:22–23,28–29)

The author of Second Maccabees is emphasizing that God, who creates everything out of nothing, is fully capable of raising the dead, even when that death has reduced the deceased to ashes. The God of mercy will reward those who have been faithful to him in the next life, especially those who have endured unjust suffering because of that choice.

This belief in the resurrection of the dead is part of Divine Revelation in Scripture. The beginnings of that Revelation appear in these later books of the Old Testament. They prefigure the fullness of this truth, which is revealed in Christ's Resurrection in the New Testament. Christ's Resurrection is the promise of our own resurrection. It is a promise that if we too are faithful to God and are willing to sacrifice and suffer for the Gospel, we will enjoy eternal

UNIT 4

MAKE IT SO

One of the Corporal Works of Mercy is to bury the dead. Generally, burying people is left to the professionals, but that does not mean you cannot participate in other ways. For example, you can attend the visitation and prayer vigil and then attend the funeral liturgy for parishioners who have recently died. Visit the graves of loved ones on their birthday or on Memorial Day. Pray for the dead and ask them to pray for you.

life and union with God in Heaven. Saint Paul states this reality beautifully in his Letter to the Romans:

> The Spirit itself bears witness with our spirit that we are children of God, and if children, then heirs, heirs of God and joint heirs with Christ, if only we suffer with him so that we may also be glorified with him.
>
> I consider that the sufferings of this present time are as nothing compared with the glory to be revealed for us. (8:16–18)

Prayer Is a Two-Way Street

Considering our belief in life everlasting, what about those who die and are not in a state of perfection? **Purgatory** is the state of final purification or cleansing, which one may need to enter following death and before entering Heaven. There is a foundation for this belief found in Second Maccabees. In this account, Judas and his army gather the dead bodies of their fellow soldiers and find idols to false gods in their tunics. Instead of writing these soldiers off as pagans, Judas leads his people to pray "that the sinful deed might be fully blotted out" (12:42), and they make an offering to God on behalf of these dead soldiers. "In doing this he acted in a very excellent and noble way, inasmuch as he had the resurrection in mind; for if he were not expecting the fallen to rise again, it would have been superfluous and foolish to pray for the dead" (12:43–44). Praying to God and petitioning him to forgive the sins of the dead is an aspect of our belief in purgatory.

UNIT 4

© Diego Grandi / Shutterstock.com

In Mexico, Día de los Muertos, or Day of the Dead, is a two-day celebration of life and death, demonstrating love and respect for deceased family members.

Purgatory ▶ A state of final purification or cleansing, which one may need to enter following death and before entering Heaven.

Praying for those who have died is rooted in our belief that there will be a **resurrection of the dead**. Every year on November 2, we celebrate **All Souls' Day** and make special intercessions on behalf of those who have died. We also pray in our liturgies and in our private prayers for the recently departed. This short prayer for the dead is said at funerals, but it can be prayed anytime:

> Eternal rest grant unto them, O Lord.
> And may perpetual light shine upon them.
> May they rest in peace. Amen.

© theasis / iStock.com

A feast day for those in hell!? The roots of Halloween, or "All Hallows' Eve," go back to a number of traditions from various cultures. One of them started in Ireland around the year 1000. On October 31, the day before All Saints' Day, the Irish people would bang pots and pans to let the damned know that they were remembered. All Saints' Day, on November 1, commemorates those saints in Heaven, and All Souls' Day, on November 2, honors the souls of the faithfully departed who might not have made it to Heaven yet. Apparently, the Irish figured that since Heaven and Purgatory were covered, all the unfortunate souls in hell might feel left out and cause trouble if they were not remembered too.

---

resurrection of the dead ➤ The raising of the righteous on the last day, to live forever with the Risen Christ. The resurrection of the dead means that not only will our immortal souls live on after death but also our transformed bodies.

All Souls' Day ➤ A holy day in the Church set aside for honoring the faithful departed, celebrated on November 2.

The Second Book of Maccabees also testifies that prayer is a two-way street between the living and the dead. To encourage his army prior to battle, Judas recalls the vision in which the former High Priest Onias "was praying with outstretched arms for the whole Jewish community" (2 Maccabees 15:12). Next, he shares the story of the prophet Jeremiah, "who loves his fellow Jews and fervently prays for the people and the holy city" (verse 14). Simply put, the living pray for the dead, and the dead pray for the living.

On November 1, the Church celebrates **All Saints' Day** to honor all known and unknown **saints**, asking them to pray for us. Saints are those who have been transformed by the grace of Christ and who reside in full union with God in Heaven. Non-Catholics sometimes confuse our practice of the **intercession** of the saints. We are not praying to them like we pray to God; rather, we are asking the saints to pray for us. Why ask them to pray for us? We can trust that those who have died have not ceased to care for us. Saint Thérèse of Lisieux said shortly before her death, "I want to spend my heaven in doing good on earth"[1] (*Catechism of the Catholic Church [CCC]*, number 956). We are grateful for their care! ✳

HMMMMMM. . . . Why is there a growing belief in the resurrection of the dead during the time of the Maccabees?

UNIT 4

All Saints' Day ➤ A feast day commemorating all of the saints of the Church, both known and unknown, celebrated on November 1. Also known as the Feast of All Saints.

saint ➤ Someone who has been transformed by the grace of Christ and who resides in full union with God in Heaven.

intercession ➤ A prayer on behalf of another person or group.

1. Explain why Judith and Esther are such unique Old Testament heroes.

2. How do the Books of Tobit, Judith, and Esther offer hope to the Jewish People of the second and first century BC?

3. How does the Greek King Antiochus IV treat the Jewish People?

4. Who are the Maccabees, and what do they do?

5. What are some differences between the First and Second Books of Maccabees?

6. Explain why Eleazar is honored among the Jewish People.

7. How does the Second Book of Maccabees address the belief of life after death?

8. Explain how the Second Book of Maccabees presents prayer as a "two-way street" between the living and the dead.

UNIT 4

ART STUDY

ORDINARY PEOPLE GIVE EXTRAORDINARY WITNESS

These images represent four people from the biblical books studied in this chapter. They are all ordinary people who became heroes because of their faith and courage.

1. Which biblical hero does each image represent?

2. Why do you think each artist has emphasized the hands of the person they've depicted?

CHAPTER 14
The Wisdom Books

HOW DO I LIVE A GOOD LIFE?

SNAPSHOT

Article 60   Page 365
Wisdom from Above
- Pre-read: Wisdom, chapters 1, 10

Article 61   Page 369
Job: Why Do Good People Suffer?
- Pre-read: Job, chapters 1–3, 38–42

Article 62   Page 376
Ecclesiastes: What's the Point?
- Pre-read: Ecclesiastes, chapters 1, 3–4

Article 63   Page 379
Song of Songs: Love Poems
- Pre-read: Song of Songs, chapters 7–8

Article 64   Page 382
Ben Sira: Wisdom Far from Home
- Pre-read: Wisdom, chapters 2, 8
- Pre-read: Wisdom of Ben Sira foreword, chapters 1, 24

Article 60
Wisdom from Above

Michelle was a fervent athlete for as long as she could remember, playing every sport her schools offered. When her junior high school did not have girls' basketball, she played on the boys' team—and was a starter! She had posters on her bedroom wall of her favorite athletes with inspirational quotes. They said things like: "It does not matter how many times you fall. It matters how many times you get back up." "If it was easy, everyone would do it." Her mother had even gotten into the act, taping a handwritten quote on her bathroom mirror that said, "God is first, family is second, school is third, and the rest is icing on the cake." These quotes helped Michelle remember what was important and inspired her to keep working on her dreams.

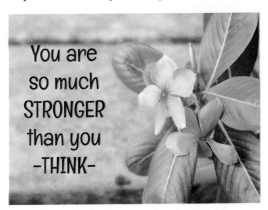

What is one of your favorite inspirational quotes?

Sometimes we need tidbits of wisdom like these to motivate and guide us. The Old Testament is a gold mine of wise sayings. In fact, short, wise sayings are the main focus of several of its Books. They are part of the wisdom literature of the Old Testament. The Wisdom Books explore the meaning of suffering, provide insights into the purpose of human life, and offer advice on how to live good and virtuous lives. Their use of poetic and symbolic language enables us to connect our hearts with God in ways that prose cannot. Though they were written thousands of years ago, they address basic human questions and situations that are still relevant today.

The Wisdom and Poetry Books

The Wisdom and Poetry Books of the Bible are distinctive among the literature of the Old Testament. These Old Testament books focus on such things as Israel's history, laws, and prophetic oracles; offer moral lessons and sage advice; guide us in our search for happiness and harmony in life; and explore life's mysteries. The Wisdom and Poetry Books are listed below, including a short description, as well as the type of writing used.

UNIT 4

Book	Description	Literary Genre
Job	a fictional story exploring why good people suffer	a combination of prose and poetry
Psalms	a collection of hymns used in prayer and worship	hymns, poetry
Proverbs	a collection of teachings and short, wise sayings	teachings, proverbs
Ecclesiastes	reflections on fairness, suffering, and the meaning of life	prose
Song of Songs	a poetic expression of human love, symbolizing God's love for humanity	love poetry
Book of Wisdom	philosophical reflections on wisdom	poetic diatribe
Wisdom of Ben Sira (sometimes called Sirach or Ecclesiasticus)	teachings on how to live right	prose, sayings, hymns, prayers, lists

Proverbs: Portable Wisdom

The first nine chapters of the Book of Proverbs are instructions from wise parents and "Woman Wisdom." In several places, the virtue of wisdom is personified, that is, given human characteristics. Wisdom is a woman seeking disciples in the city: "Wisdom cries aloud in the street, / in the open squares she raises her voice" (1:20). She asks us to call her sister (see 7:4) and invites us to dine at her house (see 9:1–16).

Chapter 10 starts a section of traditional proverbs that goes on for many chapters. A **proverb** is a short saying that is easy to recall and that communicates a wise observation on human life or expresses a religious truth. A proverb offers sound guidance, and best of all, it gets to the point quickly! Because they are easy to memorize, proverbs are kind of like portable bundles of wisdom that can be carried with you at all times. The proverbs in the Book of Proverbs cover many topics: family relationships, money, honesty, justice, laziness, truthfulness, and so on.

---

proverb ➤ A short saying that is easy to recall and communicates an astute observation on human life or expresses a religious truth.

One of the themes you will find throughout these proverbs is this advice: "Fear the Lord." In fact, it is found in the beginning of the book: "Fear of the LORD is the beginning of knowledge" (Proverbs 1:7). When the Bible tells us to "fear" God, it does not mean that we should be terrorized by him; it means that we should have a sense of awe and reverence for the Lord. For the Israelites, having a reverent attitude for God is the foundation for attaining wisdom (see 9:10). It also helps us turn away from evil (see 3:7), prolongs our life (see 10:27), and helps guide our actions (see 14:2).

Because they are easy to memorize, proverbs are kind of like portable bundles of wisdom that can be carried with you at all times!

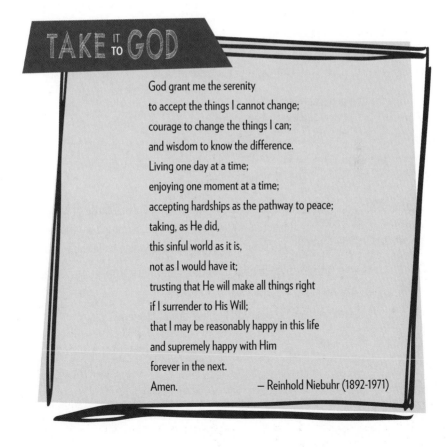

TAKE IT TO GOD

God grant me the serenity

to accept the things I cannot change;

courage to change the things I can;

and wisdom to know the difference.

Living one day at a time;

enjoying one moment at a time;

accepting hardships as the pathway to peace;

taking, as He did,

this sinful world as it is,

not as I would have it;

trusting that He will make all things right

if I surrender to His Will;

that I may be reasonably happy in this life

and supremely happy with Him

forever in the next.

Amen.   — Reinhold Niebuhr (1892-1971)

UNIT 4

The faith of the Israelites, much like Christianity, is not focused solely on beliefs but also on actions. The proverbs emphasize virtuous living, offer practical advice on how to deal with daily life, and remind us what is important and what is not. Below are some examples.

> Charm is deceptive and beauty fleeting;
> the woman who fears the LORD is to be praised.
> (Proverbs 31:30)

> Better a little with fear of the LORD
> than a great fortune with anxiety.
> (Proverbs 15:16)

> Walk with the wise and you become wise,
> but the companion of fools fares badly.
> (Proverbs 13:20)

> Open your mouth in behalf of the mute,
> and for the rights of the destitute;
> Open your mouth, judge justly,
> defend the needy and the poor!
> (Proverbs 31:8–9)

> Better a dish of herbs where love is
> than a fatted ox and hatred with it.
> (Proverbs 15:17) ✳

UNIT 4

OVERVIEW of the Book of Proverbs

- **Authors:** King Solomon is introduced as the author, probably because of his legendary wisdom. However, the actual authors are unknown, writing from the reign of King Solomon (970–931 BC) to sometime after the Babylonian Exile (587–538 BC).

- **Themes:** Seeking wisdom, avoiding foolishness and laziness, respecting parents, acting justly, trusting in God.

- **Of note:** The book is made up of several collections of proverbs.

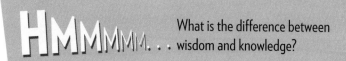

HMMMMMM. . . What is the difference between wisdom and knowledge?

Article 61
Job: Why Do Good People Suffer?

Hurricanes, murders, car accidents. Sometimes people lose their lives in the most unlikely and unjust ways. Family and friends are devastated and may agonize over why God would allow this to happen. The same goes for those who have experienced suffering through divorce, illness, poverty, and the like. What did they or those left behind do to justify such suffering? It's a very good question, one that has perplexed human beings probably for as long as our species has walked the Earth.

The Book of Job (pronounced *jōb*, which rhymes with *globe*) explores the mystery of suffering. It provides a different take on the generally accepted Israelite belief that God punishes the wicked and rewards the good in this life, and it offers a startling response to the question "Why do bad things happen to good people?"

But before going any further, let's take a step back to review a few key learnings from previous chapters that will help you better understand and appreciate this unique story.

UNIT 4

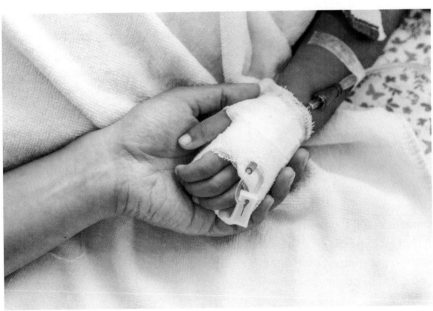

Why do bad things happen to good people? This is one of life's mysteries addressed in the Book of Job.

A Quick Review

Let's recall some of the principles for good biblical interpretation to guide our reading of the Book of Job. First, remember the cultural concept of divine retributive justice. That is, God rewards those who do good and punishes those who do wrong during this lifetime. The idea of divine retributive justice is reflected in many Old Testament books, but the Old Testament also has writings that question this concept (see articles 58 and 59). The Book of Job is one of those writings.

Second, we must consider the situation of the original audience—the Jewish People—that the human author is writing for. This closely follows the first point. The author's original audience held fast to the belief in divine retributive justice. It is this audience and their belief in divine retributive justice that the book's author seeks to challenge.

Third, consider the literary genre of Job. Knowing the literary genre used by the human author allows you to set your expectations appropriately. For example, when you hear a story that begins with "Once upon a time . . ." you understand right away that it's a fairy tale. In a fairy tale, you can expect to find fire-breathing dragons, crystal balls, and magic spells, but you wouldn't expect to find these things in a book on scientific discoveries.

The beginning of the Book of Job sets your expectations for a folktale. "In the land of Uz there was a blameless and upright man named Job" (1:1). This is followed by a short description of this faithful man and his virtuous and wonderful life (see verses 1–5). Then we listen to a conversation between God and Satan. Right away we know this is not intended to be factual history. Although the book may have been based on a real person, we know that this inspired writing is not intended to express historical fact.

Curse God and Die!

God and Satan's conversation is quite interesting! God brags about Job, saying that he is "blameless and upright, fearing God and avoiding evil" (Job 1:8), while Satan contends that Job is faithful only because God rewards him. He contends that if God took away all the nice things, "surely he will curse you to your face" (verse 11). God takes the bet and allows Satan to do whatever he wants to poor Job. (This is another sign that this is a fictional story because God does not play games with our lives.)

Job's life is perfect. He has a big family, a big house, more cattle than anyone else, and his wife and children love him. In the eyes of the ancient Israelites, these are all signs that God has rewarded Job. From the perspective of divine retributive justice, Job is someone who is faithful to God and follows the Law, and therefore nothing bad should happen to him. Wrong! What happens next completely disrupts the audience's expectations about retributive justice: bad things start happening to this good and blameless man! His goodness is emphasized by his refusal to curse God after all these horrible things happen to him.

In this painting by William Blake, Satan smites Job after betting with God that Job's faith will waiver if God takes away all good things in Job's life.

Satan has a second conversation with God, and proposes another bet, only this time, Job's suffering is even worse (see Job 1:13–2:10). In the midst of all his pain, Job's wife says: "Are you still holding to your innocence? Curse God and die!" (2:9). These two sentences get to the heart of the issue. Like Job's wife, the audience can see only two possible explanations for Job's suffering:

1. Job must be guilty. He must have done something to deserve this, and is falsely claiming to be innocent. (his wife's first sentence).
2. If God is so cruel that he would punish someone for no reason, then he is not worthy of our praise. Go ahead and curse him! (his wife's second sentence).

Job does not accept either explanation. His response to his wife? "We accept good things from God; should we not accept evil?" (Job 2:10). He sits in the difficult middle ground of maintaining his innocence and not blaming God.

UNIT 4

When have you comforted a friend who was going through a difficult time?

Don't Do Something, Just Sit There!

Job's life has been turned completely upside down. Three of his friends hear about his misfortunes and travel long distances to comfort him. They gather next to him on the ground and cry with Job for seven days and nights, "but none of them spoke a word to him; for they saw how great was his suffering" (Job 2:13).

If you ever want to assist a friend who is grieving, Job's friends are perfect role models. They sit with their friend and mourn with him, yet they keep their words to a minimum. When loved ones are experiencing a painful situation, it is natural to want to fix it, to find solutions to the problem, and make the heartache go away. But some things, like the death of a loved one, cannot be remedied. No words can repair that pain. We may feel awkward because we do not know how to respond appropriately. Probably the best thing you can do is show up and be present. Let them know that they are not alone by saying something like this: "I am here for you, and if you want to talk, I'll listen. If you just want to sit and be quiet, I can do that too."

This sympathy is short lived, however. After hearing Job complain about his pain and suffering in chapter 3, his friends respond with less than helpful arguments. Now the book uses a new literary genre, a theological debate between Job and his three friends. Job's friends argue that he must have done something to bring on his misfortunes (see Job, chapters 3–37). In response, Job continues to proclaim his innocence. This back and forth continues for thirty-five chapters!

God's Dramatic Answer!

Job desperately wants to understand why all these horrific events are occurring. He senses the need to defend his actions and make a case for his innocence. Near the end of the debate, he challenges God himself, saying "Let the Almighty answer me!" (Job 31:35). And God does. God bursts "out of the storm" and bellows: "Who is this who darkens counsel / with words of ignorance? / Gird up your loins now, like a man; / I will question you, and you tell me the answers!" (38:1–3). Uh oh!

© fstop123 / iStock.com

UNIT 4

MAKE IT SO

Almost every parish has a bereavement ministry that provides assistance for those who have recently lost a loved one. This ministry includes guidance with the funeral and burial, help finding counseling services, and support groups at the parish. This ministry also does simple things too, like organizing people to prepare meals. You (and a friend or two) can do this. Call your parish office and leave a message for the coordinator of bereavement ministry and tell them that you would like to help prepare meals for those who have recently had a death in the family. Before and after you cook the meals, say a prayer for everyone involved. In this small way, you can silently support them as they mourn.

God's response is a long and poetic reflection on nature. He repeatedly asks Job questions to which there are largely three appropriate answers: "God," "No," or "I don't know." Who decided how big the earth should be (see Job 38:4–5)? Do you know what the bottom of the sea looks like (see verse 16)? Can you tell the clouds to rain down water on the earth (see verse 34)? Who decided how long mountain goats should be pregnant (see 39:1–2)? This goes on for two chapters, until Job interrupts the Lord and admits he does not know much (see 40:4–5), but God does not relent and continues for two more chapters!

One point we can gather from God's long response is that people learn the most when they reflect on real experience. Someone can tell you that mixing yellow and blue makes green and you might believe them, but if someone gives you yellow paint and blue paint and makes you mix them, there is no way to deny it that the two colors make green. God could have just told Job, "Hey, there's a lot you don't know, buddy!" Instead, God makes Job reflect on his experience of the natural world, which in turn allows Job (and us, the readers) to realize this truth for himself.

The Book of Job teaches us that God is beyond human knowledge, and that some mysteries, including suffering, can never be completely understood, they can only be accepted.

It Will Not Fit in Our Brains

In the Garden of Eden, the serpent tempted Adam and Eve with the desire to know what God knows (see Genesis 3:5). Some people say this— assuming that we know better than God—is the root of all sin. However, there are some things that humans will never fully understand. This is the point God is making in his long speech to Job. Some things will always be a **mystery** because, simply put, we are not God.

Even though the question as to why bad things happen to good people is a mystery, it is not always *completely* mysterious. Jesus' Passion, death, and Resurrection have revealed for us that suffering can be redemptive, that we can participate in God's saving plan. But, even when it is redemptive, why some people suffer and others do not is still a mystery. When Job faces this great mystery, he responds, "I have spoken but did not understand; / things too marvelous for me, which I did not know" (Job 42:3).

When we use this word *mystery*, it is not like a mystery novel where you have to sift through the evidence and clues to figure out who committed the crime. In the religious sense, a mystery is something beyond human understanding. It is something that just will not "fit" in our brains! ✳

OVERVIEW of the Book of Job

- **Author:** Unknown, written during the sixth or fifth centuries BC.
- **Theme:** Why do good people suffer? God's power, presence, and wisdom are beyond human understanding.
- **Of note:** Job is a story within a story. Chapters 1–2 and 42:7–17 constitute a folktale. Set within that tale, 3:1–42:6 is a poetic debate about the cause of suffering.

HMMMMM. . . Why aren't Job's friends' arguments helpful to Job? Why is God's "rant" helpful?

mystery ▶ The very nature of God, who is beyond understanding; or a specific doctrine revealed by God that is beyond full human understanding.

Article 62

Ecclesiastes: What's the Point?

What is the point? I worked so hard to do a good job on that stupid biology project, and I didn't get enough points to earn even a B! Casandra worked half as hard as I did and got an A! My biology grade is still suffering and so am I!

This kind of frustration is something we all experience at some point in life. Sometimes people who do things the right way end up suffering, and people who do things wrong seem to end up on top. The Book of Ecclesiastes tackles this injustice head-on. The author is even willing to complain: "A bad business God has given / to human beings to be busied with" (1:13). Although the author of Ecclesiastes does not provide any straightforward answers, he does point to the continuous presence of God, who is there in good times and in bad.

Sometimes it seems that no matter how hard we work or how good we are or how often we do the right thing, we will still experience pain and suffering.

Vanity!

New! Improved! How often have you heard those two words in a product advertisement? Do you really believe it to be true that life could be better if you had this new and improved product? Or are you a little skeptical?

The author of Ecclesiastes, Qoheleth, wouldn't be impressed with this advertising claim. He is skeptical and won't be taken in by claims that something is new and improved. In chapter 1, Qoheleth expresses the frustration that no matter how hard we work or how good we are or how often we do the right thing, we will still experience pain and suffering: "**Vanity** of vanities! All things are vanity!" (1:2) "Nothing is new under the sun" (verse 9).

vanity ➤ Something worthless, trivial, or pointless.

If that's the case, should we just give up? Of course not! Qoheleth teaches us to put difficult times in perspective. In a famous passage, he makes the point that life has many ups and downs:

> There is an appointed time for everything,
>   and a time for every affair under the heavens.
> A time to give birth, and a time to die;
>   a time to plant, and a time to uproot the plant.
> A time to kill, and a time to heal;
>   a time to tear down, and a time to build.
> A time to weep, and a time to laugh;
>   a time to mourn, and a time to dance.
>   (Ecclesiastes 3:1–4)

He concludes, "I recognized that there is nothing better than to rejoice and to do well during life" (3:12). Does that mean we should just have fun and not worry about anything? No, again. Qoheleth means that despite our sufferings, we should do everything we can to enjoy the life God has given us. We can walk around with a sour face and complain, or we can accept our struggles, continue to do good, and enjoy the good things God provides.

UNIT 4

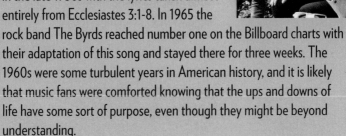

Did you know that the Book of Ecclesiastes had a hit song? The folk singer Peter Seeger wrote the original song "Turn! Turn! Turn!" in the late 1950s with the lyrics taken almost entirely from Ecclesiastes 3:1-8. In 1965 the rock band The Byrds reached number one on the Billboard charts with their adaptation of this song and stayed there for three weeks. The 1960s were some turbulent years in American history, and it is likely that music fans were comforted knowing that the ups and downs of life have some sort of purpose, even though they might be beyond understanding.

God Works in Everything

The teacher of Ecclesiastes identifies numerous reasons why our attempts to be happy are just vanity:

- Greedy people are never satisfied, because they never have enough money, or are sad when they lose what they do have (see 5:12–19).
- Humans do not have any advantages over animals, because in the end, both of us die (see 3:19–20).
- The path to wisdom is through sorrow (see 7:3).

Complaints such as these, along with posing questions with no easy answers, have earned the Book of Ecclesiastes a reputation for being a rather gloomy text! However, Qoheleth makes some important points:

- All the good that we have is a gift from God (see 5:18).
- If we accept the good, then we should accept the bad too, or at least not blame it on God (see 7:14).

Ultimately, Qoheleth accepts the mysteries of life, and encourages us to do the same, pointing us to the wonderful presence of God, "who is working in everything" (11:5). ✳

OVERVIEW of the Book of Ecclesiastes

- **Author:** A wisdom teacher, Qoheleth, writing in the fourth or third century BC.
- **Themes:** Life is not always fair. There are no easy answers. Faith in God is where true wisdom is found.
- **Of note:** The Book of Ecclesiastes is attributed to King Solomon, although he did not write it.

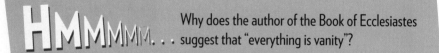

HMMMMM. . . Why does the author of the Book of Ecclesiastes suggest that "everything is vanity"?

Article 63

Song of Songs: Love Poems

Tess kept a photograph of Diego in her locker. She used the same photo as the wallpaper on her phone. Her profile picture on all her social media apps was the picture of the two of them, arm in arm, with a gorgeous mountain range behind them. She texted Diego in between classes and called him every night. He understood her like no one ever had before. They had been dating for just over a month, but she already knew deep in her heart that he was "the one." One day, they would get married, have babies and grandchildren, and live happily ever after.

Many people have had this feeling, especially when they first start dating, and though it is a wonderful feeling, only time will tell if the words "'til death do us part" will really be in their future. Even in the best of marriages, romantic feelings ebb and flow. Still, imagine what it would be like if someone felt that way about you all of the time, always wanting you near and continually caring about how you are doing. There *is* someone who loves you like this, and that someone is God.

UNIT 4

CATHOLICS **MAKING** A DIFFERENCE

Seriously? A nun who served as an inmate? Sort of. Blessed Marie-Louise Trichet was born in 1648 in Poitiers, France. At age seventeen, she met Fr. Louis de Montfort, chaplain of a badly run hospital for the poor and severely afflicted. Marie Louise decided to leave her wealthy family and devote her life to caring for the hospital's impoverished inmates. Marie Louise was unable to live at the hospital because there was no official position for her. So, she chose to enter the hospital as an "inmate." Later, she and Father Louis cofounded the religious community, the Daughters of Wisdom. Their **charism** is to gain heavenly wisdom and make known Jesus Christ, the Incarnate Wisdom, through service to the poor.

charism ➤ A special grace of the Holy Spirit given to an individual Christian or community, for the benefit and building up of the entire Church.

Sexual Attraction: It's More Than Just Sex

"Let him kiss me with kisses of his mouth, / for your love is better than wine." No, this is not the first line of a romance novel. It's the second verse of Song of Songs in the Bible (1:2). Yes, this book has a lot of sexual imagery in it. You may be wondering why. Here are some answers.

First, if we read these passages just as they are, the Song of Songs is a book of poems that affirm the goodness of sexuality. God created us male and female (see Genesis 1:27), so our sexuality is a gift from God. It is what attracts us to one another, it strengthens the union between husband and wife, and it allows us to share in the creative power of God to bring forth new life: babies! And that is good!

Second, the intimate dialogue of the man and woman in this poetry is not only about sexual attraction. The author of the Book of Song of Songs is using the attraction between a man and a woman as a metaphor: the closeness and intimacy shared between husband and wife is likened to the intimate covenant relationship between God and his people.

Song of Songs is a book of poetry that expresses the goodness of human love and God's love for his people.

The Song of Songs is not the first book to use sexual imagery as a symbol for the covenant. In the Book of Hosea, God told the prophet Hosea to marry a prostitute, Gomer (see 1:2) who was unfaithful to Hosea. Meanwhile, the Israelites had broken their covenant with God time and again by worshipping other gods. Gomer's unfaithfulness to Hosea illustrated Israel's unfaithfulness to God. In the New Testament, Saint Paul's Letter to the Ephesians (see 5:23–33) and the Book of Revelation (see 21:2) also use marriage imagery to describe the relationship between God and the Church.

A Conversation in Poems

The Song of Songs is structured as a conversation, and you will usually see the parts noted in the text: *W* stands for the woman, *M* for the man, and *D* for the Daughters of Jerusalem. The Daughters of Jerusalem act as sort of a narrator, periodically asking questions that incite responses. But the conversation is mainly between the man and the woman, who express their love and gush over one another's beauty.

You will notice that the imagery they use to flatter each other is not exactly something we would use today. "Your hair is like a flock of goats" (Song 6:5) and "Your nose [is] like the tower of Lebanon" (7:5) do not translate well in the modern world! It is highly suggested that you do not use these as compliments if you are trying to get a date for homecoming or the prom! Concepts of beauty are defined differently among cultures, and this too changes over time.

The imagery of the Song of Songs is sure to grab your attention. The fact that it is in the Bible emphasizes the importance and the goodness of our sexuality—a gift from God. Let its engaging poetry remind you of the tenderness and passion of God's love for you. ✻

"How beautiful you are, my friend, how beautiful you are!" (Song of Songs 4:1).

UNIT 4

OVERVIEW of the Book of Song of Songs

- **Author:** Unknown, probably writing after the Jews' return from the Babylonian Exile.
- **Theme:** Poetry that expresses the goodness and passion of human love and of God's love for his people.
- **Of note:** This book is sometimes called the Song of Solomon or the Canticle of Canticles.

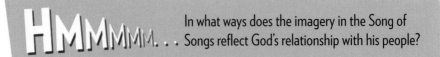

HMMMMM. . . . In what ways does the imagery in the Song of Songs reflect God's relationship with his people?

Article 64
Ben Sira: Wisdom Far from Home

Have you ever been to another country? Do you have friends who come from a culture different from your own? Perhaps you have come from another country but now live in the United States. If you've ever been in either situation, you know it can feel a little strange, even awkward, to reconcile your cultural practices and beliefs when visiting or living in another country.

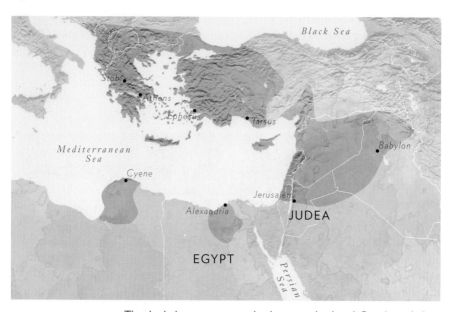

The shaded areas represent the locations the Jewish People settled in after fleeing their homes to escape persecution or foreign invasion. This movement is called the Jewish Diaspora.

    The Jewish People had a similar experience because of the Jewish Diaspora. As they formed communities in foreign lands, they faced many cultural practices and beliefs that conflicted with their own. Surrounded by Greek culture, Jewish communities worked hard to maintain their cultural identity. Two of the Old Testament books reflect this struggle: the Book of Wisdom and the Wisdom of Ben Sira.

A Woman to Guide Us

The Book of Wisdom fits in well near the Books of Job and Ecclesiastes. With the historical background of the Babylonian Exile and the domination of the Greeks, the author of Wisdom also emphasizes that suffering is not a punishment from God. So many Jewish People died because they refused to give up their faith in God. It made no sense that the Lord would punish them for that. There had to be some other explanation. Like the Second Book of Maccabees, the Book of Wisdom reflects the Jewish People's growing belief in the afterlife: "For God formed us to be imperishable; / the image of his own nature he made us" (2:23).

The Book of Wisdom is attributed to King Solomon. Although Solomon did not actually compose it, the author writes in King Solomon's voice to praise the wonders of wisdom. Like the Book of Proverbs, wisdom in the Book of Wisdom is personified as a woman who blesses and guides us to act in accordance with God's ways (see 9:1–3).

Sophia the Divine Wisdom represented in a sixteenth-century Russian icon. Sophia is the Greek word for wisdom and also a female name.

© Ivan Vdovin / Alamy Stock Photo

UNIT 4

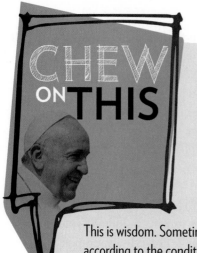

CHEW ON **THIS**

The first gift of the Holy Spirit . . . is . . . wisdom. But it is not simply human wisdom, which is the fruit of knowledge and experience. And wisdom is precisely this: it is the grace of being able to see everything with the eyes of God. It is simply this: it is to see the world, to see situations, circumstances, problems, everything through God's eyes. This is wisdom. Sometimes we see things according to our liking or according to the condition of our heart, with love or with hate, with envy. . . . No, this is not God's perspective. Wisdom is what the Holy Spirit works in us so as to enable us to see things with the eyes of God. This is the gift of wisdom. (Pope Francis, "General Audience," Saint Peter's Square, April 9, 2014)

A Different Jesus

The Wisdom of Ben Sira was written by a man named Jesus, but not the Jesus you are probably thinking of! This Jesus finished his book on wisdom around 175 BC. Almost sixty years later, his grandson translated the book from Hebrew into Greek, the common language of that time. The book contains practical advice to guide its readers toward goodness and happiness (see Ben Sira 25:1). It touches on all sorts of life situations: addressing anger (see 27:22–30), loaning money (see 29:1–20), raising children (see 30:1–13). He gives special attention to encouraging faithfulness to God's Law (see 2:15–16, 15:1, 19:20–24).

One of the highlights of the Wisdom of Ben Sira is the chapters praising the great heroes of Jewish history, from Noah to Nehemiah (see chapters 44–50). These chapters read like a "Who's Who" of Israelite history, reminding the Jews living in Diaspora of their rich history.

The Wisdom of Ben Sira contains some writing that reflects the patriarchal society of the human author. Sometimes these passages can sound quite negative about women. So as you read them, be sure not to blindly accept these negative perceptions. Passages like "I would rather live with a dragon or a lion / than live with a wicked woman" (25:16) should be read as **hyperbole** and understood to apply to men as well! ✳

OVERVIEW of the Book of Wisdom

- **Author:** Unknown, writing around 50 BC, making it the latest of all the Old Testament books.
- **Theme:** The reward of the righteous, the praise of wisdom, and the importance of trust in God.
- **Of note:** This book is not found in the Jewish canon, nor in the Protestant Bible's Old Testament canon.

OVERVIEW of the Book of Wisdom of Ben Sira

- **Author:** Jesus Ben Sira, who completed his book around 175 BC.
- **Theme:** The superiority of Jewish wisdom over Greek wisdom.
- **Of note:** Sometimes called the Book of Sirach; it is not found in the Jewish canon, nor in the Protestant Bible's Old Testament canon.

UNIT 4

HMMMMM. . . How does the Jewish People's growing belief in the afterlife affect some of the later writings of the Old Testament, such as the wisdom books?

---

hyperbole ➤ Exaggerated statements or claims not meant to be taken literally.

1. How are the Wisdom and Poetry Books different from the rest of the writings of the Old Testament?

2. What is meant by "fear of the Lord," and why is it useful?

3. What belief does the Book of Job address?

4. How does the Book of Job respond to the question of why good people suffer?

5. What does the author of Ecclesiastes suggest we do in the face of the constantly repetitive cycles of good and bad times?

6. What two things might the imagery in Song of Songs symbolize?

7. Describe the historical situation in which the Book of Wisdom and the Wisdom of Ben Sira were written.

8. What might have been a factor in leading to the Jewish People's growing belief in the afterlife?

© East Images / Alamy Stock Photo

UNIT 4

SOPHIA: LADY WISDOM

In several of the Wisdom Books, God's wisdom is personified as Sophia, or Lady Wisdom. She is portrayed as wise, strong, and beautiful.

1. In what ways has the sculptor captured Sophia's wisdom, strength, and power?

2. Why might the ancient authors have portrayed God's wisdom as a woman instead of a man?

UNIT 4 HIGHLIGHTS

CHAPTER 12   Rebuilding Jerusalem and the Temple

The Persian army conquers the Babylonians in 537 BC.

King Cyrus allows the Jewish exiles in Babylon to return to Jerusalem.

The Diaspora Jews continue living outside of Israel, worshipping in synagogues.

With leaders like Ezra and Nehemiah, the Jewish People begin rebuilding Jerusalem and the Temple.

To keep their religion pure, Ezra and Nehemiah demand that Jewish men leave their non-Jewish wives and children.

The new Temple is completed, and Temple worship is reestablished.

The returned Jews now find their religious identity in proper worship in the Jerusalem Temple.

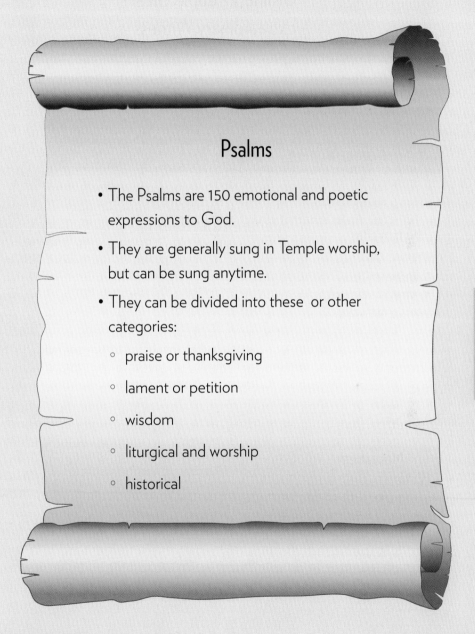

Psalms

- The Psalms are 150 emotional and poetic expressions to God.
- They are generally sung in Temple worship, but can be sung anytime.
- They can be divided into these or other categories:
  - praise or thanksgiving
  - lament or petition
  - wisdom
  - liturgical and worship
  - historical

UNIT 4

CHAPTER 13 Ordinary People Give Extraordinary Witness

The Chosen People suffer terribly under Greek rule in Judah (BC 332 to 142). But the Jews are encouraged by stories—both fictional and historical—of ordinary people who have great faith in the power of God.

The Novellas

These stories are told primarily to illustrate truths that transcend history.

Tobit is a good man who suffers so terribly he'd rather be dead. Still he trusts in God.

Judith's trust in God and courageous plan saves the Israelites from destruction.

Queen Esther, the wife of the Persian king, is secretly Jewish. Her courage saves the Jewish People from genocide.

The Maccabean History

The two books of Maccabees contain stories of violent resistance and non-violent resistance against the Greek injustices.

Judas Maccabeus, and the sacrifices his family and others made, lead the Jewish People to freedom from Greek rule.

Second Maccabees contains inspiring stories of the martyrdom of Eleazar and the mother and her seven sons.

CHAPTER 14 The Wisdom Books

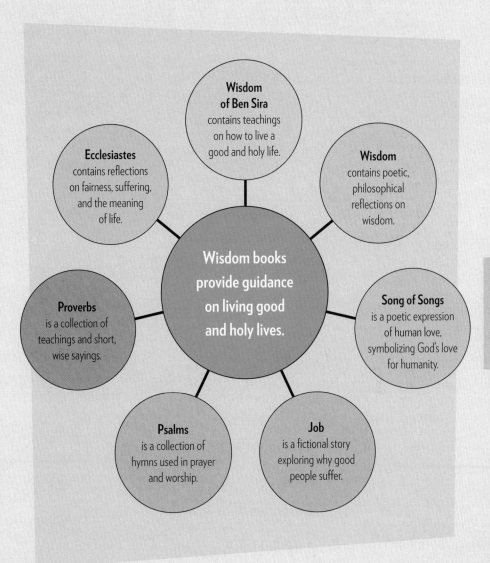

UNIT 4

UNIT 4
BRING IT HOME

HOW DO CHALLENGING TIMES DEEPEN OUR FAITH?

UNIT 4

FOCUS QUESTIONS

CHAPTER 12   Why was rebuilding the Temple so important?

CHAPTER 13   How do people face big challenges in biblical times?

CHAPTER 14   How do I live a good life?

IFE
Mater Dei High School

I understand more about where God is when times get hard. I seemed to have forgotten God's role in the hard times. I do believe my faith is like a pulley system, but this unit helped me better define it. Every time things get rough, I deepen my relationship with God, while still questioning him. In this way, I can rely on God and trust him to protect me.

UNIT 4

REFLECT

Take some time to read and reflect on the unit and chapter focus questions listed on the facing page.

- What question or section did you identify most closely with?

- What did you find within the unit that was comforting or challenging?

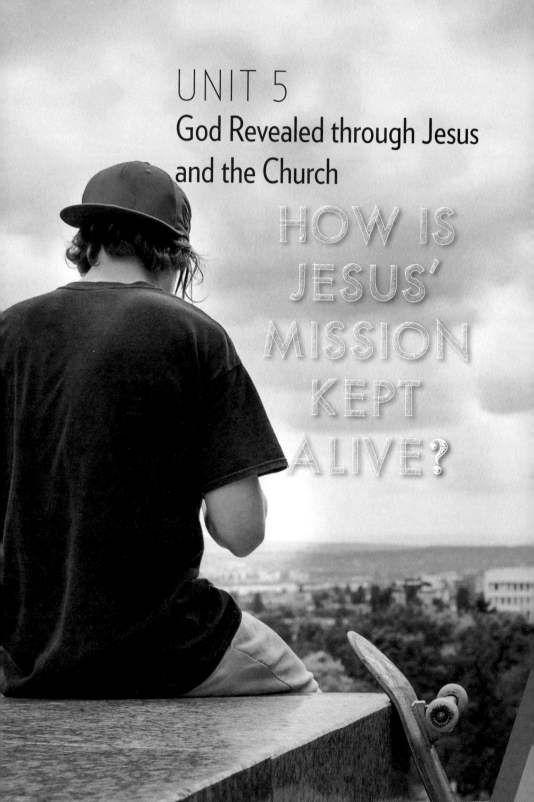

394

UNIT 5
God Revealed through Jesus and the Church

HOW IS JESUS' MISSION KEPT ALIVE?

LOOKING AHEAD

CHAPTER 15 Page 396
The Gospels

CHAPTER 16 Page 430
The Acts of the Apostles and the Letters

CHAPTER 17 Page 456
Scripture in the Life of the Church

UNIT 5

Jesus' mission is lived out every day by every one of us. When a friend is having trouble in math, you offer to help; if someone drops their things, you help pick them up; you set the dinner table so your mom doesn't have to; you pick up trash that isn't yours. If you have done any of these things, you have lived out Jesus' mission.

BELLA
Father Lopez Catholic High School

CHAPTER 15
The Gospels

DON'T THE FOUR GOSPELS SAY THE SAME THING?

SNAPSHOT

Article 65   Page 397
Sharing the Story

Article 66   Page 401
The Synoptic Gospels: Similar but Different
- Pre-read: Matthew 5:3–12, 21:1–9
- Pre-read: Luke 6:20, 19:28–38
- Pre-read: Mark 11:1–10

Article 67   Page 406
Major Events in the Synoptic Gospels

Article 68   Page 412
Jesus: Storyteller and Miracle Worker
- Pre-read: Luke 15:11–32
- Pre-read: Mark 5:21–34
- Pre-read: Matthew 14:22–32

Article 69   Page 418
From a Beloved Friend: The Gospel of John
- Pre-read: John 1:1–18, 2:1–12, 6:22–59, 13:1–20

Article 70   Page 425
Jesus: God in the Flesh
- Pre-read: John 14:1–14
- Pre-read: Colossians 1:15–23

Article 65
Sharing the Story

After watching a TV series that traces the family history of celebrities, Macy became interested in her own family history. She asked her mother if she knew anything about their ancestors. Macy's mom pointed her to a cedar box in which she found old photos, newspaper articles, and a handwritten family tree dating all the way back to the slave plantations. There was also a collection of papers stapled together, the memories of her great-great-great-grandmother who was born into slavery in 1849. This woman's strength and determination not only led to her survival but also allowed her to become a force of goodness that rippled down to Macy's mother, aunts, and uncles. The papers in her hands answered questions Macy did not even know she had. They made her feel the presence of her ancestors, as if they were just sitting right next to her sharing their stories.

The narratives of the Bible are like the family history of our ancestors in faith. How they came to us is not terribly different from how Macy learned about her family. Reflecting on the events they had experienced, and guided by the Holy Spirit, the human authors of the Bible wrote about the truth revealed to them about how God was acting in their history. Many of these accounts were passed on verbally for generations, before eventually being written down.

The narratives of the Bible are like the family history of our ancestors in faith, passed on, both through oral tradition and written tradition, from one generation to the next. What family stories have been passed on to you?

© Steven Widoff / Alamy Stock Photo

UNIT 5

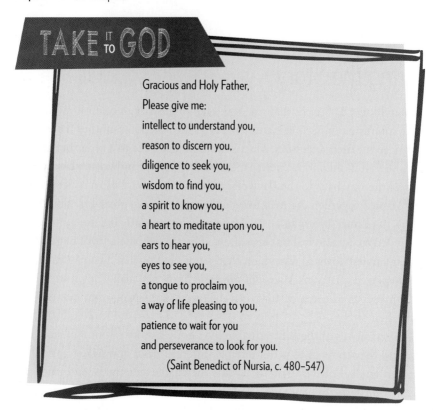

TAKE IT TO GOD

Gracious and Holy Father,

Please give me:

intellect to understand you,

reason to discern you,

diligence to seek you,

wisdom to find you,

a spirit to know you,

a heart to meditate upon you,

ears to hear you,

eyes to see you,

a tongue to proclaim you,

a way of life pleasing to you,

patience to wait for you

and perseverance to look for you.

(Saint Benedict of Nursia, c. 480–547)

Passing On the Good News

In literature, the climax of a story is when the tension in the plot reaches its highest point and decisive action is taken. That moment is the major turning point; life before and after it is radically different. The life, death, and Resurrection of Jesus Christ are the climax of the whole Bible, the turning point in salvation history, in the world's history! It is the reason that countries with Christian backgrounds date their calendar years BC (before Christ) and AD (*Anno Domini*, in the year of the Lord). The world changed and will never be the same.

Because the four **Gospels** attributed to Matthew, Mark, Luke, and John are the fullest revelation of Jesus' teachings and saving deeds, they occupy a central place in the Bible. The word *gospel* is translated from a Greek word meaning "good news." The Gospels, then, proclaim the "good news" that Jesus is God's fullest revelation to humanity. "[They] are the heart of all the Scriptures 'because they are our principal source for the life and teaching of the

Gospels ➤ Translated from a Greek word meaning "good news," referring to the four books attributed to Matthew, Mark, Luke, and John. The Gospels are the principal source for accounts of Jesus Christ's life and teaching and work of salvation.

UNIT 5

Incarnate Word, our Savior'"[1] (*Catechism of the Catholic Church [CCC]*, number 125). The Gospels are the means by which we are able to come to know and accept Jesus Christ as our Savior, and apply his teachings to our lives.

Putting It on Paper

The Gospels occupy a central place in the Bible because they are the fullest revelation of Jesus' teachings and saving deeds.

Understanding how something came to be written can sometimes help us discover its meaning. The writing of the Gospels took several decades to complete. The experiences of Jesus and his followers were first shared by word of mouth. Only after some time had passed were they finally written down in the words we have today. Scholars have identified three stages in this process of forming the Gospels.

1. **The Life and Teachings of Jesus**

   The Son of God became flesh and was born of the Virgin Mary in the land of Palestine approximately two thousand years ago. Jesus was a real person—a Jewish man living in a land occupied by the Romans. The Romans' oppressive rule showed little tolerance for dissent. Jesus' teachings, healings, and other miracles pointed toward the Kingdom of God he was establishing on Earth. He angered the religious authorities and was arrested by the Romans and sentenced to death. Through Jesus' Passion, death, Resurrection, and Ascension, his followers came to recognize him as the Messiah and Incarnate Word of God, who died for our salvation.

2. **Oral Tradition**

   After Jesus' Ascension into Heaven, and the outpouring of the Holy Spirit at Pentecost, Jesus' followers began to spread the Good News by word of mouth. Guided by the Spirit, the Apostles and disciples passed on the *kerygma*, the Good News of divine salvation, which is offered to all through Jesus Christ.

---

kerygma ▶ A Greek word meaning "proclamation" or "preaching," referring to the announcement of the Gospel or the Good News of divine salvation offered to all through Jesus Christ. *Kerygma* has two senses. It is both an event of proclamation and a message proclaimed.

UNIT 5

3. The Written Gospels

In an effort to ensure that the life and teachings of Jesus were preserved and authentically communicated to others, people in the early Church gathered various oral and written accounts of Jesus' life and teachings and used them to write the four Gospels. The need for authentic Gospels developed for two reasons. First, some misleading teachings about Jesus were being spread and they needed to be refuted. Second, the original eyewitnesses to Jesus' life began to die, and the Church wanted to preserve the truth of the message they proclaimed.

This entire process is under the guidance of the Holy Spirit. We are grateful to those who opened themselves to the guidance of the Holy Spirit, allowing his saving truth to be written and passed down to us today. ✳

A fragment of papyrus with Greek biblical text. The entire New Testament was written in Greek.

UNIT 5

HMMMMM. . .

Explain why each stage in the formation of the Gospels was important.

Article 66

The Synoptic Gospels: Similar but Different

Imagine you are a famous person, and three authors have written biographies about you. The first is by a friend from your childhood, whose account focuses on your shared experiences and the events that have formed you as a person. The second is penned by a writer who concentrates on your education and training, and the impact you've had on others. The third is written by a biographer who focuses on the charity work to which you have devoted so much of your time and energy.

Even though these three accounts share many similarities, each author tells your story in a unique way. Because they focus on specific themes, they highlight the elements important to that theme. Despite those differences, all three biographies are accurate, honest portrayals of a person whose life could never be encompassed in a single book.

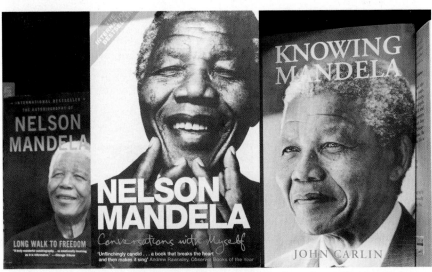

Three different biographies about Nelson Mandela, former president of South Africa, all accurate but each with its own unique focus.

UNIT 5

Jesus' life on Earth can never be fully captured by a single book. The Gospel of John even states this in its last verse: "There are also many other things that Jesus did, but if these were to be described individually, I do not think the whole world would contain the books that would be written" (21:25). Each of the four Gospels—Matthew, Mark, Luke, and John—emphasize certain aspects of Jesus' life and teachings that their communities needed to hear.

© AsiaTravel / Shutterstock.com

One Size Does Not Fit All

The Gospels offer accounts of Jesus' life, but they are not exactly biographies. Biographies generally try to tell the whole story of a person's life, attempting to accurately describe all the details. The Gospels do not do that. For example, only two of the four Gospels have accounts of Jesus' birth. Only one Gospel includes an account of Jesus as a preteen. Other than that, there is nothing else to read about Jesus' life until he begins his active ministry. The four Gospels even place the events of Jesus' life in slightly different order. It is fair to say that the Gospel authors were more concerned about the *meaning* of certain events in Jesus' life than in perfectly describing his life's every detail.

All this leads biblical scholars to describe the Gospels as a unique literary form. Think of them as religious or theological biographies that are based on the words and deeds of Jesus Christ. Guided by the Holy Spirit, the four Gospel writers, or **Evangelists**, focus on the themes and aspects of Jesus' life and teaching that are most meaningful to their respective Christian communities.

The early Christian communities could be quite different from one another, and one big difference was whether the community was predominately Jewish Christian or predominately Gentile Christian. Today, there is a clear separation between Jews and Christians, but that was not the case before and immediately after Jesus' life on Earth. Jesus was Jewish, and his earliest followers were also Jews. Even though they followed Jesus, these early Christians did not cease being Jewish. For example, the Temple was still their most important worship space (see Acts 2:46, 3:1). Even after

© Cindy Hopkins / Alamy Stock Photo

Early Christian communities didn't meet in public buildings. They first met in homes called "house churches" owned by wealthy Christians, like this ancient Roman villa in Ephesus, Turkey.

Evangelists ▶ From a Greek word meaning "messenger of good news," the title given to the authors of the Gospels of Matthew, Mark, Luke, and John.

his own conversion, Saint Paul proudly claims his Jewish faith as a descendant of Abraham (see Romans 11:1). These followers of Christ are sometimes called Jewish Christians.

But Jesus does not call only those in his own religious group to be his followers. He also comes to be "a light for revelation to the **Gentiles** [non-Jews]" (Luke 2:32). Even during his lifetime, Jesus has several encounters with Gentiles who are attracted to him and his message (see Matthew 8:5–13, John 12:20–21). After Christ's Ascension and the events of Pentecost, many Gentiles become believers. We refer to them as Gentile Christians. As you can imagine, the Gentile Christians have different concerns and questions than the Jewish Christians have.

The Look-Alikes

Because three of the Gospels—Matthew, Mark, and Luke—are similar in their style and content, they are called **synoptic Gospels**. Synoptic comes from a Greek word meaning "seeing together." Many scholars believe that Mark was the first Gospel written and that Matthew and Luke use Mark as a source for their Gospels. Matthew and Luke also seem to have some common passages that are not in Mark. Scholars theorize that these came from another common source they call **Quelle**, or the Q source. The Q source has never been discovered, but is believed to be a collection of Jesus' teachings shared among the early Christians. Matthew and Luke also contain material found only in their Gospels.

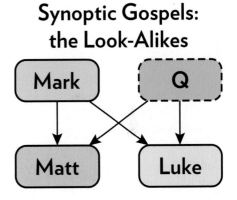

Synoptic Gospels: the Look-Alikes

Mark — Q — Matt — Luke

Gentile ➤ A non-Jewish person. In Sacred Scripture, the Gentiles were the uncircumcised, those who did not honor the God of the Torah. Saint Paul and other evangelists reached out to the Gentiles, baptizing them into the family of God.

synoptic Gospels ➤ The name given to the Gospels of Matthew, Mark, and Luke, because they are similar in style and content.

Quelle ➤ Also called the Q Source, a theoretical collection of ancient documents of the teachings of Jesus shared among the early followers of Christianity; believed by Scripture scholars to be a source for the Gospels of Matthew and Luke.

Gospel Comparisons

You will have opportunities in future courses to study the four Gospels and their unique features. For now, this chart will give you some idea of the unique characteristics of each Gospel:

	Matthew	Mark	Luke	John
Writer	Matthew, an unknown Jewish Christian, traditionally the Apostle Matthew.	Mark, a second generation Christian, possibly a follower of Peter; traditionally the John Mark mentioned in Acts 12:12.	Luke, a Gentile Christian, traditionally Luke the physician and Paul's traveling companion mentioned in Colossians 4:14.	John, traditionally the Apostle John, more likely one of his followers.
Date Likely Written	AD 75–80	AD 65–70	AD 80–85	AD 90–100
Images of Christ	Teacher and prophet like Moses, Son of God, Son of Man, Messiah, and Lord.	The suffering servant of God, Son of Man, Son of God, Messiah, and Lord.	Great healer, merciful, compassion for the poor, Son of God, Son of Man, Messiah, and Lord.	*Logos*, Word of God, Son of God, Son of Man, Lamb of God, Redeemer, Messiah, and Lord.
Likely Audience	A Jewish Christian community in Antioch, Syria.	A Gentile Christian community in Rome undergoing persecution.	Written to Theophilus (meaning "lover of God"), who possibly represents any Christian, or a Gentile Christian community in Greece.	A community of Jews, Gentiles, and Samaritans living in Ephesus, Galatia (Turkey).

	Matthew	Mark	Luke	John
Unique Themes	Jesus teaches what it means to be a member of the Kingdom of Heaven. He prepares his followers to continue his teaching and ministry.	Jesus shows that the suffering in our lives can be a source of grace when united with the sufferings of Christ.	Jesus heals long-standing divisions among people. He calls his followers to have a special compassion for those excluded from wealth and power.	Jesus is the Divine Son of God, the image of God in flesh. Salvation is available for those who believe in Jesus and commit their lives to him.
Historical Situation	Written after the Romans had destroyed all of Jerusalem, including the Temple.	The Romans subdue armed Jewish rebellions. Christians experience persecution in Rome.	Written when the persecution of Jews and Christians was intensifying.	Emperor Domitian declared himself divine and mandated that all people worship him. Jewish leaders banned Christians from the synagogues.

UNIT 5

Article 67

Major Events in the Synoptic Gospels

Though each of the synoptic Gospels emphasizes certain aspects in order to address the needs of their communities, the similarities among them far outweigh the differences. Exploring and comparing these accounts offers us unending insights into Jesus Christ's saving mission. The following similarities convey the major events in the life and ministry of Jesus.

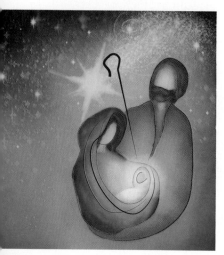

"Behold, the virgin shall be with child and bear a son, and they shall name him Emmanuel," which means "God is with us" (Matthew 1:23).

They Shall Name Him Emmanuel

The Gospels of Matthew and Luke include **infancy narratives**, accounts of Jesus' birth and childhood. These Gospels use the events surrounding Jesus' birth to express important truths about who he is.

Because Matthew's audience is Jewish, he begins his Gospel with Jesus' genealogy, emphasizing his Jewish ancestry. Jesus' coming into the world is the climax of Israel's history. The events of his conception and birth fulfill the Old Testament prophecies, informing Matthew's Jewish audience that Jesus is the Messiah for whom they had been waiting.

The author of Luke, on the other hand, is writing to a mostly Gentile audience in Greece. This community probably includes men and women from a wide variety of backgrounds and ethnicities, both rich and poor. Luke focuses attention on oppressed and marginalized people to emphasize Christ's compassion and justice. For example, the main voices in the infancy narrative are Mary and Elizabeth, two "powerless" women whose miraculous pregnancies point to the compassion of God (see 1:5–56). When the Holy Family—Joseph, Mary, and Jesus—is stranded in Bethlehem, and Mary must give birth in something like a barn, the poor shepherds are the first to recognize the Christ child (see 2:1–20).

UNIT 5

---

infancy narratives ▶ The accounts of Jesus' birth and early childhood.

"On coming up out of the water he saw the heavens being torn open and the Spirit, like a dove, descending upon him. And a voice came from the heavens, 'You are my beloved Son; with you I am well pleased'" (Mark 1:10).

My Beloved Son

All three of the synoptic Gospels recount the Baptism of Jesus in the Jordan River, which initiates his ministry and saving mission in the world. The Holy Spirit descends upon Jesus in the form of a dove, and the voice of God the Father comes from the heavens naming Jesus as his "beloved Son" (Matthew 3:17, Mark 1:11, Luke 3:22). In this event, we are able to see the union of the three Divine Persons of the Trinity—the Father, the Son, and the Holy Spirit.

Tempted

After his Baptism, Jesus is led into the desert for forty days, where he is tempted by Satan (see Matthew 4:1–11, Mark 1:12–13, Luke 4:1–13). We all know what it's like to be tempted to do something we know is wrong. And we know how difficult it can be to resist temptation. So does Jesus. The author of the Letter to the Hebrews points out that Jesus is able to sympathize with humanity because he had "similarly been tested in every way, yet [remained] without sin" (4:15).

UNIT 5

The Blessed

Matthew and Luke include some of Jesus' most profound and significant teachings, in particular the **Beatitudes**. The Beatitudes describe the actions and attitudes by which one can discover genuine happiness, and they teach us the final end to which God calls us: full communion with him in the Kingdom of Heaven. In Matthew's Sermon on the Mount (see Matthew 5:1–7:29), Jesus proclaims the New Law on a mountaintop like Moses. He does not abolish the Law of Moses, but rather invites Matthew's Jewish audience to observe the deeper meaning of the Law, loving God and loving our neighbor.

Luke's similar account, the Sermon on the Plain (see 6:20–49), is for a Gentile audience, so there is less need to connect the New Law to the Old Law. But it does offer more explicit commands to care for the poor and oppressed.

The Basilica of the Beatitudes is located on a small hill overlooking the Sea of Galilee. It is built on the traditional site of Jesus' delivery of the Sermon on the Mount.

Passion and Death

At the center of our faith are the **Passion**, death, Resurrection, and Ascension of Jesus Christ, which is called the **Paschal Mystery**. Christ's saving work is accomplished through the events of the Paschal Mystery. This is the reason the synoptic Gospels describe these events at great length, inviting us to a deeper understanding of the saving mysteries that lie at the heart of our faith.

Beatitudes ➤ The teachings of Jesus that begin the Sermon on the Mount and that summarize the New Law of Christ. The Beatitudes describe the actions and attitudes by which one can discover genuine happiness, and they teach us the final end to which God calls us: full communion with him in the Kingdom of Heaven.

Passion ➤ The suffering of Jesus during the final days of his life: his agony in the garden at Gethsemane, his trial, and his Crucifixion.

Paschal Mystery ➤ The work of salvation accomplished by Jesus Christ mainly through his Passion, death, Resurrection, and Ascension.

The Passion of Christ refers to the suffering Jesus endured in the final days of his life: his agony in the garden at Gethsemane, his trial, and his Crucifixion. Just before his Passion, Jesus institutes the Eucharist at the Last Supper. He establishes the New Covenant through his death on the cross, which we celebrate and participate in through the Eucharist: "This is my blood of the covenant, which will be shed on behalf of many for the forgiveness of sins" (Matthew 26:28).

Jesus' Passion begins with his agony in the garden at Gethsemane. In quick succession, he is betrayed by Judas, arrested, and condemned. The people behind this are the chief priests and elders, and the **Sanhedrin**, the ruling council of Jewish leaders, backs them up. They turn Jesus over to the Roman governor, Pontius Pilate, to be executed (see Mark 14:32–65). Though some of the details differ in the synoptic Gospels, they agree on these major events:

The Roman governor of Judea, Pontius Pilate, condemned Jesus to death by crucifixion, a Roman form of execution. Death was slow and painful.

- The Roman leadership alone had the legal authority to inflict the death penalty. Therefore, Jesus could only be executed with the approval of Pontius Pilate, the Roman governor of Judea.
- The soldiers mocked, tortured, and crucified Jesus. Crucifixion was a cruel and painful way to die; the victim usually suffocated to death.

The Gospel of Luke emphasizes Jesus' mercy and compassion, even during his Passion. At his death, Jesus loves even the soldiers who kill him and asks his heavenly Father to forgive them (see Luke 23:34). "By his Passion, Christ delivered us from Satan and from sin. He merited for us the new life in the Holy Spirit. His grace restores what sin had damaged in us" (*CCC*, number 1708).

UNIT 5

Sanhedrin ➤ An assembly of Jewish religious leaders—chief priests, scribes, and elders—who functioned as the supreme council and tribunal during the time of Jesus.

Death Does Not Have the Final Word: Jesus' Resurrection

We now come to the grand climax of the four Gospels, indeed, of the whole Bible. The four Gospels have different details, but they agree on the essentials. After the Sabbath, some women return to the tomb to anoint the body of Jesus and realize something is amiss. The stone has been rolled away from the tomb, and inside, Jesus' body is nowhere to be found. Soon after, Jesus begins appearing to various disciples: to Mary Magdalene (see John 20:11–16), to the Apostles (see Matthew 28:16–17), to two disciples on their way home to Emmaus (see Luke 24:13–35). These appearances surprise, shock, and give great joy. Most important, they help the disciples finally understand Jesus Christ's true identity. In the words of Thomas, the former doubter, "My Lord and my God!" (John 20:28).

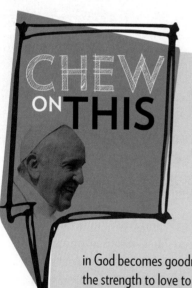

The incarnate Son of God did not remove illness and suffering from human experience but by taking them upon himself he transformed them and gave them new meaning. . . . Just as the Father gave us the Son out of love, and the Son gave himself to us out of the same love, so we too can love others as God has loved us, giving our lives for one another. Faith in God becomes goodness, faith in the crucified Christ becomes the strength to love to the end, even our enemies. The proof of authentic faith in Christ is self-giving and the spreading of love for our neighbors, especially for those who do not merit it, for the suffering and for the marginalized. (Pope Francis, "Message for the 22nd World Day of the Sick 2014," number 2)

Christ's Resurrection is the cornerstone of our faith. In his First Letter to the Corinthians, Saint Paul writes, "If Christ has not been raised, then empty [too] is our preaching; empty, too, your faith" (15:14). His Resurrection is the final sign that Jesus Christ is indeed God the Father's beloved Son, the Messiah, the Savior of the world. His Resurrection is the guarantee that all that he revealed is true. And his Resurrection is the promise and hope for our own resurrection. Without his Resurrection, there would be no Gospels, no Christian faith, no Church. It is the reason we cry out "Alleluia!" every Easter season.

Jesus Christ's Resurrection appearances end with his **Ascension**. The Ascension refers to his "going up" into Heaven forty days after his Resurrection. Before he does that, he turns his saving mission over to the leaders of his Church: "Go, therefore, and make disciples of all nations, baptizing them in the name of the Father, and of the Son, and of the holy Spirit, teaching them to observe all that I have commanded you. And behold, I am with you always, until the end of the age" (Matthew 28:19–20).

When Jesus ascended into Heaven, he passed fully and completely into the presence of God. Though we cannot see his physical presence in human form, Jesus is still present in the Eucharist and he is present in his people, the Church: "For where two or three are gathered together in my name, there am I in the midst of them" (Matthew 18:20). ✳

HMMMMM. . . Why is it better to have four Gospels rather than just one?

Ascension ➤ The "going up" into Heaven of the Risen Christ forty days after his Resurrection.

Article 68

Jesus: Storyteller and Miracle Worker

There is an old saying: "The shortest distance between human beings and the truth is a story." Somehow telling a story can capture the imagination and pass on wisdom more powerfully than facts and logical arguments. Stories have even greater impact when they are backed up by dramatic actions. Perhaps this is why Jesus is both a storyteller and a miracle worker. He masterfully uses stories to teach people about the Kingdom of God. As a miracle worker, Jesus makes the Kingdom of God a reality with his healings.

Jesus used the mustard seed as an example for the Kingdom of God. It is the smallest of seeds.

A fully grown mustard bush is large and provides very good protection for nesting birds. No wonder Jesus used it as an example of the Kingdom of God!

© Shawn Hempel / Shutterstock.com

© Hanan Isachar / Alamy Stock Photo

It's Like This . . .

Parables are one of the main teaching tools Jesus uses as a way of presenting the Good News of salvation. Parables are short stories that use everyday images to communicate religious messages. The term comes from a Greek word meaning "comparison," which is how Jesus often phrased them. For example: "What is the kingdom of God like? To what can I compare it? It is like a mustard seed that a person took and planted in the garden. When it was fully grown, it became a large bush and 'the birds of the sky dwelt in its branches'" (Luke 13:18–19).

---

parables ➤ Short stories that use everyday images to communicate religious messages. Jesus used parables frequently in his teaching as a way of presenting the Good News of salvation.

Jesus often uses parables, like this parable of the mustard seed, to offer his listeners a vision into the **Kingdom of God**. The Kingdom of God (or sometimes "Kingdom of Heaven") is the goal of God's plan of salvation, when God rules over the hearts of people, and a new social order, based on unconditional love, is established. For Jesus, the Kingdom of God is not a particular place or a particular time, rather it is the outcome of being in right relationship with God and other people. We catch glimpses of the Kingdom of God whenever people are truly living out Christ's Law of Love; however, the fullness of God's Kingdom will not be realized until the end of time.

To really understand Jesus' parables, it is helpful to know that they often end with an unexpected twist meant to surprise Christ's original audience. To really get the full effect, we must put ourselves in the shoes of the audience Jesus first addressed. In other words, we must understand their cultural values and biases. Here are two examples:

- The Jews listening to Jesus would have been shocked to hear that a Samaritan was the hero in the Parable of the Good Samaritan (Luke 10:25–37) because the Jews in Jerusalem despised the Samaritans.

- They would not have guessed the Kingdom of God would start as the tiniest seed, as Jesus taught in the Parable of the Mustard Seed (see Mark 4:30–32). In their minds, the Kingdom of God would have to have started as something large and majestic.

Parables, like the Good Samaritan, often contain a surprise twist to get the attention of listeners.

UNIT 5

Kingdom of God ➤ The culmination or goal of God's plan of salvation, the Kingdom of God is announced by the Gospel and is present in Jesus Christ. The Kingdom is the reign or rule of God over the hearts of people and, as a consequence of that, the development of a new social order based on unconditional love. The fullness of God's Kingdom will not be realized until the end of time. Also called the Reign of God or the Kingdom of Heaven.

THE PARABLES

Parable Name	Mark	Matthew	Luke
The Barren Fig Tree			13:6-9
The Dishonest Manager			16:1-13
Feasting and the Bridegroom	2:19-20	9:14-15	5:34-35
The Fig Tree	13:28-31	24:32-35	21:29-33
The Fish Net		13:47-50	
Good and Faithful Servants		24:45-51	12:42-46
The Good Samaritan			10:25-37
The Great Banquet			14:16-24
The Household Servants	13:34-37		
The Laborers in the Vineyard		20:1-16	
The Lamp	4:21	5:15	8:16-18
The Lost Coin			15:8-10
The Lost Sheep		18:12-14	15:1-7
Marriage of the King's Son		22:1-14	14:16
The Master of the House		13:51-52	
The Mustard Seed	4:30-32	13:31-32	13:18-19
New Cloth	2:22	9:16	5:36
New Wine	2:21	9:17	5:37-39
The Persistent Friend at Midnight			11:5-8
The Pharisee and the Tax Collector			18:9-14
The Prodigal Son			15:11-32
The Rejected Stone	12:10-11	21:42-46	20:17-19

THE PARABLES			
Parable Name	Mark	Matthew	Luke
The Rich Fool			12:13-31
The Rich Man and Lazarus			16:19-31
The Seed and the Harvest	4:26-29		
The Sheep and the Goats		25:31-46	
The Sower and Soils	4:1-9	13:3-23	8:4-8
The Talents		25:14-30	19:11-27
The Talents and the Servants			19:12-27
The Ten Virgins		25:1-13	
The Thief at Night		24:43-44	12:39-40
The Treasure and the Pearl		13:44-46	
The Two Debtors			7:40-45
Two Sons		21:28-32	
The Unmerciful Servant		18:23-25	
Watchful Slaves			12:35-48
The Wedding Banquet		22:1-14	14:15-24
The Wheat and the Weeds		13:28-31,36-43	
The Wicked Tenants	12:1-9	21:33-41	22:9-16
The Widow and the Judge			18:1-18
The Wise and Foolish Builders		7:24-27	6:46-49
The Worthless Salt	9:50	5:13	14:34-35
Yeast		13:33	13:20-21

UNIT 5

Actions as Loud as His Words

Jesus used not only words to teach about the Kingdom of God but also actions to show that he was already making the Kingdom present—very powerful actions called miracles. **Miracles** are signs or wonders that can only be attributed to divine power, such as healing the sick or controlling nature. Jesus' healings and other miracles reassured his followers that he was truly the Divine Son of God.

The calming of a storm on the Sea of Galilee is an example of a miracle in which Jesus controls nature.

I DIDN'T KNOW THAT!

"Just answer the question!" But sometimes answers are not always so simple and straightforward. When Jesus responds to questions in the Gospels, his answers vary: he offers indirect or mysterious answers (see Luke 13:23–25, Mark 10:26–27); he responds with another question (see Matthew 15:1–3, John 19:33–34); he doesn't answer at all (see John 19:9); his response is a parable or other metaphor (Luke 10:29–37). Jesus does not always spoon-feed simple answers, but he almost always engages our hearts and minds. This allows his listeners to discover for themselves the truth he was pointing them toward.

miracles ➤ Signs or wonders, such as healing or the control of nature, that can be attributed to divine power only.

Jesus' miracles can be categorized into four types, as this chart shows:

Type of Miracle	Event and Reference
Healings	• Jesus heals the centurion's servant (son). (Matthew 8:5–13, Luke: 7:1–10, John 4:46–54) • Peter's mother-in-law is cured of her fever. (Matthew 8:14–15, Mark 1:29–31, Luke 4:38–39) • The crippled woman is raised up straight. (Luke 13:10–13) • A man who suffers from dropsy is healed. (Luke 14:1–4) • Lepers are cleansed. (Matthew 8:1–3, Mark 1:40–42, Luke 17:12–14) • The ill and the lame are made whole. Limbs are restored. (Matthew 9:1–7, 12:9–13; Mark 2:1–12, 3:1–6; Luke 5:17–25, 6:6–11, 22:50–51; John 5:1–9) • A woman's twelve-year hemorrhage is healed. (Matthew 9:20–22, Mark 5:25–29, Luke 8:43–44) • The blind see, the deaf hear, and the mute speak. (Matthew 9:27–35, 11:5, 15:29–31, 20:29–34, 21:14; Mark 7:31–37, 8:22–26, 10:46–52; Luke 18:35–43; John 9:1–41; Acts 9:3–18) • General cures happen. (Matthew 14:34–36; Mark 6:1–6,53–56) • The sick are healed, the possessed are freed, and demons are expelled. (Matthew 8:16,28–33, 12:22, 15:21–28, 17:15–18; Mark 1:23–26, 5:1–20, 7:24–29, 9:20–26; Luke 4:33–35, 8:28–36, 9:37–42, 11:14)
Exorcisms	• Jesus heals the possessed. (Matthew 8:16, Mark 1:32–34, Luke 4:40–41) • Jesus heals a boy with a demon. (Matthew 17:14–21, Mark 9:14–29, Luke 9:37–43)
Control over Nature	• Jesus rebukes the wind and calms the storms. (Matthew 8:23–26, Mark 4:35–39, Luke 8:22–24) • Jesus walks on water. (Matthew 14:22–32, Mark 6:45–51, John 6:16–21) • Jesus makes a coin appear in the mouth of a fish. (Matthew 17:24–27) • Jesus causes a fig tree to wither. (Matthew 21:17–19, Mark 11:12–14)
Restoration of Life	• The daughter of Jairus is raised from death. (Matthew 9:18–25; Mark 5:22–24, 35–42; Luke 8:41–42,49–54) • The widow's son is raised during the funeral. (Luke 7:11–15) • Lazarus is raised and called from the tomb. (John 11:1–44)

UNIT 5

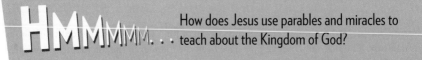

HMMMMM. . . How does Jesus use parables and miracles to teach about the Kingdom of God?

Article 69

From a Beloved Friend: The Gospel of John

Jonathan's best friend, Caleb, died in a car accident just weeks before their high school graduation. The two had met on the first day of kindergarten and had been like brothers ever since. Jonathan was asked to speak at Caleb's memorial service. He really wanted to honor his friend in that way, even though he knew it was going to be difficult. And it was. How could he possibly put into words what Caleb meant to him? Then it dawned on him: ordinary language just could not capture what was in his heart, but poetry could. At the memorial service, when it was his turn to speak, Jonathan delivered a beautiful poem honoring his best friend, expressing what was in his heart and what he wanted hearts of those present to hear.

© Life and Times / Shutterstock.com

The Gospel of John uses poetic language, which can often express one's feelings better than ordinary language. What is one of your favorite poems or song lyrics?

The use of poetic language in the Gospel of John is one of the things that sets it apart from the synoptic Gospels. John's Gospel was the last one written, and it is uniquely different; its content and poetic language clearly identify Jesus as the Divine Son of God, right from the beginning of the Gospel. It contains no parables and far fewer miracles than the synoptic Gospels. Jesus also talks a lot more, giving lengthy speeches at various times. John's Gospel also highlights the **Beloved Disciple**, who is faithful and present at critical times in Jesus' ministry.

Beloved Disciple ➤ A faithful disciple in the Gospel of John who is present at critical times in Jesus' ministry. The Beloved Disciple may have been the founder of the Johannine community.

In the Beginning . . . Again?

At the start of John's Gospel, you can tell right away that this book is going to be different. Instead of an account of Jesus' birth or early ministry, it begins with a poetic **prologue**:

> In the beginning was the Word,
>> and the Word was with God,
>> and the Word was God. (1:1)

Where else in the Bible have you heard the phrase "In the beginning"? These exact words are found in the first Creation account at the beginning of Genesis. This tells us that the beginning of the Gospel of John is also about creation—with a little bit of a twist.

First, the "Word" is a title for Jesus who was with God, who "was God" (John 1:1) from the beginning of time. Second, it is through the Word, the Son of God, that creation comes into existence: "All things came to be through him" (1:3). Third, the Word is also "the light of the human race" (1:4) who "became flesh" (1:12) and is our source of "grace and truth" (1:17). In a few short verses, the prologue establishes that Jesus Christ is the Divine, Eternal Son of God; that he participated in the work of creation; and that he has taken on our human nature to lead the human race to salvation.

"In the beginning was the Word, and the Word was with God, and the Word was God" (John 1:1).

UNIT 5

prologue ➤ A separate introduction at the beginning of a play, story, or long poem.

Not the Same and Very Different

John's Gospel provides a more mystical and divine portrayal of Jesus than any of the synoptic Gospels. The author makes it clear that knowing Jesus Christ is knowing God: "If you know me, then you will also know my Father" (John 14:7). It is clear that Jesus Christ is true God and true man.

The Gospel itself is divided into two parts. The first part, called "The Book of Signs," contains seven miracles, which John calls "signs," that point to Jesus' divine nature and show that he is the true Messiah sent by his heavenly Father.

1. Jesus changes water into wine at Cana (see 2:1–11).
2. Jesus restores the health of an official's son (see 4:46–54).
3. Jesus heals a paralytic (see 5:2–18).
4. Jesus feed the five thousand (see 6:1–15).
5. Jesus walks on water (see 6:16–21).
6. Jesus restores sight to a man born blind (see 9:1–7).
7. Jesus raises Lazarus to life (see 11:1–44).

These signs establish the Kingdom of God and point to "[Jesus'] glory, the glory as of the Father's only Son" (1:14). Some scholars have made a parallel between the seven signs and the seven days of Creation, another connection to Genesis, chapter 1.

CATHOLICS MAKING A DIFFERENCE

Courtesy Homeboy Industries

In 1986, Fr. Greg Boyle became the pastor of the Delores Mission Church in East Los Angeles. It was in one of the poorest and most violent neighborhoods in the city. Though most city leaders preferred to take a "get tough" approach to gangs, Father Greg, or G-Dog, as the homies called him, decided to befriend them. He learned that their biggest obstacle was not drugs or violence but rather a "lethal absence of hope." Father Greg started Homeboy Industries to provide work and healing, as well as a chance to escape the cycle of gang violence. It is now one of the most successful gang rehabilitation programs in the world. Father Greg says, "There is no force in the world better able to alter anything from its course than love."

Another way that John's Gospel differs from the other three Gospels is the testimony Jesus gives about himself. A good example is the seven "I Am" statements given in the first part of the Gospel. These statements intentionally echo God's revelation to Moses—"I am who am" (see Exodus 3:13-14)—implying that Jesus is also God, God in the flesh.

1. "I am the bread of life." (John 6:35)
2. "I am the light of the world." (8:12)
3. "I am the gate for the sheep." (10:7)
4. "I am the good shepherd." (10:11)
5. "I am the resurrection and the life." (11:25)
6. "I am the way and the truth and the life." (14:6)
7. "I am the vine; you are the branches." (15:5)

© kevron2001 / iStock.com

"I am the vine; you are the branches" (John 15:5).

UNIT 5

One miracle John shares with the synoptic Gospels is the account of Jesus multiplying the loaves and fish. Here too John offers a unique view by including a reflection on Jesus as the Bread of Life in chapter 6, called the Bread of Life discourse. Like the manna that God fed Moses and the Israelites in the desert (see Exodus 16:4–15), Jesus is the bread that "gives life to the world" (John 6:33). This bread, of course, is the Body and Blood of Jesus Christ, given to us in the Sacrament of the Eucharist. In the Sacrament, the Body and Blood of Jesus Christ are truly present to us through the consecrated elements of bread and wine: "Whoever eats my flesh and drinks my blood remains in me and I in him" (6:56).

Love Is Service

The second main section of John's Gospel is called the Book of Glory. This section begins with John's unique account of the Last Supper. Unlike the other Gospels, John's Gospel does not describe the Last Supper as a Passover meal. Instead, he focuses on the meaning of discipleship as a path of love and service to others. To emphasize this point, Jesus does the unthinkable:

> [During supper, Jesus], fully aware that the Father had put everything into his power and that he had come from God and was returning to God, he rose from supper and took off his outer garments. He took a towel and tied it around his waist. Then he poured water into a basin and began to wash the disciples' feet and dry them with the towel around his waist. He came to Simon Peter, who said to him, "Master, are you going to wash my feet?" Jesus answered and said to him, "What I am doing, you do not understand now, but you will understand later." Peter said to him, "You will never wash my feet." Jesus answered him, "Unless I wash you, you will have no inheritance with me." (John 13:3–8)

© Zvonimir Atletic / Shutterstock.com

Peter had good reason to object to Jesus' washing his and the other disciples' feet. Washing someone's feet was a job so low that Jewish People at the time were forbidden to make their Jewish slaves do it! In doing this menial task, Jesus demonstrates true service, telling the disciples, "If I, therefore, the master and teacher, have washed your feet, you ought to wash one another's feet" (John 13:14).

To be a disciple means following a path of love and service to others. Jesus demonstrates this by washing the feet of his disciples. In what way do you demonstrate love and service to others?

Next, Jesus gives his disciples a new commandment—love one another (see John 13:34). Here, Christ is describing *the defining characteristic* of a Christian community. "This is how all will know that you are my disciples, if you have love for one another" (13:35). In that regard, love and service are inseparably tied together. Jesus witnesses to the importance of love and service by making the ultimate sacrifice: "No one has greater love than this, to lay down one's life for one's friends" (15:13). We find no greater love than in Jesus' sacrifice on the cross.

I AM in Control

As another sign of Jesus' divinity, the Gospel of John depicts a Christ who is in control of his destiny even during his Passion and death. For example, instead of the agony in the garden, we find Jesus saying: "I came from the Father and have come into the world. Now I am leaving the world and going back to the Father" (John 16:28). Jesus is the Divine Mediator who brings together God and humanity, and then passes on his mission to his disciples (see 17:18–26).

John continues to emphasize Jesus' divinity during the accounts of his arrest and death. Right before Jesus is arrested, the soldiers announce they are looking for "Jesus the Nazorean." Jesus simply responds, "I AM" (John 18:5), and the soldiers fall to the ground in terror. When Pontius Pilate, the Roman governor who sentenced Jesus to death, asks him if he is a king, Jesus tells him that his kingdom is not in this world (see 18:36–37). The last words Jesus says on the Cross before dying signify that his divine mission is accomplished: "It is finished" (19:30). The Gospel then says that Jesus, still in control, "handed over his spirit"—it was not "taken" from him.

From Passion to Death to Resurrection: Victory!

While Jesus is still on the cross, a soldier pierces his side to make sure that Jesus is truly dead, and "immediately blood and water flowed out" (John 19:34). Blood and water are also symbols for the Sacraments of the Eucharist and Baptism. Through his death, Jesus offers his body for the salvation of the world; his blood frees us from sin and evil; and, through his life-giving water, we are reborn as children of God. The Gospel of John makes these sacramental connections to emphasize the Sacraments as important gifts God has given the world through his Church.

In the Gospel of John, Mary Magdalene is the first to go looking for Jesus, and the first one to see the Risen Christ in the garden.

UNIT 5

Beyond Jesus' death, the Gospel of John includes several Resurrection appearances. Mary Magdalene goes looking for Jesus but finds the tomb empty. She tells Simon Peter and the Beloved Disciple, who also find the tomb empty. Upon seeing the empty tombs, the Beloved Disciple immediately believes that Jesus has risen (see John 20:8). On the other hand, Mary does not quite understand what is happening until she actually sees the Risen Christ in the garden (see verse 16). Despite these eyewitness accounts, the Apostle Thomas later refuses to believe that Jesus has risen until he can place his fingers in Jesus' wounds. Jesus allows Thomas to do this (see verse 27). The Resurrection appearances are the final proof of Christ's divine nature and his victory over sin and death.

We are all like Mary and Thomas to some degree. It is difficult to believe in something that we have never physically seen. John's Gospel teaches us that we only have to be willing to trust God. Christ then closes the gap and comes to us. Jesus even refers to us in this account: "Blessed are those who have not seen and have believed" (John 20:29).

One Message of Salvation

Although the Gospel of John differs from the synoptic Gospels in some significant ways, all four Gospels together announce the same Good News: Jesus Christ, the only Son of God, became man, and through his Passion, death, Resurrection, and Ascension, he makes it possible for us to share in the divine life of the Trinity. ✳

OVERVIEW of the Book of John

- **Author:** A member of a Christian community possibly founded by the Beloved Disciple.
- **Date written:** AD 90–100.
- **Audience:** A community of Jews, Gentiles, and Samaritans of Ephesus in Turkey.
- **Images of Jesus:** *Logos,* Word of God, Son of God, Son of Man, Lamb of God, Redeemer, Messiah, Lord.

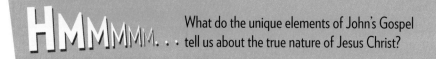

HMMMMM. . . What do the unique elements of John's Gospel tell us about the true nature of Jesus Christ?

Article 70
Jesus: God in the Flesh

Jackson had always wanted to go rafting down the Colorado River in the Grand Canyon. But he didn't own a raft, he didn't know how to paddle one, and he didn't even know how people got the boats into or out of the canyon. One day his dad's best friend, Marlon, was visiting. Marlon was a river guide in the Grand Canyon. When Jackson found out about this, he asked Marlon all sorts of questions. At the end of their conversation, Marlon invited Jackson to be his assistant on his next trip, promising to show him what to pack, how to tow the boat, how to paddle through the dangerous rapids, and everything else he needed to know to manage his way down the river.

Knowing someone who has the experience and wisdom to guide us makes all the difference in the world. Jesus Christ has "been there" and is our ultimate guide in life. He is not the kind of guide who calls down to us from above the canyon to tell us how to paddle our raft. He is a guide who is in the boat with us. Being both true God and true man, he shares in our humanity, yet he has the infinite wisdom of the Father. He is the Word of God that guides us on the river of life.

MAKE IT SO

The Son of God became human in order to make God known to us. Now it's our turn to make God known to others. Besides living good and holy lives, we can also spread the Good News in other ways. One way to do this is to volunteer in your parish's religious education program. They often allow high school students to assist, or sometimes even teach the younger religious education classes on Sundays. Children look up to and sometimes even idolize teenagers. Just by your being with them, either assisting or teaching, you can really have a positive impact in their lives!

UNIT 5

True God and True Man

In studying Scripture, especially the Gospels, we come to know Jesus Christ more fully and more intimately. The Gospels help us understand that Jesus is God's Word Made Flesh, and through him, God is most fully revealed to us. Saint Paul says that Jesus Christ "is the image of the invisible God" (Colossians 1:15). Jesus, himself, said, "Whoever has seen me has seen the Father" (John 14:9).

Another way to state this is that Jesus Christ is one Divine Person with two natures—a human nature and a divine nature. He walked on this Earth as a man. He ate food, slept, laughed, cried, and experienced all the things that we do (see Hebrews 4:15). He is also truly God, with divine knowledge and divine power. This mystery—Jesus Christ, the Divine Son of God, becoming man—is called the **Incarnation**. In the Incarnation, Jesus Christ became truly man while remaining truly God.

© Zvonimir Atletic / Shutterstock.com

The first and last letters of the Greek alphabet, *alpha* and *omega*, are painted on the dome of an Austrian Cathedral. In the Book of Revelation, Christ is called the Alpha and the Omega.

Incarnation ▶ From the Latin, meaning "to become flesh," referring to the mystery of Jesus Christ, the Divine Son of God, becoming man. In the Incarnation, Jesus Christ became truly man while remaining truly God.

Because Jesus Christ is true God and true man, he is the fullness of Divine Revelation: "God has revealed himself fully by sending his own Son, in whom he has established his covenant for ever. The Son is his Father's definitive Word; so there will be no further Revelation after him" (*CCC*, number 73). Christ is "the Alpha and the Omega, the first and the last, the beginning and the end" (Revelation 22:13).

Your Participation Is Required

Because Jesus Christ is the fullness of God's Revelation, our salvation depends on being in communion with Christ. For this to happen, our active participation is required. We can find his presence in God's Word, Sacred Scripture. The Gospels invite us to put our complete faith and trust in him. We deepen our relationship by receiving him in the Eucharist and applying his teachings to every part of our life. We can participate in his mission through our active involvement with his mystical presence on Earth, the Body of Christ—his Church. ✳

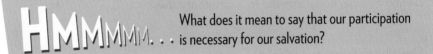

HMMMMMM. . . What does it mean to say that our participation is necessary for our salvation?

1. What are Gospels, and what does the word *gospel* mean?

2. What are the three stages in the formation of the Gospels?

3. Why are the Gospels different from one another?

4. What are the synoptic Gospels?

5. What should we remember to help us better understand Jesus' parables?

6. Define *miracle*, and name the four different types.

7. Describe the prologue in John's Gospel.

8. How is John's account of the Last Supper different from the accounts in the synoptic Gospels?

9. Why is there no further need for more of God's public Revelation?

© jozef sedmak / Alamy Stock Photo

UNIT 5

THE FOUR EVANGELISTS

We do not know much for sure about the human authors of the four Gospels. But artists, like the one who painted this image, have done their best to portray them based on what we do know.

1. Why do you think the artist painted the four Evangelists so close to one another?

2. Which Evangelist do you think is Matthew? Mark? Luke? John? What clues might help you?

3. Why is there only one open book on the table, and why might the four men be looking so intently at it?

CHAPTER 16
The Acts of the Apostles and the Letters

WHO GOT THE CHURCH GOING AFTER JESUS' ASCENSION?

SNAPSHOT

Article 71   Page 431
Acts of the Apostles: Passing the Baton
• Pre-read: Acts, chapters 1–4, 7–9, 15

Article 72   Page 437
Paul's Letters: Time Machine and Guidebook
• Pre-read: Galatians 1:11–2:14
• Pre-read: Romans 3:21–31
• Pre-read: Philippians 4:4–9
• Pre-read: Colossians 1:15–20
• Pre-read: 1 Timothy 4:6–16

Article 73   Page 442
Letters to Everyone: The Non-Pauline Letters
• Pre-read: Hebrews 4:14–16
• Pre-read: James 1:19–27, 2:14–26
• Pre-read: 1 John 4:7–21

Article 74   Page 445
The Book of Revelation: A Message of Hope
• Pre-read: Revelation 1:1–20, 12:1–6, 13:11–18, 17:1–18, 21:1–27

Article 75   Page 450
Passing It On
• Pre-read: Matthew 28:16–20

UNIT 5

Article 71

Acts of the Apostles: Passing the Baton

You are probably familiar with the relay race, a track and field team sport consisting of four athletes who run a preset distance. As they run, they carry a baton. Running a good relay race depends on the commitment of all the team members to go their required distance and efficiently pass the baton to the next runner.

Passing on the faith isn't a race, but in some ways, it can be likened to a relay. Before his Ascension into Heaven, Jesus passed his saving mission to the Apostles. The "baton" was now in their hands; it was their turn to pass on the Good News of our salvation. The accounts of where, when, and how the early Church picked up where Jesus left off are told in the Acts of the Apostles.

We Are Not Alone

When you read the first line of Acts of the Apostles, do you notice to whom the book is written? If you go back and read the first verse of the Gospel of Luke, you will see that it is addressed to the same person: Theophilus. This is because the Acts of the Apostles is part

Jesus passed the "baton" of his saving mission to the Apostles, who in turn, passed it on to others. How do you pass on the Good News of our salvation?

two of Luke's account. Acts picks up where Luke left off. It describes the main events of the early Church, starting with the Church's humble beginnings as a small, mainly Jewish community in Palestine. By the end of Acts, the Church has grown to include thousands of believers in numerous communities all around the Mediterranean Sea.

Although the author of Luke already briefly addressed Jesus' Ascension at the end of the Gospel, he covers it in a little more detail in Acts. As the Apostles see Jesus taken into Heaven, we can almost hear them asking, "Now what do we do?" Two men dressed in white mysteriously appear and ask them, "Men of Galilee, why are you standing there looking at the sky?" (Acts 1:11). In other words, "Pick up the baton and go!"

UNIT 5

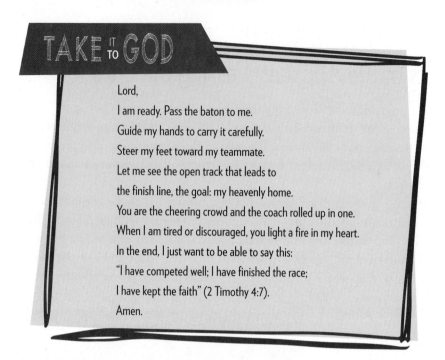

TAKE IT TO GOD

Lord,

I am ready. Pass the baton to me.

Guide my hands to carry it carefully.

Steer my feet toward my teammate.

Let me see the open track that leads to

the finish line, the goal: my heavenly home.

You are the cheering crowd and the coach rolled up in one.

When I am tired or discouraged, you light a fire in my heart.

In the end, I just want to be able to say this:

"I have competed well; I have finished the race;

I have kept the faith" (2 Timothy 4:7).

Amen.

After the Apostles choose a successor for Judas (see Acts 1:15–26), they observe the Feast of Pentecost. Pentecost is a Jewish feast celebrating the offering of the harvest's firstfruits to the Lord (see Leviticus 23:15–22). This feast also memorializes God giving his Law at Mount Sinai to guide the Israelites (see Exodus, chapters 19–20). The new Pentecost in Acts tells how Jesus sent the Holy Spirit to guide the Church (see Acts 2:1–13). As Jesus promised, the Church is not left alone to carry out its mission (see 1:4). The Holy Spirit was, and still is, our guide on the path.

UNIT 5

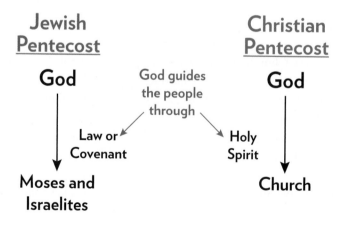

Jewish Pentecost

God

Law or Covenant

Moses and Israelites

God guides the people through

Christian Pentecost

God

Holy Spirit

Church

When the Holy Spirit descends upon the Apostles, "there appeared to them tongues as of fire, which parted and came to rest on each one of them" (Acts 2:3). As Moses and the Israelites are making their escape from slavery and heading toward the Red Sea, the Lord guides them "by means of a column of fire" (Exodus 13:21). In both of these situations, God offers his people guidance and strength to bravely carry out his will. It takes incredible courage for Peter to make that speech at Pentecost. Less than two months prior to this, the Jewish leaders handed Jesus over to the Roman authorities to have him crucified. Here Peter publicly announces, "Let the whole house of Israel know for certain that God has made him both Lord and Messiah, this Jesus whom you crucified" (Acts 2:36). By saying this, Peter has aligned himself with an enemy of both his religion and government. The Holy Spirit gives us the fiery courage we need to be Jesus' disciples.

In the account of the Tower of Babel (see Genesis 11:1–9), the people arrogantly try to build a tower to the heavens so they can be like God. Because of this, God confuses their language and spreads them all over the Earth. The account of the Pentecost is a reversal of this confusion. Though the people gathered in Jerusalem speak different languages, they can all still understand Peter's preaching. The Tower of Babel account shows us how sin separates us from God and one another, while the events at Pentecost teach us that our true faith unites us with God and one another.

Fire is one of many symbols for the Holy Spirit. "Then there appeared to them tongues as of fire . . . and they were all filled with the holy Spirit" (Acts 2:3–4).

UNIT 5

This Is the Way

Members of the earliest Church communities were not called Christians. That name comes a little later. The Acts of the Apostles records the name first being used to describe the believers in Antioch (see Acts 11:19–26). "The Way" is one of the earliest names for the Christian community (see 9:2). The term *way* implies a practice or a method used to accomplish something. The members of the Way devote themselves to the teachings of the Apostles, communal life, the breaking of the bread, and prayer (see 2:42–47).

The Acts of the Apostles portrays the Christian community in Jerusalem as nearly ideal. These Christians share everything in common, and because of this there are no needy people among them (see Acts 4:32–36). Still, the community is not without its problems. Acts tells of the challenges the first Christians face, from both outside and inside the Christian community.

The troubles from outside the community are primarily persecutions, starting with persecution by the Jewish community in Jerusalem (see Acts 5:17–42). This leads to the Church's first martyr when the deacon, Stephen, is stoned (see 7:54–60). A **Pharisee** named Saul is present at that murder, overseeing the arrests of Christians in an effort "to destroy the church" (8:3). We will learn more about him later.

Saint Stephen (AD c. 5–34) was a deacon in the early Church who was stoned to death for teaching about Jesus. He is considered the first Christian martyr.

Pharisee ➤ A Jewish sect at the time of Jesus known for its strict adherence to the Law.

Rather than discouraging the growth of the Church, the martyrdom of Christians like Stephen has the opposite effect. The courage and faith of these martyrs encourages those who are already Christian and inspires more people to join the Church. Tertullian (c. AD 155–240), an early Christian theologian, is so impressed with their witness and its importance that he claims, "The blood of the martyrs is the seed of the church."

The troubles inside the community are caused primarily by quarrels between groups of Christians. The biggest disagreement is over what to do with Gentile believers. Specifically, do the Gentile believers need to follow Jewish Laws to be Christians, especially the laws on food and circumcision? There are opposing viewpoints on this issue. Many Jewish Christians feel it is only right for Gentile Christians to follow Jewish Laws because Jesus was Jewish, and he followed the same laws. The Gentile Christians disagree with this, believing they do not need to follow the laws meant primarily for the Jewish People. Ultimately the Council of Jerusalem, the Church's first **Ecumenical Council**, resolves this question. They decide that the Gentiles do not have to be circumcised and only need to follow the laws that are more universal, reflecting God's moral law for all people (see Acts 15:1–21).

The New Guy

Remember Saul, the man who oversees Stephen's martyrdom? Acts describes him as "breathing murderous threats against the disciples of the Lord" (9:1). Saul is a passionate Jew, a Pharisee who does not believe in Jesus as the Messiah. He sees the Jews who follow Jesus as a danger to true Jewish faith and tries to stop the spread of their beliefs. Then something miraculous happens. On his way to arrest some Jewish Christians in Damascus, Saul has an incredible vision of Christ saying to him, "Saul, Saul, why are you persecuting me?" (verse 4). This vision completely changes Saul's life (see verses 1–19)—he quickly converts and is baptized a Christian. Naturally, many of the Christians do not initially trust him, but ultimately his efforts to spread the Gospel convince everyone of his sincerity. Saul becomes an Apostle and is better known by the Greek version of his name: Paul.

UNIT 5

Ecumenical Council ➤ A gathering of the Church's bishops from around the world convened by the Pope or approved by him to address pressing issues in the Church and in the world.

Most of the second half of the Book of Acts covers the travels of Saint Paul and his companions in the lands around the Mediterranean Sea. In three separate journeys, Paul focuses his missionary work on spreading the Good News of Jesus Christ to the Gentiles. While on these journeys, Paul is run out of town by an angry mob (see Acts 17:1–9); is nearly beaten to death, arrested, and imprisoned (see 21:27–40); and is shipwrecked on an island (see 27:6–44). Saint Paul is truly committed to his mission as "a minister of Christ Jesus to the Gentiles" (Romans 15:16). ✳

The Conversion of St. Paul, by artist Ignacio de Ries, shows Paul receiving his life-changing vision of Christ while on his way to Damascus to arrest some Jewish Christians.

OVERVIEW of the Acts of the Apostles

- **Author:** Often identified as Luke, who also wrote the Gospel of Luke.
- **Date Written:** Approximately AD 80.
- **Time period:** Around AD 30-65.
- **Audience:** Gentile (Greek) Christians represented by Theophilus.
- **Of note:** Despite the title, the Acts of the Apostles focuses mainly on Peter and Paul.

HMMMMM. . . Why was it particularly difficult for the Gentiles to become Christians?

Article 72

Paul's Letters: Time Machine and Guidebook

When not geographically near family and friends, how do most people your age communicate with one another? Texting, right? If cell phones existed almost two thousand years ago, Paul would have most certainly texted the early Christian communities who were spread all around the Mediterranean Sea. Sending an electronic message would have been much easier and faster than writing letters. Alas, Paul did not have that luxury; he had to communicate through carefully written letters. For us, that's a good thing! His letters survived and became the first books of the New Testament.

As the early Christian communities are getting started, they often face challenges in their efforts to follow Jesus Christ. To help them, Saint Paul writes many letters, or **epistles**, to these communities and their leaders, offering advice, criticism, and encouragement. Not only do his letters offer us a glimpse into the life of the early Church, buy they also provide guidance for our lives today.

If you didn't have a mobile device, how would you communicate with a distant family member or friend?

Perfect Person for the Job

Saint Paul is sometimes called the Apostle to the Gentiles, and it would be difficult to find someone better for this task. He was born in Tarsus (located in modern-day Turkey) which makes him a Roman citizen—a status that affords him important privileges (see Acts 22:22–29). He is also a well-educated Jew who is fluent in Hebrew and Greek. He is passionate in his beliefs and free to travel. These attributes combine to make Paul the perfect person to preach the Gospel to people from a variety of backgrounds.

UNIT 5

epistle ➤ Another name for a New Testament letter.

Prior to his conversion, Paul had studied with a respected rabbi (see Acts 22:3) and had become a zealous Pharisee. The Pharisees were a Jewish group at the time of Jesus known for their strict adherence to the Mosaic Law. In the Gospels, Jesus criticizes the Pharisees for being more committed to the Law than to the Law's purpose: to instill love of God and love of neighbor. Given this history, the Pharisees have no affection for the Jews who follow Jesus' teachings and proclaim him as the Messiah. Paul is so committed to his Pharisaic beliefs that he persecutes Christians before his conversion to Christianity (see Galatians 1:13–17).

After becoming a Christian, Paul soon gains favor with the Christian community and is appointed to leadership roles in the Church. His Jewish education and linguistic talents allow him to convincingly preach to Jews and Gentiles alike (see Galatians 2:9). He travels throughout the Mediterranean with associates like Timothy, Barnabas, and Titus. They establish and support new Christian communities in places like Corinth, Galatia, Ephesus, and Philippi. Paul continues to offer these communities his guidance and encouragement through a series of letters. It is believed that Paul was executed by the authorities in Rome sometime around AD 64. His letters still inspire and guide the Church today.

UNIT 5

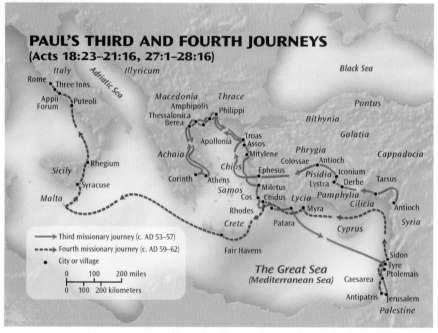

Paul made four journeys over a period of ten years,
spreading the Gospel throughout the Mediterranean.

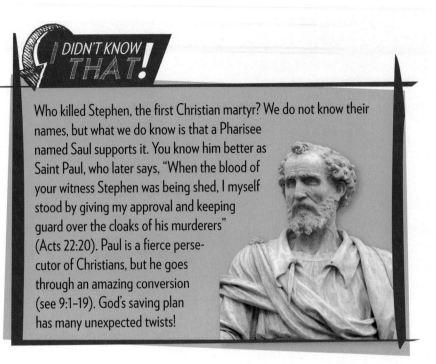

I DIDN'T KNOW THAT!

Who killed Stephen, the first Christian martyr? We do not know their names, but what we do know is that a Pharisee named Saul supports it. You know him better as Saint Paul, who later says, "When the blood of your witness Stephen was being shed, I myself stood by giving my approval and keeping guard over the cloaks of his murderers" (Acts 22:20). Paul is a fierce perse-cutor of Christians, but he goes through an amazing conversion (see 9:1–19). God's saving plan has many unexpected twists!

The Letters

There are thirteen **Pauline letters** in the New Testament, written by Saint Paul or by disciples who wrote in his name. Nine of the letters are addressed to entire communities. The other four are letters to individuals. Three of these are called **Pastoral** Letters (First and Second Timothy and Titus) and are ad-dressed to leaders, or pastors, of a community. The Pastoral Letters are named after the community or individual to whom they are addressed. ✳

UNIT 5

Pauline letters ➤ Thirteen New Testament letters attributed to Saint Paul or to disciples who wrote in his name. The letters offer advice, pastoral encouragement, teaching, and community news to early Christian communities.

pastoral ➤ From the Latin *pastor*, meaning "shepherd" or "herdsman"; refers to the spiritual care or guidance of others.

LETTERS TO COMMUNITIES			
Letter	**Author**	**Date**	**Themes Addressed**
Romans	Paul	AD 56–58	• the cross • resurrection of the body • justification by faith; salvation for Jews and Gentiles through Jesus Christ • hope and joy
1 Corinthians	Paul	AD 56	• the cross • moral advice • Christian unity • diverse spiritual gifts • the Church as the Body of Christ • the resurrection of the body
2 Corinthians	Paul	AD 57	• false preaching • Paul's ministry to the Corinthians
Galatians	Paul	AD 54–55	• false preaching • freedom from Jewish Laws • the Christian community • the cross and Christ's death
Ephesians	likely a follower of Paul	AD 90–100 (after Paul's death)	• the Church as the Body of Christ • Christian unity • daily conduct and love
Philippians	Paul	AD 55 or AD 59–63	• imitation of Christ • Christian unity • joy and peace
Colossians	Paul or more likely a follower of Paul	AD 61 if by Paul, around AD 80 if by a follower	• the divinity of Christ • false preaching • moral advice
1 Thessalonians	Paul	AD 51	• endurance through persecution • resurrection of the dead • vigilance in faith
2 Thessalonians	Paul or more likely a follower of Paul	AD 51 if by Paul, AD 90–100 if by a follower	• endurance through persecution • the second coming of Christ

UNIT 5

LETTERS TO INDIVIDUALS			
Letter	**Author**	**Date**	**Themes Addressed**
1 Timothy	likely followers of Paul	Around AD 100	• false preaching • advice on Church leadership • responsibilities of Church members • wealth
2 Timothy	likely followers of Paul	Around AD 100	• endurance through persecution • false preaching • encouragement to be Christlike • moral advice
Titus	likely followers of Paul	Around AD 100	• advice on Church leadership • moral advice
Philemon	Paul	AD 54–56 or AD 61–63	• Paul's plea for Philemon to release his slave Onesimus, who was imprisoned with Paul

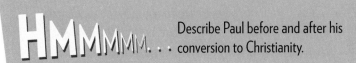

HMMMMM. . . Describe Paul before and after his conversion to Christianity.

UNIT 5

Article 73

Letters to Everyone: The Non-Pauline Letters

There are eight non-Pauline letters in the New Testament. The first is the Letter to the Hebrews whose author is unknown, and whose title comes from the audience it addresses. The rest of the letters are called **Catholic letters**. In this context, *Catholic* does not specifically refer to the Catholic Church. The word *catholic* is originally a Greek word meaning "universal." These letters were not written to specific communities or individuals, but rather to the universal Church—all the Christian communities. Most of the Catholic letters get their names from the authors each one is attributed to.

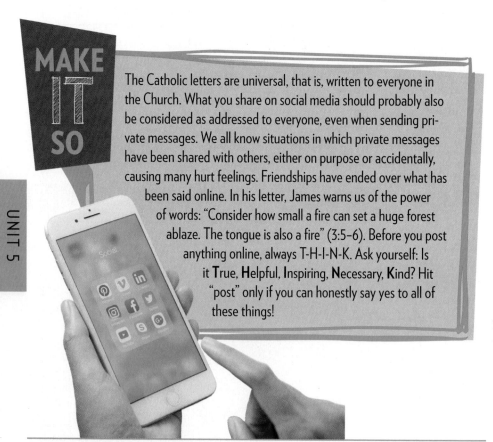

MAKE IT SO

The Catholic letters are universal, that is, written to everyone in the Church. What you share on social media should probably also be considered as addressed to everyone, even when sending private messages. We all know situations in which private messages have been shared with others, either on purpose or accidentally, causing many hurt feelings. Friendships have ended over what has been said online. In his letter, James warns us of the power of words: "Consider how small a fire can set a huge forest ablaze. The tongue is also a fire" (3:5–6). Before you post anything online, always T-H-I-N-K. Ask yourself: Is it True, Helpful, Inspiring, Necessary, Kind? Hit "post" only if you can honestly say yes to all of these things!

© aPhoenixPhotographer / Shutterstock.com

UNIT 5

Catholic letters ➤ The eight non-Pauline letters in the New Testament that were addressed to the universal Church.

Letter	Author	Date	Themes Addressed
Hebrews	Unknown	AD 80–90	• endurance through persecution • Jesus' death on the cross as perfect sacrifice and sign of the New Covenant • Jesus Christ is our high priest • the divinity of Christ
James	James, the relative of Jesus, but more likely a later admirer of James	AD 57–62 if by James, AD 70–110 if a later admirer	• Christians' actions should reflect their beliefs • care for the poor • warnings against wealth • endurance through suffering
1 Peter	Peter, but more likely a later disciple of Peter	AD 60–63 if by Peter, AD 70 to 90 if by a later disciple	• endurance through persecution • embracing suffering with hope • moral advice
2 Peter	Unknown person writing in Peter's name	AD 100–125	• arguments against false teachers • the second coming of Christ • encouragement to be patient and remain faithful
1 John	Unknown person associated with the community that produced the Gospel of John	around AD 100	• God's love and love for one another • false teachings • true belief in Jesus Christ who is both true God and true man
2 John	(same as above)	(same as above)	• love for one another
3 John	(same as above)	(same as above)	• encouragement to offer hospitality to fellow Christians
Jude	Unknown, traditionally thought to be Jude, the brother of James	AD 80–90	• warnings about false teachers • encouragement to keep their faith

UNIT 5

These letters cover a variety of issues troubling the early Christian communities. The author of the Letter to the Hebrews explains how Jesus is the High Priest and the fulfillment of Jewish history. James's letter is a strong admonishment that worship alone is not enough, and that we need to live out our faith by caring for one another. Peter addresses the Christian communities who are suffering from persecution, offering them encouragement to persevere in their faith. John centers his message on the key teaching of Christ: love one another. Jude warns the Church about teachers who are leading the people away from the true faith.

In each of their own ways, these letters offer us a glimpse into the questions and the problems the early Christian communities faced. They also provide us with timeless insights on how to address similar problems today: compassion for one another, faithful endurance through hard times, and sharing God's love with all people. ✳

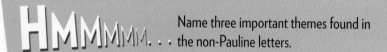

HMMMMM. . . Name three important themes found in the non-Pauline letters.

Article 74

The Book of Revelation: A Message of Hope

Jeremiah Denton was a pilot in the United States Navy, fighting in the war in Vietnam. While on a mission over North Vietnam, his fighter jet was shot down. Denton parachuted safely into enemy territory but was quickly captured. For nearly eight years, he was tortured and kept in isolation for long periods of time. In a televised interview, his captors questioned him about his conditions. Denton offered positive comments about how he was being treated, but his eyes told a different story. By blinking his eyes in Morse Code, he was able to convey a message his captors could not understand: "t-o-r-t-u-r-e."

In the late first century, many Church communities were persecuted by the Romans, particularly the seven churches of Asia. The Revelation to John was written to offer hope to these Christians, encouraging them to keep the faith despite these hardships. John uses a literary style filled with symbols and dramatic imagery, a style Jews and early Christians associated with times of crisis. Its coded language may have also helped avoid putting readers at risk by using imagery that only Christians would understand.

Like John, author of the Book of Revelation, former Vietnam captive Rear Admiral General Denton conveyed his message of torture to the world using a code his captors couldn't understand.

UNIT 5

It's More About the Past

The Revelation to John (sometimes called The Book of Revelation) might be one of the most misunderstood books in the Bible. Some people wrongly use it to try to predict the end of the world. Though Revelation does offer its readers the assurance of Christ's second coming, it does not offer a prediction of when and how it will occur. The book actually tells us more about the past than it does the future. It takes a little study to understand its mysterious imagery.

The Book of Revelation is an example of **apocalyptic literature**, a literary form that uses dramatic and symbolic language to offer hope to a people in crisis. In the first century, the Church went through intense periods of persecution, depending on the temperament of the Roman emperor. Christian persecutions peaked under two emperors, Nero (AD 54–68) and Domitian (AD 81–96). During this period, Roman emperors were believed to be divine, and Christians were sometimes forced to worship them. Refusal to offer incense at a Roman altar could mean death. Many Christians chose to give up their lives rather than deny their faith.

The Book of Revelation was written by the Christian prophet John, possibly around AD 92–96, during the reign of Emperor Domitian. John had been exiled to the Greek island of Patmos for preaching the Gospel. Although he was no longer able to preach in person, John put pen to paper and preached through the written word.

UNIT 5

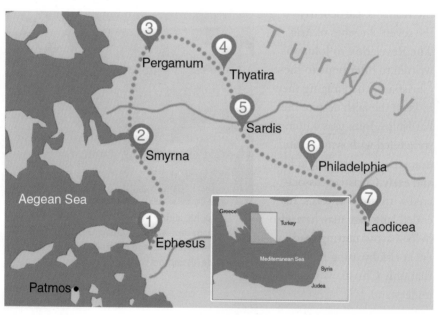

The Christian prophet John wrote the Book of Revelation from the Island of Patmos to seven churches located in what is now Turkey.

apocalyptic literature ➤ A literary form that uses highly dramatic and symbolic language to offer hope to a people in crisis.

Cracking the Code

To better understand the message of Revelation, it is important to understand a few key images and symbols used by the author. For example, recall that numbers often have significant meaning in the Bible.

Seven signifies perfection or completion. The Lord rested on the seventh day of creation, after its completion (see Genesis 2:1–3). Jesus said we should forgive "not seven times but seventy-seven times" (Matthew 18:22). In other words, our forgiveness should be the maximum we can offer. Four means universal, like the four directions of the compass. Six is one less than seven, so it is imperfect. A multiple of six, such as 666, would imply great imperfection, or evil. Also, if numbers are multiplied, their meaning is magnified. The bigger the number the greater the emphasis that is placed on its meaning. For example, 1000 refers to a quantity too big to count.

Twelve is also a symbolic number. In the Old Testament, we find the Twelve Tribes of Israel. In the New Testament we have the Twelve Apostles. This helps us understand this verse in Revelation: "Then I looked and there was the Lamb standing on Mount Zion, and with him a hundred and forty-four thousand who had his name and his Father's name written on their foreheads" (14:1). A common misinterpretation of this text is that only 144,000 people are destined to be saved at Christ's second coming. Considering the current population of the world is over seven billion people, 144,000 is not a lot! But if you look at the number symbolically—12 Tribes of Israel x 12 Apostles x 1,000—it means the fullness of God's people, so many you cannot count them.

Other symbolism found in the Book of Revelation includes:

lampstand = God's presence
horn = power
eyes = knowledge
dragon = evil
Lamb = Christ
Babylon = Rome
New Jerusalem = heaven
white = victory
red = bloodshed, martyrdom

UNIT 5

Consider the following verse: "They have washed their robes and made them white in the blood of the Lamb" (Revelation 7:14). This would tell the audience that those who had martyred (blood) for Christ (the Lamb) had found victory (white robe). Not all of the imagery is this straightforward, but knowing and understanding some of the clues can help your understanding.

A Message of Hope

The imagery of the Book of Revelation can be quite graphic and scary. Certainly, the Christians enduring persecution could easily relate to the fearsome beast representing the Roman Empire. But we miss the point of this book if we get overly fixated on the haunting imagery. John's writing offers encouragement, comfort, and hope to his original audience. They probably know fellow Christians in their community who have been martyred. They fear for their lives and the lives of their friends and family.

The Book of Revelation sends a message that is loud and clear to these persecuted Christians: have courage and keep the faith, even in the face of death. There is a heavenly reward awaiting you; your martyred loved ones are already experiencing that reward. John reminds them that God is with them, even in their darkest and most painful moments.

This advice is timeless, making it incredibly relevant to us today too. John gives the reason for our hope in his vision of a new Heaven and a new Earth:

Jesus, the Lamb of God, lying on the seven sealed book, Revelation 5:1–14. The cross and banner symbolize Christ's victory over death.

I heard a loud voice from the throne saying, "Behold, God's dwelling is with the human race. He will dwell with them and they will be his people and God himself will always be with them [as their God]. He will wipe every tear from their eyes, and there shall be no more death or mourning, wailing or pain, [for] the old order has passed away."

The one who sat on the throne said, "Behold, I make all things new."

(Revelation 21:3–5) ✳

CATHOLICS MAKING A DIFFERENCE

In 2010, Asia Bibi was sentenced to death for blasphemy in Pakistan, where Christians are a persecuted minority. Her conviction originated from a dispute she had with her Muslim neighbors who accused Bibi, a Roman Catholic, of insulting the prophet Muhammed. She firmly denied this. Despite inconsistent witness testimony, she was still convicted and sentenced to death. In an appeal in 2018, the Supreme Court of Pakistan acquitted her due to insufficient evidence. In May of 2019, she relocated to Canada. While living in solitary confinement, she did not waver in her faith: "All of us must learn from the teaching and sacrifice of Christ who was crucified for us and who forgave all those who harmed him. . . . I ask Christians in Pakistan to live and pray for peace" ("Asia Bibi Asks the Prayers of Pope Francis," Vatican Radio, June 4, 2015).

© See Li / Alamy Stock Photo

Free Asia Bibi

Sentenced to death in Pakistan

Asia Bibi's faith did not waver, even in the face of death.

UNIT 5

OVERVIEW of Revelation to John

- **Author:** A Jewish-Christian prophet named John.
- **Date written:** Probably around AD 92–96.
- **Audience:** Christian churches in Asia Minor during a time of Roman persecution.
- **Themes:** Christ will come again in full glory; in the final judgment, good will be rewarded, evil punished; hope and courage in the face of persecution.

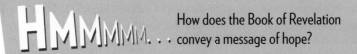

HMMMMM. . .

How does the Book of Revelation convey a message of hope?

Article 75

Passing It On

When Jesus commissioned the Apostles to carry on his mission, they did not just memorize his words and then repeat them. They also had to pass on "his way of life and his works"[1] (*Catechism of the Catholic Church [CCC]*, number 76): "All power in heaven and on earth has been given to me. Go, therefore, and make disciples of all nations, baptizing them in the name of the Father, and of the Son, and of the holy Spirit, teaching them to observe all that I have commanded you" (Matthew 28:18–20).

With these words Jesus commissioned the Apostles to authentically teach and interpret the sacred truths he revealed to them. Guided by the Holy Spirit, they proclaimed the Good News with their preaching, by being living examples, by establishing the institutions needed to keep the Church alive and well, and through their writings. The process of passing on the Gospel message is called **Sacred Tradition**, which continues "under the inspiration of the Holy Spirit, to all generations, until Christ returns in glory" (*CCC*, number 96).

© alefbet / Shutterstock.com

Jesus commissioned the Apostles to authentically preach the Gospel and make disciples of all nations.

Sacred Tradition ➤ The process of passing on the Gospel message. Sacred Tradition, which began with the oral communication of the Gospel by the Apostles, was written down in Sacred Scripture, is handed down and lived out in the life of the Church, and is interpreted by the Magisterium under the guidance of the Holy Spirit.

The responsibility of passing on Sacred Tradition given to the Apostles and their successors is called **Apostolic Succession**. This is the reason Sacred Tradition is also called the Apostolic Tradition. It refers to the uninterrupted transmittal of apostolic preaching and authority from the Apostles directly to their successors, the bishops. Every bishop can trace his authority back to the Apostles. This authority is conveyed through the laying on of hands when a bishop receives the Sacrament of Holy Orders as instituted by Christ. The office of bishop is permanent, because at ordination a bishop is marked with an indelible, sacred character; it can never be erased.

The Two Pillars: Sacred Tradition, Sacred Scripture

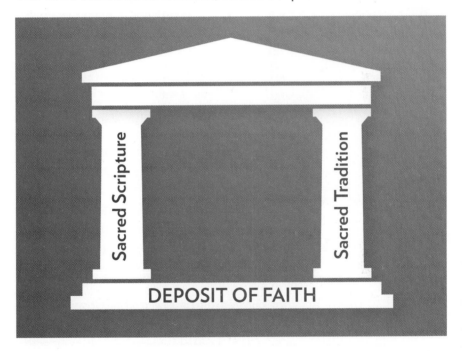

In keeping with the Lord's command, the Gospel is handed on through two means: Sacred Scripture and Sacred Tradition. Recall that Sacred Scripture is the Word of God, the Good News of Jesus Christ. Sacred Tradition refers to the words and actions of the Apostles, who were already passing on the

Apostolic Succession ▶ The uninterrupted passing on of apostolic preaching and authority from the Apostles directly to all bishops. It is accomplished through the laying on of hands when a bishop is ordained in the Sacrament of Holy Orders as instituted by Christ. The office of bishop is permanent, because at ordination a bishop is marked with an indelible, sacred character.

UNIT 5

teachings of Jesus before the books of the New Testament were written. Sacred Tradition "transmits in its entirety the Word of God which has been entrusted to the apostles by Christ the Lord and the Holy Spirit" [2] (*CCC*, number 81).

These two means of transmitting the faith both flow from a single source: the **Deposit of Faith**. Sacred Tradition and Scripture are two distinct modes of expressing the one Deposit of Faith, but both allow us to come to know the truth revealed by Jesus Christ. Through the power of the Holy Spirit, this living transmission of Sacred Tradition and Sacred Scripture remains active and present in the life of the Church today.

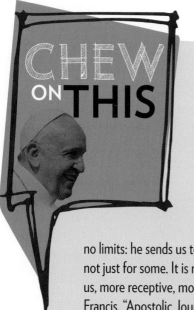

Jesus did not say: "Go, if you would like to, if you have the time," but he said: "Go and make disciples of all nations." Sharing the experience of faith, bearing witness to the faith, proclaiming the Gospel: this is a command that the Lord entrusts to the whole Church, and that includes you. . . . . Where does Jesus send us? There are no borders, no limits: he sends us to everyone. The Gospel is for everyone, not just for some. It is not only for those who seem closer to us, more receptive, more welcoming. It is for everyone. (Pope Francis, "Apostolic Journey to Rio De Janeiro on the Occasion of the XXVIII World Youth Day, 2013," number 1)

Deposit of Faith ➤ The heritage of faith contained in Sacred Scripture and Sacred Tradition. It has been passed on from the time of the Apostles. The Magisterium takes from it all that it teaches as revealed truth.

The responsibility of passing on and interpreting the Deposit of Faith belongs to the Magisterium. The **Magisterium** is the Church's living teaching office, which consists of all bishops, in communion with the Pope. Guided by the Holy Spirit, the Magisterium is responsible for teaching and defining **dogma**, the central teachings of the Church that are considered definitive and authoritative.

The job of passing on the faith does not only belong to the Church hierarchy. "All the faithful share in understanding and handing on revealed truth. They have received the anointing of the Holy Spirit, who instructs them[3] and guides them into all truth[4]" (*CCC*, number 91). We do this by teaching the truths of our faith to others, through our words and actions. Acting in harmony with the Magisterium, we all play a part in passing on the Good News of Jesus Christ.

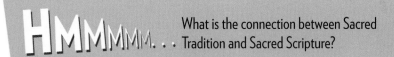

HMMMMM. . . What is the connection between Sacred Tradition and Sacred Scripture?

Magisterium ➤ The Church's living teaching office, which consists of all bishops, in communion with the Pope, the bishop of Rome. Their task is to interpret and preserve the truths revealed in both Sacred Scripture and Sacred Tradition.

dogma ➤ Teachings recognized as central to Church teaching, defined by the Magisterium and considered definitive and authoritative.

1. What two things does Pentecost celebrate during Jesus' time?

2. To what four activities do the early Christians devote themselves?

3. What is it about Paul's background that helps make him an effective preacher?

4. What are the Pauline letters? What are some of their themes?

5. What are the Catholic letters? What are some of their themes?

6. Why is the Book of Revelation so difficult to understand?

7. What is the point of the Book of Revelation?

8. What is the Deposit of Faith?

9. Who makes up the Magisterium, and what is their job?

New Testament Time Line

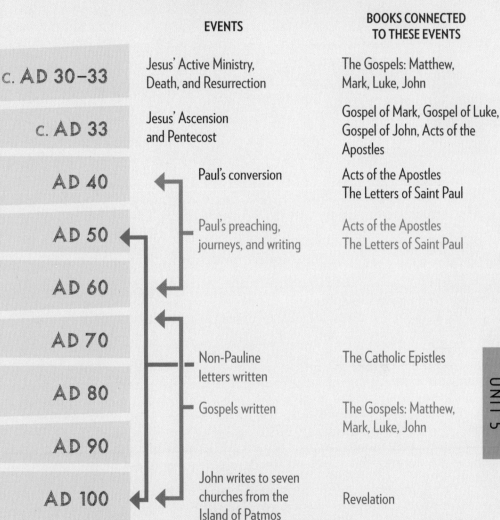

	EVENTS	BOOKS CONNECTED TO THESE EVENTS
c. AD 30–33	Jesus' Active Ministry, Death, and Resurrection	The Gospels: Matthew, Mark, Luke, John
c. AD 33	Jesus' Ascension and Pentecost	Gospel of Mark, Gospel of Luke, Gospel of John, Acts of the Apostles
AD 40	Paul's conversion	Acts of the Apostles The Letters of Saint Paul
AD 50	Paul's preaching, journeys, and writing	Acts of the Apostles The Letters of Saint Paul
AD 60		
AD 70		
AD 80	Non-Pauline letters written	The Catholic Epistles
	Gospels written	The Gospels: Matthew, Mark, Luke, John
AD 90		
AD 100	John writes to seven churches from the Island of Patmos	Revelation

UNIT 5

1. Based on this infographic, which New Testament books were written first? Which book was most likely written last?

2. What event or events were critical for Christianity to emerge as a major world religion? Explain.

CHAPTER 17
Scripture in the Life of the Church

HOW CAN I USE THE BIBLE TO PRAY?

SNAPSHOT

Article 76   Page 457
Sacred Scripture: Food for the Soul
- Pre-read: 2 Timothy 3:16–17

Article 77   Page 460
The Prayer of the Church: Getting into the Rhythm

Article 78   Page 465
The Lord's Prayer: An Essential Conversation
- Pre-read: Matthew 6:5–15
- Pre-read: Luke 11:1–4

Article 79   Page 468
The Right Thing to Do: Morality in the Bible
- Pre-read: Exodus 20:1–17
- Pre-read: Matthew 5:1–7:29
- Pre-read: John 15:1–17

Article 80   Page 472
Lectio Divina: Listening to the Word

Article 81   Page 476
Common Catholic Devotions

Article 76
Sacred Scripture: Food for the Soul

Complicated. That's one word that's been used to describe the Bible. Even though we've learned much about the Bible in this course, it still seems to come back to that realization, doesn't it? The Bible was written thousands of years ago to an audience who spoke a different language and lived in a culture unlike our own. The good news is that we do not have to be Scripture scholars to read the Bible and deepen our relationship with God. However, it will require a commitment to take the time in our busy lives to study Sacred Scripture. Our reward will be accessing this "food for the soul, and a pure and lasting fount of spiritual life"[1] (*CCC*, number 131).

Scripture: The Way to Know and Love Jesus Christ

The heart of Sacred Scripture is the Revelation of our Triune God: Father, Son, and Holy Spirit. Just as the Church is both nourished and guided by God's Word, so too are we as individuals. By reading Scripture we come to know God better, deepening and strengthening our commitment to live as disciples of Jesus Christ. As Paul said to Timothy: "All scripture is inspired by God and is useful for teaching, for refutation, for correction, and for training in righteousness, so that one who belongs to God may be competent, equipped for every good work" (2 Timothy 3:16–17).

A unique sculpture of the Holy Trinity stands tall in Budapest. The Revelation of our Triune God is at the heart of Scripture.

UNIT 5

The way you get to know someone is by talking with them, listening to them, and spending time with them. It's the same thing in getting to know and love Jesus. There are several ways to get to know Jesus, but a primary way is Sacred Scripture. Saint Jerome (345–420) wisely taught that "ignorance of the Scriptures is ignorance of Christ"[2] (*CCC*, number 133). This means that to be an effective disciple of Jesus Christ, we need to spend time reading and studying his life and teachings as found in the Bible. Knowing, praying with, and understanding Scripture, then, is a basic necessity for every Christian. We can study and pray with Scripture individually and with others. And we can do it anywhere: at home, at school, in our parish, or anywhere a group of faithful people is gathered.

How can we get to know God's Word better? Here are some ways:

- Set aside 10 minutes to read and reflect on the readings for Sunday Mass.
- Pay close attention to the homily.
- Join a Bible study at your church or school. If there aren't any Bible studies available, start one with a few friends.
- Drop by a Catholic bookstore to see what prayer books they have for teens.
- Become a lector at your church.

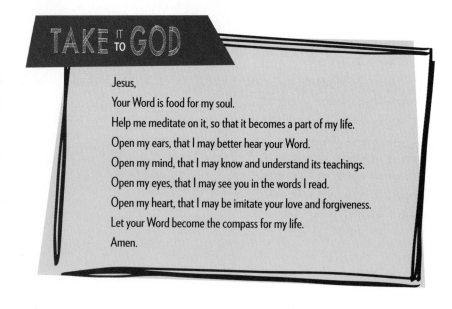

TAKE IT TO GOD

Jesus,

Your Word is food for my soul.

Help me meditate on it, so that it becomes a part of my life.

Open my ears, that I may better hear your Word.

Open my mind, that I may know and understand its teachings.

Open my eyes, that I may see you in the words I read.

Open my heart, that I may be imitate your love and forgiveness.

Let your Word become the compass for my life.

Amen.

All of these ways of studying and praying with Scripture can help you deepen your relationship with God's Word. The rest of this chapter will give you many other ideas for making the Bible a regular part of your spiritual life and practice. ✳

© sturti / iStock.com

Joining a Bible study group is an excellent (and fun!) way to learn about Scripture.

Why does Sacred Scripture require that we do more than just read it? Why do we have to study it?

Article 77

The Prayer of the Church: Getting into the Rhythm

Ever since Stanley's first week of school in kindergarten, he and his father have gone out to breakfast every Friday. Over the years, the conversation has progressed from talking about cartoons and teachers to discussing basketball and girls. And sometimes Stanley and his dad are quiet and don't say anything. Regardless, Stanley can always count on having his dad's attention. There is rhythm to this tradition, which gives Stanley comfort and strengthens his relationship with his dad.

Traditions, such as celebrating holidays with family or having breakfast every Friday with a friend, provide a rhythm and sense of comfort to our lives and strengthen our relationships.

Similarly, the Church offers prayer traditions that can give us comfort and help strengthen our relationship with God: the Liturgy of the Hours and the celebration of the Eucharist. These two Scripture-based prayers are tied to the rhythms of the Church year, as well as to the beat of our daily lives. The prayerful reading of Sacred Scripture is an integral element of both of these traditions, allowing the living Word of God to shape our lives.

UNIT 5

On the Hour

Before proceeding further, it is important to know that **liturgy** is the Church's official, public, communal prayer. "It is the whole *community*, the Body of Christ united with its Head, that celebrates" (*CCC*, number 1140). The word *liturgy* comes from the Greek word *leitourgia*, meaning "work of the people." Liturgy is the work of the whole People of God.

The Liturgy of the Hours, also known as the Divine Office, is the official public, *daily* prayer of the Catholic Church. The Divine Office provides standard prayers, Scripture readings, and reflections at regular hours throughout the day. The recitation of the Psalms is at the heart of the Divine Office. Along with the Psalms, the Divine Office incorporates meditations, hymns, and other scriptural readings in order to express "the symbolism of the time of day, the liturgical season, or the feast being celebrated" (*CCC*, number 1177). It can be prayed alone or with other people.

"Seven times a day I praise you" (Psalm 119:164). The Liturgy of the Hours is arranged into four-week cycles that are adjusted for specific feast days and other seasonal celebrations. The daily practice is centered on two primary "hours" each day: morning and evening. Additional prayers bring the total to seven times each day. The prayers for the Liturgy of the Hours are found in a book called the **breviary**.

A page from a fourteenth-century English breviary, a book that contains the Liturgy of the Hours.

UNIT 5

---

liturgy ➤ The Church's official, public, communal prayer. It is God's work, in which the People of God participate. The Church's most important liturgy is the Eucharist, or the Mass.

breviary ➤ A prayer book that contains the prayers for the Liturgy of the Hours.

Hour	Latin Name	Themes
Morning Prayer	*Lauds*	Christ's Resurrection, praise for creation, dedication, light, dawn
Midmorning Prayer	*Terce*	New life, beginnings
Midday Prayer	*Sext*	Renewed commitment to the mission of Christ
Midafternoon Prayer	*None*	Awareness of the end of life and time
Evening	*Vespers*	Gratitude for Christ, reflection of Christ's Passion and burial, thanksgiving for the day, repentance for sin
Night Prayer	*Compline*	Divine protection and peace, restful sleep and happy death
Office of Readings	*Matins*	Wisdom revealed in the words of Scripture, writings of the Church Fathers, and lives of the saints

CATHOLICS MAKING A DIFFERENCE

"If Jerome doesn't know, nobody does, or ever did!" These words are credited to Saint Augustine of Hippo (354–430) speaking about his peer, the mid-fourth-century theologian Saint Jerome (c. 345–420). Saint Jerome was one of the Church's first biblical scholars. He had an amazing intellect and great knowledge of the biblical texts. He wrote many commentaries on Scripture as well several books on Church history. However, Saint Jerome is most well-known for translating the Bible into Latin, the common language at the time. This translation is called the Vulgate (from the Latin word meaning "common") and was the translation used in Church liturgies for centuries. Because of his many contributions to Catholic theology, Saint Jerome is also a Doctor of the Church.

The Bible and the Sacraments

At Mass, the Sacrament of the Eucharist, we are fed by "the bread of life, taken from the one table of God's Word and Christ's Body"[3] (*CCC*, number 103). When we gather to celebrate Mass, we experience the presence of Christ in several ways and every one of those ways is based in Scripture:

- We experience Christ in the People of God who gather to celebrate the Mass. And why do we gather? Because in the Gospels, Christ commands that we gather to eat his Body and drink his Blood. In fact, we use the term **Body of Christ** to refer to Jesus' Body and Blood in the Eucharist and also to refer to the entire Church.

- We experience Christ in the celebrant, the priest or bishop who presides over the liturgy. The celebrant represents Christ, our great High Priest (see Hebrews 4:14–16).

- We experience Christ in the Liturgy of the Word, which is most of the first half of the Mass. The Liturgy of the Word is completely based on Scripture. On most Sundays and holy days, the Liturgy of the Word includes readings from the Old Testament, the Psalms, the Gospels, and the New Testament letters. The **homily** offers a reflection on how we can put the teachings from Scripture into practice. In all of these, we are nourished by God's Word.

- We experience Christ in the **Liturgy of the Eucharist**, which is most of the second half of the Mass, when we eat the Body and Blood of Jesus Christ in the form of the consecrated bread and wine. The various forms of the **Eucharistic Prayer** contain many biblical images and phrases. The words of consecration spoken by the priest during the Eucharistic Prayer are taken from the Last Supper accounts in the synoptic Gospels (see Matthew 26:26–29, Mark 14:22–24, Luke 22:19–20).

UNIT 5

Body of Christ ➤ A term that when capitalized designates Jesus' Body in the Eucharist, or the entire Church, which is also referred to as the Mystical Body of Christ.

homily ➤ A brief liturgical sermon that explains the Scripture readings, helps the People of God accept Sacred Scripture as the Word of God, and encourages them to put the teachings of Scripture into practice in their daily lives.

Liturgy of the Eucharist ➤ This term refers to the second part of the Mass that includes the offertory, the prayers of consecration and invocation of the Holy Spirit, the reception of Communion, and the dismissal.

Eucharistic Prayer ➤ The part of the Mass that includes the Consecration, beginning with the Preface and concluding with the Great Amen.

Like the Eucharist, the other sacraments, from Baptism to Anointing of the Sick, incorporate Sacred Scripture into their celebrations, drawing strength and inspiration from the Word of God. In this way, Sacred Scripture forms the foundation for all our liturgical celebrations. Through the sacraments, we enter into the presence of God: Father, Son, and Holy Spirit. ✳

© wideonet / iStock.com

The words of consecration spoken by the priest during the Eucharistic Prayer are taken from the Last Supper accounts in the synoptic Gospels.

UNIT 5

HMMMMM. . . What do you find most meaningful in the Scripture used in the Mass?

Article 78
The Lord's Prayer: An Essential Conversation

Prayer is lifting up of one's mind and heart to God. It is the essential conversation we have with God. If you need to be reminded how important prayer is, remember that even Jesus prayed . . . and often! (See Matthew 14:23, Mark 14:32, and Luke 6:12.)

Although there are a multitude of prayers and ways of praying, the Lord's Prayer is the most central prayer to our faith. For many of us, it was the first prayer we learned, and it might be the last prayer we offer before our death. We say it in times of trouble and in moments of gratitude. It is a prayer that binds all Christians together and guides us on our spiritual journey.

Joining hands when praying with others can create a powerful bond among the participants. When have you joined hands in prayer with others?

prayer ➤ Lifting up of one's mind and heart to God or the requesting of good things from him. The five basic forms of prayer are blessing, praise, petition, thanksgiving, and intercession. In prayer, we communicate with God in a relationship of love.

THE Prayer

When Jesus' disciples ask him how to pray, he gives them this advice: "When you pray, do not be like the hypocrites, who love to stand and pray in the synagogues and on street corners so that others may see them. . . . But when you pray, go to your inner room, close the door, and pray to your Father in secret" (Matthew 6:5–6). Then he teaches them the Lord's Prayer, also known as the Our Father. The Lord's Prayer we use at Mass is based on Matthew's Gospel (see 6:9–15). The Gospel of Luke has a version that is slightly different (see 11:1–4).

Seven Petitions, Seven Requests

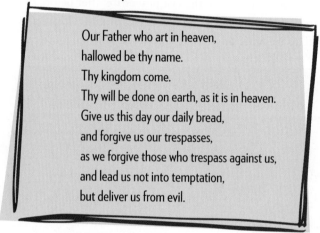

Our Father who art in heaven,
hallowed be thy name.
Thy kingdom come.
Thy will be done on earth, as it is in heaven.
Give us this day our daily bread,
and forgive us our trespasses,
as we forgive those who trespass against us,
and lead us not into temptation,
but deliver us from evil.

The Lord's Prayer is made up of seven petitions, or requests, for grace or blessings from God. These petitions offer us a model for Christian prayer:

1. "Hallowed be your name" asks that our words and deeds reflect our reverence for the name of God.
2. "Your kingdom come" expresses our desire to bring about the Kingdom of God on earth, as well as our hope for the second coming of Christ.
3. "Your will be done on earth, as it is in heaven" asks for the encouragement and strength needed to follow God's will.
4. "Give us this day, our daily bread" is a request for not only our physical needs but our spiritual ones as well. It is an expression of our ultimate reliance on God for all we need.
5. "Forgive us our trespasses, as we forgive those who trespass against us" requests that God forgive us in the same manner that we forgive others. This certainly should encourage our willingness to pardon others!

6. "Lead us not into temptation" asks for the strength to withstand the attraction to do wrong.

7. "Deliver us from evil" is a request to keep us safe from Satan. It is a sign of our desire to spend our eternal life with God.

The Lord's Prayer "is truly the summary of the whole gospel"[4] (*CCC*, number 2774). It has an essential role in the Sacraments of Baptism, Confirmation, and the Eucharist. It holds a place of comfort and guidance in both our personal and communal prayers. It is a prayer held in common with other Christians. And so it should be. After all, the prayer is the words of Jesus, the Word of God. ✳

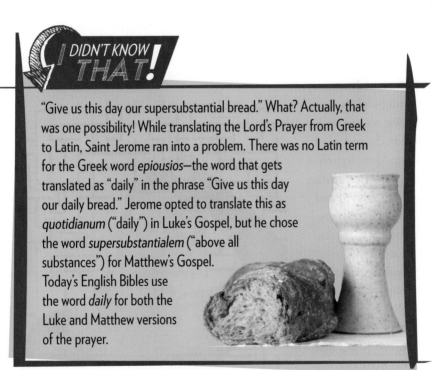

I DIDN'T KNOW THAT!

"Give us this day our supersubstantial bread." What? Actually, that was one possibility! While translating the Lord's Prayer from Greek to Latin, Saint Jerome ran into a problem. There was no Latin term for the Greek word *epiousios*—the word that gets translated as "daily" in the phrase "Give us this day our daily bread." Jerome opted to translate this as *quotidianum* ("daily") in Luke's Gospel, but he chose the word *supersubstantialem* ("above all substances") for Matthew's Gospel. Today's English Bibles use the word *daily* for both the Luke and Matthew versions of the prayer.

UNIT 5

HMMMMMM. . .

What does the verse "forgive us our trespasses, as we forgive those who trespass against us" in the Lord's Prayer mean?

Article 79

The Right Thing to Do: Morality in the Bible

How does one know what is the right thing to do in any given situation? Sometimes the answer to that question is obvious, like choosing not to cheat on a test because we know that would be dishonest. But sometimes we are faced with a dilemma and don't know what is the right thing to do. The Ten Commandments in the Bible can offer useful guidance when answers are not easy to come by. By opening ourselves to the guidance of the Holy Spirit, Sacred Scripture can guide us toward the best path, even when the path may at first seem unclear.

Guidelines for Doing Good

When we face dilemmas concerning what is right and wrong, we are walking within the realms of **morality**. Morality refers to what is good and what is bad, what is right and what is wrong in terms of the choices we make. God created human beings with an ability to reason, and gave us free will so that each of us can "initiate and control his own actions" (*CCC*, number 1730). We can choose what is morally good or evil. Sacred Scripture is one of God's gifts to help us discern what is good for ourselves and others.

Sometimes it's very difficult to choose what is the right thing to do when we're faced with a dilemma. What guides you in making the right decision?

---

morality ▶ Refers to the goodness or evil of human acts. The morality of an act is determined by the nature of the action, the intention, and the circumstances.

Praying regularly and reading and studying he Bible are key ways to establish a foundation for a good moral life. "We must assimilate [the Word of God] in faith and prayer and put it into practice" (*CCC*, number 1785). We should all be familiar with some proven biblical guidelines for our moral faith: the Ten Commandments (see Exodus 20:1–17), the Beatitudes (see Matthew 5:1–12, Luke 6:20–23), the Sermon on the Mount (see Matthew, chapters 5–7), and the Great Commandment (see Matthew 22:34–40), to name a few. In the Ten Commandments, God directs us to honor him, the Sabbath, and our parents. He also prohibits us from doing harm to ourselves and one another (see Exodus 20:1–17). Jesus' Beatitudes lead us on the path to true happiness (see Matthew 5:3–12). In the Sermon on the Mount, Jesus teaches us the basics of Christian discipleship: loving our enemies, praying, and putting God first in our lives, among others. And when Jesus is asked which is the greatest commandment, he shows the essential connection between the love of God and the love of our neighbor.

The Bible offers wonderful role models to whom we can look for guidance in living a moral life. Mary, the Mother of God, offers us an unparalleled example of faithfulness and obedience to God (see Luke 1:38). Though there are numerous other examples, remember that some of the most faithful of God's servants, like David, were often flawed (see 2 Samuel, chapter 11). People must discern their actions in light of the teachings of the whole Bible and Church teachings. Just because people are good does not mean everything they do is good.

Mary's faithfulness and obedience to God is a prime example of how to live a moral life.

UNIT 5

The Rule of Love

"This is my commandment: love one another as I love you. No one has greater love than this, to lay down one's life for one's friends" (John 15:12–13). If there is any one moral law that Jesus placed above any other, it would be the Law of Love. This is why we sometimes call the New Law of Christ the Law of Love. When asked what was the greatest commandment, Christ said that we should love God and love our neighbor (see Matthew 22:34–40). The love he is talking about is not a feeling but the act of placing someone else's needs ahead of your own. It is an act of sacrificing your own wants and needs for another. The moral guidance to love one another includes loving one's enemies (see Luke 6:27).

When have you placed the needs of someone else ahead of your own?

Jesus is our shining example of what it means to live a moral human life. The biblical accounts of his words and deeds provide us with a template on which to model our lives. He cared for the outcasts and oppressed (see Mark 2:15–17). He healed the sick and fed the hungry (see Matthew 15:29–39). His goodness is most evident in his sacrifice on the cross and his forgiveness of the people who killed him (see Luke 23:34).

The way we may be sure that we know him is to keep his commandments. . . . Whoever keeps his word, the love of God is truly perfected in him. This is the way we may know that we are in union with him: whoever claims to abide in him ought to live [just] as he lived. (1 John 2:3,5–6) ✱

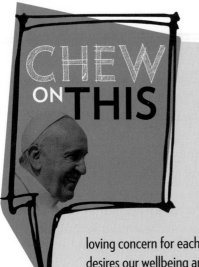

CHEW ON THIS

As we can see in Sacred Scripture, *mercy* is a key word that indicates God's action towards us. He does not limit himself merely to affirming his love, but makes it visible and tangible. Love, after all, can never be just an abstraction. By its very nature, it indicates something concrete: intentions, attitudes, and behaviours that are shown in daily living. The mercy of God is his loving concern for each one of us. He feels responsible; that is, he desires our wellbeing and he wants to see us happy, full of joy, and peaceful. (Pope Francis, Bull of Indiction of the Extraordinary Jubilee of Mercy [*Misericordiae Vultus*, 2015], number 9)

HMMMMM. . .

What does it require of you to truly love others as your brothers and sisters?

UNIT 5

Article 80

Lectio Divina: Listening to the Word

"We have two ears and one mouth, so we can listen twice as much as we speak." These wise words are attributed to the Greek philosopher Epictetus, sometime around AD 55. He makes a good point. Obviously, talking is an important part of conversation, but so is listening—perhaps even more so. Listening is a powerful tool that allows us to learn and grow. It can be likened to opening a door and waiting for something new and different to come in.

The same is true regarding prayer. Certainly, talking to God is important, but that's only one side of the conversation. Prayer is a two-way street. Listening to God is absolutely necessary if we want to deepen our spiritual life. Taking the time to listen is a way to learn what God wants for us. Without doing so, how can we accomplish "thy will be done"?

© saksorn kumjit / Shutterstock.com

Listening in prayer can be likened to opening a door and waiting for something new and different to come in.

© 4Max / Shutterstock.com

The best way to get comfortable with this form of praying with Sacred Scripture is by continually practicing, using the steps outlined in this chapter. The following Scripture passages can be particularly fruitful for *lectio divina*:

- Genesis 45:4–8 (Joseph reunites with his brothers.)
- Jeremiah 1:4–10 (Jeremiah is called by God.)
- Mark 4:35–41 (Jesus calms a storm at sea.)
- Mark 2:1–12 (Jesus heals a paralyzed man.)

It is also good to keep a journal handy in case you want to write down something that touches your heart. If at first you find yourself easily distracted, don't worry about it. Simply continue following the steps. The more you return to *lectio divina*, the more comfortable you will become with it.

Paying Attention

Learning to listen to God's voice isn't as complicated as you might think. One way we can do this is by reading Scripture using an ancient form of prayer called *lectio divina*. *Lectio divina*, a Latin term meaning "divine reading," is a form of meditative prayer focused on a Scripture passage. It involves repetitive readings and periods of reflection "where the Word of God is so read and meditated that it becomes prayer" (*CCC*, number 1177). It is a way of reading the Bible that invites us to slowly and mindfully pay attention and "taste" each word.

UNIT 5

---

lectio divina ➤ A Latin term meaning "divine reading." *Lectio divina* is a form of meditative prayer focused on a Scripture passage. It involves repetitive readings and periods of reflection and can serve as either private or communal prayer.

To give you a sense of what it means to "taste" each word of Scripture, imagine yourself sitting at the table with your favorite meal in front of you. You are fully and completely attentive to this delicious food. For a moment, you close your eyes and enjoy the pleasant aroma. As you take your first bite, you chew your food slowly and deliberately, noticing its texture and taste. After you've finished your meal, the taste still lingers in your mouth, and you feel very peacefully content.

Lectio divina is much like this. In fact, since ancient times, this spiritual practice has been compared to a cow quietly chewing its cud. It has become a symbol of how we are to **ruminate** on the Word of God.

How to Do It

Guigo II, a Carthusian monk in the twelfth century, wrote the book *The Ladder of Monks*. In this text, he describes how to do *lectio divina* in four stages. It can be done silently or aloud, by yourself or with a group of people. To begin, find a Scripture passage—maybe one of Jesus' parables or miracles. Then find a comfortable place to sit, where you won't be disturbed. It's important that you have absolute quiet. Start with a few minutes of silence to calm your mind before proceeding through these four stages:

1. *Lectio* (Reading)

   Read the passage one time through to get an idea of what the reading is about. Then reread it slowly and prayerfully several times. Pay attention to each word. It sometimes helps to read it aloud. Listen for a word or phrase that sticks out or grabs your attention. The word or phrase does not have to make sense. Listen with what Saint Benedict of Nursia (c. 480–547) called "the ear of your heart." Continue to slowly reread the passage until that word or phrase becomes obvious.

2. *Meditatio* (Meditation)

   Meditate on the Scripture passage or word that grabbed your attention. Say that word passage either silently or aloud. Repeat it slowly over and over at about the rate of your breathing. Ruminate on it, savor it. Every time you exhale, say the word or phrase. Do this for several minutes.

---

ruminate ➤ To think deeply about something; to contemplate, meditate on, ponder over, chew on.

UNIT 5

3. *Oratio* (Prayer)

This time is spent talking to God. You can talk to God like you would a friend. You can ask for forgiveness, or offer an intention for yourself or someone else. Simply follow whatever your heart wants to say.

4. *Contemplatio* (Contemplation)

Here we simply and silently rest in the presence of God. As much as we are able to, we put ourselves in the presence of God. Our intention is to put aside all words and thoughts and simply let the love of God embrace us. Often our mind wanders, so it might help to focus on our breathing, or the repetition of a sacred word (such as *Lord, Jesus, God, Spirit,* and so on). Just be still and be present with your whole body.

Sometimes afterward, people like to add another stage called *actio* (action). This can be done a number of ways, such as writing in a journal alone or talking in a discussion group. This stage addresses how God, through Sacred Scripture, is calling you to act in the world. Through *lectio divina*, we hope "to deepen our convictions of faith, prompt the conversion of our heart, and strengthen our will to follow Christ" (*CCC*, number 2708). ✳

The spiritual practice of *lectio divina* has been compared to a cow quietly chewing its cud. It has become a symbol of how we are to ruminate on the Word of God.

UNIT 5

HMMMMM . . .

How is *lectio divina* similar to eating a meal slowly and mindfully?

Article 81
Common Catholic Devotions

Throughout the centuries, Sacred Scripture and Sacred Tradition have inspired a number of **devotional prayers**. Devotional prayers, also known simply as devotions, are personalized prayers that have developed outside the liturgy of the Church but should lead us to it. Two of the most well-known and commonly practiced devotions are the Stations of the Cross and the Rosary.

© Zvonimir Atletic / Shutterstock.com

Station 2, Jesus is given his cross. The Stations of the Cross is a devotion commonly practiced during the season of Lent.

---

devotional prayers ➤ Also known as devotions, these are personalized prayers that have developed outside, but should lead to, the liturgy of the Church.

Stations of the Cross

In the years after Jesus' Resurrection and Ascension, early Christians would sometimes make pilgrimages to Jerusalem. While there, they prayerfully walked the **Via Dolorosa** (Latin for "way of sorrow"), the path Jesus walked in the last hours of his life.

The **Stations of the Cross** became a popular devotion in the Middle Ages. Because it was not easy to make a pilgrimage to the Holy Land, churches developed a "virtual" way for people to travel the Via Dolorosa, creating artistic representations of the events in Jesus Christ's Passion and death. People would walk and pray before these representations, just as people did along the Via Dolorosa. The number of stops, or stations, varied until 1731, when Pope Clement XII standardized the practice of the following fourteen stations:

1. Jesus is condemned to death.
2. Jesus bears his cross.
3. Jesus falls the first time.
4. Jesus meets his mother.
5. Simon of Cyrene helps Jesus to carry his cross.
6. Veronica wipes the face of Jesus.
7. Jesus falls a second time.
8. Jesus meets the women of Jerusalem.
9. Jesus falls a third time.
10. Jesus is stripped of his garments.
11. Jesus is nailed to the cross.
12. Jesus dies on the cross.
13. Jesus is taken down from the cross.
14. Jesus is placed in the tomb.

These stations are rooted in the scriptural accounts of Jesus' Passion and death. However, some of the events—such as stations 3, 4, 6, 7, and 9—are not found in the Bible, but they are supported by Sacred Tradition.

UNIT 5

Via Dolorosa ➤ Latin for "way of sorrow," referring to the path Jesus journeyed in the last hours of his life, which is commemorated in the devotion of the Stations of the Cross.

Stations of the Cross ➤ A devotion for prayer and reflection, popular during Lent, that retraces the events of Jesus' Passion and death in fourteen "stations," represented by artistic depictions. Most Catholic churches have artistic representations of the fourteen Stations of the Cross. Also called the Way of the Cross.

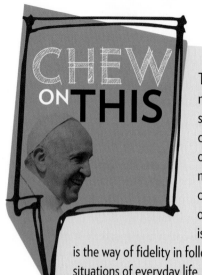

This evening, dear friends, the Lord once more asks you to be in the forefront of serving others. He wants to make of you a concrete response to the needs and sufferings of humanity. He wants you to be signs of his merciful love for our time! To enable you to carry out this mission, he shows you the way of personal commitment and self-sacrifice. It is the Way of the Cross. The Way of the Cross is the way of fidelity in following Jesus to the end, in the often dramatic situations of everyday life. It is a way that fears no lack of success, ostracism or solitude, because it fills ours hearts with the fullness of Jesus. The Way of the Cross is the way of God's own life, his "style," which Jesus brings even to the pathways of a society at times divided, unjust and corrupt. (Pope Francis, "Way of the Cross with the Young People," July 29, 2016)

Whether the events are from Scripture or Tradition, or both, the Stations of the Cross invite us to reflect on Jesus' sacrifice that led to his Resurrection, and our salvation. In 1991, Pope Saint John Paul II introduced the following scriptural Stations of the Cross, which more accurately reflects Christ's Passion and death as told in the biblical accounts:

1. Jesus is in the garden of Gethsemane.
2. Jesus is betrayed by Judas and is arrested.
3. Jesus is condemned by the Sanhedrin.
4. Jesus is denied by Peter.
5. Jesus is judged by Pilate.
6. Jesus is scourged and crowned with thorns.
7. Jesus bears the cross.
8. Jesus is helped by Simon the Cyrenian to carry the cross.
9. Jesus meets the women of Jerusalem.
10. Jesus is crucified.
11. Jesus promises his Kingdom to the good thief.
12. Jesus speaks to his mother and the disciple.
13. Jesus dies on the cross.
14. Jesus is placed in the tomb.

When you walk into a Catholic church, you'll find the fourteen Stations of the Cross artistically represented on its walls. Usually there are gaps, or open wall space, between each station. To pray the Stations, you must walk to each station, mimicking the Via Dolorosa.

The Rosary

Truths from Scripture and Tradition are also expressed in another popular Catholic devotion called the **Rosary**. The Rosary is a devotional prayer that honors the Virgin Mary and helps us meditate on Christ's life and mission. We pray the Rosary using rosary beads, which are grouped into five "decades"—a series of ten beads. Each decade consists of praying the Lord's Prayer followed by ten Hail Mary's and the Glory Be.

The Rosary is a devotional prayer that honors the Virgin Mary and helps us meditate on Christ's life and mission. If you haven't prayed the Rosary before, give it a try!

UNIT 5

© Philip Yb Studio / Shutterstock.com

Rosary ➤ A devotional prayer that honors the Virgin Mary and helps us meditate on Christ's life and mission. We pray the Rosary using rosary beads, which are grouped into "decades." Each decade consists of praying the Lord's Prayer followed by ten Hail Mary's and the Glory Be while meditating on an event from Christ's life and mission.

As we pray each decade, we meditate on an event from Christ's life. The events are grouped into the three categories, called "Mysteries," that focus on Jesus' birth, Passion, and Resurrection. They are the Joyful Mysteries, the Sorrowful Mysteries, and the Glorious Mysteries, respectively. The Rosary (from the Latin *rosarium*, meaning "garland of roses") is made up of 150 Hail Marys, mirroring the 150 Psalms. In 2002, Pope Saint John Paul II added another series called the Luminous Mysteries, which focus on Christ's public ministry.

The Joyful Mysteries (Jesus' Birth)

- The Annunciation
- The Visitation
- The Birth of Our Lord
- The Presentation of Jesus in the Temple
- The Finding of Jesus in the Temple

The Sorrowful Mysteries (Jesus' Passion and Death)

- The Agony in the Garden
- The Scourging at the Pillar
- The Crowning with Thorns
- The Carrying of the Cross
- The Crucifixion

The Glorious Mysteries (Jesus' Resurrection and Ascension)

- The Resurrection of Jesus
- The Ascension of Jesus into Heaven
- The Descent of the Holy Spirit on the Apostles (Pentecost)
- The Assumption of Mary into Heaven
- The Crowning of Mary as Queen of Heaven

The Luminous Mysteries (Jesus' Public Ministry)

- The Baptism of Jesus
- Jesus Reveals Himself in the Miracle at Cana
- Jesus Proclaims the Good News of the Kingdom of God
- The Transfiguration of Jesus
- The Institution of the Eucharist

Praying the Rosary is a meditative experience that offers a deep sense of peace that springs from God's grace. Prayerfully focusing on Jesus' life brings us into a deeper relationship with Christ, through whom God brings about our salvation. ✳

Prayers and Parts of the Rosary

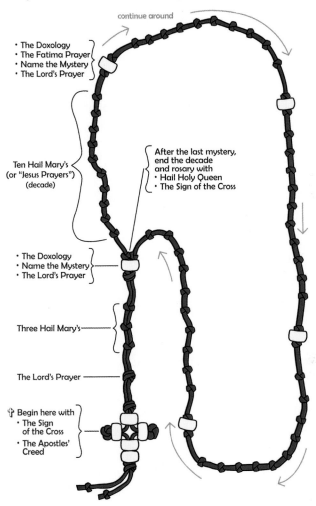

continue around

- The Doxology
- The Fatima Prayer
- Name the Mystery
- The Lord's Prayer

After the last mystery, end the decade and rosary with
- Hail Holy Queen
- The Sign of the Cross

Ten Hail Mary's (or "Jesus Prayers") (decade)

- The Doxology
- Name the Mystery
- The Lord's Prayer

Three Hail Mary's

The Lord's Prayer

✝ Begin here with
- The Sign of the Cross
- The Apostles' Creed

UNIT 5

HMMMMM. . . How is praying the Stations of the Cross similar to making a pilgrimage to the Holy Land?

1. What did Saint Jerome mean when he said, "Ignorance of the Scriptures is ignorance of Christ"?

2. List at least three ways to deepen your relationship with Sacred Scripture.

3. What is the Liturgy of the Hours? What part of Scripture is its main focus?

4. What role does Sacred Scripture play in the celebration of the Mass?

5. Why is the Lord's Prayer so important?

6. How does reading Scripture help us come to know what is morally good?

7. Why is listening to God an important element in prayer?

8. What are the four stages of *lectio divina?*

9. What are devotional prayers? Name two examples.

Holy Hotline

The Bible is a wonderful place to turn to express one's feelings in prayer. Reading and praying with the Bible can draw you closer to God's presence and power. If you want to take it a step further, memorize a few passages so you can pray them anytime! Here are some to get you started:

PSALM 23	When I am worried . . .	**JOSHUA 1:5**	When I need courage and strength . . .
JAMES 5:7-8	When I am impatient . . .	**MATTHEW 7:7-11**	When I am in need . . .
2 CORINTHIANS 4:8-9	When I am discouraged . . .	**JOHN 14:1**	When I am troubled . . .
JEREMIAH 1:5-8	When I feel inadequate . . .	**PSALM 51:3-4**	When I feel guilty for my sins . . .
1 PETER 5:7-9	When I am facing adversity . . .	**ROMANS 8:28**	When things don't go my way . . .
PHILIPPIANS 4:6-7	When I feel stressed out . . .	**1 CORINTHIANS 10:13**	When I am tempted to do wrong . . .
PROVERBS 3:5-6	When I am confused . . .	**ISAIAH 43:1-3**	When I am afraid . . .
DEUTERONOMY 31:6	When I feel alone . . .	**MATTHEW 11:28-30**	When I am feeling overwhelmed . . .

UNIT 5

UNIT 5 HIGHLIGHTS

CHAPTER 15   The Gospels

The Gospels

There are four:

- Mathew
- Mark
- Luke
- John

The Gospels are like religious or theological biographies based on Jesus' life and teachings.

They are the principal source for understanding Jesus Christ's life and teaching—the turning point in salvation history.

The synoptic Gospels—Matthew, Mark, and Luke—are similar in their style and content.

Many scholars believe that Mark was written first and that Matthew and Luke used Mark as a source for their Gospels.

John's Gospel provides a more divine portrayal of Jesus than the synoptic Gospels.

Each Gospel author emphasizes certain aspects of Jesus' life and teachings.

Jesus brought about the Kingdom of God through his life, teachings (especially the parables), and miracles.

Jesus brought about the Kingdom of God most especially through his Passion, death, Resurrection, and Ascension.

Jesus Christ, the beloved Son of God, is God's Word Made Flesh, true God and true man, the fullness of Divine Revelation.

CHAPTER 16 The Acts of the Apostles and the Letters

Acts of the Apostles	The Letters	The Book of Revelation	The Deposit of Faith
• Jesus ascends into Heaven. • On Pentecost, Jesus sends the Holy Spirit to guide the Church. • The Apostles continue Jesus' mission. • Saint Paul, a Jewish Pharisee, persecutes the Church. Paul converts to Christianity.	• Paul wrote many letters to the early Gentile Christian communities. • There are eight non-Pauline letters in the New Testament. • The Catholic letters are written by various Church leaders and are addressed to all of the Christian communities.	• This book was written by the Christian prophet John during a period of intense persecution (AD 92–96). • It uses lots of symbolic language and imagery. • This book encourages the Christians to remain faithful and confident that Christ will triumph over all evil.	• is contained in Sacred Scripture and Sacred Tradition
			The Magisterium
			• consists of all bishops in communion with the Pope • is responsible for passing on and interpreting the Deposit of Faith

CHAPTER 17 Scripture in the Life of the Church

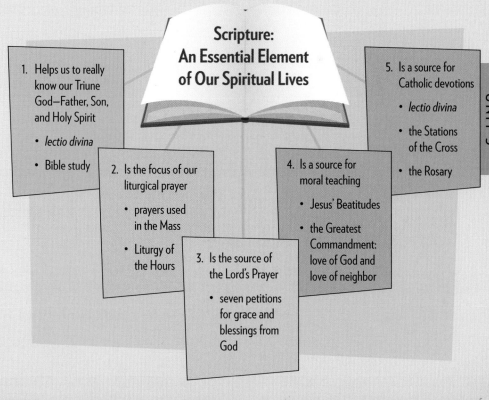

Scripture:
An Essential Element of Our Spiritual Lives

1. Helps us to really know our Triune God—Father, Son, and Holy Spirit
   - *lectio divina*
   - Bible study

2. Is the focus of our liturgical prayer
   - prayers used in the Mass
   - Liturgy of the Hours

3. Is the source of the Lord's Prayer
   - seven petitions for grace and blessings from God

4. Is a source for moral teaching
   - Jesus' Beatitudes
   - the Greatest Commandment: love of God and love of neighbor

5. Is a source for Catholic devotions
   - *lectio divina*
   - the Stations of the Cross
   - the Rosary

UNIT 5

UNIT 5
BRING IT HOME

HOW IS JESUS' MISSION KEPT ALIVE?

FOCUS QUESTIONS

CHAPTER 15   Don't the four Gospels say the same thing?

CHAPTER 16   Who got the Church going after Jesus' Ascension?

CHAPTER 17   How can I use the Bible to pray?

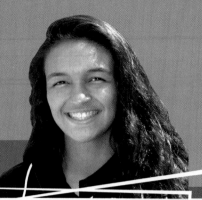

BELLA
Father Lopez Catholic High School

Jesus' mission is caring for God's creation and spreading the Good News. Be proud of your faith. When you hear an ambulance, make the sign of the cross; if your friend is having problems, ask if he'll pray with you. Faith is a powerful thing. It gives us a greater purpose. We aren't on this Earth just for ourselves. We are all part of a plan.

UNIT 5

REFLECT

Take some time to read and reflect on the unit and chapter focus questions listed on the facing page.

- What question or section did you identify most closely with?

- What did you find within the unit that was comforting or challenging?

APPENDIX
Challenge Questions

The content of this course raises some important questions for those who think seriously about their faith. This is especially true today, when many people are asking hard questions about religious beliefs. We are not afraid of these hard questions, because an honest search for answers will deepen our faith and understanding of what God has revealed. Here are some common questions with some key points for how to answer them. The references to paragraphs in the *Catechism of the Catholic Church (CCC)* are for further reading if you want to explore these questions more deeply.

QUESTION 1: Is it true that Catholics do not use or read the Bible?

Of course not! Catholics read the Bible regularly. Back in the fourth century, Saint Jerome, the brilliant Scripture scholar, said, "Ignorance of the Scriptures is ignorance of Christ." The Catholic Church takes this admonition seriously, which is why reading and hearing the Sacred Scriptures is woven into everything Catholics do.

For example, our liturgies, especially the Mass, are filled with Scripture. Many of the prayers and responses in the Mass are taken directly from Scripture: "Holy, holy, holy," "Our Father, who art in Heaven," "Lord, I am not worthy . . . ," "Do this in remembrance of me," to name just a few. At every Mass, we also listen to three or four readings from the Bible, followed by the priest or deacon preaching on them during the homily. The Liturgy of the Hours, the official daily prayer of the Church, is based mostly on readings from the Bible as well.

Catholics are also strongly encouraged to make reading Scripture part of their personal prayer life. The bishops of the Second Vatican Council "earnestly and especially urge[s] all the Christian faithful, especially Religious, to learn by frequent reading of the divine Scriptures the 'excellent knowledge of Jesus Christ' (Phil. 3:8)" (*Dogmatic Constitution on Divine Revelation* [*Dei Verbum*, 1965], number 25). We see evidence of Catholics studying the Bible in the great variety of Catholic Bibles and Bible study aids available, and in the large number of parish groups studying and praying with Scripture.

QUESTION 2: Isn't the Bible just another piece of literature?

Although the Bible does contain many types of literary genres, it is more than just literature. The critical difference is that the Bible is the inspired Word of God. This means that unlike other books, we can count on Sacred Scripture as a source of Divine Revelation. Through it, our triune God—Father, Son, and Holy Spirit—is revealed to us. By reading and praying with the Bible, we strengthen our relationship with God and grow deeper in our knowledge of God's saving plan.

Because the Bible is the Word of God, we do not read or understand it in the same way as other literature. We approach it in faith, with the expectation that we will meet the living God through its words. We understand that we must always read and interpret the Bible with the help of the Church and under the guidance of the Holy Spirit.

QUESTION 3: Is the Bible always literally true?

The Bible is always true when it teaches what God wants us to know for our salvation. Whether certain passages in the Bible are historically or scientifically true depends on the context, such as the human author's background, their intended purpose for writing, and the literary genre they are using. Because of this, Catholics do not read the Bible literally, in the sense that many fundamentalist Christians do; rather, we take a contextualist approach in interpreting biblical passages. The Church provides us with guidelines for interpreting the Bible in context (see chapter 4 of this book).

Although the Church does not claim that the Bible's purpose is to present scientific or historical facts, Catholics do believe that events told about in both the Old and New Testaments are historically based. This is especially true for the Gospels; they are accurate in recounting the words and deeds of Jesus Christ. The fact that Jesus is a real historical figure is verified even by non-Christian sources.

QUESTION 4: Isn't the Bible about the past? Why do people today think it applies to them?

Although the Bible does contain history, stories, and teachings about events in the past, its message is timeless and universal. The Bible includes accounts of regular people who struggle with things like greed, lust, jealousy, and other sinful behavior. They wonder why God allows bad things to happen to good people. We still struggle with many of the same questions and problems that faced human beings faced when the Bible was written thousands of years ago. God inspired the human authors of Scripture to write down the things God wanted us to know and understand, things that remain just as true for us today. Considering the literal and spiritual senses of Scripture (allegorical, moral, and anagogical) helps to provide us with direction and spiritual answers for these questions and problems. It helps us to see who God is, who we are in relation to God and creation, and how we can be part of God's grand saving plan. How could this not apply to us today?

Scripture is the living Word of God, with God as its author. It is not a dead word, frozen in history. Through the guidance of the Holy Spirit, God continues to speak to us through these writings. This is why the celebration of the Sacraments always includes readings from Scripture. This is also why reading the Bible should be a regular part of our prayer life.

QUESTION 5: Why do Catholics maintain beliefs and practices that are not in the Bible?

Anyone who asks this question is making a big assumption. They are assuming that God would choose only one way to reveal divine truth. This is simply not the case, testified to by the Bible itself. The Gospel of John says, "Now Jesus did many other signs in the presence of [his] disciples that are not written in this book" (20:30). The Bible is not the sole means that God chose to hand on the truths of Divine Revelation. Everything that Jesus taught to the Apostles and early disciples was passed down to us at first by word of mouth. These teachings, called the Apostolic Tradition (or Sacred Tradition), include some things that were not recorded in Scripture. This is why Catholic beliefs and practices are based on both Sacred Scripture and Sacred Tradition. Scripture and Tradition are the two complementary ways Divine Revelation is passed down.

Even though Sacred Tradition includes some things not found in the Bible, it is important to note that Sacred Tradition never contradicts the Bible, and the Bible never contradicts Sacred Tradition. They support and reinforce each other.

GLOSSARY

A

All Saints' Day ➤ A feast day commemorating all of the saints of the Church, both known and unknown, celebrated on November 1. Also known as the Feast of All Saints.

All Souls' Day ➤ A holy day in the Church set aside for honoring the faithful departed, celebrated on November 2.

analogy of faith ➤ The coherence of individual doctrines with the whole of Revelation. In other words, as each doctrine is connected with Revelation, each doctrine is also connected with all other doctrines.

anawim ➤ A Hebrew word for the poor and marginalized.

apocalyptic literature ➤ A literary form that uses highly dramatic and symbolic language to offer hope to a people in crisis.

apocrypha ➤ Writings about Jesus or the Christian message not accepted as part of the canon of Scripture.

apostasy ➤ The act of renouncing one's faith.

Apostolic Succession ➤ The uninterrupted passing on of apostolic preaching and authority from the Apostles directly to all bishops. It is accomplished through the laying on of hands when a bishop is ordained in the Sacrament of Holy Orders as instituted by Christ. The office of bishop is permanent, because at ordination a bishop is marked with an indelible, sacred character.

archaeology ➤ The study of human activity and history by means of excavating and analyzing the artifacts and other physical materials.

Ark of the Covenant ➤ A sacred chest that housed the tablets of the Ten Commandments, placed within the sanctuary where God would come and dwell.

Ascension ➤ The "going up" into Heaven of the Risen Christ forty days after his Resurrection.

B

Babylonian Exile ➤ The period in Israelite history during which the Israelites of the ancient kingdom of Judah were held in captivity in Babylon. The period began with the Babylonians' destruction of the Temple and the city of Jerusalem in 587 BC and lasted until 539 BC.

ban ➤ The practice of destroying everyone and everything in a defeated town and burning it as a sacrificial offering to God.

Beatitudes ➤ The teachings of Jesus that begin the Sermon on the Mount and that summarize the New Law of Christ. The Beatitudes describe the actions and attitudes by which one can discover genuine happiness, and they teach us the final end to which God calls us: full communion with him in the Kingdom of Heaven.

Beloved Disciple ➤ A faithful disciple in the Gospel of John who is present at critical times in Jesus' ministry. The Beloved Disciple may have been the founder of the Johannine community.

Bible ➤ The collection of Christian sacred writings, or Scripture, accepted by the Church as inspired by God and composed of the Old and New Testaments.

biblical exegesis ➤ The critical interpretation and explanation of Sacred Scripture.

biblical inerrancy ➤ The doctrine that the books of Sacred Scripture are free from error regarding the truth God wishes to reveal through Scripture for the sake of our salvation.

bishop ➤ One who has received the fullness of the Sacrament of Holy Orders and is a successor to the Apostles.

Body of Christ ➤ A term that when capitalized designates Jesus' Body in the Eucharist, or the entire Church, which is also referred to as the Mystical Body of Christ.

breviary ➤ A prayer book that contains the prayers for the Liturgy of the Hours.

C

canon (of Sacred Scripture) ➤ The books of the Bible officially recognized by the Church as the inspired Word of God.

canonize ➤ The act by which the Church officially recognizes a deceased Catholic as a saint.

Catholic letters ➤ The eight non-Pauline letters in the New Testament that were addressed to the universal Church.

charism ➤ A special grace of the Holy Spirit given to an individual Christian or community, for the benefit and building up of the entire Church.

Chosen People ➤ Also called the Israelites or the Jews, these are the descendants of Abraham, Isaac, and Jacob, whom God entered into a special covenant with at Mount Sinai. God chose them to prepare for the coming of his Son, Jesus Christ, the Messiah and Savior of the world.

Church ➤ The term *Church* has three inseparable meanings: (1) the entire People of God throughout the world; (2) the diocese, which is also known as the local Church; and (3) the assembly of believers gathered for the celebration of the liturgy, especially the Eucharist.

circumcision ➤ The act, required by Jewish Law, of removing the foreskin of the penis. Since the time of Abraham, it has been a sign of God's covenant relationship with the Jewish People.

concupiscence ➤ The tendency of all human beings toward sin, as a result of Original Sin.

conscience ➤ The "inner voice," guided by human reason and Divine Law, that enables us to judge the moral quality of a specific action that has been made, is being made, or will be made. This judgment enables us to distinguish good from evil, in order to accomplish good and avoid evil.

contextualist approach ➤ The interpretation of the Bible that takes into account the various contexts for understanding. These contexts include the senses of Scripture, literary forms, historical situations, cultural backgrounds, the unity of the whole of Sacred Scripture, Sacred Tradition, and the analogy of faith.

covenant ➤ A solemn agreement between human beings or between God and a human being in which mutual commitments are made.

creed ➤ A short summary statement or profession of faith. The Nicene and Apostles' Creeds are the Church's most familiar and important creeds.

D

Deposit of Faith ➤ The heritage of faith contained in Sacred Scripture and Sacred Tradition. It has been passed on from the time of the Apostles. The Magisterium takes from it all that it teaches as revealed truth.

deuterocanonical ➤ Books of the Old Testament that do not appear in the Hebrew Scripture but are accepted by the Church as part of the canon of Scripture.

deuteronomic cycle ➤ The pattern repeated by the Israelites found in the writings of the Deuteronomist. The pattern was: (1) the Israelites forget their covenant commitments and fall into sin; (2) God's punishes them, allowing them to be conquered by their enemies; (3) the people repent and cry for God's mercy; and (4) God hears their cry and sends a leader to deliver them.

devotional prayers ➤ Also known as devotions, these are personalized prayers that have developed outside of, but should lead to, the liturgy of the Church.

Diaspora ➤ In general, the movement, migration, or scattering of a people away from an established or ancestral homeland.

Divine Inspiration ➤ The divine assistance the Holy Spirit gave the authors of the books of the Bible so the authors could write in human words the message of salvation God wanted to communicate.

divine retributive justice ➤ The belief that God punishes people for their sins during this lifetime.

Divine Revelation ➤ God's self-communication through which he makes known the mystery of his divine plan. Divine Revelation is a gift accomplished by the Father, Son, and Holy Spirit through the words and deeds of salvation history. It is most fully realized in the Passion, death, Resurrection, and Ascension of Jesus Christ.

Doctor of the Church ➤ A title officially bestowed by the Church on saints who are highly esteemed for their theological writings as well as their personal holiness.

dogma ➤ Teachings recognized as central to Church teaching, defined by the Magisterium and considered definitive and authoritative.

dynasty ➤ Any sequence of powerful leaders of the same family.

E

Ecumenical Council ➤ A gathering of the Church's bishops from around the world to address pressing issues in the Church and society. Ecumenical Councils are usually convened by the Pope or are at least approved by him.

Emmanuel ➤ A Hebrew word meaning "God is with us."

encyclical ➤ A teaching letter from the Pope to the members of the Church on topics of social justice, human rights, and peace.

epistle ➤ Another name for a New Testament letter.

Essenes ➤ A group of pious, ultraconservative Jews who left the Temple of Jerusalem and began a community by the Dead Sea, known as Qumran.

Eucharist ➤ The celebration of the entire Mass. The term can also refer specifically to the consecrated bread and wine that have become the Body and Blood of Christ.

Eucharistic Prayer ➤ The part of the Mass that includes the Consecration, beginning with the Preface and concluding with the Great Amen.

Evangelists ➤ From a Greek word meaning "messenger of good news," the title given to the authors of the Gospels of Matthew, Mark, Luke, and John.

F

faith ➤ From the Latin *fides*, meaning "trust" or "belief," faith is the gift of God by which one freely accepts God's full Revelation in Jesus Christ. It is a matter of both the head (acceptance of God's revealed truth) and the heart (love of God and neighbor as a response to God's first loving us). Also, one of the three Theological Virtues.

Fall, the ➤ Also called the Fall from Grace, the biblical revelation about the origins of sin and evil in the world, expressed figuratively in the account of Adam and Eve in Genesis.

fundamentalist approach ➤ The interpretation of the Bible and Christian doctrine based on the literalist meaning of the Bible's words. The interpretation is made without regard to the historical setting in which the writings or teachings were first developed.

G

genealogy ➤ Known as family history, is the study of families and the tracing of their lineages.

genocide ➤ The systematic and planned extermination of a national, racial, ethnic, or cultural group.

Gentile ➤ A non-Jewish person. In Sacred Scripture, the Gentiles were the uncircumcised, those who did not honor the God of the Torah. Saint Paul and other evangelists reached out to the Gentiles, baptizing them into the family of God.

Gnostic ➤ Referring to the belief that salvation comes from secret knowledge available to only a select few.

Gospel ➤ Translated from a Greek word meaning "good news," referring to the four books attributed to Matthew, Mark, Luke, and John. The Gospels are the principal source for accounts of Jesus Christ's life and teaching and work of salvation.

H

Heaven ➤ A state of eternal life and union with God, in which one experiences full happiness and the satisfaction of the deepest human longings.

Holocaust ➤ In the Old Testament, this refers to a sacrifice consumed by fire. In the twentieth century, *Holocaust* is the widely used term to designate the attempted extermination of the Jews by the Nazis during the Second World War (1939–1945).

holy ➤ To be dedicated to God; to reflect some aspect of God's being.

Holy of Holies ➤ The most holy place in the Tabernacle and later the Temple in Jerusalem, where the Ark of the Covenant was kept. Only the High Priest could enter, and he only once a year. **homily** ➤ A brief liturgical sermon that explains the Scripture readings, helps the People of God accept Sacred Scripture as the Word of God, and encourages them to put the teachings of Scripture into practice in their daily lives.

hyperbole ➤ Exaggerated statements or claims not meant to be taken literally.

Incarnation ➤ From the Latin, meaning "to become flesh," referring to the mystery of Jesus Christ, the Divine Son of God, becoming man. In the Incarnation, Jesus Christ became truly man while remaining truly God.

infancy narratives ➤ The accounts of Jesus' birth and early childhood.

intercession ➤ A prayer on behalf of another person or group.

Israel ➤ This name comes from Jacob's experience of "wrestling with God" (see Genesis 32:28) and is used in different ways: (1) the Twelve Tribes of Israel as descendants of the twelve sons of Jacob, (2) the Chosen People or Jewish People as a whole, (3) the northern kingdom (Israel) in contrast to the southern kingdom (Judah), and (4) the modern nation of Israel.

Jerusalem ➤ From the Hebrew meaning "foundation of peace," the name of the city in Palestine that was Israel's capital where Solomon built the Temple and where Jesus was crucified.

Jews ➤ The term used to refer to all of the physical and spiritual descendants of Jacob (Israel) as well as to the patriarchs Abraham and Isaac and their wives. Originally referred specifically to the members of the tribe of Judah.

Judaism ➤ This word (which has been traced to Judah, the fourth son of Jacob and the tribe descended from him) refers to the monotheistic religion of the Jewish People who trace their origin to Abraham and whose religious observance is based on the Torah and Talmud.

judges ➤ The eleven men and one woman who served the Hebrew people as tribal leaders, military commanders, arbiters of disputes, and enliveners of faith.

kerygma ➤ A Greek word meaning "proclamation" or "preaching," referring to the announcement of the Gospel or the Good News of divine salvation offered to all through Jesus Christ. *Kerygma* has two senses. It is both an event of proclamation and a message proclaimed.

Kingdom of God ➤ The culmination or goal of God's plan of salvation, the Kingdom of God is announced by the Gospel and is present in Jesus Christ. The Kingdom is the reign or rule of God over the hearts of people and, as a consequence of that, the development of a new social order based on unconditional love. The fullness of God's Kingdom will not be realized until the end of time. Also called the Reign of God or the Kingdom of Heaven.

kosher laws ➤ A set of dietary and food preparation restrictions that govern the foods Jewish people can and cannot eat.

Latin Vulgate ➤ The Vulgate is a Latin version of the Holy Bible, and largely the result of the labors of Saint Jerome (c. 345–420), who was commissioned by Pope Damasus I in AD 382 to make a revision of the old Latin translations.

Law of Moses ➤ Also called the Mosaic Law, the first five books of the Old Testament, which are also called the books of the law or the Torah. God gave Moses the tablets summarizing the Law (see Exodus 31:18), which is why it is also called the Law of Moses, or the Mosaic Law.

lectio divina ➤ A Latin term meaning "divine reading." *Lectio divina* is a form of meditative prayer focused on a Scripture passage. It involves repetitive readings and periods of reflection and can serve as either private or communal prayer.

literal sense ➤ A form of biblical interpretation that considers the explicit meaning of the text. It lays the foundation for all other senses of Sacred Scripture.

literary forms (genres) ➤ Different kinds of writing determined by their literary technique, content, tone, and purpose.

liturgy ➤ The Church's official, public, communal prayer. It is God's work, in which the People of God participate. The Church's most important liturgy is the Eucharist, or the Mass.

Liturgy of the Eucharist ➤ This term refers to the second part of the Mass that includes the offertory, the prayers of consecration and invocation of the Holy Spirit, the reception of Communion, and the dismissal.

Liturgy of the Hours ➤ Also known as the Divine Office, the official public, daily prayer of the Catholic Church. The Divine Office provides standard prayers, Scripture readings, and reflections at regular hours throughout the day.

Liturgy of the Word ➤ This term refers to the first part of the Mass that includes the introductory rite, the readings from Scripture, the homily, and the prayers of the faithful.

M

Magisterium ➤ The Church's living teaching office, which consists of all bishops, in communion with the Pope, the bishop of Rome.

martyr ➤ A person who suffers death because of his or her beliefs. The Church has canonized many Christian martyrs as saints.

Messiah ➤ Hebrew word for "anointed one." The equivalent Greek term is *Christos*. We call Jesus the Christ and the Messiah because he is the Anointed One who brings salvation through his life, death, and Resurrection.

messianic prophecy ➤ A message, communicated on behalf of God by his messengers, that points toward the coming of the Savior, Jesus Christ. Messianic prophecies were often expressed as words of hope and comfort to those living in times of darkness and despair.

miracles ➤ Signs or wonders, such as healing or the control of nature, that can be attributed to divine power only.

monarchy ➤ A government or a state headed by a single person, such as a king or queen. As a biblical term, it refers to the period of time when the Israelites existed as an independent nation.

morality ➤ Refers to the goodness or evil of human acts. The morality of an act is determined by the nature of the action, the intention, and the circumstances.

mystery ➤ The very nature of God, who is beyond understanding; or a specific doctrine revealed by God that is beyond full human understanding.

N

Nag Hammadi manuscripts ➤ Fourth-century writings, discovered in 1945 near the village of Nag Hammadi in Upper Egypt, that are invaluable sources of information regarding Gnostic beliefs, practices, and lifestyle. Gnosticism was an early Church heresy claiming that Christ's humanity was an illusion and the human body is evil.

natural revelation ➤ The process by which God makes himself known to human reason through the created world.

nazirites ➤ People who were consecrated to God through a vow to remain in a holy state, which required that they refrain from drinking alcohol, stay away from dead bodies, and keep their hair uncut.

New Covenant ➤ The covenant or law established by God in Jesus Christ to fulfill and perfect the Old Covenant or Mosaic Law. It is a perfection here on Earth of the Divine Law. The law of the New Covenant is called a law of love, grace, and freedom. The New Covenant will never end or diminish, and nothing new will be revealed until Christ comes again in glory.

New Jerusalem ➤ In the Book of Revelation, a symbol of a renewed society in which God dwells; a symbol of the Church, the "holy city," the assembly of the People of God called together from "the ends of the earth"; also, in other settings, a symbol of Heaven.

New Law ➤ Divine Law revealed in the New Testament through the life and teaching of Jesus Christ and through the witness and teaching of the Apostles. The New Law perfects the Old Law and brings it to fulfillment. Also called the Law of Love.

New Testament ➤ The twenty-seven books of the Bible, which have the life, teachings, Passion, death, Resurrection, and Ascension of Jesus Christ and the beginnings of the Church as their central theme.

O

Old Covenant ➤ The original covenant God established with Abraham and renewed with the Chosen People at Mount Sinai, in which he promised to be their God and they promised to be his people, obeying his Law and worshipping him alone.

Old Law ➤ Divine Law revealed in the Old Testament, summarized in the Ten Commandments. Also call the Law of Moses.

Old Testament ➤ The Christian name for those biblical writings that record God's Revelation to the Chosen People. Christians believe the Old Testament anticipates and prepares for the New Testament.

oral tradition ➤ The handing on of the message of God's saving plan through words and deeds.

original holiness ➤ The original state of human beings in their relationship with God, sharing in the divine life in full communion with him.

original justice ➤ The original state of Adam and Eve before the Fall, a state of complete harmony with themselves, with each other, and with all of creation.

Original Sin ➤ From the Latin *origo*, meaning "beginning" or "birth." The term has two meanings: (1) the sin of the first human beings, who disobeyed God's command by choosing to follow their own will and thus lost their original holiness and became subject to death, and (2) the fallen state of human nature that affects every person born into the world, except Jesus and Mary.

P

parables ➤ Short stories that use everyday images to communicate religious messages. Jesus used parables frequently in his teaching as a way of presenting the Good News of salvation.

particular good ➤ Something that shares in the goodness of God but ultimately leaves you unsatisfied.

Paschal Lamb ➤ In the Old Testament, the sacrificial lamb shared at the Seder meal of the Passover on the night the Israelites escaped from Egypt; in the New Testament, the Paschal Lamb is Jesus, the Incarnate Son of God who dies on a cross to take away "the sin of the world" (John 1:29).

Paschal Mystery ➤ The work of salvation accomplished by Jesus Christ mainly through his Passion, death, Resurrection, and Ascension.

Passion ➤ The suffering of Jesus during the final days of his life: his agony in the garden at Gethsemane, his trial, and his Crucifixion.

Passover ➤ The night the Lord passed over the houses of the Israelites marked by the blood of the lamb, and spared the firstborn sons from death. It also is the feast that celebrates the deliverance of the Chosen People from bondage in Egypt and the Exodus from Egypt to the Promised Land.

pastoral ➤ From the Latin *pastor*, meaning "shepherd" or "herdsman"; refers to the spiritual care or guidance of others.

patriarch ➤ The father or leader of a tribe, clan, or tradition. Abraham, Isaac, and Jacob were the patriarchs of the Israelite people.

Pauline letters ➤ Thirteen New Testament letters attributed to Saint Paul or to disciples who wrote in his name. The letters offer advice, pastoral encouragement, teaching, and community news to early Christian communities.

Pentateuch ➤ A Greek word meaning "five books," referring to the first five books of the Old Testament.

pharaoh ➤ A ruler of ancient Egypt.

Pharisee ➤ A Jewish sect at the time of Jesus known for its strict adherence to the Law.

prayer ➤ Lifting up of one's mind and heart to God or the requesting of good things from him. The five basic forms of prayer are blessing, praise, petition, thanksgiving, and intercession. In prayer, we communicate with God in a relationship of love.

prefigure ➤ Similar to foreshadowing, it is an indication of a type of thing, person, or event that points to its future fulfillment. The meaning of what is contained in the Old Testament is unveiled in the New Testament.

prologue ➤ A separate introduction at the beginning of a play, story, or long poem.

prophet ➤ A person God chooses to speak his message of salvation. In the Bible, primarily a communicator of a divine message of repentance to the Chosen People, not necessarily a person who predicted the future.

proverb ➤ A short saying that is easy to recall and communicates an astute observation on human life or expresses a religious truth.

Psalter ➤ The Book of Psalms of the Old Testament, which contains 150 Psalms.

Purgatory ➤ A state of final purification or cleansing, which one may need to enter following death and before entering Heaven.

Q

Quelle ➤ Also called the Q Source, a theoretical collection of ancient documents of the teachings of Jesus shared among the early followers of Christianity; believed by Scripture scholars to be a source for the Gospels of Matthew and Luke.

R

redemption, redemptive ➤ From the Latin *redemptio*, meaning "a buying back," referring, in the Old Testament, to Yahweh's deliverance of Israel and, in the New Testament, to Christ's deliverance of all Christians from the forces of sin.

resurrection of the dead ➤ The raising of the righteous on the last day, to live forever with the Risen Christ. The resurrection of the dead means that not only will our immortal souls live on after death but also our transformed bodies.

Rosary ➤ A devotional prayer that honors the Virgin Mary and helps us meditate on Christ's life and mission. We pray the Rosary using rosary beads, which are grouped into "decades." Each decade consists of praying the Lord's Prayer followed by ten Hail Marys and the Glory Be while meditating on an event from Christ's life and mission.

ruminate ➤ To think deeply about something; to contemplate, meditate on, ponder over, chew on.

S

saint ➤ Someone who has been transformed by the grace of Christ and who resides in full union with God in Heaven.

salvation history ➤ The pattern of specific events in human history in which God clearly reveals his presence and saving actions. Salvation was accomplished once and for all through Jesus Christ, a truth foreshadowed and revealed throughout the Old Testament.

Samaritan ➤ An inhabitant of Samaria. The Samaritans rejected the Jerusalem Temple and worshipped instead at Mount Gerizim. The hostility between Jews and Samaritans is often recounted in the New Testament.

Sanhedrin ➤ An assembly of Jewish religious leaders—chief priests, scribes, and elders—who functioned as the supreme council and tribunal during the time of Jesus.

scholastic theology ➤ The use of philosophical methods to better understand revealed truth. The goal of scholastic theology is to present the understanding of revealed truth in a logical and systematic form.

Second Vatican Council ➤ The Ecumenical or general Council of the Roman Catholic Church that Pope Saint John XXIII convened as Pope in 1962 and that continued under Pope Saint Paul VI until 1965. Also called Vatican Council II.

Seder ➤ The Hebrew word meaning "order" or "procedure" that refers to a Jewish ceremonial meal, usually celebrated at home during Passover, in commemoration of the Exodus of the Chosen People from Egypt.

Septuagint ➤ A Greek translation of the Old Testament begun about 250 BC. The Septuagint included the forty-six books of the Old Testament. It is often referred to by the Roman number LXX, which means seventy, in honor of the legendary seventy rabbis who translated the Hebrew text into Greek in supposedly seventy days.

servant leadership ➤ A type of leadership based on humble service to all God's people.

sign ➤ An object, event, or action that conveys a meaning or represents something else.

sin ➤ Any deliberate offense, in thought, word, or deed, against the will of God. Sin wounds human nature and injures human solidarity.

Sinai Covenant

(also Mosaic Covenant) ➤ The covenant established with the Israelites at Mount Sinai that renewed God's covenant with Abraham's descendants. The Sinai Covenant establishes the Israelites as God's Chosen People.

Son of Man ➤ A messianic title from the Book of Daniel, used to describe a figure who receives authority over other nations from God; the only messianic title in the Gospels used by Jesus to describe himself.

soul ➤ Our spiritual principle, it is immortal, and it is what makes us most like God. Our soul is created by God at the moment of our conception. It is the seat of human consciousness and freedom.

spiritual sense ➤ A form of biblical interpretation that builds on the literal sense to consider what the realities and events of Sacred Scripture signify and mean for salvation.

Stations of the Cross ➤ A devotion for prayer and reflection, popular during Lent, that retraces the events of Jesus' Passion and death in fourteen "stations," represented by artistic depictions. Most Catholic churches have artistic representations of the fourteen Stations of the Cross. Also called the Way of the Cross.

synagogue ➤ This word (from the Greek *synagōgē*, meaning "meeting" or "assembly") refers to the worship assemblies of Jews to celebrate the Sabbath; Jesus is depicted in the Gospel of Luke (see 4:14–30) as beginning his Galilean ministry in the synagogue at Nazareth.

synoptic Gospels ➤ The name given to the Gospels of Matthew, Mark, and Luke, because they are similar in style and content.

T

Tabernacle ➤ In the Old Testament, the portable tent that was used as a sanctuary for the Ark of the Covenant during the Israelite's migration in the desert.

Ten Commandments ➤ Sometimes called the Decalogue, the list of ten norms, or rules of moral behavior, that God gave Moses and that are the basis of ethical conduct.

theophany ➤ God's manifestation of himself in a visible form to enrich human understanding of him. An example is God's appearance to Moses in the form of a burning bush.

Torah ➤ A Hebrew word meaning "law," referring to the first five books of the Old Testament.

Tradition or Sacred Tradition ➤ The process of passing on the Gospel message. Sacred Tradition, which began with the oral communication of the Gospel by the Apostles, was written down in Sacred Scripture, is handed down and lived out in the life of the Church, and is interpreted by the Magisterium under the guidance of the Holy Spirit. Both Sacred Tradition and Sacred Scripture have their common source in the Revelation of Jesus Christ and must be equally honored.

tribute ➤ A payment by one ruler or state to another, usually as an acknowledgment of submission.

typology ➤ The discernment of God's work in the Old Testament as a prefiguration of what he accomplished through Jesus Christ in the fullness of time. Typology illuminates the unity of God's plan in the two Testaments but does not devalue the Old Covenant or its ongoing relevance and value for the Jewish people.

U

ultimate good ➤ The source of our complete fulfillment, which can be found only in our union with God.

V

vanity ➤ Something worthless, trivial, or pointless.

Via Dolorosa ➤ Latin for "way of sorrow," referring to the path Jesus journeyed in the last hours of his life, which is commemorated in the devotion of the Stations of the Cross.

W

written tradition ➤ Under the inspiration of the Holy Spirit, the synthesis in written form of the message of salvation that has been passed down in the oral tradition.

Y

Yahweh ➤ The most sacred of the Old Testament names for God, which he revealed to Moses. It is frequently translated as "I AM" or "I am who am."

Z

Zion (also Sion) ➤ This word originally referred to the mountain on which stood the Canaanite fortress that was captured by David. Later it was used to designate the Temple built on that location, and then eventually it referred to the whole city of Jerusalem, Israel's capital; the term is also used to refer to the New Jerusalem, the heavenly city of the future.

INDEX

Note: Charts and maps are indicated with "C" and "M," respectively.

A

Aaron, 136, 153

Abraham, 47, 59, 78, 113–118, 120–121, 299

Acts of the Apostles, 431–436

Adam, 12, 15–16, 23–25, 276, 375

Adonai, 135

adultery, 245–246, 380

afterlife, 356–359

Ahab, 238

Ahasuerus, 345–346, 347

All Saint's Day, 361

All Soul's Day, 360

Amos, 248–250

analogy of faith, 90

anawim, 151, 248, 307

ancestry, 186, 289–290, 397, 406

Antiochus IV, 350–352

apocalyptic literature, 95C, 446

apostasy, 354

Apostles, 50, 60, 399, 411, 431, 432–433, 450. See also specific names of Apostles

Apostolic Succession, 451

Apostolic (Sacred) Tradition, 70, 71, 87, 90, 101, 450–452

Aquinas, Thomas, 17, 41–43, 44

archaeology, 98–100, 101

Ark of the Covenant, 142–144, 169, 182, 198–199, 209, 324

Ascension, 50, 411, 431, 480

Assyria, 229, 259, 260–261, 321, 328, 341–344

Augustine of Hippo, 17, 39, 462

B

Babylon, 29, 261–263, 265–266, 269–270, 273, 275–276, 313

Babylonian Exile, 62–63, 269–270, 276–285, 319, 321

bans, 164–165

Baptism, 237, 407, 423, 464

Bathsheba, 201, 202, 206

Beatitudes, 408, 469

Beloved Disciple, 418, 424

Bible (Sacred Scripture), overview. See also New Testament; Old Testament; specific books

archaeological artifacts, 99–100

authorship of, 20, 51–53

canons of, 68–71

climax of, 398

composition of, 59–66, 66C

defined, 47

Divine Revelation in, 11, 20, 31–32, 47–50

as faith transmission method, 451, 452

interpretation of, 21–22, 54–55, 85–101, 95C, 96C

morality in, 468–470

organization of, 67–68

prayer traditions from, 460–467, 462C, 472–475

reading and studying purpose, 457–459

Sacraments based on, 463–464

science and understanding, 20–21

translations of, 69, 72–74, 86, 462

truth of, 22, 53

word origins and meaning, 67

Blood of Christ, 421, 423, 463

Body of Christ, 16, 143, 421, 461, 463

Booths, Feast of, 150C

C

Cain and Abel, 26–27

Canaan (Promised Land), 47–48, 152–153, 169–172

canonize, 33

Canticle of Mary, 179, 179C

Catholic Bibles, 69

Catholic letters, 442–444, 443C

Catholic Worker Movement, 235, 266

Christ (Messiah), 48, 77, 78, 293, 307, 399

Chronicles, 323, 325

Church

as Body of Christ, 16, 461, 463

defined, 15

early history of, 50, 60, 399, 402–403, 411, 431–435, 439–444

Jesus' presence in, 411
Old Testament prefiguration of, 15
prayer traditions of, 460–467, 462C
teaching office of, 85–86, 101, 453
circumcisions, 116, 118, 170, 350, 435
cleanliness, 148, 149–150
Colossians, 426, 440C
compassion, 16, 151, 406, 409
complaints, 64, 136, 139, 152–153, 172
concupiscence, 31
conscience, 45
Corinthians, 411, 440C
covenants. See also Old Covenant
  contracts compared to, 117C
  definition, 28, 116
  and deuteronomic cycle, 173, 177, 280–281
  as eternal, 144
  marriage metaphors, 117, 118–119, 140, 144, 245–246, 380
  New, 77–78, 186, 291, 409
  renewals of, 140
  signs for, 28, 118
Creation, 12–14, 18, 38–40, 419, 420
Crucifixion, 80C, 99, 301, 409, 423, 480
Cyrus, 284–285, 320

D

Daniel, 276
David, 186, 193–206, 202C, 325
Day of Atonement, 150C, 324
dead, 149, 176, 357–360, 359–360, 417C
Dead Sea Scrolls, 99–100
death, 195, 342, 356–359, 417C, 418. See also Crucifixion; martyrs
Deborah, 175
Deposit of Faith, 452–453
deuterocanonical writings, 69
deuteronomic cycle, 173, 177, 280–281
Deuteronomy, 141, 154, 157, 217C
Diaspora, 321–322
Divine Inspiration, 20, 51–55
Divine Office, 335, 461
divine retributive justice, 162–167, 209, 280–281, 299, 346, 369–375
Divine Revelation, 11, 20, 31–32, 38–50, 51–55, 234, 358, 427
divorce, 76, 191, 252

dogma, 453
Domitian, 446

E

Ecclesiastes, 366C, 376–378
Ecumenical Councils, 70, 70M, 87, 89, 435
Eleazar, 355
Elijah, 238–242, 242C, 243
Elisha, 241–242, 242C, 243, 243C
Emmanuel, 267, 294
Ephesians, Letter to the, 380, 440C
epistles (letters), 95C, 437, 439, 440–441C, 442–444, 443C
Esau, 123–125
Essenes, 100
Esther, 345–348
Eucharist, 143, 409, 411, 421, 423, 460, 463, 467
Evangelists, 402. See also specific Gospels of Matthew, Mark, Luke, and John
Eve, 12, 15–16, 23–25
evil, 23, 27, 29, 357, 447, 466
Exodus, 66C, 133–144, 148, 163, 217C, 304–305, 304C
exorcisms, 417C
experience, 227, 227C, 374, 425
Ezekiel, 274–278
Ezra, 325, 329–330, 331

F

faith
  defined, 116
  effects of, 16–17, 23, 186, 285
  hypocrisy and, 249, 250
  judgment based on, 245–246, 281
  martyrdom and, 350, 353, 354, 355–358, 435, 447, 448
  mentors for, 181
  persecution and, 444, 445, 446
  as relationship with God, 16–17, 23, 119, 181
  renewal of, 171
  renouncing, 353, 354
  as salvation requirement, 427
  suffering and, 129, 341–342
  tests of, 121, 371–374
  as trust in God, 136–137, 153–154, 157, 193–194, 260–261, 301, 341–342, 424
Fall, the, 23

fear of the Lord, 367–368
Flood, the, 27–28
foreigners, 151, 184–187, 211, 226, 248, 252, 329–220
forgiveness, 124, 127–129, 144, 359–360, 409
free will, 24, 29, 162, 468

G

Galatians, 438, 440C
Genesis, 11–18, 23–29, 66C, 276
Gentiles
    as agents of God, 184–187, 285
    as Christians, 402, 403, 406, 435
    defined, 403
    intermarriage with, 211, 226, 238, 252, 329–330
Gideon, 176
Gnosticism, 71, 100
God
    call of, 114–115, 135–137, 231, 252, 258, 268
    as Creator, 12–13
    existence of, 41–45, 43C
    fear of, 367–368
    goodness of, 20, 39, 378
    grace of, 129
    guidance of, 433
    image of, 14, 32, 39
    justice of, 162–167, 209, 280–281, 299, 346, 369–375
    knowing, 20, 38–55, 234, 358, 375, 426–427
    manifestations of, 134, 143, 433
    names and titles of, 135
    nature of, 14–15, 38–39
    presence of, 143–144, 169, 182, 240–241, 447
    voice of, 239–241
Goliath, 193, 307
Gomer, 245–246, 380
goodness, 13–14, 17, 20, 39, 208, 378
Gospels, See also specific Gospels of Matthew, Mark, Luke, and John
    authorship and sources for, 403
    characteristics and comparisons, 404–405C
    composition stages, 399–400
    content overview, 68, 81, 398–399, 401–402
    defined, 398
    events in, 406–411, 422–424

    infancy narrative comparisons, 304–305, 304C
    laws in, 408, 422, 470
    literary form of, 402
    messianic prophecies of, 294–295, 295C
    parables in, 412–413, 414–415C
    portrayals of Jesus, 144, 418–421
    synoptic, 403
    word meaning, 398
    writing dates vs. historical period, 66C
Great Commandment, 76, 156, 469, 470
Greece, 341, 349–352, 354
Greek (language), 69, 72, 345, 350

H

Hagar, 120, 121
Haman, 346
Hannah, 178–179, 179C
Hanukkah, 351
happiness, 16–17, 19, 23, 141, 162, 378, 408
Heaven, 50, 278, 411, 431
Hebrew (language), 72, 345
Hebrews, Letter to the, 299, 407, 443C
Hezekiah, 260–261
High Priest, 299, 463
holiness, 23, 24, 145–151, 183, 299
Holocaust, 346–347
Holofernes, 343—344
holy days, 150, 150C
Holy of Holies, 143, 324
Holy Orders, 451
Holy Spirit, 51–55, 90, 399, 400, 407, 432–433, 450
Hosea, 245–247, 250, 380
Hoshea, 229
hypocrisy, 249–250, 266

I

"I Am" statements, 421, 423
idolatry
    as infidelity to God, 144, 176, 212, 246, 259
    intermarriage and risk of, 211, 226, 238, 252, 329–330
    warnings on, 48, 182, 211, 266
Incarnation, 49–50, 399, 426
infancy narratives, 304–305, 304C, 406, 480
intercessions, 361

intermarriage, 211, 226, 238, 252, 329–330

Isaac, 121–123

Isaiah (book)

composition dating, 284

First, 264–265, 264C, 266–267, 284

Second, 264, 264C, 266, 283, 284–285, 294, 296–297, 320

Third, 264, 264C, 266, 294

Isaiah (prophet), 48, 260, 261

Ishmael, 120, 121

Israel

defined, 125

northern kingdom, 125, 212, 213M, 228, 245–250, 259, 311C, 341–344

Twelve Tribes of, 125, 147, 170 , 172, 305, 324

united kingdom, 212, 213M, 226, 228

Israel (Jacob), 114, 123–126

J

Jacob (Israel), 114, 123–126

James, Letter of, 443C, 444

Jehoiachin, 279

Jephthah, 176

Jeremiah, 268–273, 272C, 361

Jeroboam, 212, 227, 228

Jerome, 72, 458, 462

Jerusalem (Zion/Sion), 197. *See also* Temple of Jerusalem

Assyrian attack, 260

early Christian Church in, 434

early history and significance, 197–198

fall of, 263, 275–276, 279

messianic prophecies on, 79C, 295C

pilgrimages to, 477

post-exile reconstruction of, 320, 322, 327, 330

post-exile return to, 284–285, 319, 321, 328

Jesus. See also messianic prophecy

Ascension of, 50, 411, 431, 480

Baptism of, 407

biblical sections about, 68, 81, 398–399, 401–402

birth and childhood, 304–305, 304C, 406, 480

compassion of, 406, 409

death of, 80C, 99, 301, 409, 423, 480

on divine retributive justice, 166, 167, 299

as Divine Revelation, 49–50, 234, 427

genealogy of, 186, 199

as guide for life, 425

Hebrew name of, 305

humanity of, 144, 276, 407

humor of, 251

Incarnation, 49–50, 399, 426–427

knowing, 457–459

as Messiah, 77, 78, 299, 307, 399

miracles of, 243C, 295C, 416, 417C, 420, 421

mission to Apostles, 50, 60, 411, 431, 450

natures of, 426

New Covenant of, 77–78, 186, 291, 409

New Law (Law of Love), 78, 156, 330, 408, 422, 470

Old Testament quoting of, 76

parables as teaching tools, 412–413, 414–415C

Passion of, 297, 300, 302, 408–409

prayer advice of, 466

prefiguration of, 243, 243C, 303–307, 304C

presence of, 411, 421

on religious hypocrisy, 250

Resurrection of, 173, 253, 358–359, 410–411, 480

sacrifice of, 122, 138, 447

self-descriptions, 276, 295C, 421, 423

Sermon on the Mount and Beatitudes, 305, 408, 469

on service, 422

as Son of God, 80C, 144, 418, 419, 426

as Son of Man, 244, 253, 276, 295C

temptation of, 407

as Word of God, 419, 425

Jewish Christians, 402–403, 435

Jewish Scripture, 69. *See also* Old Testament

Jews (Judeans)

as Christians, 402–403, 435

defined, 319, 321

of the Dispersion, 321–322

early Christian persecution by, 434–435

genocides of, 346–347

as Gospel audience, 406

Greek persecution of, 350, 353–354

religion and worship assemblies, 321–322

Jezebel, 238, 240

Job, 239, 366C, 369–375

John (letters), 443C, 444

John (prophet), 446. *See also* Revelation, Book of

John, Gospel of
Beloved Disciple in, 418
characteristics and comparisons, 404–405C
content and themes, 420, 422
Jesus portrayals in, 144, 418–421, 423, 424
miracles in, 420, 421
overview, 424
prologue of, 419
Resurrection, 410, 424
on writings about Jesus, 401
writing style of, 418

John the Baptist, 48, 234, 241, 243, 244, 285

Jonah, 251–255

Jonathan, 194, 196

Jonathan Maccabee, 351–352

Joseph (foster father of Jesus), 99, 199, 406

Joseph (son of Jacob), 126–129

Joshua, 153, 156, 168–171, 241–242, 242C, 305–306

Josiah, 261–262, 268, 279

Judah
Assyrian threats to, 260–261
behavior in, 263, 268
fall of, 212, 262–263, 266, 279
kingdom of, 213M, 228
leadership descriptions, 212, 259–262, 279
prophets of, 265, 268–271, 274–278, 312C

Judaism, 155–156, 321–322, 355, 402–403

Judas Maccabee, 351, 359, 361

Jude, 443C, 444

Judges, 172–183

judgment, 25, 26–27, 45, 208

Judith, 343–344, 348

justice
of God, 154, 162–167, 209, 280–281, 299, 346, 369–375
lack of, as sinful behavior, 211, 212, 226
loss of, as consequence of sin, 30
original, 23, 30

K

kerygma, 399

Kingdom of God [Heaven], 75, 307, 408, 412–417, 414–415C, 417C, 420

Kings, First, 183, 205–212, 226, 238–240, 324

Kings, Second, 183, 212, 238, 241–244, 259–261, 265, 279

knowledge
with experience, 227, 227C, 374, 425
of God, 20, 38–55, 234, 358, 375, 426–427
of Jesus, 457–459
as relationships, 247
through reason, 20, 40, 44–45

kosher laws, 148, 354

L

Lamb of God, 122, 138, 447

Lamentations, 281

lamentations, 333, 335

Leah, 126

lectio divina, 473–475

Leviticus, 141, 145–151, 162, 217C

literal sense, 91

literary forms (genres), 89, 94–95, 95C, 101, 366C, 373, 402

liturgy, 333, 335, 461

Liturgy of the Eucharist, 463

Liturgy of the Hours, 335, 461

Liturgy of the Word, 335, 355, 463

Lord's Prayer, 465–467, 479

love
biblical stories of, 124
Catholic letters on, 444
and dating, 379
forgiveness as, 128
God and, 14, 116, 165, 438, 470
Jesus' Law of, 78, 156, 330, 408, 422, 470

Luke, Gospel of
audience of, 406
authorship and sources for, 403
bibical books as second part of, 431
characteristics and comparisons, 404–405C
content and themes, 406–408, 410
Lord's Prayer in, 466
messianic prophecies in, 294–295
parables in, 412–413, 414–415C

M

Maccabees, 349–361

Magisterium, 85–86, 101, 453

Malachi, 294

Mark, Gospel of, 403, 404–405C, 407, 410

marriage
  as covenant metaphor, 117, 118–119, 140, 144, 245–246, 380
  crisis strengthening, 320
  and divorce, 76, 191, 252
  mixed, 211, 226, 238, 252, 329–330
  polygamy, 116, 126, 201, 211, 226

martyrs
  afterlife beliefs and, 357–358
  defined, 353
  early Christian, 434–435
  as faithfulness examples, 350, 353, 354, 355–358, 446
  modern, 236, 292, 353, 449
  Revelation to John symbolism of, 447

Mary, Mother of God, 199, 406, 469

Mary Magdalene, 410, 424

Mass, 335, 458, 463

Matthew, Gospel of
  audience of, 406
  authorship and sources for, 403
  characteristics and comparisons, 404–405C
  content and themes, 186, 304–305, 304C, 406–408, 410
  Lord's Prayer in, 466
  messianic prophecies in, 294–295
  parables in, 412–413, 414–415C

Messiah (Christ), 48, 77, 78, 293, 299, 307, 399

messianic prophecy
  definition and descriptions, 292–293
  New Testament fulfillment of, 77–81, 79–80C, 294–295, 295C
  Old vs. New Testament, 294–295, 295C
  in Prophetic Books, 242, 267, 272–273, 272C, 285, 294, 296–297
  in Wisdom Books, 298, 299–302

Micah, 237, 294

miracles, 243C, 295C, 416, 417C, 420, 421

Miriam, 153

Moabites, 184–187

monarchies, 182–183, 191–192, 204

morality, 468–470

Mordecai, 345–346

Mosaic Law (Old Law), 48, 141–142, 144–151, 155, 432, 469

Moses
  biblical story of, 133–144, 152–155
  Jesus' narrative comparisons, 304–305, 304C, 421
  Jesus' Transfiguration appearance of, 244
  literary parallels, 241–242, 242C
  number symbolism, 28
  as prophet, 233, 233C

Mount Sinai (Mount Horeb), 28, 140, 155, 240

N

Nag Hammadi manuscripts, 100

Naomi, 184, 185

Nathan, 199, 202, 233

natural revelation, 38–40

nazirites, 176

Nebuchadnezzar, 263, 279, 343

Nehemiah, 325, 330, 331

Nero, 446

New Covenant, 77–78, 186, 291, 409

New Jerusalem, 198, 278

New Law (Law of Love), 78, 156, 330, 408, 422, 470

New Testament, See also Gospels
  afterlife beliefs in, 356, 358–359
  composition process of, 60–63
  content descriptions, overview, 53, 68
  defined, 60
  as God's Revelation, 48–50
  Old Testament relationship to, 75–81, 79–80C, 290–291
  original language of, 72
  prophets of, 234

New Year's Day, 150C

Ninevites, 253–255, 341

Noah, 27–28, 47

Numbers, 141, 152–154, 157, 217C

number symbolism, 28, 154, 447

O

Old Covenant
  Abrahamic, 78, 116–118, 168
  Mosaic, 141, 144, 171, 173
  New Covenant relationship with, 77–78, 291
  Noahic, 28, 47
Old Law (Mosaic Law), 48, 141–142, 144–151, 155, 432, 469
Old Testament (Jewish Scripture)
  archaeological artifacts of, 100
  composition process of, 60–63
  content descriptions, overview, 53
  dreams in, 126
  historical context and dating, 62–63
  humor in, 251
  as Jewish Scripture, 69
  laws in, 145–151, 150C
  messianic prophesies in, 77–78, 79–80C, 292–297, 295C
  New Testament relationship to, 75–81, 79–80C, 290–291
  organization of, 67
  original language of, 72
  prophets of, 78, 79–80C, 233, 311C, 312C
  reward and punishment themes, 162
oral traditions, 60–61, 280, 397
Original Sin, 23, 30–31
Our Father, 465–467, 479

P

parables, 95C, 124, 251, 412–413, 414–415C
Paschal Lamb, 138
Paschal Mystery, 408–409
Passion, 297, 300, 302, 408–409, 423, 480
Passover, 138, 150C, 170, 262
patriarchs, 113–129
Paul (Saul)
  background, 434, 435, 437–438
  conversion of, 435
  death of, 438
  as Jewish Christian, 403
  letters of, 66C, 437, 439, 440–441C
  missionary travels of, 436, 438, 438M
  teachings of, 16, 38, 115, 285, 359, 380, 411, 426, 457
Pauline letters, 66C, 437, 439, 440–441C
Pentateuch (Torah), 67, 141, 145–151, 150C

Pentecost, 150C, 399, 432–433
People of God, 15, 198, 461, 463
persecution, 350, 353–354, 434–435, 444, 445, 446, 448. *See also* martyrs
Persia, 284–285, 320, 321M, 345–347, 349
Peter (apostle), 422, 424, 433
Peter (letters), 443C, 444
petitions, 359, 466
pharaoh, 116, 126, 133, 136
Pharisees, 434, 438
Philemon, 441C
Philippians, 440C
Philistines, 182, 193, 195, 196, 200
Pilate, Pontius, 409, 423
plagues, 137–138
poor people, 151, 211, 236, 248, 249, 266, 368, 408
prayer(s)
  benefits of, 465
  Church traditions, 335, 460–464, 462C
  for dead, 359–361
  defined, 465
  devotional, 476–481
  intercessions, 361
  Jesus' teachings on, 466–467
  listening and meditative, 472–475
  as literary form, 95C
  petition, 359, 466
  psalms for, 336
Promised Land, 47–48, 152–153, 169–172
Prophetic Books, 66C, 238–255, 274–278, 294
prophets, 48, 230–237, 311C, 312C. *See also* messianic prophecy; specific names of prophets
Protestant Reformation, 69
Proverbs, 95C, 366–368, 366C
Psalms (Psalter), 298, 299–301, 302, 332–336, 366C, 461
purgatory, 359
purification, 28, 147, 359
Purim, 347

Q

Qoheleth, 376–378
Quelle (Q Source), 403
Qumran, 100

R

Rachel, 126
reason, 20, 40, 44–45
Rebekah, 123
rebellions, 349–352
reconciliation, 129, 144
Red Sea, 139, 433
Rehoboam, 227, 228
repentance, 144, 173, 177, 253–254
Resurrection, 253, 278, 358–359, 410–411, 424, 480
resurrection of the dead, 357–360
retribution, 162. See also divine retributive justice
Revelation. See Divine Revelation
Revelation, Book of (Revelation to John), 68, 198, 380, 445–449, 446M
Roman Empire, 399, 409, 423, 433, 445, 446, 447
Romans, Letter to the, 359, 440C
Rosary, 479–481
Ruth, 184–187

S

Sacred Scripture. See Bible
Sacred (Apostolic) Tradition, 70, 71, 87, 90, 101, 450–452
sacrifices, 116, 121–122, 138, 147–148, 270, 324, 334
saints, 44, 361. See also specific names of saints
salvation, 412, 413, 424, 427
salvation history, 31–32, 47–50, 67, 140, 246, 290, 303–307
Samaritans, 329, 413
Samson, 176–177
Samuel (books), 178–183, 191–200
Samuel (prophet), 164, 178–183, 191–193, 233
Sarah (Book of Tobit), 342
Sarah (Sarai), 113–118, 120–121
Satan, 370, 371, 407, 466
Saul, King, 164, 183, 191–192, 194–195
scholastic theology, 41–43
science, 18–22
Second Vatican Council, 87, 89
Seder, 138
Septuagint, 69
Sermon on the Mount, 305, 408, 469

Servant Songs, The, 284, 296–297
service, 422
sexuality, 245–247, 379–381
Shamgar, 174–175
Shema, 155–156
sin
  as biblical theme, 11
  consequences of, 23–27, 30–31, 202–204
  cycle of repentance and, 173
  forgiveness of, 124, 127–129, 144, 359–360, 409
  human tendency toward, 31
  nature of, 24, 225
  origins of, 23
  prophets' roles on, 235
  temptation of, 23, 204, 407, 466
slavery, 126, 129, 133, 156, 211, 212, 226, 349
Solomon, 206–211, 226–227, 309, 324, 325, 368, 378
Song of Songs, 366C, 379–381
Son of God, 80C, 144, 418, 419, 426
Son of Man, 244, 253, 276, 295C
spiritual sense, 92–93, 101
Stations of the Cross, 477–479
Stephen, 434–435
suffering
  benefits of, 125, 299, 375
  of Christ, 297, 302, 408–409
  compassion and unity in, 16, 372
  as consequence of sin, 24, 30
  faithfulness during, 341–342, 444, 445, 448
  God as source of, 154, 161, 162–166
  injustice of, 369–378
  of Messiah, 284, 296–297, 300
  of religious persecution, 350, 353–354, 434–435, 444, 445, 446, 448
Suffering Servant, 284, 296–297
synagogues, 322
synoptic Gospels, 403, 404–405C, 406–413, 414–415C, 416, 417C

T

Tabernacle, 142, 143, 324
Temple of Jerusalem
  accessibility issues, 228, 322
  construction of, 209, 324
  descriptions, 324
  desecration of, 259, 350

destruction of, 268–269, 273, 279

Jesus at, 234, 307

purpose of, 198–199, 209, 324

reconstruction of, 277–278, 322, 327–328

rededication of, 351

renovations and law discoveries, 262

worship in, 323–326, 332–334

Ten Commandments, 48, 78, 141, 142, 469

theophany, 134, 143, 433

Thessalonians, 440C

Timothy, 439, 441C, 457

Titus, 438, 439, 441C

Tobit, 341–342, 348

Torah (Pentateuch), 67, 141, 145–151, 150C

Tower of Babel, 29, 433

Transfiguration, 244

truth, 19–20, 22, 52, 91, 181

Twelve Apostles, 305

Twelve Tribes of Israel, 125, 147, 170, 172, 305, 324

typologies, 290–291

U

Uriah, 201–202, 202C

W

wisdom, 207–208, 333, 336, 365, 366, 366C

Wisdom, Book of, 302, 366C, 383

Wisdom of Ben Sira, 366C, 384–385

Word of God, 68, 76, 419, 425

written tradition, 62

Y

Yahweh, 135. *See also* God

Z

Zedekiah, 270, 279

Zion/Sion, *See also* Jerusalem

ACKNOWLEDGMENTS

The scriptural quotations in this publication marked *NRSV* are from the *New Revised Standard Version of the Bible*, Catholic Edition. Copyright © 1989, 1993 by National Council of the Churches of Christ in the United States of America. All rights reserved worldwide.

The scriptural quotations in this publication marked *GNT* are from the *Good News Translation®* (Today's English Version, Second Edition). Copyright © 1992 by the American Bible Society. All rights reserved. Bible text from the *Good News Translation (GNT)* is not to be reproduced in copies or otherwise by any means except as permitted in writing by the American Bible Society, 1865 Broadway, New York, NY 10023 (*www.americanbible.org*).

The scriptural quotations in this publication marked *NJB* are from the *New Jerusalem Bible (NJB)*. Copyright © 1985 by Darton, Longman and Todd, London; and Doubleday, a division of Bantam Doubleday Dell Publishing Group, New York. All rights reserved.

All other scriptural quotations are taken from the *New American Bible, revised edition* © 2010, 1991, 1986, 1970 Confraternity of Christian Doctrine, Inc., Washington, D.C. All Rights Reserved. No part of this work may be reproduced or transmitted in any form or by any means, electronic or mechanical, including photocopying, recording, or by any information storage and retrieval system, without permission in writing from the copyright owner.

The quotations throughout this publication marked *CCC* are from the English translation of the *Catechism of the Catholic Church* for use in the United States of America, second edition. Copyright © 1994 by the United States Catholic Conference, Inc.—Libreria Editrice Vaticana (LEV). English translation of the *Catechism of the Catholic Church: Modifications from the Editio Typica* copyright © 1997 by the United States Catholic Conference, Inc.—LEV.

The quotations by Pope Leo XIII on pages 18 and 20 are from "Encyclical on the Study of Holy Scripture" *["Providentissimus Deus"]*, number 23, at *http://w2.vatican.va/content/leo-xiii/en/encyclicals/documents/hf_l-xiii_enc_18111893_providentissimus-deus.html* Copyright © Libreria Editrice Vaticana (LEV.)

The excerpt on page 21 is from "Greeting of His Holiness Pope Francis to Participants at the Conference Organized by the Vatican Observatory," May 12, 2017, at *https://w2.vatican.va/content/francesco/en/speeches/2017/may/documents/papa-francesco_20170512_specola-vaticana.html*. Copyright © LEV.

The excerpt by Pope Francis on page 38 is from his "General Audience," Saint Peter's Square, May 21, 2014 at *http://w2.vatican.va/content/francesco/en/audiences/2014/documents/papa-francesco_20140521_udienza-generale.html*. Copyright © LEV.

The quotation on page 38 is from the transcript of an oral history interview with Edward Hopper, June 17, 1959, in the Smithsonian Archives of American Art. For more of the interview, go to *www.aaa.si.edu/collections/interviews/oral-history-interview-edward-hopper-11844*. Copyright © 2017 Archives of American art, Smithsonian Institution.

The quotations on pages 51, 87, 89, and 488 are from *Dogmatic Constitution on Divine Revelation [Dei Verbum, 1965]*, numbers 11, 12, 12, and 25, at *www.vatican.va/archive/hist_councils/ii_vatican_council/documents/vat-ii_const_19651118_dei-verbum_en.html*. Copyright © LEV.

The quotation by Saint Teresa of Calcutta on page 54 is from *Mother Teresa: Her Essential Wisdom*, edited by Carol Kelly-Gangi, page 54. Copyright © 2006 by Barnes & Noble Publishing, Inc.

The quotations on pages 68 and 97 are from "Address of Pope Francis to the Members of the Pontifical Biblical Commission," April 12, 2013, at *https://w2.vatican.va/content/francesco/en/speeches/2013/april/documents/papa-francesco_20130412_commissione-biblica.html*. Copyright © LEV.

The excerpt on page 122 is from "Message of His Holiness Pope Francis for the 49th World Communications Day," 2015, at *https://w2.vatican.va/content/francesco/en/messages/communications/documents/papa-francesco_20150123_messaggio-comunicazioni-sociali.html*. Copyright © LEV.

The excerpt on page 146 is from Pope Francis's *Angelus*, Saint Peter's Square, October 26, 2014, at *https://w2.vatican.va/content/francesco/en/angelus/2014/documents/papa-francesco_angelus_20141026.html*. Copyright © LEV.

The "Twelve Leadership Lessons from Pope Francis" on page 174 are from his homily at Casa Santa Marta, January 19, 2016. Copyright © LEV.

The excerpt on page 206 is from Pope Francis's radio address, Vatican City, Mass at the chapel of Casa Santa Marta, January 19, 2016.

The excerpt on page 235 is from "Apostolic Journey of His Holiness Pope Francis to Sarajevo (Bosnia and Herzegovina)," June 6, 2015, at *https://m.vatican.va/content/francesco/en/speeches/2015/june/documents/papa-francesco_20150606_sarajevo-giovani.html*. Copyright © LEV.

The quotation on page 246 is from "Apostolic Journey of His Holiness Pope Francis to Cuba, to the United States of America, and Visit to the United Nations Headquarters: Visit to the Joint Session of the Unites States Congress," September 24, 2015, at *https://w2.vatican.va/content/francesco/en/speeches/2015/september/documents/papa-francesco_20150924_usa-us-congress.html*. Copyright © LEV.

The quotation on page 266 is from "The Zwicks: Faith People," by Michael Serazio, quoted in the HoustonPress, May 5, 2005, at *www.houstonpress.com/news/the-zwicks-faith-people-6549513*.

The excerpt on page 271 is from Pope Francis's "Letter to Young People on the Occasion of the Presentation of the 15th Ordinary General Assembly of the Synod of Bishops," January 13, 2017, at *https://*

Acknowledgments

w2.vatican.va/content/francesco/en/letters/2017
/documents/papa-francesco_20170113_lettera-giovani-
doc-sinodo.html. Copyright © LEV.

The excerpt on page 294 is from "Apostolic Journey
of His Holiness Pope Francis to Georgia and Azerbaijan," October 2, 2016, at https://w2.vatican.va/content
/francesco/en/homilies/2016/documents/papa-francesco
_20161002_omelia-azerbaijan.html. Copyright © LEV.

The quotation on page 328 is from Pope Francis's
"Apostolic Journey to Rio de Janeiro on the Occasion
of the XXVIII World Youth Day," July 27, 2013, at
https://w2.vatican.va/content/francesco/en/speeches/2013
/july/documents/papa-francesco_20130727_gmg-veglia-
giovani.html. Copyright © LEV.

The excerpts on pages 337 and 471 are from Pope
Francis's Bull of Indiction of the Extraordinary Jubilee of
Mercy [Misericordiae Vultus, 2015], numbers 6 and 9, at
https://w2.vatican.va/content/francesco/en/apost_letters
/documents/papa-francesco_bolla_20150411_misericordiae-
vultus.html. Copyright © LEV.

The excerpt on page 350 is from Pope Francis's
morning meditation "Why We Go to the Temple,"
November 22, 2013, at https://w2.vatican.va/content
/francesco/en/cotidie/2013/documents/papa-francesco-
cotidie_20131122_temple.html. Copyright © LEV.

The excerpt on page 384 is from Pope Francis's
"General Audience," Saint Peter's Square, April 9,
2014, at https://w2.vatican.va/content/francesco/en/audi-
ences/2014/documents/papa-francesco_20140409_udienza
-generale.html. Copyright © LEV.

The excerpt on page 410 is from Pope Francis's
"Message for the 22nd World Day of the Sick 2014,"
number 2, at https://w2.vatican.va/content/francesco/en
/messages/sick/documents/papa-francesco_20131206_
giornata-malato.html. Copyright © LEV.

The quote by Asia Bibi on page 449 is from "Asia
Bibi Asks the Prayers of Pope Francis," Vatican Radio,
June 4, 2015.

The excerpt on page 452 is from Pope Francis,
"Apostolic Journey to Rio De Janeiro on the Occasion
of the XXVIII World Youth Day, 2013," number 1, at
http://w2.vatican.va/content/francesco/en/homilies/2013
/documents/papa-francesco_20130728_celebrazione-xx-
viii-gmg.html.Copyright © LEV.

The excerpt on page 478 is from Pope Francis's
"Way of the Cross with the Young People," July 29,
2016, at https://w2.vatican.va/content/francesco/en/speeches
/2016/july/documents/papa-francesco_20160729_polonia
-via-crucis.html. Copyright © LEV.

To view copyright terms and conditions for internet materials cited here, log on to the home pages for
the referenced websites.

During this book's preparation, all citations, facts,
figures, names, addresses, telephone numbers, internet
URLs, and other pieces of information cited within
were verified for accuracy. The authors and Saint
Mary's Press staff have made every attempt to reference
current and valid sources, but we cannot guarantee the
content of any source, and we are not responsible for
any changes that may have occurred since our verifi-
cation. If you find an error in, or have a question or
concern about, any of the information or sources listed
within, please contact Saint Mary's Press.

Endnotes Cited in Quotations from the
Catechism of the Catholic Church, Second Edition

Chapter 1
1. Dei Filius 4: Denzinger-Schönmetzer, Enchiridion Symbolorum, definitionum et declarationum de
   rebus fidei et morum (1965) 3017.
2. Dei Verbum 11.

Chapter 2
1. Pius XII, Humani Generis, 561: Denzinger-
   Schönmetzer, Enchiridion Symbolorum, definitionum et declarationum de rebus fidei et morum
   (1965) 3876; cf. Dei Filius 2: Denzinger-
   Schönmetzer Enchiridion Symbolorum, definitionum et declarationum de rebus fidei et morum
   (1965) 3005; Dei Verbum 6; St. Thomas Aquinas
   Summa Theologiae I, 1, 1.
2. Dei Verbum 12 § 3.

Chapter 3
1. Cf. Dei Verbum 14.
2. Dei Verbum 18.

Chapter 4
1. Dei Verbum 10 § 2.
2. Dei Verbum 12 § 3.

Chapter 11
1. Cf. Saint Augustine, Quaest. in Hept. 2, 73:
   J. P. Migne, ed., Patrologia Latine (Paris:
   1841–1855) 34, 623; cf. Dei Verbum 16.

Chapter 14
1. St. Thérèse of Lisieux, The Final Conversations,
   tr. John Clarke (Washington: ICS, 1977), 102.

Chapter 15
1. Dei Verbum 18.

Chapter 16
1. Dei Verbum 7.
2. Dei Verbum 9.
3. Cf. 1 John 2:20, 27.
4. Cf. 1 John 16:13.

Chapter 17
1. Dei Verbum 21.
2. Dei Verbum 25. cf. Phil 3:8 and St. Jerome,
   Commentariorum in Isaiam libri xviii prol.:
   J. P. Migne, ed., Patrologia Latina (Paris:
   1841–1855) 24, 17b.
3. Cf. Dei Verbum 21.
4. Tertullian, De orat. 1 J. P. Migne, ed., Patrologia
   Latina (Paris: 1841–1855) 1, 1251–1255.